Bert Bielefeld (Ed.)

Architectural Presentation

BAS

Bert Bielefeld (Ed.)

Architectural Presentation

BIRKHÄUSER
BASEL

Contents

CAD _163

Modelbuilding _247

Architectural Photography _319

Foreword

For architects, illustrating their own designs is essential for work and communication. This includes the first sketched ideas, technical illustrations, drawings made by hand or with the aid of CAD programs, and elaborate presentation drawings, as well as the closely related tools, models and photography. In designing and planning, architects must repeatedly move between different illustration and drawing techniques in order to concretise and consolidate the creative process. They also need illustration techniques to communicate with their clients and to present themselves to the specialist world.

This compendium, which covers the various facets of these techniques and aids, comprises five important *Basics* volumes on the topic. Readers are given tools that are immensely useful in defining ideas, making studies during the design process, presenting and documenting their own work, and working towards technical implementation and documentation.

Developing a building in design terms and presenting it to third parties by means of freehand drawings makes several demands on the draughtsman or woman. Naturally, practice is required here, but this skill can also be acquired systematically – for instance by constructing perspectives. The volume *Freehand Drawing* provides knowledge about the materials, aids and techniques that can be used during the design process and in recording architecture on site. It is precisely the subjective quality of the freehand drawing that helps one to organise one's own thoughts and to identify the important design approaches.

The volume *Technical Drawing* begins at the point where the formulation of the idea has advanced to such a stage that the design can now be continued in technical drawings made to scale. These provide a concrete image of what is to be developed in design or construction terms, and the detailing process that they involve is an important step on the path to the completed building. This book conveys the basic material needed to prepare the different kinds of plans and drawings in the planning process – with the goal of enabling students to depict their ideas and designs quickly and confidently in construction drawings.

Today, producing design and detailed drawings without the aid of the computer is almost inconceivable. The complexity of large building projects requires the smooth flow of data between all the planners involved, with regular modifications and alterations to the plans on the path to producing the drawings that will be used to erect the building. The volume *CAD* offers a general overview of the basic principles of Computer Aided Design (CAD) in that it provides a general understanding of the functions, structures and work processes that traverse the boundaries between different programs, and are therefore useful for concrete work with a specific CAD program.

An important means of depicting architecture is the model, which offers a spatial impression of the planned building. But models are also a useful tool in the search for proportions and forms, as they allow ideas that exist on paper to be examined and developed further in three dimensions. The volume *Modelbuilding* deals with various model typologies and the important aids, tools and machines used in building models. Suitable materials and their particular qualities are presented systematically and explained in terms of their impact on the composition.

The volume *Architectural Photography* deals with yet another form of illustrating and documenting architecture that is used widely in publications, magazines, office brochures, or on websites. As well as being employed for presentation purposes, photography can also play other roles in the architect's daily life. Just like the sketchbook, the camera can be a companion that accompanies architects on every site visit and trip they make to record buildings, impressions and stimuli that they can later use in their own work. In addition to the basic photographical and technical material, the typical design parameters of an architectural photograph are described, to illustrate the ideal approach to taking photographs.

Bert Bielefeld, Editor

Florian Afflerbach

Freehand Drawing

Basic principles of freehand drawing

DISTINCTIONS AND TERMS

The theory of art defines sketches and drawings as part of the graphic arts. The instruments used for drawing (pencil, pastels etc.) are abraded as they are drawn across a substrate, generally paper, or form a liquid film (ink, watercolours etc.). The most obvious difference from painting is that lines are dominant rather than areas of colours. Consequently, sketches and drawings remain just a composition of lines, not colours and are therefore never paintings. What the hand, using the drawing instrument, puts on paper are the primary means of a drawing: point, line and surface. Sketches and drawings can be given greater expressive power by using complementary means such as spatial staggering in depth, colour, or the depiction of light and shade.

Freehand drawing is the basis for many kinds of artistic work: painting, sculpture and also architecture. It includes the sketch, a rapidly produced drawing in which depicting the typical characteristic is often more important than reproducing individual qualities and which, even more so than the drawing, aims at achieving a maximum of expression and power

Fig. 1: The Tagblatt Tower in Stuttgart, drawn using four different techniques (clockwise from top left): pencil with watercolours, pencil, chalk on brown paper, charcoal

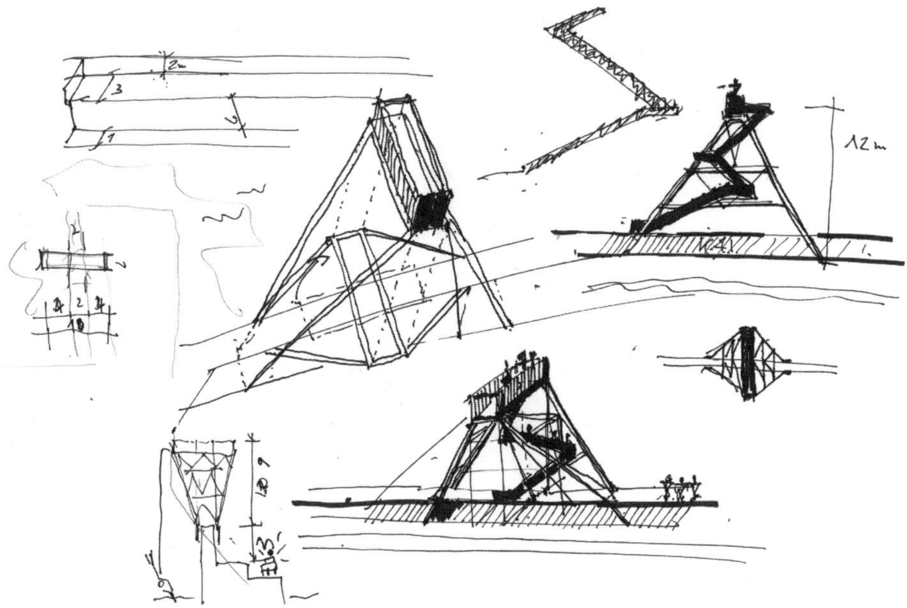

Fig. 2: Spontaneous sketches of ideas on a paper napkin (Antalya observation tower)

with little expenditure of technique and material. The drawing therefore always offers more information than the sketch.

Freehand sketching and drawing is generally used during the early stages of an architectural design, to depict ideas or concepts or to clarify basic questions about the form, construction or urban situation of a building. Sketches and drawings made at this phase can provide the basis for architectural models or technical drawings, which then make the design more concrete. They can also be made with rulers and stencils, if they have a design character. The boundary to technical drawing is blurred. The sketch can also be used in the later phases of a project, for example to show a detail for the detail design stage, > Fig. 54, page 57 or to provide instructions for skilled tradesmen working on the building site.

If architecture is drawn on site, the sketch is not based on imagination but is the depiction of a concrete reality based on looking directly at the building. > Fig. 3

Sketches and drawings are always a highly individual mirror as the skilled hand, raw force and tenacious impatience can be read from them,

Fig. 3: Architectural sketch made on site (Fundação Iberê Camargo, Alvaro Siza, Porto Alegre)

telling us much about how they were made and the particular nature of the author. In contrast to photography they are made gradually and thus interact with the person who produces them, who is in permanent visual contact with what he or she has already put on paper.

Drawing and sketching in architectural design or drawing architecture on site is determined by a selective way of working. Certain things are omitted so that they do not distract, or important aspects are emphasised so as to depict them in a focused way. It can therefore be said that the expressive content of the empty, untouched areas of a drawing is equal to that of the treated areas. This moment of imprecision further distinguishes the drawing from photography, which generally records everything within the viewing angle of the lens, or from the CAD drawing, which often includes unnecessary information. > Fig. 80, page 81: the brain can imagine the appearance of the annexes as they have similar building forms.

DESIGN MEDIUM

Freehand sketching is an elementary part of all design phases that call for design, functional or construction-related decisions. It functions as intellectual preparatory work, which is repeatedly rejected and renewed until the pure drawing of the final version is produced using the methods of technical drawing.

The combination of a roll of sketching paper and pencil, a place to build models and the CAD program is the ideal workplace for the designing architect. Freehand drawing is particularly useful for spontaneous and creative work, as ideas can be put down directly on paper with minimal interruption to the flow of thought.

The early sketch made during the design stage, still unaffected by any kind of political, financial or constructional pressure, is the moment when the architect's idea appears in its pure and unadulterated form. This spontaneity and intuition underline the subjective nature of the freehand drawing which, as it is made by hand, is directly connected to the author and thus to the architect's drawing language.

The increased use of CAD programs in the early design stages makes drawing styles seem more uniform and interchangeable. Designers subject themselves to the rules of the CAD system in terms of graphics, scale and norms, although the sketch is in fact graphically independent, without scale and non-binding. A gap that apparently can no longer be closed is opening up between the architect's understanding and his hand, as something that is virtual – the design – is also being produced virtually.

Later design phases, too, throw up problems that call for new ideas, variations and improvements. Freehand sketching and drawing can also use a greater degree of detail and a different scale to arrive at solutions and can therefore accompany a project right up to its completion. > Chapter Freehand drawing in architectural design, Continuing the design

INSTRUMENT OF COMMUNICATION

The architect must be able to communicate his or her ideas and concepts in a way that can be correctly read and understood by the viewer. While still a student, teachers and fellow students are the main recipients for these ideas, whereas in professional life it is colleagues, clients, tradespeople, public authorities or the general public to whom certain contents must be conveyed quickly and directly.

The drawing is the language of the architect. As part of the design process sketches are made all the time during brainstorming sessions, and on the building site sketches are used daily in discussions with construction workers. If the descriptive perspective drawing, legible by a lay public, that is frequently called for in architecture competitions is drawn freehand this has the advantage that, unlike finely detailed, photorealistic computer renderings, it does not yet have a final character and does not lay down a detailed architectural direction. Here it is not decisive whether a perspective drawing is made with the help of technical drawing

Fig. 4: Hand-drawn perspective for a competition

instruments (ruler, compass, parallel straightedge or similar) or is drawn freehand. The important aspect is the unfinished and incomplete quality of the drawing, which leaves leeway for the imagination of viewers who may have little understanding of architecture. The drawing becomes an intermediary. > Fig. 89 below, page 90

PERCEPTION

Drawing buildings directly on site offers an excellent opportunity to understand architecture better. The permanent interplay between direct observation and the drawing being created allows the structures, proportions and other formative aspects that describe the building to be grasped precisely. What is seen and then drawn imprints itself on the memory. The information gained in this way can be used for comparative purposes in the next on-site architectural drawing, or in a future design project. Architectural drawing on site does not mean simply the depiction of what is seen but the reflective processing of form, function or construction.

The drawing is a collection of transported and interpreted impressions that have made their way onto paper. The lines, colours and hatch-

Fig. 5: Visit to the Müller House (Adolf Loos, Prague)

ing are metaphors for what has been perceived. In recognising what was drawn the viewer converts these metaphors back into reality. The drawing is therefore not simply a tool for depicting but also (for both draughtsperson and viewer) an intellectual tool. The drawing illustrates what has been considered and records what has been perceived. In precisely observing the subject, the person drawing it is confronted with new questions.

The city provides excellent opportunities for the architectural draughtsperson who wishes to draw on site, through the abstract aspect of the drawing it is broken down from three to two dimensions. Perspective drawing in the city includes making use of certain rules and guidelines in order to depict the architecture correctly and with a high level of content. By adding people, vegetation, cars, data and atmospheric impressions, snapshots are made that illustrate experiences of time and space. Yet the architectural drawing can never replace actually making a visit to a building.

Tools and techniques

DRAWING SUBSTRATES

Drawing boards, drawing tables and T-squares have become so rare in the professional life of the architect today that large sheets or rolls of paper are practically never used. CAD programs with an infinitely larger user interface and plotters that transfer the drawing to paper take over the large-scale work. Consequently, the selection below is restricted to drawing substrates in the form of smaller sheets of paper.

First of all we should focus on those substrates that can be considered for the design process. Essentially, every kind of paper substrate can be used as the basis for a freehand drawing – including scraps of paper, notes or even beer mats or paper napkins.

Sketchbooks are valuable companions both during the design process and for the architectural drawing on site. Information, ideas, architecture sketches and interesting things from everyday life can be recorded in them permanently and developments documented.

Working with the sketching paper roll

The most important kind of paper in the design process is the sketching paper roll. This is very thin, transparent paper rolled around a cylindrical cardboard core. The sketching paper roll is generally around 30 cm wide and has a length of between 20 and 100 m. It is available in different paper strengths from 20 to 40 g/m^2 of wood-free cellulose, the thicker papers (unit: g/m^2) being less translucent. It is generally transparent-white; brownish or corn yellow sketching paper rolls are rarer. They offer the advantage that white pencils or chalks can be used on them to emphasise certain lines and surfaces.

The sketching paper roll can be used in every design phase whenever ideas and studies must be given a sketched visual form and different versions and examinations are necessary. It offers a number of advantages.

Sketching paper rolls are relatively inexpensive. This aids the creative flow, as there are no financial repercussions if a sketch just made has to be torn off the roll, crumpled up and tossed into the waste-paper basket. This paper is there to be thrown away, as in this phase sheets from rolls of sketching paper are the bearers of a wealth of good and bad ideas that are examined on the next piece of paper from the long roll. In this way the design gradually grows more concrete.

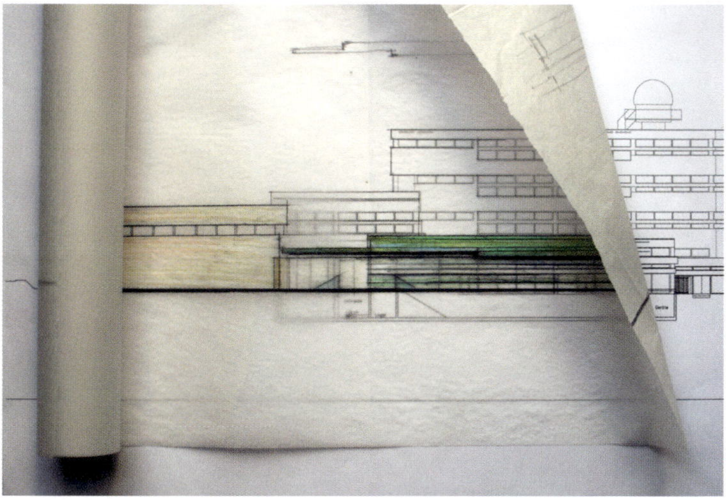

Fig. 6: Roll of sketching paper with a design sketch laid over as-built drawing

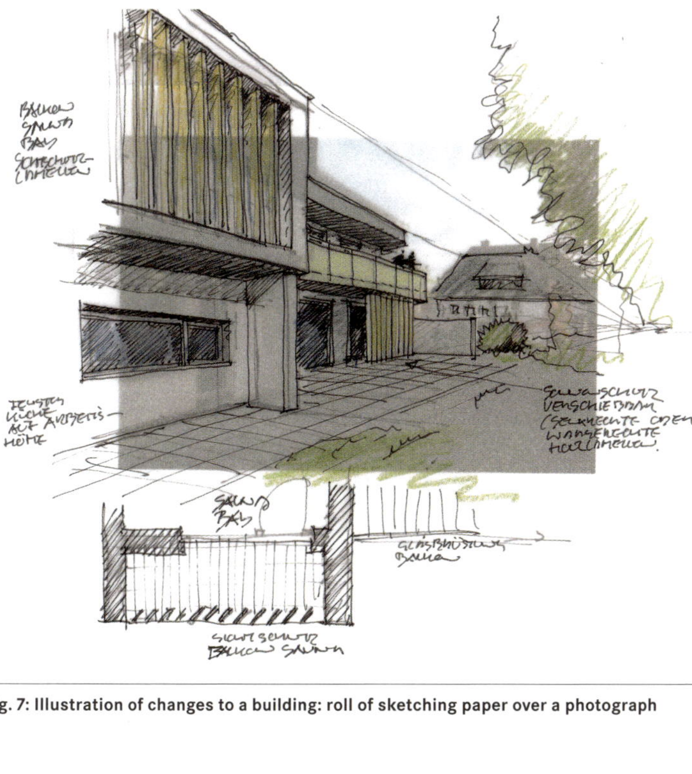

Fig. 7: Illustration of changes to a building: roll of sketching paper over a photograph

Fig. 8: Alternatives, produced with the roll of sketching paper

To produce different versions and variations and to examine their contents, the roll of sketching paper is laid over an existing drawing. Here it does not matter whether this is one's own drawing, a drawing by a colleague, as-built plans from a current project, or plans made with the computer. The roll of sketching paper can be laid over every kind of drawing – and even across the computer screen.

Changes or improvements are repeatedly drawn on new translucent layers of paper. The paper's translucency makes direct comparison with the earlier sketch possible. This procedure can be repeated until the desired goal is achieved.

But the sketching paper roll can also be used as drawing substrate without any other drawing beneath it. In particularly tall or long buildings, situations can arise where a long piece of paper is needed in order to draw an elevation, a section or a certain perspective.

In drawing perspective by the intersection point method the sketching paper roll can also be used. > Chapter Freehand drawing in architectural design, Drawing types The drawings needed for this method (elevation and plan) are placed beneath the translucent paper and fixed in position. This allows the perspective to be made on its own sheet of paper, separated from the elevation and plan. > Fig. 64, page 64

Tracing paper

If the paper in the sketch roll is found to be too thin or not sufficiently resistant, another kind of paper combines the quality of the sketching paper roll with that of normal paper: tracing paper. It is thicker than sketching paper (80 to 200 g/m²) and consequently less transparent, which can lead to the problem that the drawing beneath is not completely legible.

Tracing paper generally comes in sheets in DIN A formats and also, but more rarely, in rolls. Compared to the sketching paper roll, tracing paper is more suitable for drawing instruments with hard tips such as ballpoint pens and classic ink pens with different line widths. Incorrect lines can be scratched away using a razor blade or special kinds of erasers. However, this also removes the uppermost layer of the tracing paper and care must be taken to avoid scratching a hole in the paper.

Drawing paper

The most undemanding paper for freehand drawing is simple, brilliant white, wood-free drawing paper or drawing card, which resembles multi-function printer paper. It has the character of an empty sheet of paper and at the start of a project represents in a metaphorical sense a "tabula rasa" for free drawing without any influences.

It is available in different thicknesses from 80 to 300 g/m² and generally in DIN A formats. It is not ideally suited to any specific drawing instrument. > Tab. 1 This kind of paper is more an "all-rounder". Lines drawn on it with water- or alcohol-based pens bleed easily. If they are too watery, watercolours cause the paper to tear or to become wavy. Hard tips, such as ballpoint pens and hard pencil leads, often print through the paper and, if a pad or block is being used, leave a relief-like imprint on the next page. Lined paper is not really suitable for sketching. If a design is being drawn at a particular scale, squared paper provides beginners with a sure guide as regards dimensions. ○

Grey and brown paper

Compared to white papers, of which there is a wide range, greyish and brownish paper offer the advantage that white lines and areas can be draw on them, and the brightest part of the drawing does not have to be paper untouched by the drawing, as is the case with white paper.

○ **Note:** The rule of thumb is: the finer the grain, the thinner the paper, and the smoother the surface of the paper the more suitable it is for hard drawing instruments such as pencils or ink and felt pens. Markers can also be used more easily on smooth paper, as the lines and areas of colour do not bleed to such an extent. Conversely, coarse-grained paper is better for watercolours, soft pencils or charcoal and pastels. It should be acid-free as this means it is resistant to ageing and can also be used for inks and watercolours.

Fig. 9: Heights and depths using white and black on brown paper

Fig. 10: Heights and depths with white and black on yellow paper

This is ideal for emphasising areas or surfaces, space and atmosphere. For instance: in a perspective, colouring the sides of the building that stand in the sun white and those in the shade black makes the line drawing more spatial and atmospheric. It is also easier to indicate differences in the materials used in the planned buildings. The grey or brown area of the paper that remains untouched by lines and blocks of colour then stand for a middle tonal value that is in neither sun nor shade. > Fig. 9

Sketchbooks

The prospective architect should keep a sketchbook in which the progress of a design can be documented and which offers the opportunity to note down an idea, something seen or a piece of information. Sketchbooks are available in wide variety of shapes and sizes, but for an architect's purposes some kinds are more suitable.

A freehand sketch or drawing is generally not to scale and therefore is as large as you draw it. Nevertheless, the size of the sketchbook page should be at least DIN A5 in horizontal or upright format. A large drawing surface offers the advantage that, for example, the vanishing points of a perspective frequently still lie on the sheet, or there is room enough for a further idea on the same sheet. Therefore small sketchpads and ring books with individual pages are unsuitable. If you need to make a smaller drawing you can drawn a small frame or outline on the existing sheet.

Tab. 1: Combinations of different drawing grounds and drawing instruments (++ very good, + good, o middling, - bad, – very bad)

	Sketching paper roll	Tracing paper	Drawing paper	Multifunction paper up to 120 g/m²	Multifunction paper from 120 g/m²	Grey and brown paper	Watercolour paper	Marker paper
Hard pencil	-	++	o	+	+	o	o	-
Soft pencil	++	+	+	o	++	++	+	-
Coloured pencil	+	+	+	o	+	o	o	–
Felt pen	++	+	o	+	o	+	-	o
Ink pen	++	++	+	+	+	+	-	+
Ballpoint pen	–	-	+	o	o	o	–	o
Pastels and charcoal	-	–	o	o	++	++	+	-
Markers	++	+	-	-	-	–	-	++
Watercolours	–	–	+	o	+	–	++	o

Sketchbooks need to be filled. Drawing by drawing a fine collection can be built up, a travel sketchbook, or the chronology of one's own progress. Sketchbooks accompany their owner over a longer period of time and should therefore have a sturdy cover with thread-stitched pages. This kind of cover also can serve as a base or support when drawing. The paper should be acid-free and have a thickness of at least 150 g/m². The kind of paper depends entirely on the drawing instrument chosen. If you use mainly pencil and watercolours, you should choose coarse-grain or even watercolour paper. For markers and ballpoint pens smooth paper is more suitable. > Tab. 1 ■

■ **Tip:** This technique can also be used with sketching paper or tracing paper. If using tracing paper the white is applied to the back to avoid contact with the pencil or ink lines drawn on the front. This also has the advantage that the area to be covered in white can be drawn more clearly.

■ **Tip:** Some sketchbooks have useful features that improve everyday (sketching) life. Some have an attachment to hold the pencil, other have a pocket inside the back cover to take visiting cards or similar information. With smaller sketchbooks an external rubberised band is an advantage, as it prevents the book from opening accidentally when in a bag or satchel. Sketchbooks with rounded corners prevent dog-ears.

Fig. 11: Sketchbooks of different sizes and with different kinds of paper, some with a bookmark or rubber band

Keeping a sketchbook

Everything that interests an architect can be kept in a sketchbook: from sketched ideas about town planning to a window detail, written notes and illegible doodles made during a talk given by a colleague, architectural drawings made during travels, everyday situations and objects of all kinds that are sufficiently interesting to make a drawing worthwhile.

In drawings with an informative or even narrative character, writing can be a meaningful addition. Some things are best understood in a drawing, others are better written down: assessments about a material, smells, descriptions of a colour for making a wash later, names (or even personal signatures) of people you have to deal with in a project, or references to certain impending or past events which you wanted to note quickly.

If a sketchbook is used chronologically, it can develop into a kind of personal life story with the character of a diary that you can use as an encyclopaedic store of knowledge for future design projects. Known as journaling, this aspect is illustrated by the constantly growing range of notebooks now available that cater for different professions, places or personal interests.

Fig. 12: Open sketchbooks with notes, design sketches and on-site drawings

Keeping a sketchbook also forms a counterpart to digital photography, which makes it possible to take large numbers of pictures everywhere and at all times. Sketchbooks you have filled yourself are full of your own observations and through the author's subjectivity they acquire a pure form of individual identity. You can also record you own memories in them. On looking later at sketches you have made, you recall the subjects and being reminded of them again may even mean that they are stored in your long-term memory.

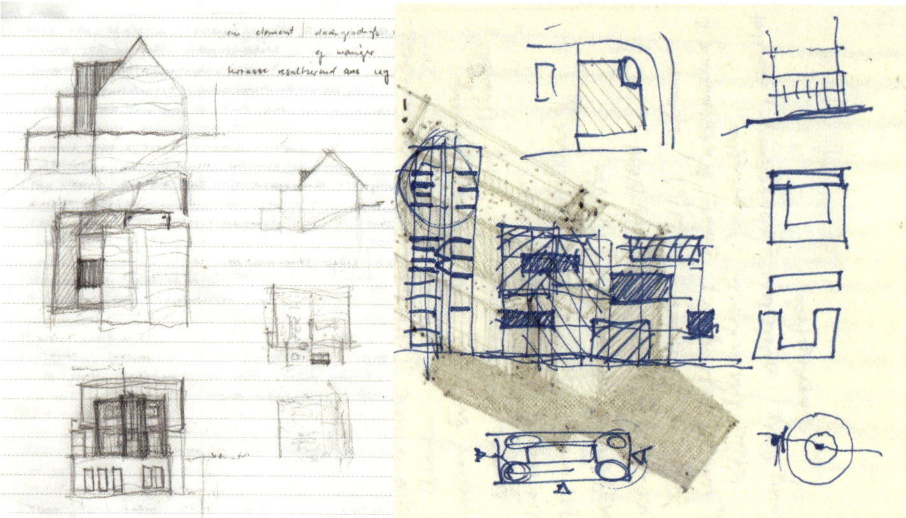

Fig. 13: Somewhat illegible, intimate design sketches

LINES AND THE INSTRUMENTS FOR DRAWING THEM

Lines

Like the technical drawing, a freehand drawing also consists largely of lines that vary in terms of form and weight from drawing to drawing. They can be used to depict almost everything in drawing and sketching architecture: from site boundaries, building outlines and edges to individual storeys and to wall constructions, furniture and door handles. But it is only through accentuation, different kinds of lines and the differentiated use of strokes in different sizes and scales of drawings that the sketch becomes legible and understandable. Sketches illegible to outside observers are intended only for the author and help transfer important information to the next design stage. > Fig. 13

The lines that gradually create the design grow more concrete over the course of time to form a sketch or drawing. Here the draughtsman or woman constantly improves what has been drawn, rejects it, erases it or – in the best case scenario – finds it good. The draughtsperson always sees what has been "done" a moment previously, engaging in an emotional relationship with what has been drawn. Object – eye – hand – pencil – paper: a complex sequence of activities and reactions is concealed behind creative drawing.

In on-site architectural drawing the dimension of this interaction changes: you do not compare what has been drawn with the image in

Fig. 14: On-site architectural drawing, where edges, changes of material, colour and light (here shown as dotted lines) are abstracted and depicted as strokes.

your head but with the depiction of real architecture. We do not draw imaginary lines but rather we abstract outlines that do not exist in real nature. > Fig. 14 We interpret them as lines, although in fact only a change of volume, material, colour or light takes place. We therefore draw the visual boundary between two volumes (or material or colours), a boundary between light and shade or between a volume and the air surrounding it as a line. ○

Types of lines

Although freehand drawing and sketching tends to be a relatively fast activity and must not comply with the rules of technical drawing, it nevertheless makes sense to differentiate between the most common types of lines: full lines, dashed or broken lines, and dotted lines. Differences cannot be made between line thicknesses, as in each sketch this depends on the instrument with which the lines are drawn. Nevertheless, sketches that use a wide variety of different line thicknesses are more vivid and more legible.

○ **Note:** The dot-dash line familiar from technical drawing is not commonly used in freehand drawing, as it denotes axes and section lines, which are generally not considered in the early design stages.

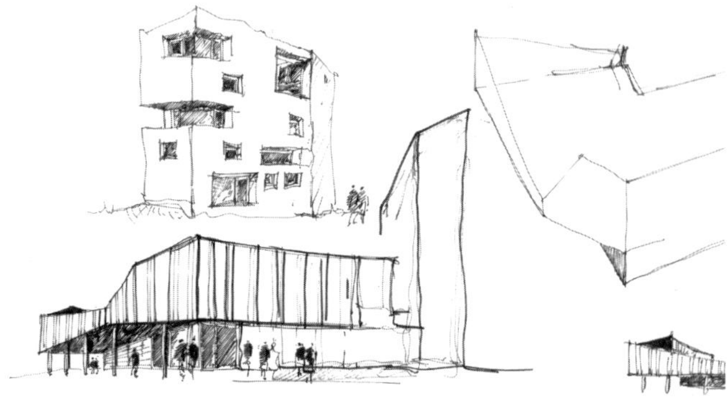

Fig. 15: Sketch elevation made with different line thicknesses; the volume at the bottom left is emphasised by the use thicker outlines.

Full lines are those used to describe all the visible edges of objects and building parts in a depiction. In section drawings the parts of the buildings cut through are indicated by the use of thicker lines. In elevations the line of the ground is emphasised. Buildings in the foreground are often given heavier outlines and shown with thicker lines than the less important edges or parts of the building in the background. > Fig. 25, page 35

Broken lines (also known as dashed lines) denote volumes, building parts, or other important edges that lie behind or beneath the actual depiction. Dotted lines, on the other hand, describe the edges of building parts that are over or above what is depicted. Dotted lines should truly consist of dots. The need to use dashed or dotted lines in depicting building parts arises particularly frequently in floor plans or section drawings. > Chapter Architectural drawing on site, Drawing types

Drawing correctly

Straight lines should be drawn straight. Frequent mistakes include lines that, due to the given radius between wrist and arm, are drawn curved although in fact they should be straight. Care should also be taken that a line consists of only a single line. To draw straight ground lines the little finger can be led along the edge of the table or of the sketchbook at the same time drawing a straight line parallel to this edge. A second line should not be drawn over an interrupted or broken line in order to correct it. The interrupted line can be continued at a slight distance. > Fig. 16

Lines that represent building corners, for example, should always consist of two intersecting lines. The lines of a volume that lie behind

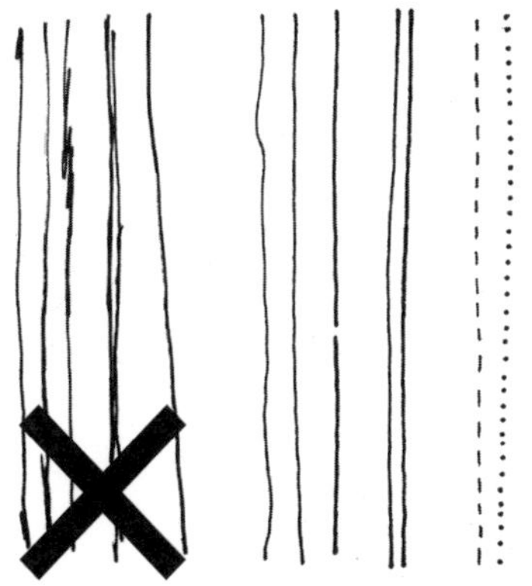

Fig. 16: Incorrectly and correctly drawn lines, full lines, dashed lines and dotted lines

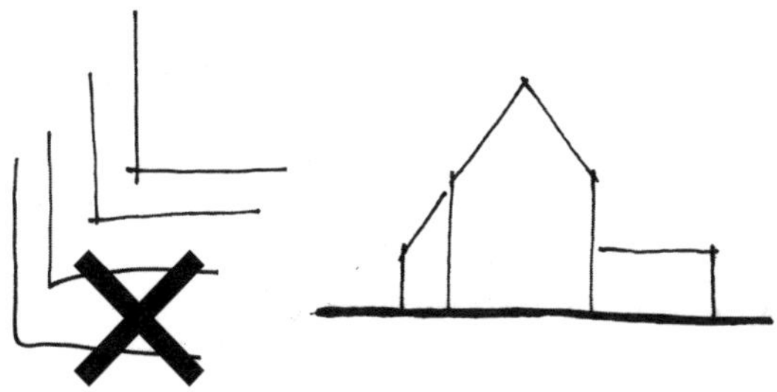

Fig. 17: Correct and incorrect corners, the lines of the building volumes in the background are separated somewhat from the main volume.

another volume should not cut its lines and should be drawn somewhat separated.

Hatching

Hatching allows us to create surfaces, shadows or to indicate materials with the use of lines. It should not be confused with the different kinds of hatching used to denote specific materials in technical drawings. Essentially, we distinguish between angled hatching, cross-hatching and dotted hatching.

Diagonal hatching, whether simple or crosshatched, is intended to emphasise the flatness of a building part or to indicate that part of a building lies in shadow. Then the lines of the hatching run in the direction of the light source. If simple hatching is made vertically or horizontally this can also indicate the material to be used. > Fig. 21, page 32 It is also possible to make hatching denser at an edge or corner as a way of depicting curvature. ■

■ **Tip:** Hatching ought not to be drawn too rapidly. Snaking thin lines, irregular distances between the lines or changes in direction give an impression of carelessness. The individual lines of the hatching should be drawn right up to the borders of the area to which the hatching is applied. This calls for patience and precision but it is the only way to achieve the desired effect, the depiction of a flat area.

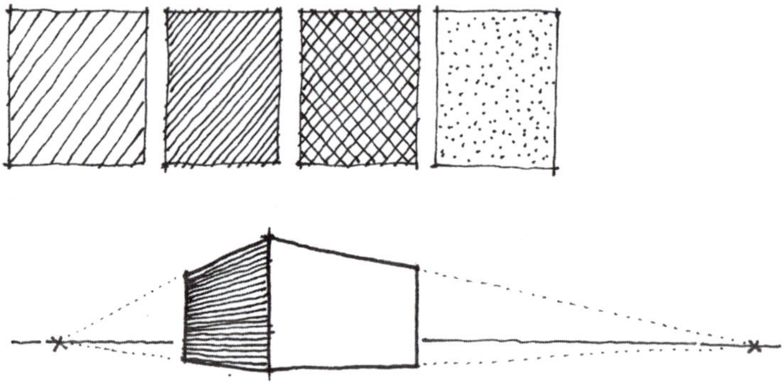

Fig. 18: Different kinds of hatching, in the perspective the hatching lines recede towards a vanishing point

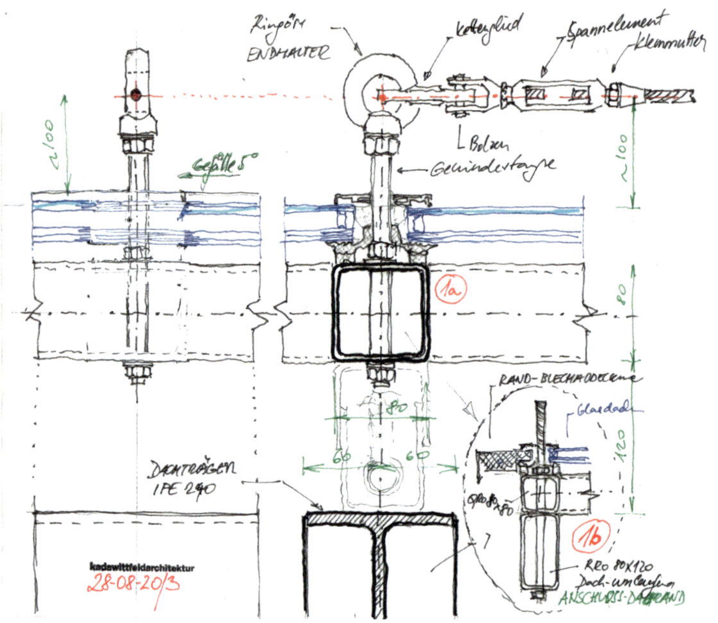

Fig. 19: Detail drawings (sections and isometric) of a facade construction with different line types and hatching

Fig. 20: Pencils, clutch pencils, graphite stick, eraser, sharpener and cutting knife

Pencils

The lead pencil, which is actually made of graphite with a clay binder that is encased in wood, is one of the most important sketching tools. It is undemanding, fast and flexible, economically priced and resistant to ageing. It is a sensitive drawing medium: you can draw both quick sketches and detailed studies with it. A low amount of pressure on the pencil creates a fine line that has a searching character. Once the perfect line has been found you can, using the same pencil, increase the pressure to produce a more definite line.

For sketching the most suitable pencils are grades B to 4B (soft to medium soft, B standing for black). The grading ranges from 8H (very hard) to H, HB (normal), B to 8B. If you use pencils of different hardness (or fineliners with different line thicknesses) in the same drawing, the difference in emphasis can produce a lively depiction. In general such drawings seem to have greater variety, but the beginner is advised to use just one pencil in a drawing. In this way you can begin to achieve full mastery of the pencil, whereas changing pencils during drawing reduces spontaneity and interrupts the important continuity of the drawing process.

As well as the classic wood pencil there are also propelling pencils. Clutch pencils have the same leads as pencils and are therefore also suitable for drawing. They are also available with very strong leads (approx. 6 mm thick) and these resemble graphite sticks, whose thick lead is covered only by a plastic coat. Graphite sticks can be used to draw flat areas. Fine propelling pencils should not be used, as their extremely thin leads do not allow different line thicknesses or heavy finger pressure. They are

Fig. 21: Tchoban Foundation, Museum for Architectural Drawing, Berlin

Fig. 22: Design for a weather station

more suitable for technical drawing. As, after a time, using a drawing instrument that is too short causes cramps in the hand, an extender should be attached to a pencil when half of it has been used up. ■

The eraser should be as white and soft as possible but at the same time it should have distinct edges so that lines can be properly removed. Blurring, that is rubbing lines and hatching with the finger, sheet or handkerchief should be avoided. Every individual line, even in close hatching, should remain visible. ■

■ **Tip:** If the complete drawing can be approximately imagined before the first line is drawn it is worthwhile, if you are right handed, to begin the drawing at the top left and to end in the direction of bottom right (for a left-hander from top right to bottom left). This prevents smudging the drawing surface with your hand. This applies to pencils, charcoal sticks and pastels.

■ **Tip:** A (cutter) knife should be used to sharpen pencils or coloured pencils, as it can produce a very long exposed lead. This lasts for a long time and does not have to be re-sharpened during the drawing. If you regard it as important to have a lead point that remains the same, then a standard pencil sharpener will also do.

Fig. 23: Design perspective: a world of colour produced by combining different coloured pencils

Coloured pencils

Coloured pencils are made in the same way as normal pencils. A pressed lead made of colour pigment is encased in wood. They are also sensitive to pressure, allowing deep and light shades of a hue to be produced with the one pencil.

For sketching, 15–20 different colours are generally sufficient, as coloured pencils can also be combined with each other. In sketching they are particularly suitable for making the first colour concepts or for indications and information; in the later design process the use of coloured pencils creates atmosphere and liveliness. ■

Felt pens

There is an extremely large range of different felt pens (also fibre pens, fineliners etc.). Essentially, all kinds of felt pens can be used for sketching and drawing; the fine differences are only revealed in the detail. Thicker felt pens are more suitable for freehand sketching; thin pens (up to 1 mm point thickness) are also suitable for drawings made with the use of a ruler and stencils.

■ **Tip:** Wooden planking can be depicted by parallel lines of red, brown, blue and green made with coloured pencils. A metallic surface is produced by combining lines of blue, green and grey.

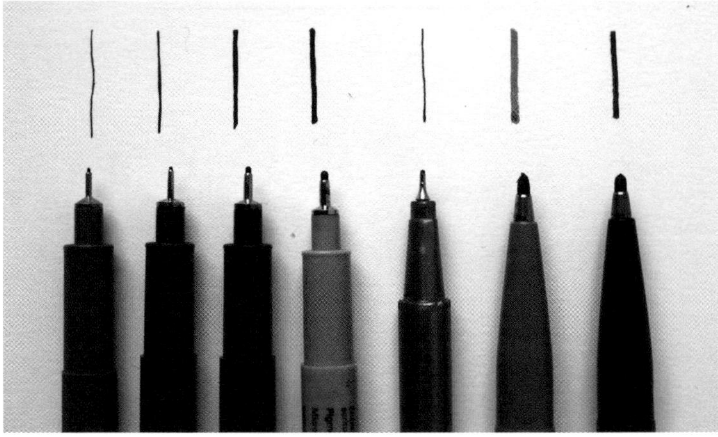

Fig. 24: Ink pens with different line widths and felt-tip pens

In choosing felt pens, solubility in water is an important criterion (e.g. on contact with watercolours). Water-resistant felt tip pens such as pigment ink pens are also fade-resistant. They can be obtained in different thicknesses and therefore resemble ink drawing instruments from the technical drawing field (DIN 15). Water-soluble felt pens are available in many different colours and can be used to show design changes or re-workings, or for general notes.

Ballpoint pens

Ballpoint pens produce lines by means of a small ball that transfers the viscous ink in the pen to the paper. The ballpoint is a pressure-sensitive drawing tool: if the pressure is increased a thicker line is produced, and if less pressure is used the line is thinner. This variety of line thicknesses makes the ballpoint suitable for depicting spatial volumes.

The ballpoint pen is an undemanding and speedy drawing tool. It can be used on all sorts of paper, but the hard ceramic surface of the ball makes it difficult to use on thin sketching paper. Only lines produced with document-quality ballpoint pens are resistant to ageing and do not change their appearance.

Fig. 25: Ink pigment drawing using different line thicknesses to emphasise the volumes of the building, felt pens used to indicate shadow

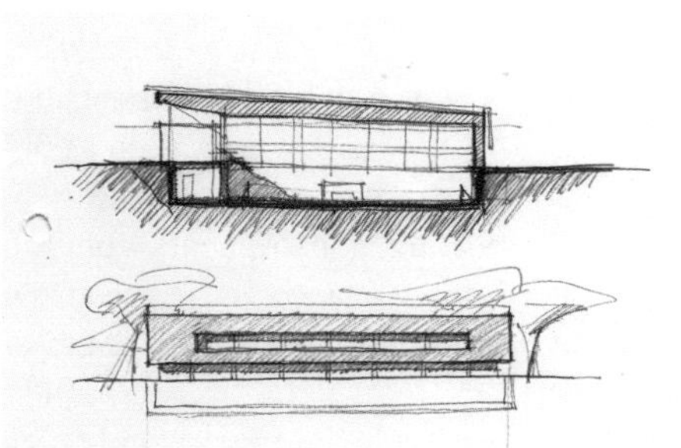

Fig. 26: Design drawing (section and elevation) made with a ballpoint pen

Fig. 27: On-site drawing made with a ballpoint pen

Fig. 28: Solid tone (opaque), halftone (transparent) and structured surface

SURFACES AND THE INSTRUMENTS FOR DRAWING THEM

Areas

A great deal can be achieved with pure line drawings, but some situations require instruments that can create flat areas or surfaces. If surfaces are used in part of a sketch it stands out very clearly from the rest of the drawing.

Hatching, which consists of individual lines, comes very close to a drawing made with surfaces. But making hatching can be extremely tedious and time-consuming. In addition, hatching only achieves monochrome suggestions of space or the nature of a material. In contrast, the implements for creating surface areas can be used rapidly, and using multiple tone values can heighten the depiction of space. Materials and surfaces can be drawn in a way that is much closer to nature, while a number of the instruments used to create surface areas can produce more authentic shadows.

Types of surfaces

It is far easier to distinguish between different types of lines than types of surfaces, as the latter are almost always tied to the kind of instrument used. However, the difference between solid tones, halftones and structured surfaces is important. > Fig. 28

Solid tone surfaces are surfaces that are drawn with full tonal value and are therefore opaque. Halftone surfaces do not have a full tonal value, are not opaque and therefore have a transparent quality. They seem predestined for use in depicting shadows. With structured surfaces the white of the paper may appear through at certain places. This has to do directly with the instrument being used. Common to all instruments used to create surfaces or areas is that they do not produce any visible lines.

Fig. 29: Form studies (pastels)

Pastels and charcoal sticks

Structured surfaces can be drawn with pastel chalks and charcoal sticks. The uneven abrasion on the paper creates interesting structures, which frequently have the appearance of stone surfaces. Due to their porosity, drawings made with pastels or charcoal must be given a coat of fixative.

Grey and brown pastels are generally sold in boxes. They are available in black, white, ochre, sepia, red chalk, and various shades of grey. A special effect can be achieved when they are used on paper other than white. > Chapter Tools and techniques, Drawing substrates The rough quality of pastel drawings makes it necessary to use large sheets of paper. They are particularly useful during the early design stages for making studies of form, light and shadow. The hard contrasts produced by the full tone colours give the drawings a particularly dramatic quality. > Fig. 1 below left, page 12 ■

■ **Tip:** Brown and grey pastels are often only 7 mm thick, with a length of approx. 8 cm. Therefore it is a good idea to break them into pieces 2–3 cm long before using them. This makes them easier to handle and also means that, in addition to the short end, the other side, which is then not so long, can also be used to create flat areas of colour.

Fig. 30: Neue Pinakothek Munich sequences (charcoal pencil)

Fat-free charcoal pencils are available in different degrees of hardness. Their great advantage is that they can be easily used when one is on the move as they have the same form as the standard pencil and therefore are not so easily broken. They produce a very dense black that allows strong contrasts to be made. Charcoal drawings are generally highly expressive and particularly effective for depicting cubic, voluminous buildings. Charcoal pencils are somewhere between line and surface drawing instruments. They produce lines that are very thick and clear, but it is also very easy to create surfaces and structures, for example of masonry, with them.

Fig. 31: Marker pens with different kinds of tips

Marker pens

Alcohol-based marker pens are excellent for indicating colour, materials and shadows when drawing and sketching architecture. Sketches coloured with marker pens have a vivid spatial quality. You have to work very fast with markers as the sketch dries almost immediately.

Most alcohol-based marker pens have drawing tips at either end of the pen, which have a different shape and degree of hardness. There are softer brush tips, with which one can work in a painterly way, and harder wedge or trapezoid-shaped tips that can be used to create areas of colour or lines of different thicknesses.

They are available in several hundred colours; however you really only need various warm and cold shades of grey, a lighter and a darker red, green, blue and yellow, as well as a few brown and beige shades, and of course black. Marker colours are often stronger than you might think. Before sketching, the shade of colour should be tested. To create different shades of a colour, a blender pen is needed that dissolves the colour of the marker by means of a solvent. ○

○ **Note:** The blender pen (frequently called: "0") can lighten an area of colour at any required place or at the edges. A colour gradient is obtained by first applying the required colour with a marker pen to a smooth surface (e.g. a sheet of glass). The colour is then taken up by the blender. The colour gradient is now drawn, the colour initially appearing in full tone and then gradually thinning out to transparent white.

Fig. 32: Design sketch with markers, using different colour gradients

Fig. 33: Design fantasy, pencil coloured with marker pens, drawn on special paper with shadows depicted transparently

Alcohol-based marker pens can be used on many different kinds of paper. However, standard, open-pored paper absorbs a lot of the marker colour, giving the drawing a more powerful quality. In sketchbooks a rough sheet of paper must be inserted between the page being used and the next one to prevent the colour soaking through. For drawing areas of colour smooth papers are most suitable, for instance the roll of sketching paper.

Fig. 34: Kolumba Cologne, purely marker pen drawing, made on site

Drawings made exclusively with marker pens have a particularly three-dimensional and atmospheric effect. Here one works from the lightest to the darkest layer of a "family" of markers (e.g. warm shades of grey). At those parts of the building that face towards the light the white of the paper should be allowed to shine through, without a layer of marker ink. ■

■ **Tip:** Materiality can also be excellently depicted with marker pens. Horizontal or vertical clapboard cladding can be shown by minimal overlapping of the individual lines drawn with the broad, trapezoid-shaped tip of the pen. The overlapping creates darker areas of the colour used, which suggests the shadow joints between the wooden boards. Concrete surfaces are often vertically structured at their upper and lower ends due to weathering. This impression can be created with the tip of the light grey marker. The outlines of the individual formwork panels and the turnbuckles are drawn with darker grey.

Fig. 35: Watercolour box with brushes and a paper handkerchief as absorbent surface

Watercolours

In some cases it is essential to show the colour of the parts of a building, the vegetation or the sky. This can be in an architectural design or while making drawings of existing architecture on the move. Watercolours enable you to depict the colouring of materials, atmosphere and nature in a realistic way.

A (metal) watercolour box is the most suitable; the standard kinds available generally have between 12 and 24 colour pans. However, all you really need are the primary colours yellow, red and blue (not necessarily the richest shades) and 1–2 natural shades of green, a brown and an ochre shade, and black. Brushes should be the series 4, 12 and 24. A larger watercolour box may also have a surface on which to mix colours and a compartment to store the brushes so that they are protected against fraying.

Watercolours generally take the form of pressed, dried colour pigments with which different shades or intensities of a basic colour can be obtained by mixing them with water. This mixing also gives the watercolour a glazing, i.e. translucent, quality. Layers of watercolour can be placed one on top of the other, provided you have the necessary patience, as you must wait until one layer has dried before applying the next one, if you wish to avoid the new colour blending with the earlier one. In using watercolours you generally work from light to dark areas on the sheet. At the brightest part of the drawing there should be no layer of watercolour, just the white of the paper. > Fig. 38 Monochrome watercolours are also fascinating.

The translucent quality of watercolour paints makes them suitable for depicting shadows. You do not always have to use a watercolour based on black that depicts shadows as a grey film and darkens the area of colour beneath it. Depending on the particular mood of the drawing, shadows can also be made using dark violet, dark blue or dark green hues.

A colour gradient to depict vaulted areas or the sky can be easily produced using watercolours. First the basic colour required is mixed. The area that will finally have the deepest colour is painted first; this is generally done with a size 12 brush. Then the brush is very gently washed in a glass of water and excess water equally gently removed by using a paper handkerchief. The brush still holds the same colour, but the intensity is slightly reduced. Now painting is continued on the still wet paper, again covering only a small area at a time. This procedure is repeated until the entire area required is painted or until the brush holds water only, without any trace of colour. ■

■ **Tip:** If you are painting larger areas with watercolours it is helpful to raise the sheet on the side further away from you. The colour mix should be applied downwards, causing it to flow towards you. Watercolour is applied until the lower edge of the painted area is formed in the shape of a long drop. Then brush can be filled again with colour and continued at the area already painted without creating any visible edges or lines.

Fig. 36: Monochrome design watercolour

Fig. 37: Depicting curved or vaulted surfaces with watercolours requires the use of colour gradients.

A pencil drawing coloured with watercolours is a delightful mix. Generally, it is difficult to draw in pencil on coarse, thick, watercolour paper and therefore a smoother paper must be used, but this does not easily allow several layers of watercolour to be applied. A compromise is necessary. As few as possible layers of colour should be applied in order to avoid damaging the paper. On this account this technique is not a pure

Fig. 38: Sketched, naturalistic colours of a building and its surroundings

watercolour but a colouring. The use of watercolours allows the important things to be easily separated from the unimportant, and the composition is simplified. When not all of the drawing is coloured and it thus becomes clear where the focus lies, the concentration makes the depiction more interesting. ■ ○

■ **Tip:** If using watercolours while on the move it is useful to carry with you a small screw-top jar filled with water. Paper handkerchiefs can be used to dry the brush and to clean the box after drawing.

○ **Note:** Watercolours are not only available in the form of compressed colour blocks. Watercolour pencils look much the same as normal coloured pencils but are water-soluble and can be painted over with water later. Liquid artists watercolours in tubes offer more intense colours than the blocks, but they are complicated to mix on palettes and therefore not so suitable for rapid freehand drawing.

Fig. 39: On-site drawing made with ink pen and watercolour pencils, later given a water wash

Fig. 40: Pencil drawing with watercolours: a classic in the illustration of architecture (building site Grossmarkthalle Frankfurt am Main)

SPECIAL INSTRUMENTS USED IN ARCHITECTURAL DESIGN

Triangular scales

The triangular (architect's) scale is a drawing and measuring tool, about 30 cm long, with which one can draw and measure lines at different scales. It is an indispensable tool in architectural design. On each of the three faces there are two different scales, giving a total of six usable scales. Each edge is allocated to a particular scale or pair of scales (e.g. 1:2, 1:5, 1:10, 1:20, 1:25, 1:33, 1:50, 1:75, 1:100, 1:125, 1:150, 1:200, 1:250, 1:500 or 1:1000).

Triangular scales can be made of plastic or aluminium. If buying one you should ensure that it has as many possible different scales as possible. Of course, the scale 1:2 can be easily converted to use for drawings at a scale of 1:20 and 1:200 and so forth.

A triangular scale is placed on a scale design sketch in order to determine the scale, to check a particular dimension in the sketch, or to change a dimension. The triangular scale is also suitable for measuring existing plans or drawings that have no dimensions, but whose scale is known. If you draw freely without any existing basis you can draw the desired length in metres directly to the desired scale.

Fig. 41: Measuring a sketched elevation (scale 1:500) with the triangular scale

Fig. 42: Ruler, set square, triangular scale, French curve, circle template

Rulers, set squares and templates

Rulers and set squares can be used to check rapidly made sketches to see whether their dimensions and proportions need to be developed further. Straight-edge rulers produce mono-dimensional drawings. Their disadvantage is that they are suitable only for drawing straight lines. They are, however, ideal for constructing perspectives with one or more vanishing points. > Fig. 23, page 33 The transparent set square, which is also used for technical drawing, is very useful for drawing parallels and lines at right angles, or any other angle required, to a given line. The length of the hypotenuse (the long side of the triangle) should be 32 cm. A grip makes this implement easier to use.

French curves are available as prefabricated stencils. They come from the field of mathematics, where they are used to draw parabolas and functions. In architecture they are particularly useful for drawing round design elements, especially in perspective. If a particular curve is not available a flexible curve can be used. A circle template with circles of different diameters is always useful.

Freehand drawing in architectural design

DRAWING TYPES

Generations of architects have debated and examined which form of illustration is most suitable for conveying an impression of their building to themselves and to different groups of people. Looking at the depictions of architecture as described in contracts and the basic forms of depiction used by architects work we find the following range of drawings: site plan, floor plan, elevation, section, detail, perspective and then, less commonly, axonometric. Architects use these drawings to express different aspects of their designs. These aspects can be roughly broken down into the following architectural categories: the urban situation, the function, the construction, the proportions, the configuration of building volumes, the way the building parts fit together, and the materials used in the building. This applies to technical drawings made to a particular scale as well as to freehand sketches, which at the start of a design are generally made without any scale. When the design becomes more concrete or when the planning commission is based on an existing building, the freehand sketches also employ a scale. You discover which drawing at which scale is ideal for conveying the intended content through individual experience and by drawing regularly. Designs should be continually developed and examined in several types of drawings.

Site plan, floor plan, section and elevation are planar depictions, i.e. simple projections. They are not experienced in reality, as the elevation, for instance, is an "unrealistic" drawing, made at right angles to the building from an infinite distance. We experience a real building very differently. The site plan and elevation describe the exterior of a building, while the floor plan and section provide mostly information about the internal configuration of the building. Axonometric projections are based on planar depictions but also show the third dimension, height. Perspectives are central projections and are based on one or more vanishing points.

Pictogram

Pictograms are a special case. These are symbolic graphics that attempt only to convey the design idea or design variations. They must not be based on any of the drawing types referred to above and must not provide any concrete information or data about the design. The drawn form of the pictogram is very free, but generally extremely clear in graphical terms. They do not use any scale. > Fig. 44

Fig. 43: Sketches of different projections: floor plan, section, elevations (developed design)

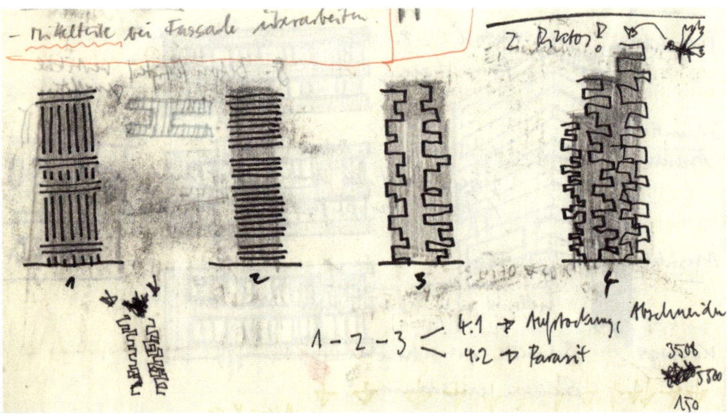

Fig. 44: Pictograms of different facade versions (conversion of an existing high-rise)

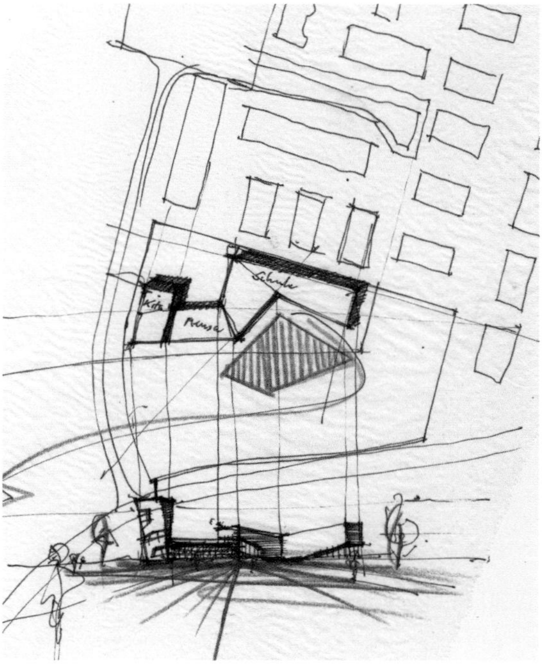

Fig. 45: Site plan with neighbouring buildings and a perspective with the first impression of the exterior

Site plan

The largest scale drawing of an individual building or complex of buildings is the site plan. The site plan shows the location of all building parts on the site and its immediate surroundings, whose surface areas are also shown. The building that is the subject of the design is shown as a top view. Site plans are generally drawn at a scale of 1:500, at earlier design stages and in larger building projects also at 1:1000.

It makes sense also to show the immediate surroundings of the planned building. These can include neighbouring buildings, vegetation or infrastructure elements. Site plans often contain legends, levels (height above sea level) and arrows that indicate entrances or circulation. North is generally to the top of the sheet, a north arrow (or pointer) should always be used. The building should be drawn in such a way that it stands out clearly from the surrounding developments. This can be achieved by heightening the contrast, by using thicker lines, or by the use of colour or surface textures. > Figs. 36, page 44, and 45 The site boundaries are indicated with a dashed line. > Figs. 46 and 47

Fig. 46: Immediate surroundings highlighted by use of coloured areas on the computer

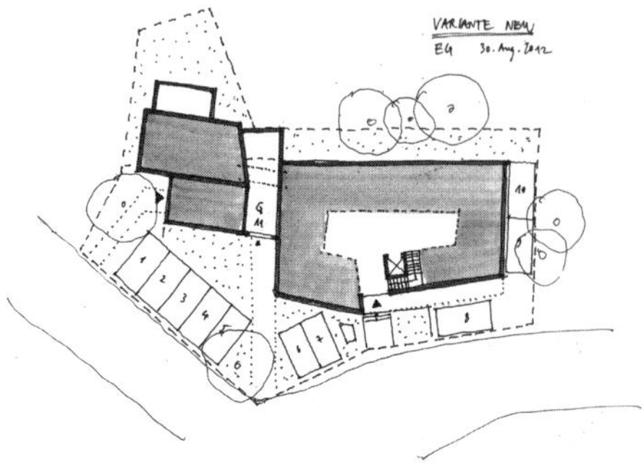

Fig. 47: Schematic ground floor plan with depiction of the site

Floor plan

A floor plan is a horizontal cut through a building. Architects always look down from above, that is to say, a cut is made through the building and everything that can be seen below the line of the cut is shown. This line is chosen so that all the openings and the circulation systems can be seen. The floor plan shows the arrangement of rooms on the different floors, each floor being drawn separately. Floor plans reveal spatial sequences and functions. Sketches of ground floor plans should show the nature of the surrounding area of the site.

Dark or black-coloured walls outlining white rooms are one of the principal characteristics of a floor plan sketch. They reveal the building typology, separate rooms from each other, or indicate the structural system. In the early stages of the design the floor plan sketches do not yet have these typical characteristics. In such cases, simple coloured areas may be used to indicate sequences of spaces that will eventually provide the configuration of the building. > Fig. 48 Floor plans of this type are generally at a scale of 1:200. In the later planning stages floor plans must be drawn at scales of up to 1:50.

■ **Tip:** If the shape or position of the further floors of the building differs from the floor plan shown it makes sense to indicate them using full, dashed or dotted lines (see Chapter Tools and techniques, Lines and the instruments for drawing them).

Fig. 48: A floor plan takes shape through the arrangement of rooms, sorted by colour according to their function.

Fig. 49: Sketch section at the design stage with depiction of the surroundings

Section

The section is made by placing a vertical section plane in the design on which everything that you see when looking in a specific horizontal direction is then depicted. The section plane should be chosen in such a way that all the important room heights, the way the structure works and the circulation of the building can be read. What lies close to the section plane is drawn clearly; building parts that are further away can be drawn more lightly in elevation. > Fig. 50

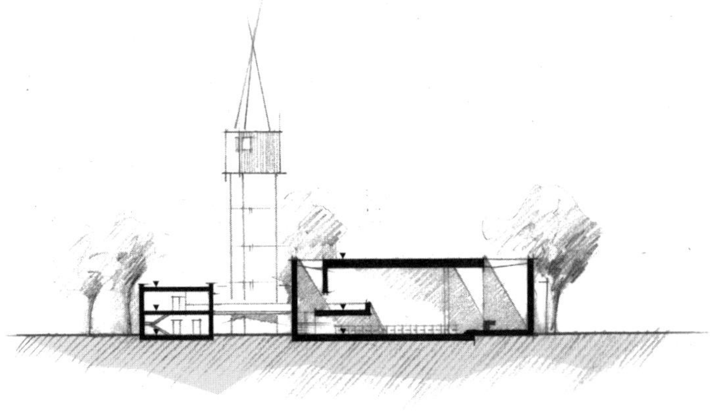

Fig. 50: Sectional drawing made at the design stage showing surrounding buildings and trees

During the early design phases the sketched section is a most important means of illustration. Often it is needed in order to clarify decisive spatial situations. The scale of building sections and elevations depends on how far the design of the floor plans has advanced. If the floor plans are drawn at a scale of 1:100 it makes sense to draw the sections and elevations at this scale too. Urban planning sections through terrain are generally drawn at a scale of 1:500.

To grasp the complexity of a building a number of sections are generally needed (at least one cross section and one longitudinal section). As with the floor plan the walls and ceiling slabs cut through are coloured dark or crosshatched, and important edges that are not directly visible are indicated by dashed or dotted lines. The position of the top of the surrounding terrain should be shown in every section and is depicted by a strong line. If the design involves changing this level the original edge of the terrain can be shown as a dashed line. Elements that provide a sense of scale, such as people, vehicles and vegetation, give section and elevation drawings a certain lively quality and make them easier to read.

> Chapter Freehand drawing in architectural design, Indicators of scale

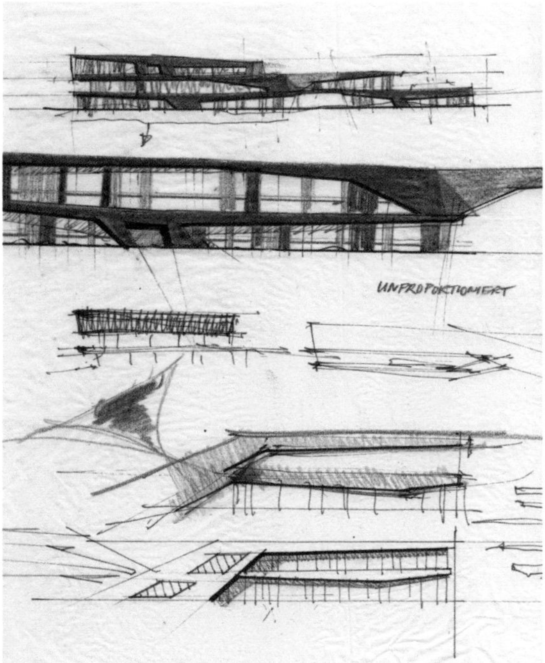

Fig. 51: Elevations of one design at different scales in a sketch

Elevation

The elevation (or view) is a planar drawing that shows one external face of a building. It could be regarded as a sectional drawing in which, however, the section plane is not inside the building but outside and directly in front of it. The elevation depicts the proportions of a design or reveals the relationship of the planned building to its surroundings (neighbouring buildings, nature etc.). The relief of a building (facade, windows, projections) should also be visible and can be shown by means of shadows. This gives an essentially planar drawing such an elevation a certain depth. Building parts in the background are, as in the section, drawn more faintly and with separated lines.

During architectural design the elevation can be sketched directly beside, above, or below a plan drawing, as the lengths required are already given. It is important that the ground line on which the building stands be emphasised, and that the planned building be clearly distinguished in the drawing from the neighbouring buildings.

Fig. 52: Elevation developed from sketched floor plans

Detail

If you wish to define the construction or materials of a building precisely, you must proceed to drawing at a smaller scale. What are called the details of the building are shown in section, elevation or perspective drawings. Particularly important are detail sketches of those places where the different parts of the building are pieced together, where materials meet, where construction meets design. The term "detail drawing" can cover drawings made at very different scales. A very detailed depiction at the scale of 1:1 to 1:5 is clearly a detail, but so is the depiction of a facade at the scale of 1:50, as this offers far more detailed information than the scale normally used for an elevation drawing.

In detail sketches it may be necessary to define certain materials precisely. There are standards that lay down the kind of hatching or lines used to depict materials. In a large-scale section the cut building parts are indicated by thicker lines. To allow visual checks to be made frequently, a part of the relevant internal and external elevation and a floor plan are drawn alongside the detail section drawing (vertical or horizontal section).

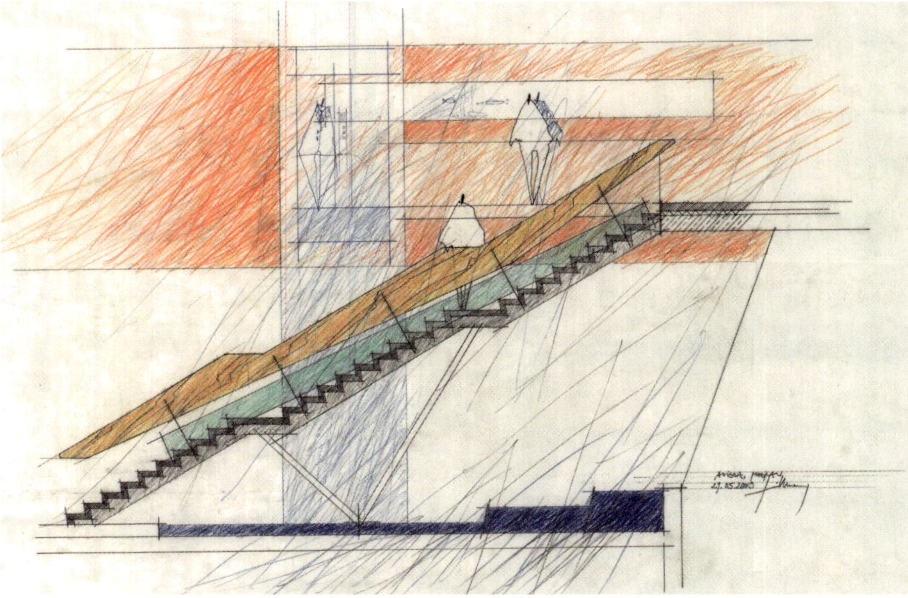

Fig. 53: Large-scale staircase detail with indication of colours and materials

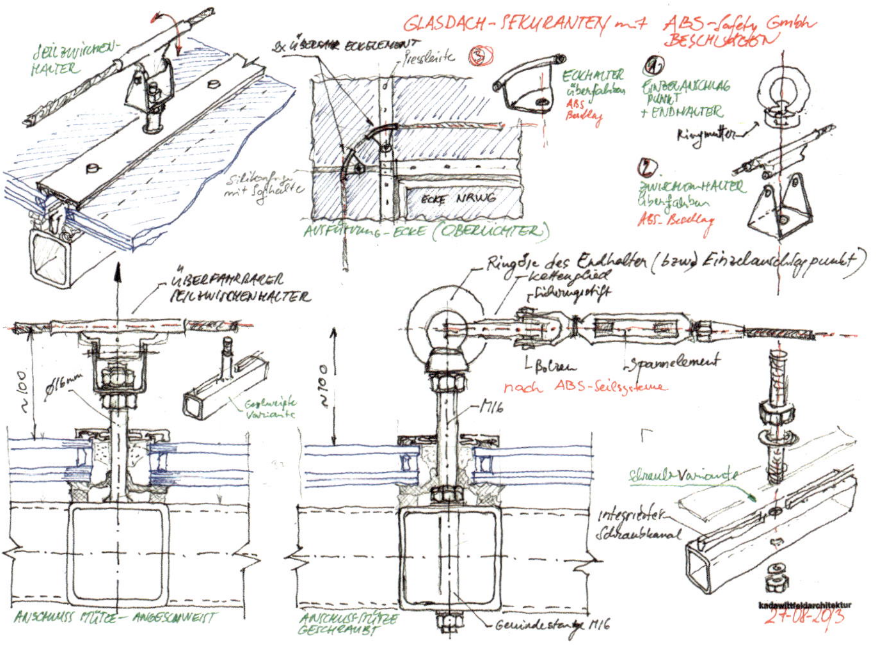

Fig. 54: Small-scale development of details using different types of drawing

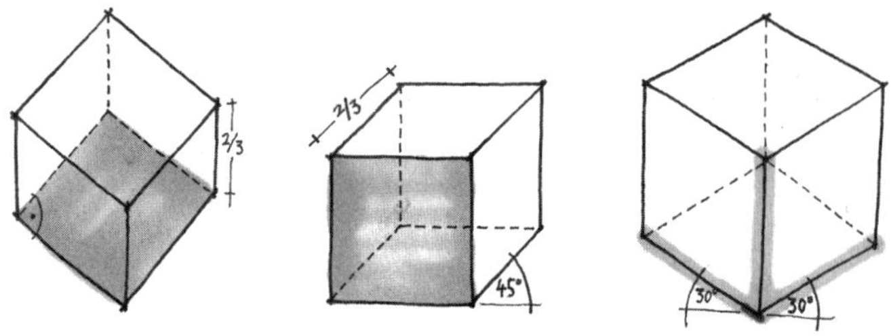

Fig. 55: Floor plan axonometric, elevation axonometric and isometric projection.

Axonometric projections

Axonometric projections combine the advantages of planar and three-dimensional drawings as they combine both kinds of depictions: in some kinds of axonometric projections, the depths and heights of rooms can be measured from the drawing. These drawings are frequently used in the architect's daily life to depict simple spatial relationships. They are often based on existing drawings and in such cases adopt the scales of these drawings. The three simplest and most common axonometric projections used in architectural design are the floor plan axonometric, the elevation axonometric, and the isometric projection. > Fig. 55

The floor plan axonometric projection (or military projection) is based on the floor plan, i.e. the dimensions of the floor plan are retained and can read off the constructed axonometric projection. The heights are generally reduced by one third. If a floor plan drawing of a current design already exists, then a spatial depiction can be very quickly drawn using a roll of sketching paper. The disadvantage of the floor plan axonometric is the large visible surface of the top view.

The floor plan axonometric as an exploded drawing (which can also be made on the basis of an isometric) is very informative but relatively time-consuming. Here, the different floors, building parts or planes of the construction are shown separated from each other but linked by connecting lines and by the geometric severity of the axonometric projection.

The elevation axonometric projection (also sometimes called cavalier projection) is based on the elevation. The elevation of the building is viewed frontally; the volume develops behind it at an angle. The depth of the building volume is shortened, generally by a third or a half. This form of axonometric projection is easy to produce if an elevation of the design is already available.

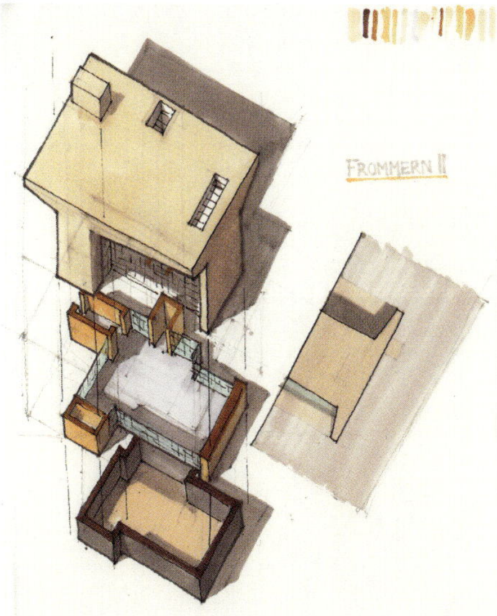

Fig. 56: Floor plan axonometric projection as an exploded drawing

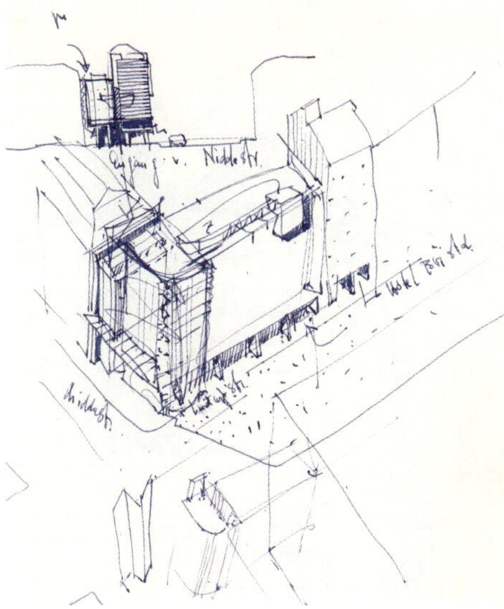

Fig. 57: Rapidly sketched isometric to explain a spatial situation, with elevation

The isometric ("iso" comes from the ancient Greek and means equal) offer true lengths in all directions, however the floor plan is distorted and shown without a right angle. Therefore the isometric cannot be made on the basis of an existing drawing. > Chapter Freehand drawing in architectural design, Continuing the design But the additional effort involved in making this kind of drawing is worthwhile, as the isometric has the illustrative character of a bird's eye view. The isometric is often used in drawing overview plans.

Free perspectives

A perspective drawing differs in one important point from the floor plan, elevation, section and axonometric: it has one or more vanishing points. That is to say parallel edges, building parts or buildings are not drawn parallel to each other but meet at a vanishing point. Perspectives are particularly suitable for making a building understandable in a clear, communicative way that lay people can grasp. Such perspectives are often drawn from the eye level of someone passing by a building, as the aim is to depict spatial impressions realistically. In addition to the outer spatial configuration, the perspective also shows particularly clearly the form and proportions of a building and how it is integrated in urban design. > Fig. 39, page 46

In situations in which designs based on planar drawings such as floor plan, section and elevation must be quickly examined in spatial terms,

Fig. 58: Rapidly drawn perspective (not constructed) at the height of a passer-by for an urban design ideas competition

Fig. 59: Sectional perspectives of sports halls

bird's eye perspectives, sectional perspectives and perspectivised elevations are used. These are rarely based on the laws that govern the construction of perspectives but nevertheless communicate the design idea.

In the perspective that a lay person can easily read, the horizon, which in such rapidly made perspectives is generally not drawn, usually lies in the area of the ground floor of the building. This creates the illusion of a realistic passer-by's view of a building in its spatial setting, whether this is the city or the country.

Bird's eye perspectives are three-dimensional drawings looking down from the sky, i.e. the station point of the perspective is above the building. Like the site plan they show both the building and its surroundings. You see a distorted top view of the building itself and at least one elevation. > Fig. 37, page 44

The combination of section and perspective known as the sectional perspective is a most communicative form of depiction. It can show the architectural characteristics known from the section, while giving the drawing a spatial dimension.

The perspectivised elevation suggests, in perspective, an area in front of a building, and in this way counteracts the absence of perspective in a classic elevation. > Fig. 43 below, page 50, and Fig. 45, page 51 As long as the elevation does not suffer in graphical terms, it can improve the otherwise rather abstract elevation of a building.

Constructed perspective

Freely drawn perspectives cannot always completely satisfy or convince the designer and the viewer, as they are not geometrically constructed and are consequently imprecise. To produce a correct perspective, even in freehand drawing, a construction method that comes from descriptive geometry can be used. The basis of this method is shown below for an orthogonal building, using two vanishing points.

To construct a perspective in this way you require a floor plan and at least one elevation of the design. These drawings must be put on the paper, at the same scale, before the perspective is constructed – in the form of a sketch, copy or print. Ideally, however, the perspective should be drawn on transparent paper; the drawings referred to above can be placed beneath the transparent sheet. > Fig. 64, page 64

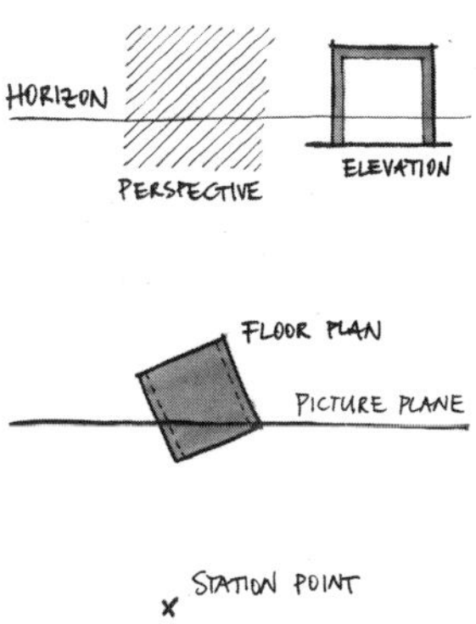

Fig. 60: Schematic construction of a perspective (the perspective will be drawn in the crosshatched area)

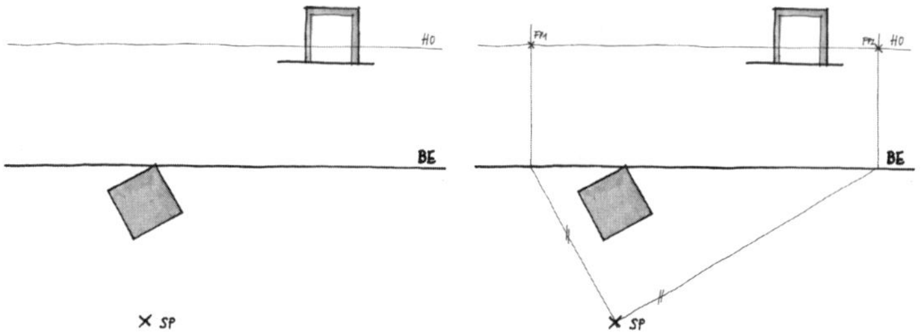

Fig. 61: Preparation and construction of the vanishing points

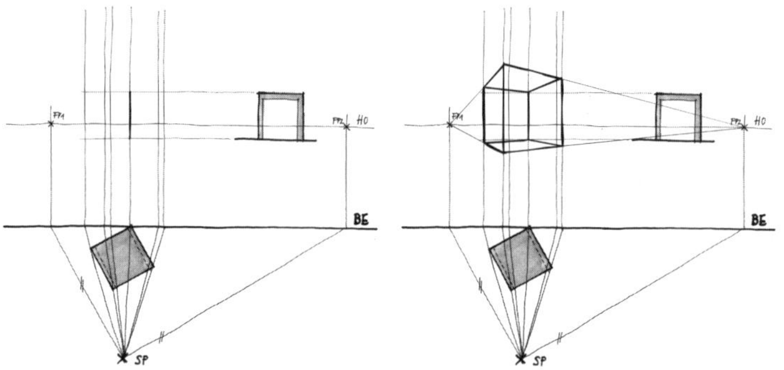

Fig. 62: Transfer of the true height and construction of the perspective

On the sheet the perspective is constructed from bottom to top. Near the bottom edge of the sheet is the station point (SP). Now the floor plan must be positioned in such a way that the desired perspective can be drawn. The distance to the station point must be determined, and the floor plan must be swivelled until an interesting view is found. The elevation is placed above the floor plan, not centrally but to the left or right of the floor plan. The perspective is created alongside the elevation and above the floor plan. The picture plane (PP) is drawn through the floor plan as a horizontal line, parallel to the ground line of the elevation. Its position determines the size of the final perspective. Ideally it should be positioned so that it cuts at least one important corner or edge of the building. In the elevation drawing the vertical position of the horizon (HO) is chosen. It is drawn parallel to the ground line of the elevation and to the picture plane in the upper part of the sheet. > Fig. 60

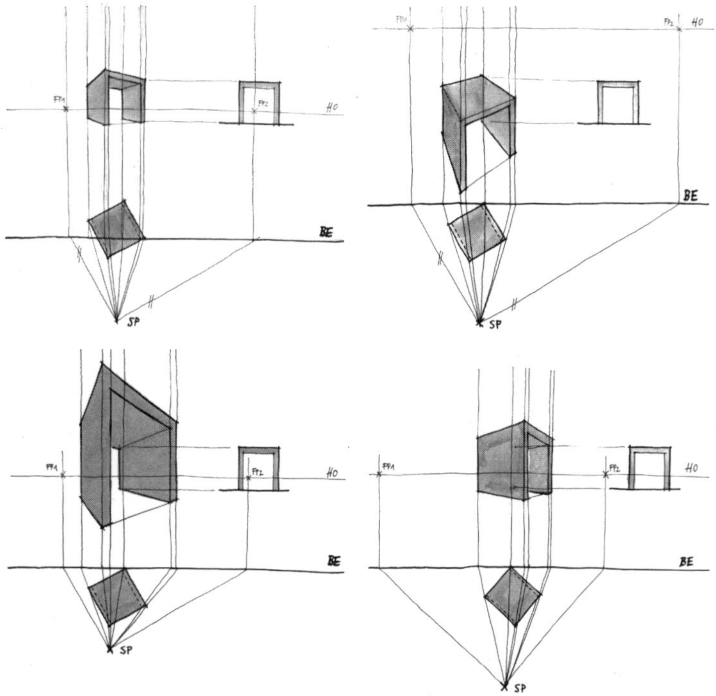

Fig. 63: Changing the position of the picture plane, the horizon and the station point and swivelling the building

This preparatory work should be carried out before constructing the perspective. Now the vanishing points needed are constructed. To do this lines are drawn parallel to the orthogonal outside edges of the floor plan and are extended to meet the picture plane. At each of the points where they meet this plane a vertical line is drawn up to the horizon. These two new points are the two vanishing points. > Fig. 61 ○

○ **Note:** Although this construction method is relatively time consuming it produces only a small perspective. It also requires a good understanding of the procedure and the variables. Only the main principles are presented in this book. Construction methods employing one or three vanishing points are not dealt with, nor are the construction of shadows or perspectives of non-orthogonal floor plans.

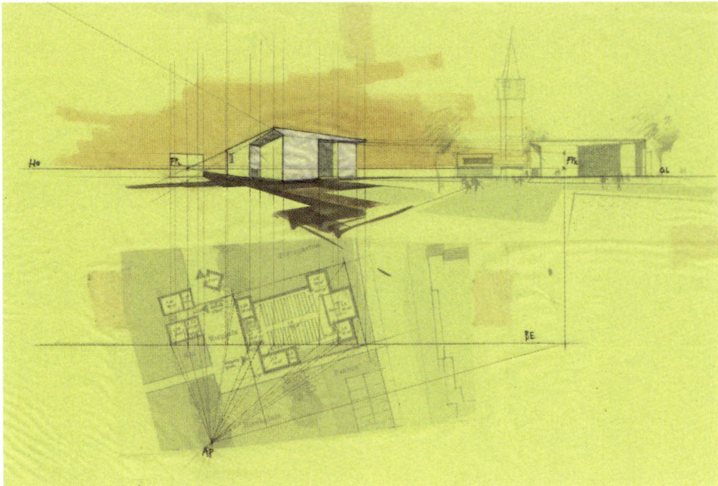

Fig. 64: Perspective based on the point projection construction method

In the next step the building volume is transferred from the plan to the perspective to be drawn. To do this lines are drawn from the station point to the important corner points of the building in plan and continued to the picture plane. From these points on the picture verticals are drawn. Here the corner point of the floor plan that cuts the picture plane should also be included. Only at those points where the plan drawing cuts the picture plane can real heights be transferred from the elevation to the perspective.

Now the perspective can be created step by step. From the first edge of the building vanishing lines are drawn to the next building edge, the position of which has been defined by the verticals already drawn. Seen from the eye-point the right-hand sides of the building sides always vanish to the right vanishing point and left-hand sides to the left vanishing point. > Fig. 62

In this method, four variables determine the appearance of the constructed perspective. > Fig. 63 If you change the position of the picture plane in relation to the floor plan this changes the size of the drawing. Only those building parts on the picture plane retain their size. The horizon determines the vertical height of the station point. If the elevation drawing cuts the horizon you obtain a view of the building from above or below. Shifting the station point immediately changes the perspective. If it is close to (far from) the floor plan the perspective can seem very dramatic (flat). If the floor plan is turned until it reaches the desired position in relation to the station point, this changes the position of the vanishing points. > Fig. 63

INDICATORS OF SCALE

In the technical architectural drawing – such as the floor plan – familiar forms for fittings or furnishings such as toilets, staircases or doors serve as a scale that gives the viewer a grasp of the proportions. These indicators of scale are enormously important for the outside viewer, whether clients, colleagues or lay people. They should be included in all architectural drawings –both the architectural design and the drawing made on site. They also include drawings of trees and plants, people, street furniture, vehicles, and in some cases also the sky.

People

Showing people in architectural drawings is of great importance. They give the virtual building a vertical dimension that everyone can immediately understand. They are indispensable above all in elevations and sections; > Fig. 49, page 53 and in perspectives passers-by or users of the building dimension the space that the design intends to convey. > Fig. 23, page 33 They are more rarely found in floor plans where they are not obligatory. The manner in which people are depicted depends on whether they accompany the design in an additive manner or are intended to indicate how the space is dimensioned. Like everything else people can be depicted in a variety of ways. > Figs. 15, 53, 58, 74 and 90

Views of architecture drawn on site can also be given a scale by adding people. If these drawings are perspectives then, before starting to draw, you should consider your position relative to other people. If you stand when drawing then (assuming a straight plane) the heads of all standing adults should be shown on the horizon line, no matter how near or far away they are. > Fig. 74, page 76 Here, too, you are confronted with the basic decision about what level of importance should be given to the people depicted. The main focus should always be on the architecture.

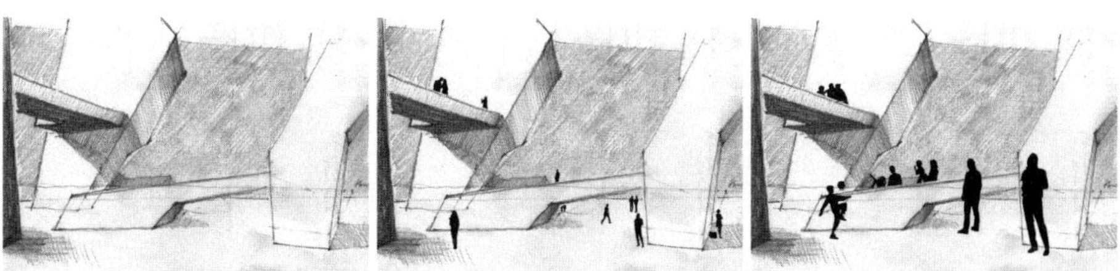

Fig. 65: A sketch of a space initially without dimensions. Attempts to dimension it with different depictions of people give the space very different sizes.

Fig. 66: Trees as positive and negative, the focus is on the composition as a whole

Vegetation

Where they seem relevant in a drawing, trees can be depicted in many different ways. There are innumerable kinds of trees and many of them change their appearance with the seasons. How one depicts trees is always a question of the composition or the focal point on the sheet. If the attention is to be directed to a building that is surrounded by trees, these should be drawn faintly and vaguely. > Fig. 50, page 54 If the drawing is intended more to convey an overall impression, the trees and the building can be given roughly equal emphasis. > Fig. 66 Whatever the case, the depiction of vegetation helps to integrate the architecture into its established setting. > Fig. 25, page 35 Trees should not be drawn too small, as this makes the building appear proportionally too large.

To make a (deciduous) tree appear more three-dimensional in summer the mass of leaves with the trunk should first of all be shown as an outline drawing. The trunk and the branches can be added, but it is more important to break the tree up into so-called "leaf-clouds" whose structure is more defined on their shadow side. It should be noted that "leaf-clouds" that have one side in shadow and one in the light appear more three-dimensional. > Fig. 10, page 22, and Fig. 27, page 35 Conversely, in winter trees consist only of the structure of the trunk and the branches, which grow thinner towards the top of the tree. In depicting trees a combination of line drawing (pencil or fineliner) with a number of surface areas (marker pen or watercolours) is particularly charming. > Fig. 36, page 44

Fig. 67: Different kinds of trees

Bushes, grass and other kinds of incidental vegetation should be indicated only by a variety of lines or suggestions of irregular textures, and should never be too dominant.

Vehicles

Much like architecture and the human body, motorised vehicles are made up almost exclusively of basic geometric shapes added together. Most of the parts of a car can therefore be constructed relatively simply in a drawing. In elevation and sections they are generally needed only in the form of silhouettes, but in perspectives they are three-dimensional volumes. In designs that stand on busy streets in particular, cars must be drawn so that they fit properly into the given space in terms of perspective – i.e. they must be drawn correctly with regard to the vanishing point. > Fig. 68

Sky

If the horizon (the horizon that actually describes the top of the visible land or building mass) can be seen on the sheet, the depiction of the sky acquires particular importance. Like almost everything else the sky can be depicted in a number of different ways. Hatching can convey a certain dramatic quality if the lines become denser towards the horizon or point towards a vanishing point. This effect can also be achieved by a gradient using watercolours or marker pens. Whatever the case, care should be taken that the upper area of clouds is not given any colour but

Fig. 68: Like the buildings, the car on the road vanishes towards the vanishing point.

is left white. Only the underside of the clouds should be depicted. > Fig. 38, page 45 The same applies when you hatch clouds: in the lower part of the cloud close to the horizon the hatching lines are condensed, and the upper part of the cloud is left untouched. A sky can be edged with nearby trees, neighbouring buildings or electricity wires, no matter whether it is just hatched or depicted with watercolours. Whether and in what way the sky is present in an elevation or a perspective can also supply information about the topographical surroundings of the site of the planned building.

Degree of abstraction

A floor plan at a scale of 1:100 is intended for a certain stage of the planning process (design planning). This scale also suggests that, in comparison to earlier planning stages, the drawing is larger in terms of the area of paper needed, and that more must be depicted. This could take the form of the way rooms are furnished, details of the construction or of the building services. In contrast in such plans the urban context will hardly be visible.

It is not only in the field of technical drawing that particular scales are allocated to the different planning stages. Freehand drawing should also obey certain rules in order to ensure that legibility is preserved, for lay people as well. This is a difficult topic to deal with as sketching is always dependent on the individual style and expression of the draughtsperson. Essentially, however, the size of the drawing should always match the content shown.

A design is often made on the basis of an existing drawing with a known scale. Where this is not the case, a triangular scale can help. Freehand sketches without a basis should not be too large, as they are generally used in the early planning stages where details have yet to be clarified.

In architectural drawing on site, the size of a perspective can greatly influence its expressive strength. People, vegetation, vehicles and urban furniture enrich every drawing through atmosphere and by suggesting dimensions. They function extremely well in terms of indicating scale, whereas other things tend to hinder the understanding of space. The depiction of individual stones in a wall or roof tiles from a great distance can strongly influence the apparent size. In addition, repetition of the same structures can often seem childish; it is far preferable merely to suggest such structures. As in the early planning stage of a design, a greater distance from the object being drawn demands a higher degree of abstraction.

CONTINUING THE DESIGN

Only the very first sketch of a design consists of pure thoughts, and every sketch that follows reacts to what has been drawn before by rejecting it, accepting it or developing it further. But sometime or other the point comes where the information in the sketches must be carried a step further. The sketch consolidates at a certain scale and finds the way from abstraction to concretisation.

The steps that a design has to undergo before it is realised are in principle comparable to the architect's services, as described in the professional scale of fees. During the basic evaluation, the design and approval plans and the later technical and economic design phases, the design constantly changes in the way it is depicted and, as a result, also changes the scale. The types of drawing that emerge show the design from all side and at different levels of depth, support it or reveal its flaws.

The freehand sketch reveals its advantages as a mediator between the different scales and planning stages. A drawing that previously only existed at a larger scale can be transferred to a different scale through the draughtsperson's experience. The visual language changes. At this stage, leave may be taken of the medium of freehand drawing in order to concretise and dimension the design by producing technical drawings. If what had been hoped for does not emerge as a result the sketch can be used again, which advances the design even though it involves going back a step in either scale or thought. This is how a design develops, through advances and setbacks, and the design method does not compete but switches between freehand and technical drawing, model and simulation, and engages with them in a meaningful symbiosis.

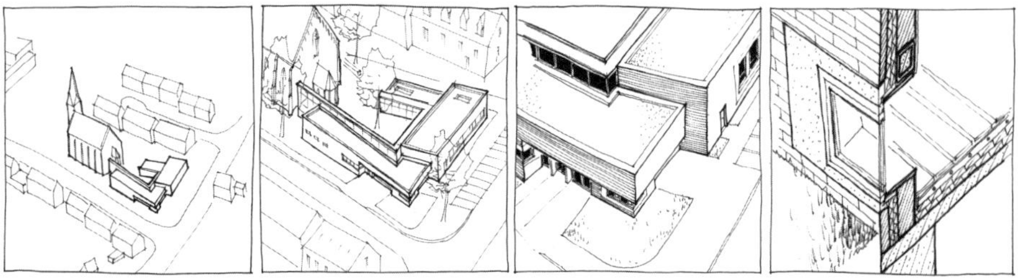

Fig. 69: Changing visual languages in consecutive design steps

Based on a printed-out photo of a model, the building volume can be examined using a roll of sketching paper. CAD applications often have axonometric view areas in which planar drawings such as floor plans or elevations can be shown in parallel perspective. If we print out this view area it can provide the basis for a useful and informative axonometric. > Fig. 56, page 59 Equally, a digitalised drawing can be imported into any CAD program. It is positioned so that it lies visibly on its own construction plane so that the lines conceived can be drawn over with vectors.

When the end of a design phase approaches and concrete results are required, the medium of freehand drawing need not be abandoned. For example, competition entries that use plans and perspectives drawn freehand stand out among many presentation plans made completely on the computer. Their authenticity gives the viewer the feel that the author has holistically engaged with his or her work. Hand-drawn details are just as suitable as CAD details to accompany the specifications for a particular trade. > Fig. 19, page 30 The points of contact between analogous and digital design media are numerous and varied.

Architectural drawing on site

The special thing about drawing on site – however banal it may sound – is being present in front of the architecture, its phenomenological appearance, observing the building directly and then transferring this to the drawing. Drawing on site means drawing an existing piece of architecture which our eyes see and which penetrates our brain and which, with our hand, we reproduce on a sheet of paper. This illustrates the difference both to design sketches, which are derived from the imagination, and to photography, which rarely works in a cognitive way.

Through the repeated act of looking closely, drawing on site encourages the development of a building archive in which patterns, geometries, structures, forms and typologies can be stored. The draughtsperson appropriates a building individually and produces a two-dimensional equivalent of the image that he or she has perceived, at an undefined scale. ■

DRAWING TYPES

When we look at a building on site, we find ourselves in a specific relationship to it in terms of perspective. This means that the perspective is the sole realistic type of drawing you can draw without a further examination of the building. This is the great difference from projection drawings. A site plan, an elevation, or an axonometric cannot be produced on site without walking around the building; you will not be able to draw an elevation correctly if you are not positioned at right angles to the building; you will not be able to draw a floor plan or a section if you have only looked at the building from outside.

■ **Tip:** A drawing that you have started on site should, wherever possible, also be finished on site. You should never draw from photographs as this prevents atmospheric and spatial impressions from appearing in the drawing, neglects some aspects and exaggerates others. Drawing on site offers an opportunity to refine your perception and therefore a chance to show by means of particular aspects what was important to you at the particular time. Nobody can assume another person's perception. Nevertheless the scene should also be photographed so that afterwards you can compare the reality with what you have perceived.

Fig. 70: Drawing excursion to Runkel: despite similar conditions and the same rules of drawing, individual drawing styles still emerge.

Fig. 71: Drawing excursion to Dietkirchen: the choice of drawing instruments influences the depiction.

However, since an architect uses a variety of methods of illustration in order to make certain ideas in the design understandable, you should attempt on site to make other drawings as well as perspectives. If, say, the focus of interest is on the construction of the building, you should try to make a section or draw a detail. However, this means you must first enter the building, walk around it and examine it closely. This inspection encourages the cognitive penetration of the building through understanding the logic of its structure.

PERSPECTIVE DRAWING

Someone who makes freehand drawings of real architecture cannot use the constructed perspective method as they do not have the floor plan and elevation needed. Nevertheless, by observing certain principles rules and laws it is still possible to draw a correct perspective. Perspective is particularly useful for the depiction of space. A measurable spatial depth, which is imitated in all perspectives, cannot be taken a freely drawn perspective, as perspectives do not have any scale.

The depiction of space is regulated by five principles:

1. The first principle of perspective illustration is that of the spatial constant. It describes the relationships between the sizes of objects in the depth of the space. Objects of the same size are shown smaller the further away they are.
2. The principle of staggering is that any object behind another is hidden. Care should be taken that the lines do not overlap, as if they do they cannot be interpreted in spatial terms.
3. The principal of correct level of detail can be compared with architects' plans, which use different scales. Objects in the foreground are close and are therefore depicted in detail; objects that are closer to the horizon are further away and therefore some of the precise detail is lost. Here the draughtsman or woman varies the degree of abstraction.
4. Someone who has a good long-distance view in the city or the country recognises that the layers of air and vapour cause tonal values to fade or grow weaker towards the horizon. This is the atmospheric principle. The same object, seen at a greater distance, tends to blur visually in the background.
5. The fifth principle of perspective drawing deals with shadows, which with all their different facets can create strong spatial effects.

The way the picture is built up is an important decision that must be made before starting every drawing, and may decide on the success or failure of the work. A drawing is always only a depicted part of the surroundings. There are complicated ways of showing the whole of these

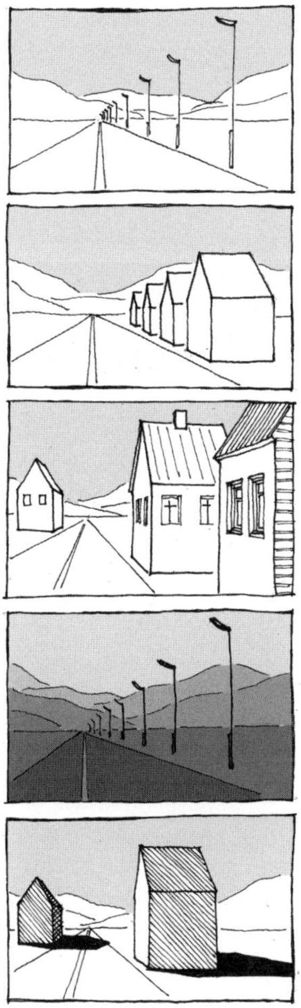

Fig. 72: The five principles of perspective illustration: spatial constant, staggering, correct level of detail, atmosphere, shadows

surroundings in perspective, but essentially a part or section must be chosen – consciously or unconsciously. First of all, the picture plane must be determined, that is, you must decide what you want to draw. The imaginary picture plane (PP) lies between you and the object you draw. > Fig. 73 It is like an invisible plane slid between draughtsperson and subject, and projects what the observer sees onto the drawing sheet at a reduced scale.

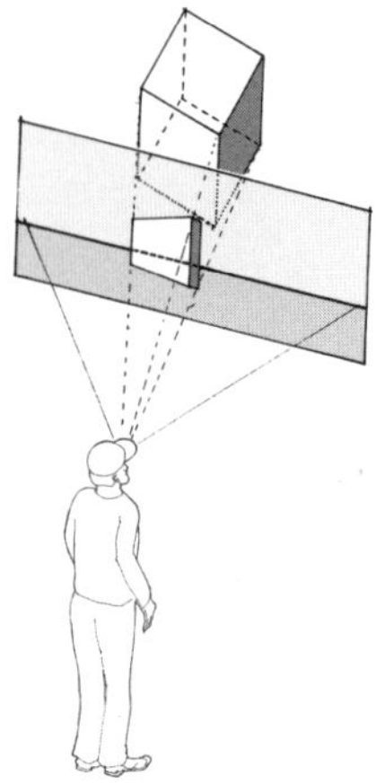

Fig. 73: Between architecture and draughtsman lies the picture plane: the drawing sheet.

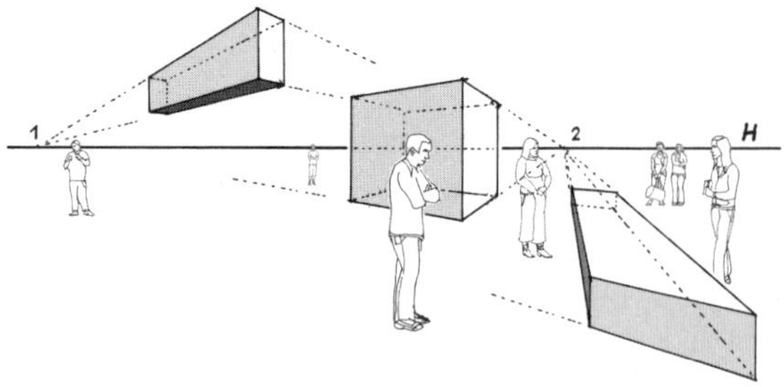

Fig. 74: Three-dimensional volumes in relation to the position of the horizon

Before starting the drawing you must discover your relationship to the subject of the drawing. Is it above or below you? Where is the horizon? How many vanishing points are there? The horizon (H) is always at our eye level, whether we are lying on the ground (frog perspective), sitting or standing. If all the people gathered on a level square were of the same size, then their eyes would all be at the same height and therefore directed towards the line of the horizon. > Fig. 74 Depending on interest the subject of the (draughtsperson's) desire is either above the horizon (H), at the same height as the horizon or below it. Vanishing points (VP) always lie on the horizon line (except for tilted planes and three point perspectives).

The station point from which a building is viewed influences the kind of perspective (central, two-point or three-point perspective). If you look at a building or an interior space at right angles, you must draw the perspective with a single vanishing point (central perspective). The special aspect of the central perspective is that only the lines of building edges that are parallel and run in space converge at the central vanishing point; all the other lines have no vanishing point and therefore never meet. If you are not looking at the building at right angles but at an outside corner of the building, you have a diagonal or two-point perspective. Left-hand building parts converge towards a left hand vanishing point, right hand building parts towards the right-hand point. As the name suggests, the two-point perspective has two vanishing points. All the vertical edges of the rectangular volume remain vertical. If we draw an angled view and at the same time look upwards, for instance at the base of a high-rise) or

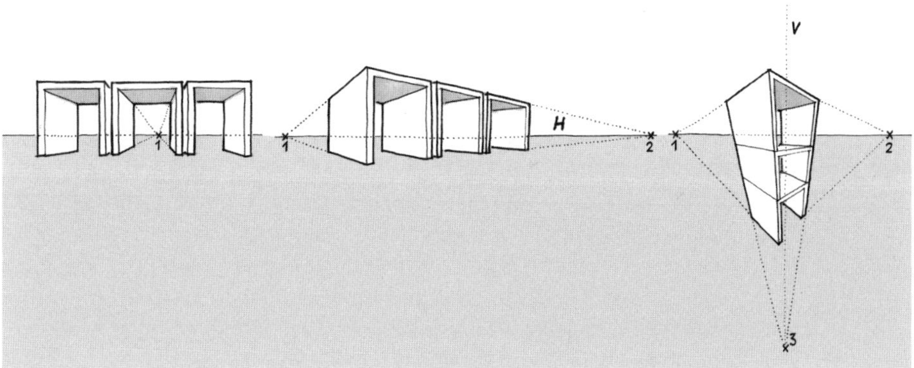

Fig. 75: System of the central perspective, two-point perspective, and three-point perspective

look downwards, (for instance out of the window of a high-rise building), a third vanishing point is added. This is then – with a rectangular building – the <u>three-point perspective</u>. Theoretically we could draw a spherical perspective that depicts the space surrounding us in all directions. In a rectilinear world one would always have six vanishing points, four them every 90° in the four points of the compass and one each for the high point and the low point. The high point and low point lie on what is called the "<u>vertizon</u>" (V), the equivalent of the horizon. ■ ●

■ **Tip:** Essentially, the nearer you are to the building you are drawing, the closer together the vanishing points are on the drawing sheet (see Fig. 63, page 63). If you move further away from the building and draw it again you will notice that in relation the vanishing points are now further away from the building, possibly even no longer on the drawing sheet. In single point perspectives the vanishing point is generally near the centre of the sheet.

● **Important:** A significant difference from the technical architectural drawing is the depiction only of what is visible, i.e. no edges of volumes that lie behind or in front of the building being drawn are indicated by dashed or dotted lines. Unless, that is, various lines are needed to construct building parts: lines to discover the horizon, vanishing points or construction lines for complicated building parts can be retained in the finished drawing, as they form part of the development and comprehension process of the drawing. Corrections are also allowed. The aim is to find the correct line and to depict the subject of the drawing correctly.

Construction of an on-site perspective

The perspective most commonly used in on-site drawing is the diagonal or two-point perspective with two vanishing points. The individual steps of the construction are described below.

If, with your arm outstretched, you hold the pen or pencil horizontally in front of your eyes and imagine the line produced, you obtain the position of the horizon. This can be transferred to the sheet as a straight horizontal line. In the present situation this can be done on the lower part of the sheet, as at the moment the level of your eyes (approx. 1.50 m above the level of the ground) is in the lower part of the building. Now you can see what is to be drawn above and below the horizon. With a two-point perspective it is advisable to draw the building edge closest to the point where you are standing as a vertical. > Fig. 76

Finding the vanishing points is most important. First of all, the actual length of the building edge is drawn on the verticals. This also determines the size of the drawing. The pencil is an ideal instrument for measuring the lengths, angles and proportions. It can be placed directly against the lines of streets, building edges, or sloping roofs. If you measure the angles of the lines running from the end points of the building edges and continue these lines to the horizon you obtain the two vanishing points. The width and height of the building you are looking at can be measured with the pencil: fix your thumb at a certain point on the pencil and read this length in relation to the entire length of the pencil. > Fig. 77

Taking further measurements completes the volume of the building in all directions. The position of the projecting pediment can be determined by drawing two diagonals through the rectangular area. The main openings of the building are also drawn. > Fig. 78

■ **Tip:** To arrive at comparable results you should always hold your arm outstretched against the subject of the drawing, no matter what you wish to measure. In measuring angles a watch face can also be helpful. A sloping roof must not always be described by a number of degrees, the detail "two o'clock" can also suffice.

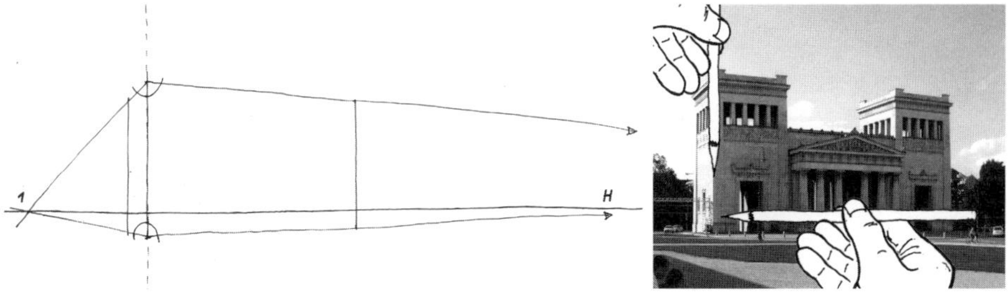

Fig. 76: Determining the position of the horizon and a near building corner with the drawing pen or pencil

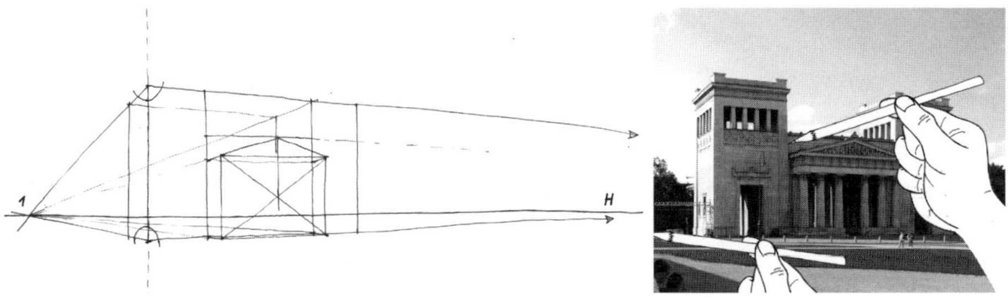

Fig. 77: Finding the vanishing points and measuring the building's height and width

Now the drawing can be completed. Secondary openings, ornament and details are added. The foreground and background frame the building. Applying shadows gives the architectural drawing a certain plasticity. > Fig. 79

In the simpler central perspective first of all look you for the point on the end face (for instance of the building) that is exactly at right angles to the station point. This point lies on the horizon. From the corner points of the end face of the building – or perhaps an opening or an imaginary surface – lines are drawn from the direction of the vanishing point. > Figs. 90 and 91, page 91

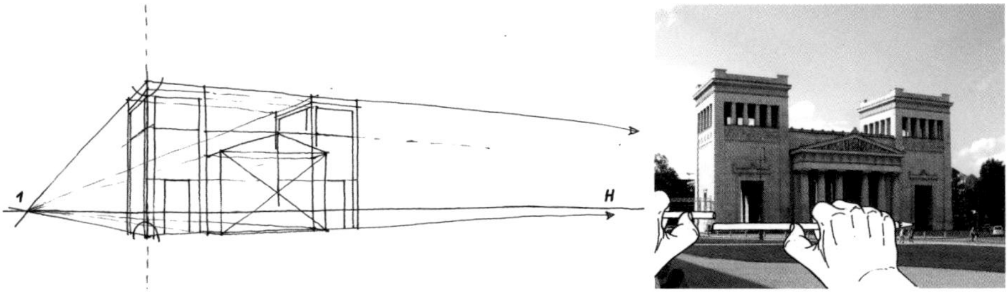

Fig. 78: Completing the volume by measuring

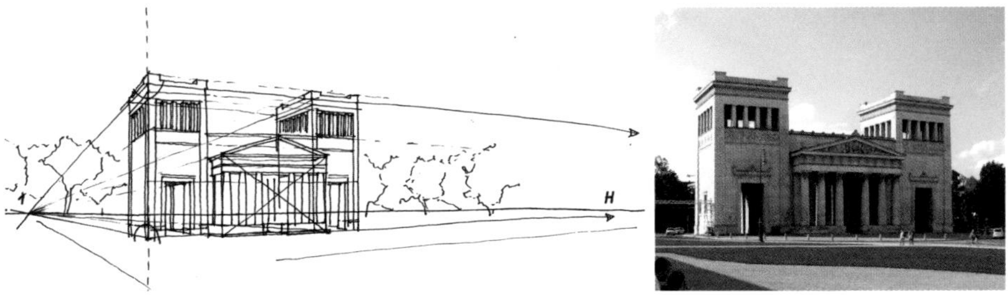

Fig. 79: Completing the drawing

Site plan and floor plan

If you wish to have an overview of the place where the building stands a small site plan sketch is ideal. The site plan is essential for depicting the urban setting. You can attempt to survey the space with the help of the perspective but walking across it is also extremely useful. Walk around the building, which is ideally freestanding, taking paces of equal length. To make an approximately correct site plan, it is useful first of all to draw a chequerboard grid on the sheet. Then – depending on the size of the place – the width and length of each square represents ten to twenty paces. You should now walk across the area and attempt to insert the building at the right position in this grid. You can also do it at a smaller scale by just looking at the building and drawing its outline rather than a site plan. Here you walk around the outsides of a freestanding building and count your paces. This helps you discover the outline or footprint, i.e. the relationship of width to length. If it is possible to get inside the building you wish to draw, you can continue drawing the floor plan in the interior and in this way depict the building's function.

Fig. 80: Axonometric projection made on site

Floor plan axonometric

If the outline of the floor plan has been drawn you can attempt a further type of architectural drawing, the axonometric depiction. This is, alongside the perspective, the drawing that is best able to provide information about the configuration of the building volume. On the basis of the plan drawing (generally immediately above or below it) using extended construction lines, make an attempt to depict the building in three dimensions. Walls and columns, for example, are given certain heights. Through further observations, as the result of walking around and inside the building several times, you can then complete the drawing.

Elevation and section

If you wish to convey the special proportions of the building on site the elevation drawing is recommended. Alongside the perspective this is most useful drawing for depicting the proportions of a building. You can achieve command of the correct degree of abstraction at different scales (i.e. drawing sizes) by producing several elevations, each time at a different distance from the building. You should attempt to ignore the marginal central perspective offered by your view of the building. With access to the building, you can sketch a cross section based on the elevation, which shows the structural system of the building or its circulation system.

AIDS

Grid and frame

With a transparent grid of lines or a mesh, which can easily be made on a sheet of film, you can recognise several important aspects. If, like most sheets of drawing paper, the sheet of film is roughly in the format 2:3 it can be used as a basis for positioning a drawing on the sheet, by holding it at the desired distance away from yourself and looking at the building through the transparent film. If you hold one of the horizontal lines directly in front of your eyes you also obtain the horizon. You also see all the building verticals, which for a one- or two-point perspective, are always drawn as verticals. The transparent grid provides further aid if you have difficulty in transferring the correct proportions of the building and its surroundings to the sheet of paper. The structure of the gridded sheet of film can be applied lightly to the sheet with the drawing. You now examine the "contents" of each square and draw these, square by square, onto the sheet. Gradually the sheet is filled with the correct proportions.

A frame, which can also be made with the thumb and index finger of both hands, can help to find the section or part of the reality in front of you that you wish to draw. It gives you a feeling for what you can fit on the sheet, and helps avoid unpleasant surprises with regard to the size of drawing. The area of the frame always represents the drawing sheet.

Preliminary sketch

Before making a larger perspective drawing it is sometimes advisable first of all to draw a small preliminary sketch of what you plan to do. This should help deal with problems as regards the relationship in which you stand to the building, where the horizon is, and how many vanishing points there are and whether they are on the drawing sheet at all. It should give you a feeling for how the drawing can be positioned on the sheet. The frame of the preliminary drawing represents the outer edges of the drawing sheet. The horizon is quickly found and entered in the lower third of the sheet, then by measuring the angles the two essential vanishing points can be found. The rough outline of the building can now be added faintly. The quick note represented by the preliminary drawing trains your ability to grasp and perceive, both of which are essential for drawing on site. The miniature drawing also helps to decide how large to make the drawing that follows the preliminary one.

Fig. 81: Using a sheet of film with a grid of lines that divides up the building, which is distorted in perspective, into areas of equal size

Fig. 82: Use of the frame

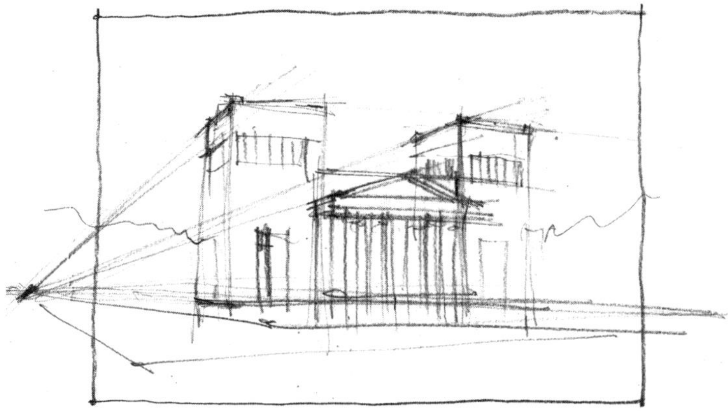

Fig. 83: Miniature preliminary drawing based on the content of the frame (here a two-point perspective, station point in the lower part of the building)

Construction aids

In diagonal perspectives the sides of buildings are often so distorted that you cannot grasp the visual centre point of the building without being irritated by this distortion. To determine where the visual centre point of a building seen in perspective lies, take the pencil with your thumb at the centre of its length and hold it in front of your eyes. Now move the pencil towards or away from you until the length of the pencil exactly covers the building that you want to draw. If you look again at your thumb and note the point of the building that is hidden behind it, you obtain the centre point of the building and of the drawing you are about to make and can position it better on the sheet.

For instance, in order to depict regularly spaced street lamps in perspective you must first of all choose a distance (D) between two street lamps. Then you determine the middle line (M) of the two lamps and connect this with the vanishing point (VP). From the top of the first lamp you now draw a diagonal through the middle point of the second lamp and extend it to meet a bottom point on the lower vanishing line. This is the point at which the third lamp stands.

You find the middle point of vertical lines in a perspective by measuring the actual length or height of the lines. In contrast, the middle point (M) of rectangular areas is found by drawing an “X” through a rectangular area in perspective. Centrally positioned building elements (flags, towers, windows) can then be more easily constructed from this middle point.

Fig. 84: Finding the visual focus of the building

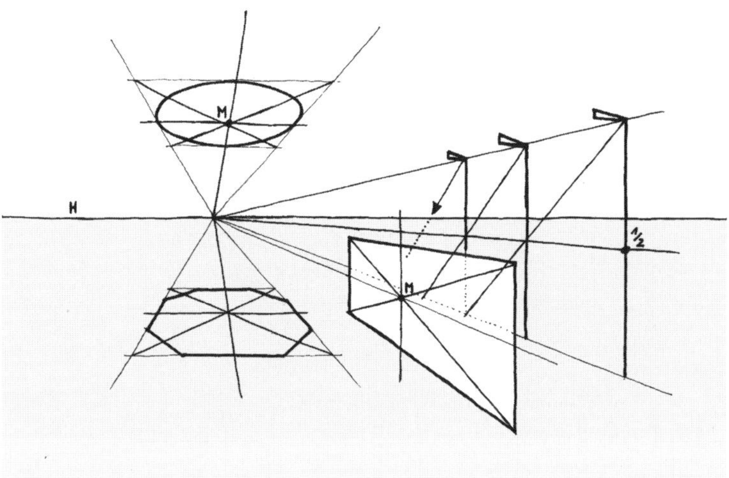

Fig. 85: Construction aids

Circles are always found within squares, ellipses within a rectangle. From the square or rectangle with an "X" drawn through it we arrive at the circle or the ellipse through the intermediate step of the octagon.

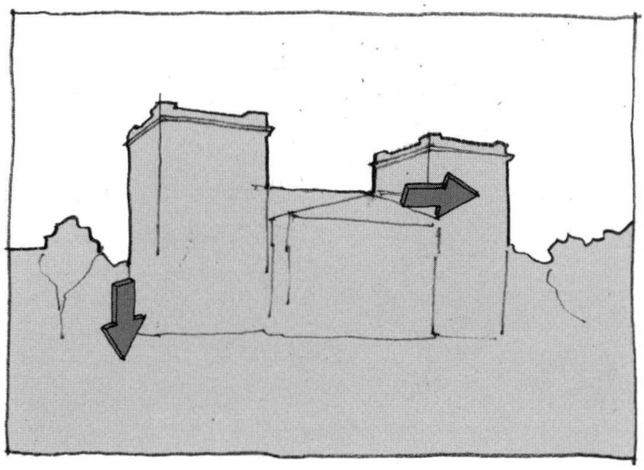

Fig. 86: Approach to drawing with outlines (see also Fig. 73, page 76)

Outlines

Drawing a perspective correctly is often difficult. There are, however, a number of approaches to depicting the object correctly. In drawing outlines or intermediate spaces first of all the contour is depicted that separates, say, the stone building from the airy sky or defines the void/space between two volumes. On this basis the relationships between two volumes are first determined, not the volumes themselves. Once the main outline, which can be drawn intuitively or by measuring, is established on the sheet the building can be completed below the outline. While making the outline compare the lengths, angles and relationships just drawn with those you drew just a short time earlier. The outline is thus a scale for itself and later has a considerable influence on the composition of the drawing as a whole.

Shadows

Light makes buildings, objects and people visible but it is shadows that make them seem alive in reality. If you are able to identify and depict shadows a drawing becomes more spatial and has greater relief. There are different ways of transferring this spatiality to the two-dimensional drawing substrate. The path of the sun should be noted and followed while making a drawing, as in the course of producing an elaborate drawing it can change (and along with it the shadows). When the sun shines different kinds of shadows can be identified on buildings. The side facing towards the light of a rectangular building is brighter than the side of the building opposite. The sides of the building between them are,

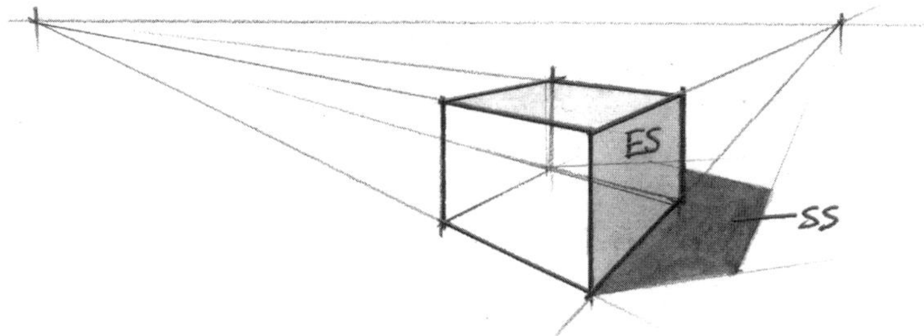

Fig. 87: An object's own shadow and cast shadow (light source on the left)

in terms of brightness, somewhere in between. A distinction is drawn between own shadow and cast shadow. Own shadow (OS) is, as a rule, lighter than cast shadow (CS). If own shadow and cast shadow meet they produce what is called core shadow. Pure shadow drawings have a special kind of attractiveness. Here the focus is on depicting the different tonal values of the shadows. Medium light tones are avoided and particularly light and dark areas are exaggerated. The brightest surface remains white. If the drawing is made on grey or brown paper the brightest area can also be made using a white pencil, which achieves a similar effect.
> Fig. 10, page 22

Instruments for when you are on the move

You should feel at ease with your own drawing instruments or utensils. They should be agreeable to use and, for daily use, they should all fit easily into a bag. The equipment needed for drawing in the city need not be elaborate; it must only suffice for what you intend to do.

A fisherman's seat, a stool or even a draughtsman's stool are recommended to every urban draughtsman or woman. If you do not have a stool you have to find a position where you can sit comfortably for a length of time, but which then may not offer the view you want. During the colder part of the year, fingerless gloves, which allow you to hold the pencil properly, are very useful. What are known as fold-back clips are handy to prevent the wind whipping up the pages while you are drawing on site. Drawings made with a lot of graphite or charcoal should be treated with a

Fig. 88: The draughtsperson's utensils

fixative to ensure a long life. If you do not have this protective layer (generally available in spray cans) with you, a temporary solution is to lay a ■ ○ loose empty sheet over your drawing.

■ **Tip:** Drawing architecture on site marked by external influences: a strong wind, hot sun, bright backlight, annoying pigeons and inquisitive passers-by or unpleasant smells, the public realm that cannot be influenced, atmospheric morning light or a spontaneous feeling for a particular piece of architecture. Drawing buildings on site also means observing rules. You should be certain that it is permitted to draw at the chosen spot. It is indeed often the case that drawing is allowed where photography is forbidden, but where this is uncertain you should make enquiries.

○ **Note:** In public space, your choice of drawing subjects may place you at prominent and busy places and squares. You should not let yourself be discouraged by the comments of passers-by. If you feel watched by an audience behind you, you should close your sketchbook briefly until the inquisitive glances have turned elsewhere. You do not need to put up with this kind of thing: after all, the author of the drawing is the only relevant person, not the public at large. You should observe the influences and rules, particularly if the drawing takes a longer period of time.

Further development

AS-BUILT DRAWING

Design sketching can also be combined with drawing architecture on site. For instance, where you intend to prepare a design for an empty inner city site, you should first of all visit the site. With the sketchbook all the relevant data and impressions of the site can be noted and the spatial situation recorded in a drawing. After this urban design analysis a perspective of the empty site, without the future design, can be made directly. You should look for a perspective that shows the main characteristics of the site.

When the design has matured in terms of function and form it can be integrated into the drawing made on site using sketching paper or tracing paper. The planned volume, which previously existed only in the form of planar projections, can now be evaluated in spatial and urban planning terms. Care should be taken to insert the design correctly into the drawing in terms of perspective, taking into account the horizon and vanishing point(s).

Naturally, this can also be done on the basis of a photograph of the site or even of the model of the surroundings. First of all, however, the horizon and vanishing points must be determined, which can be drawn using sketching paper.

DIGITALISATION AND IMAGE EDITING

Freehand drawings are always originals, of which only one exists. In some cases, however, digital reproductions are needed, whether for screen presentations, presentation drawings or website contents. The digitalisation of a drawing is almost always followed by editing the image on the computer, no matter whether the drawing was pixelated by a scanner or a camera. This is true of both design drawings and on-site drawings.

Digitalisation

If sketches or architectural drawings are required in digital form for a particular purpose, there are essentially two ways in which this can be done.

Scanning drawings with a flatbed image scanner is a very good and authentic solution. The scanner has image processing software that allows the settings to be adjusted. The resolution should be 300 dpi, which is high, but still acceptable in terms of data volume. The drawing is laid flat and evenly on the scanner. As a result the distance of the drawing to

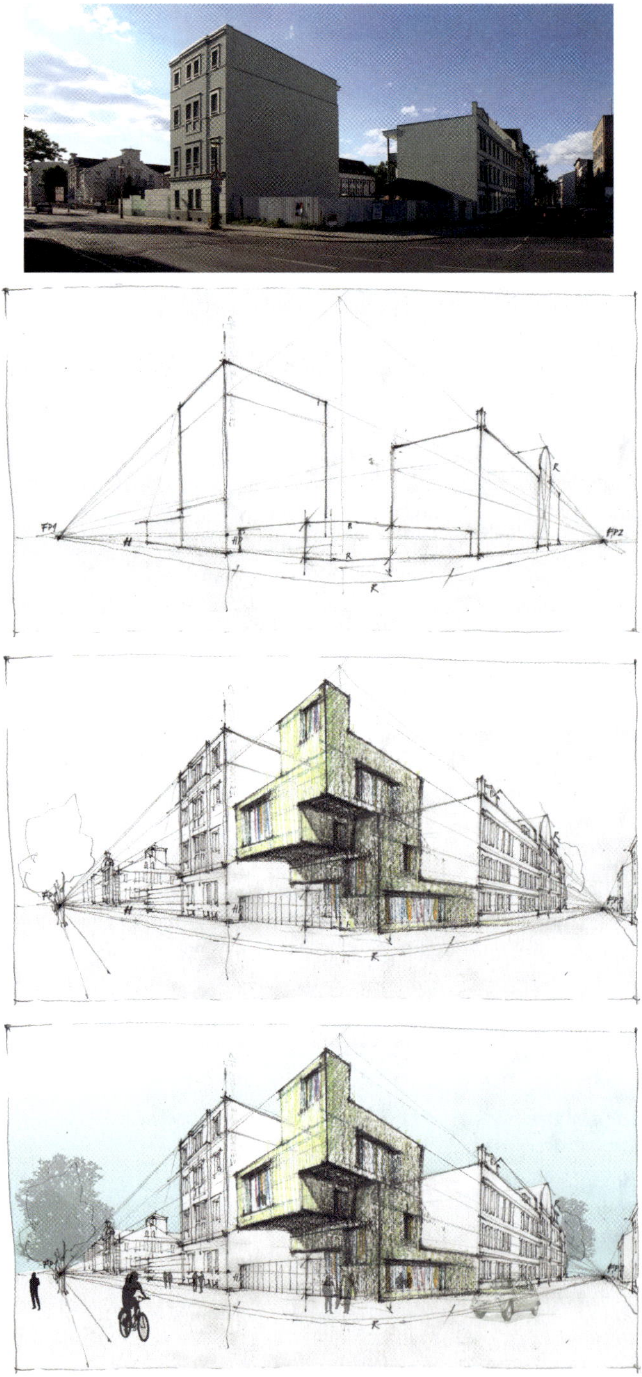

Fig. 89: Photograph of the empty site, construction of the perspective, insertion of the design volume, developing the image, completing the illustration

Fig 90: Scanning vs. photographing a drawing

Fig. 91: Drawing before and after cleaning

the light source remains the same, allowing you to expect a homogenous result. If only a DIN A4 scanner is available, larger documents can be scanned in sections and later pieced together with the image editing program in the panorama or sorting function. Care should be taken that the individual data are always scanned and saved in the same way.

Drawings can also be <u>photographed</u>. If you want to do this indoors you should ensure even, ideally indirect, lighting so that no reflections impair the depiction of the drawing. Reflections occur in particular with pencil drawings and drawings made on tracing paper. The photograph must be taken perpendicular to the drawing so that it is not distorted. The photographer's shadow should not be cast. The direct flash function of the camera should always be deactivated. If you attempt to make a photographic reproduction outdoors, in principle the same rules apply: no reflections, no shadows, and even lighting. In this way, both with an overcast sky and in bright sunshine, good results can be achieved.

Postprocessing a design drawing

After the drawing has been digitalised, image editing is usually necessary to allow the drawing to be used for other purposes. For instance, after a drawing on sketching paper has been scanned or photographed, grey areas and edges caused by unevenness may often impair the image. Bleeding may be evident directly beside lines, or the original grey or black of the lines may not be recognisable.

With a purely line drawing for which only pencil or fineliner was used it makes sense to reduce the saturation level of the entire image so that it still has a number of different shades of grey (caution: do not active "greyscale" editing as this changes the compatibility of the file). If the drawing now looks rather pale, correcting the gradation curve can help. Using the white pipette (black pipette) a white (black) area is marked in the drawing. In this way all blurred grey areas in the drawing can be removed, and the individual lines now appear more clearly. Changes to image brightness and contrast produce similar results.

Having been cleaned up the drawing offers a good basis for further editing and processing with areas of colour, colour gradients and transparencies. A collage-like mounting of people, trees and other indicators of scale in a hand drawing can achieve a delightful effect. Here, it is important that the additional elements be allocated to a separate layer in the image editing program so that later changes can be made. > Fig. 89 below

Postprocessing an on-site drawing

An architectural drawing that was made on site can also be subsequently edited, for instance on the basis of a photograph. Care should be taken that the place remains authentic and is not falsified by incorrectly cast shadows, exaggerated colours, or changes to the depictions of material.

In Fig. 92 right, the background was first completely covered with a mid-grey and then the lightest areas (the windows and the soffit of the arch) created by removing this colour. Special effects here include the angled entry of light, created by means of a white transparent surface, and the reflections on the floor, transparent duplicates, turned upside down, of the respective original layers in the image editing program. Fig. 93 underlines the horizontality of the design by the atmospheric addition of sky and vegetation as a gradient and through the emphasis of the horizon. Here, too, the depicting the shadows correctly is most important.

Fig. 92: Original and digitally processed on-site drawing

Fig. 93: Digital processing of on-site drawings

In conclusion

Drawing is the architect's language. The technical drawing is not as personally formulated as the freehand sketch but is tied to certain conventions. When such a drawing is made by hand the placing of focal points and particular care can create an individual style. However, the use of CAD programs in the early design stages makes drawing styles more uniform and interchangeable and increasingly reduces the proportion of freely drawn ideas in a design. Even while still a student the growing complexity of the tasks that confront the architect reduces the use of the freehand drawing, which is often seen as excessively time-consuming.

But it is precisely the spontaneous and intuitive freehand drawing that can transfer the ideas of the designer to a sheet of paper in a pure manner. Here, sketching is learnt by trial and error. To be able to use this medium in a confident and effective way, certain techniques and tools must be tried out. In the later stage of the design it forms a perfect synthesis with model building and technical drawing.

Sketching architecture on site provides a valuable service. It offers the draughtsman or woman a very personal abstraction of what has been perceived. The archive of architectural structures and quotations that is gradually built up through drawing existing architecture can be later drawn upon when designing. But here, too, drawing architecture cannot claim to replace other disciplines of architectural education. Visiting a building in its setting in urban space or in the landscape, going inside it, touching it and discovering its various functional, constructive or design characteristics are also an essential part of perceiving and understanding a building.

Bert Bielefeld, Isabella Skiba

Technical Drawing

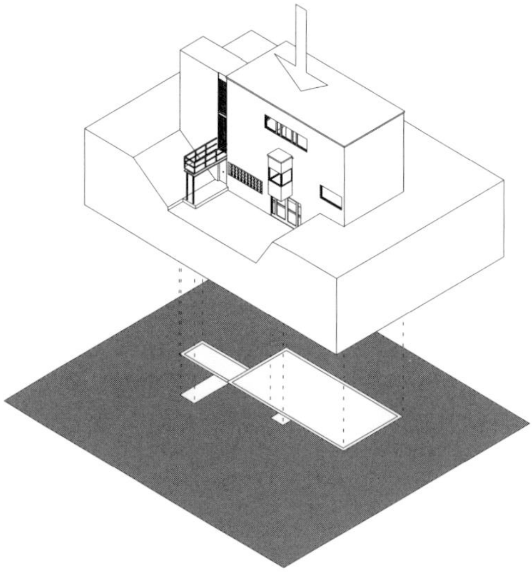

Fig. 1: Top view principle

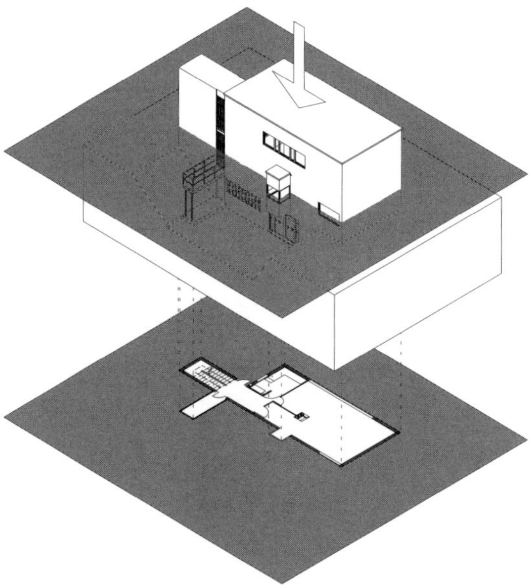

Fig. 2: Plan view principle

Projection types

Buildings are drawn in the form of sketches and free perspectives, but also using various structural drawing approaches. A fundamental distinction is made between top view and elevation for the exterior, and between plan view and section when drawing the interior of a building.

TOP VIEW (OR ROOF PLAN)

Top view drawings present a view or projection of the building seen from above. A top view (also often called roof plan) is important for the location plan, for example, which defines the building's position on the plot.

PLAN VIEW

In the same way, a plan shows a single floor of the building. Here a section is taken through the building at a height of about 1 to 1.5 m above the floor, to include as many apertures (doors, windows) in the masonry as possible. To make the drawing comprehensive, the heights of all the relevant structural sections (sill to floor height, aperture height, ground level, floor height) are given, as well as all the relevant horizontal dimensions. The height of the horizontal section may be changed to illustrate as many special features of the design as possible and to represent any windows that may, for example, be higher. (The different position of the window is then clarified by giving the sill to floor height.) For the direction of the plan, there are two basic possibilities:

- The downward direction of view used in architects' plans (top view), which makes it possible to record room structures, form and size.
- The reflected plan views from below showing construction elements that lie above the horizontal section level. - Structural engineers prefer this view, which shows the loadbearing construction elements in the ceiling above. >Chapter Planning Stages, Specialist planning

Designating plan views

Plan views are generally designated according to the floor they apply to, e.g. cellar floor plan view, ground floor plan view, 1st floor plan view, attic floor plan view etc. If it is not possible to identify floors clearly in a design, e.g. when floor levels are offset, the obvious thing to do is to name the plan views after particular levels: e.g. level -3 plan view, underground car park. ○

○ **Note:** As a rule, plans with top and plan views are "northed," in other words, north is at the top edge of the plan and is indicated by a north arrow.

ELEVATION

Elevations (also called views in the ISO standards) show the outside of the building with all its apertures. Views of the cubature of a building provide information about its relationship to its environment, its form and proportions, and the construction type and material qualities where applicable. Along with the plan views and sections, elevations complete the overall design.

Elevations are parallel projections, seen from the side, onto a building facade. The projection lines run at right angles to the projection plane, so offset sections are not shown in their true size.

An elevation generally shows the immediate surroundings, with the lie of the terrain and links to any existing building development where appropriate.

Designating elevations

Elevations are identified according to their position on a point of the compass. The north arrow on the location plan and on the plan views defines the orientation of the building. Hence, the following designations are used for each of the four elevations: view north, south, east and west (or northeast, southwest etc.). If only two elevations are visible (as in terraced houses), they can also be defined in relation to the building's position on the plot, or the position of the development as a whole. But this means that only two sides are fixed unambiguously, e.g. the garden or courtyard side and the street side. The labelling of the elevations must be clear for anyone – even if they are not familiar with the area.

SECTION

A section is created by making a vertical cut through a building and considering this as a view in parallel projection. Sections are intended to provide information about floor heights, material quality and the building materials to be used for the planned building.

The section line must be entered on the plan view or all plan views. It is identified by a thick dash-dot line and the direction of view. Arrows and two capital letters of equal size fix the direction and the designation of the section. The section is taken in such a way that all the information relevant to the building can be recorded, which means that the section

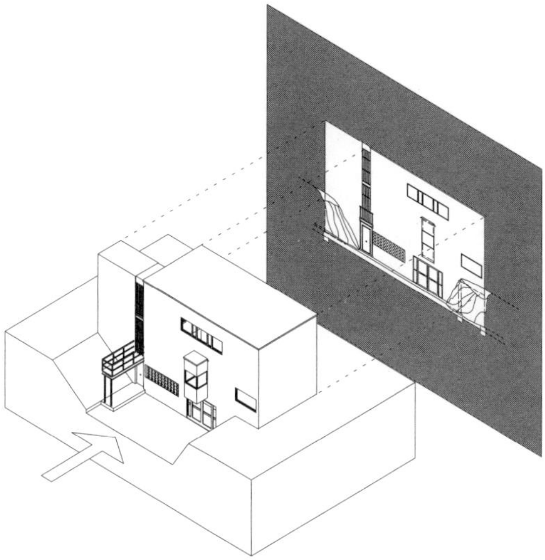

Fig. 3 : Elevation principle

line may deviate occasionally. This deviation must be at right angles, and must be identified in the plan view.

Elements of a section

Important elements shown in a section include the structure of the roof, the floors and ceilings, the foundations, and the walls with their apertures. The section should also show access to the building via stairs, lift, ramp etc.

Designating sections

Sections taken parallel through a main axis of the building are called longitudinal and cross sections. A longitudinal section cuts the building along the longer side and the cross section along the shorter. If more than two sections are taken, they are usually designated by capital letters or numbers. As the section lines on the plan views are identified by the same letters on both sides, the section designations are, correspondingly, section A–A, section B–B or section C–C etc.

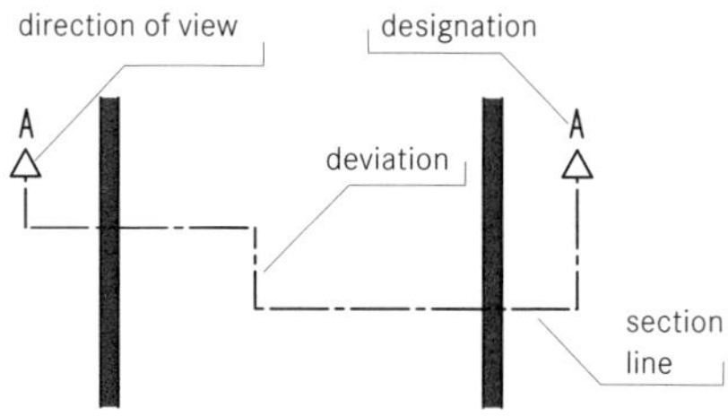

Fig. 4: Section line

THREE-DIMENSIONAL VIEWS

Axonometric projections

Axonometric projections are plan views or views with a third plane added - height. They are generally used as three-dimensional views at the planning stage, and give a spatial impression of the building. They are used for construction plans only in exceptional cases, for example to show the design of a corner.

It is easy to develop three-dimensional views from a two-dimensional drawing. A distinction is made between different projections (even though the term "projection" is misleading here):

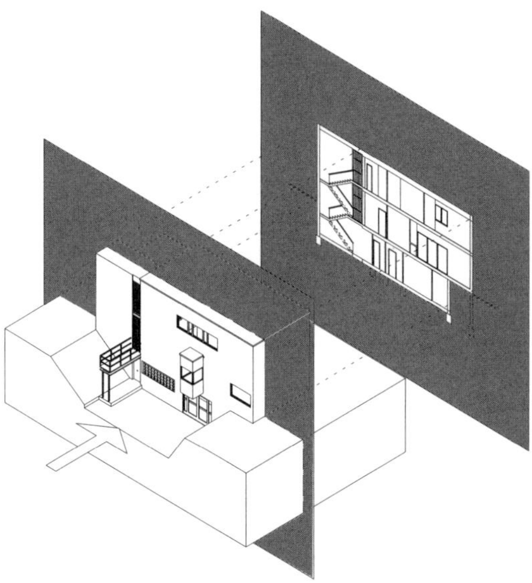

Fig. 5: Section principle

- The “military projection,” where the plan view is rotated through 45° at one corner and completed vertically by adding the heights.
- The “architects’ projection,” where the plan view is again rotated at one corner - through 30° or 60°.
- The “cavalier projection,” where an elevation or section acquires a third dimension by the addition of lines at an angle of 45°.

Isometric and dimetric projections

It is possible to create a better three-dimensional impression by moving away from the right angle as a base. Isometric and dimetric projections are used to do this.

Isometric drawings place each of the two plan view axes at an angle of 30° to the horizontal base line, and the height axis is plotted onto the plan view axes. This means that the object represented is not so distorted as in the three methods given above, but the drawing must be constructed more elaborately.

For a dimetric projection the two plan view axes are placed at angles of 7° and 42°. The line lengths of the latter should be shortened by factors of 0.5 or 0.7.

Perspective drawings

Perspective drawings differ from axonometric, isometric and dimetric projections in that they do not present the lines lying on an axis as parallel, but in perspective. Since perspective drawings are not generally used as construction plans, but only for presentation purposes, they fall into the field of descriptive geometry and are not examined further here.

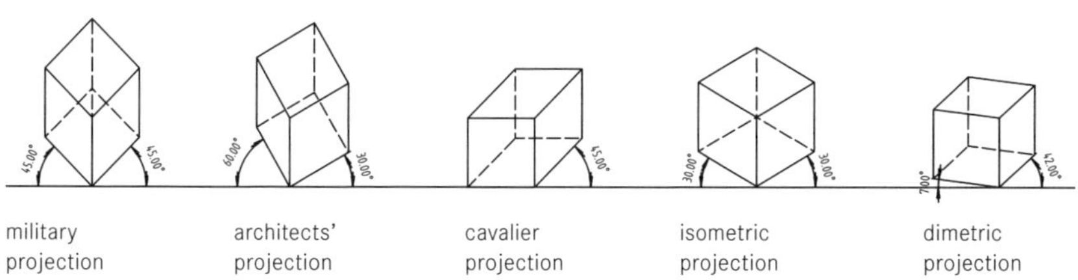

Fig. 6: Axonometric, isometric and dimetric projections

Principles of representation

AIDS

Basically there are two different methods for producing construction plans:

- Hand drawing
- CAD

Drawing tables

Hand drawing is carried out either at special drawing tables fitted with a pair of sliding rulers set at right angles, which can be adjusted; or using drawing rails, which are screwed onto an existing desktop and slid vertically on stretched wires. Both variants make it possible to draw lines parallel or at right angles.

Pens and pencils for hand drawing

Hand drawings are usually made with pencils or ink pens. Pencils are available in various hardness grades, which affect the thickness and visual effect of a line: the harder the pencil, the finer the line, because ■ little lead is rubbed off onto the paper. So various grades of pencil are needed for drawings, to be able to make lines of different widths.

■ Ink pens exist in various forms (e.g. with or without cartridges) and nib widths. The nibs mentioned in the chapter on lines are available individually.

Rulers and set squares

A variety of rulers, protractors, triangles, set squares and stencils are available to make drawing simpler. Rulers, triangles and adjustable set squares are used to draw in the geometrical dimensions. Lengths on

■ **Tip:** Pencils ranging from grade B (soft) via F (medium) to H to 3H (various degrees of hardness) are used for construction plans. Harder pencils should be used first, to avoid smudging the softer, thicker lines.

■ **Tip:** Ink pens come with and without cartridges in various colors. The latter are cheaper in throwaway versions, but more expensive if a lot of drawing is to be done. The thinner the line produced by an ink pen, the greater is the danger that the pen may dry up if stored for a long time. Sometimes the pigments in the nib of the pens can be moistened in a bath of water. If lines that have already been drawn need to be removed, special ink erasers can be used. But careful scratching with a razor blade is quicker.

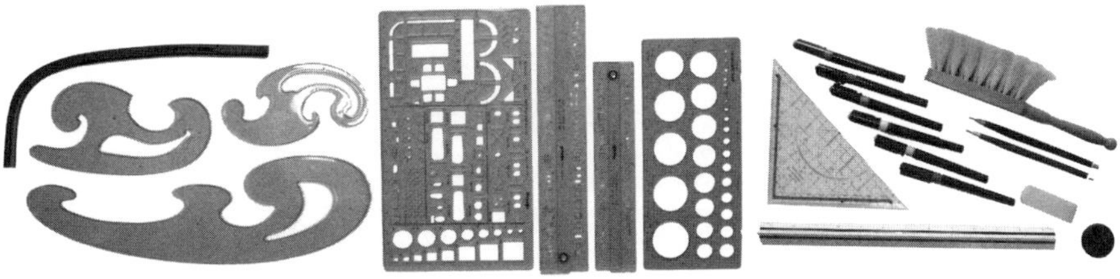

Fig. 7: Typical aids

plans are generally measured with a set square, a triangular ruler including six different scales with a length scale for each.

Stencils

Stencils are available for almost all typical drawing symbols (e.g. for furniture, electrical connections or bathroom facilities). There are also stencils for standard typefaces. All stencils are dependent on line thickness and scale.

CAD programs

● ■

CAD drawings are made using a computer. You need a CAD (Computer Aided Design) program intended specially for construction drawing. Various programs are available on the market, but they differ considerably in ease of use, performance and price. Almost all providers offer student and school versions.

● **Important:** Some universities allow students to draw using CAD when they first begin their studies, whilst others allow students to do so only after they have completed a number of foundation semesters. In most of the planning firms that students will encounter in their subsequent careers, most drawing will be done using CAD. As a fundamental principle, however, there are many situations in which it is important to be competent in drawing by hand, as sketching a specific detail on paper during a discussion leads to a solution being reached far more quickly than drawing it on a computer at a later point.

■ **Tip:** It makes sense to look at what several providers offer before working your way into a program. Prices vary considerably even between the student versions, and it is also important for fellow students or colleagues to use the same program, so that working experiences can be shared.

Further information on drawing with CAD can be found in *Basics CAD*, page 163 ff.

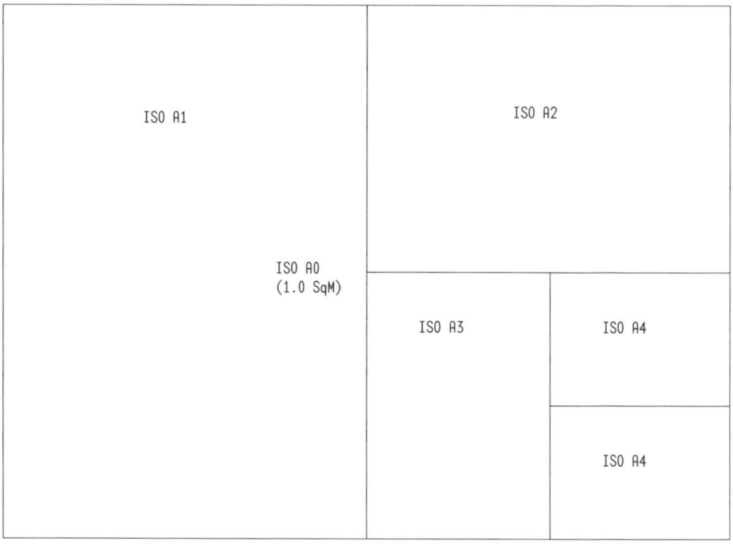

Fig. 8: Paper format relationships in the ISO-A series

PAPER FORMATS AND PAPER TYPES

Paper formats

DIN 476-1 or ISO 216 define various paper formats based on a page ratio of 1:√2. The advantage of this page ratio is that a large sheet can always be divided into smaller formats without waste.

There are various series within the DIN or ISO standards; the DIN-A or ISO-A series is generally used for plans.

As losses occur when cutting to size and folding, sheet formats distinguish between trimmed and untrimmed sheets. There are also format categories like DIN A3 Plus on the paper market, but these were created by printer manufacturers and are not further standardized.

Tab. 1: ISO/DIN series A–E (mm × mm)

	A–	B–	C–	D–	E–
2-0	1,189 × 1,682	1,414 × 2,000			
0	841 × 189	1,000 × 1,414	917 × 1,297	771 × 1,091	800 × 1,120
-1	594 × 841	707 × 1,000	648 × 917	545 × 771	560 × 800
-2	420 × 594	500 × 707	458 × 648	385 × 545	400 × 560
-3	297 × 420	353 × 500	324 × 458	272 × 385	280 × 400
-4	210 × 297	250 × 353	229 × 324	192 × 272	200 × 280

Tab. 2: Untrimmed and trimmed DIN-A series papers (mm × mm)

DIN	untrimmed	trimmed	edge distance
2-AO	1,230 × 1,720	1,189 × 1,682	10
A0	880 × 1,230	880 × 1,230	10
A1	625 × 880	594 × 841	10
A2	450 × 625	420 × 594	10
A3	330 × 450	297 × 420	5
A4	240 × 330	210 × 297	5

The paper formats described above are recognized and used in most countries; but in North America in particular, some inch-based formats are used that are based on ANSI standards.

Tab. 3: ANSI paper formats

Series	Engineers	Architects	Engineers	Architects
A	8½ × 11	9 × 12	216 × 279	229 × 305
B	11 × 17	12 × 18	279 × 432	305 × 457
C	17 × 22	18 × 24	432 × 559	457 × 610
D	22 × 34	24 × 36	559 × 864	610 × 914
E	34 × 44	36 × 48	864 × 1,118	914 × 1,219
F	44 × 68		1,118 × 1,727	
	inch × inch		mm × mm	

Paper types

Various paper types are distinguished, as well as paper formats. As a rule, tracing paper is used for hand drawings, as it has the advantage that other drawings can be placed underneath it to be traced. This considerably simplifies construction (e.g. of upper storeys or sections). Tracing paper also makes it possible to duplicate the original drawing simply, using blueprints.

In the inventory field, drawing films are often used, as they hold their shape even at higher temperatures, and thus measurements can be read off them reliably even after a long time.

For technical drawings made with CAD programs, normal white paper in roll or sheet form is usually used for plotting. Coated papers, or photographic or glossy papers are often used for presentation drawings, as they have a high-quality surface.

SCALE

Every type of plan mentioned in the first chapter (Projection types) is a reduction in a certain ratio to the built reality, i.e. it is drawn on a particular scale. The scale used must be marked on every drawing, in the form of the word scale and two figures separated by a colon (e.g. Scale 1:10).

Definition of scale

A scale describes the relationship between the dimensions of an element in a drawing and in the original size. A distinction is made between three principal scale types:

- Original scale (scale 1:1) as the natural scale
- Enlarged scale (scale x:1), in which one element is drawn larger than its natural size by a certain multiple
- Reduced scale, (scale 1:x), in which one element is reproduced smaller than its actual size by a certain multiple

Thus, for example, a wall drawn on a scale of 1:100 will be one hundred times smaller than the original.

Typical scales

Reduced scales are almost always used for construction drawings, as the object represented is usually larger than the paper. As precision and detail in the design process increase, the reduction becomes less, so the object itself is represented as larger.

Location plans and rough surveys are often drawn on a scale of 1:500 (or 1:1,000), design drawings on the scales of 1:200 or 1:100. For working plans, the scales of 1:50, 1:25, 1:20, 1:10, 1:5, 1:2 and 1:1 are used.
> Chapter Planning stages

Converting scales

If a wall 5.5 m long is to be represented on the scale of 1:50, its length must be divided by the reduction factor: thus, 5.5 m/50 = 0.11 m.The ■ length drawn is thus 11 cm. It becomes more difficult when an object that is already drawn on a reduced scale has to be converted to a different one. If a door with a drawn length of 5 cm at a scale of 1:20 is then shown on a scale of 1:50, the two scales must be calculated against each other. Thus, the length is 5 cm *20/50 = 5 cm/factor 2.5 = 2 cm.

Scales for CAD programs

CAD programs simplify the scale conversion problem. Here the building is usually input on a scale of 1:1, i.e. a wall 5.5 m long is drawn at this length. The drawing is additionally provided with an output or reference scale, which defines the scale on which the drawing will be printed and output later. Pen and lettering widths also adapt to this reference scale when viewed on the monitor, so that the ultimate result can be seen.

■ **Tip:** The best way to convert original measurements into typical scale model measurements is to use a triangular ruler (see Fig. 7). Alternatively, one can calculate the to-scale length as follows:

- scale 1:10, scale 1:100, scale 1:1,000 – move the comma by the number of zeroes. Or: change the unit of measurement from m to cm for M 1:100 or to mm for M 1:1,000
- scale 1:20, scale 1:200 – move the comma as above, additionally halving the number (an original measurement of 1 m gives a scale of 1:200 0.5 cm)
- scale 1:5, scale 1:50, scale 1:500 – move the comma by the number of zeroes plus one place, additionally multiplying the number by 2 (an original measurement of 1 m gives scale 1:50 2 cm)

LINES

A technical drawing consists of lines that differentiate things according to their type and width. Here a distinction is made between line types and line widths, though their significance can vary from scale to scale.

Line types

The are four principal types of line: the unbroken line, the dashed line, the dash-dot line and the dotted line, and other intermediate forms can be developed from these.

Line widths

The following line widths are customary, although as a rule only widths up to 0.7 mm are used: 0.13 mm, 0.18 mm, 0.25 mm. 0.35 mm, 0.5 mm, 0.7 mm, 1 mm, 1.4 mm, 2 mm.

Using unbroken lines

The unbroken line is used for all visible objects and visible edges of building sections; boundaries of sectional areas are also identified by unbroken lines. When parts of a building are cut in sections on the scale of 1:200 and 1:100, unbroken lines 0.25–0.5 mm wide are generally used; on scales from 1:50 a width of 0.7–1 mm is recommended. Unbroken lines for auxiliary constructions, dimension lines or secondary top or plan views are drawn more finely: 0.18–0.25 mm wide for a scale of 1:200 or 1:100, and 0.25–0.5 mm from 1:50. ○

Using dashed lines and dotted lines

Dashed lines are used for concealed edges of building parts (e.g. the under-step in details of stairs) in line widths of 0.25–0.35 mm for scales of 1:200 and 1:100, and 0.5–0.7 mm for scales from 1:50.

Dash-dot lines define axes and section runs. As section runs need to be immediately recognized on the drawing, they are drawn at a line width of 0.5 mm for scales of 1:200 and 1:100, and 1 mm for scales from

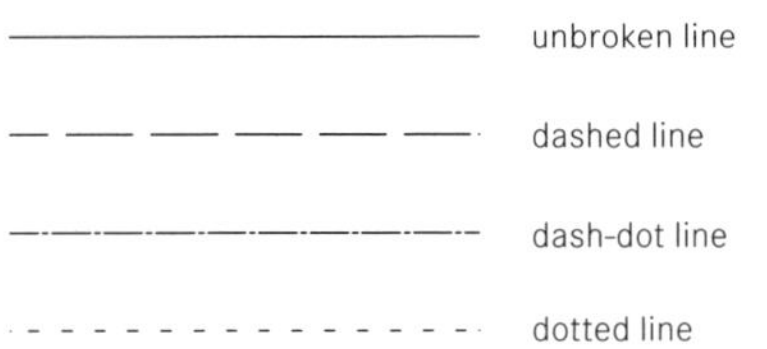

Fig. 9: Line types

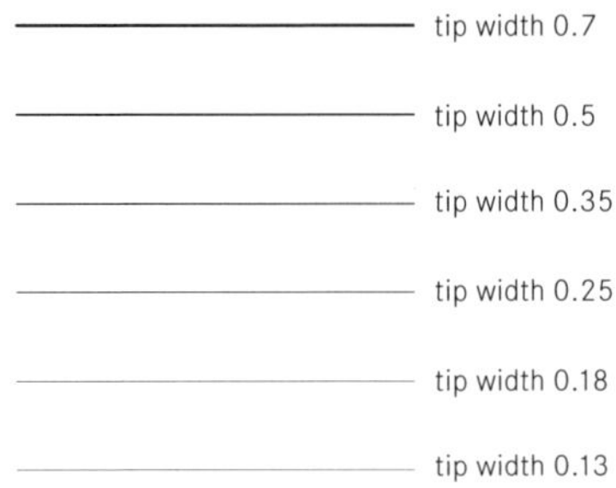

Fig. 10: Line widths

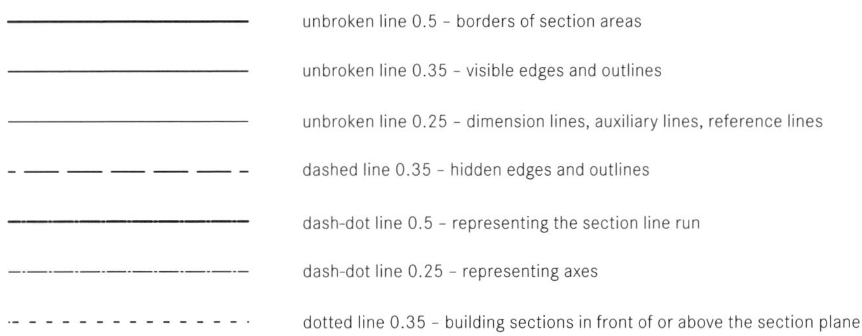

Fig. 11: Line types and widths, scale 1:100

Fig. 12: Line types and widths, scale 1:50

1:50. Axes, on the other hand, are usually drawn in lines 0.18–0.25 mm wide for scales of 1:100 or 1:200, and 0.35–0.5 mm from 1:50.

Dotted lines identify the edges of building section that can no longer be represented because they are placed behind the section plane. > Chapter Projection types Here a line width of 0.25–0.35 mm is used for scales of 1:100 and 1:200, and 0.5-0.7 mm from 1:50.

HATCHING

Hatching is intended to simplify representing individual elements in ■ drawings, and to make them more intelligible. Hatching appears in section plans (plan views, sections) and provides information about the nature of the representation, and the qualities of the materials and components used in the planning. When sections are taken through parts of a building the lines around them are usually filled in with hatching. Most statements about the way hatching is presented have been summed up in national standards. > Appendix, page 394 Basically, there is a distinction between section areas that are not dependent on the materials, such as diagonal hatching or filler areas, and material-dependent representations. > Fig. 13 A material-dependent representation identifies the material to be used for the part of the building through which the section has been taken. In the preliminary design phase, walls with a section through them are often shown only by filled areas of material-independent diagonal hatching on the plan view, to emphasize the solid parts of the building. Material-dependent hatching is not usually deployed until the working plan stage (e.g. masonry or reinforced concrete), as the appropriate materials will already have been chosen at this point.

Principles of hatching

Hatching can be presented as lines, dots, grids or geometrical figures. If the interfaces of several parts of the building are juxtaposed, then the direction of the hatching will change as well. Hatching is usually drawn at 45° or 135°.

○ **Note:** The above-mentioned line widths should be understood as guidelines, because of the current use of CAD. Today's CAD programs offer users pen categories that can be tailored to individual needs. So at times smaller line widths are used than in hand drawings. Test printouts should however be made at the beginning of a drawing to be able to estimate the effect of the line width on an output scale, as the on-screen effect often does not reflect the printed reality because of zoom functions and presentation that is independent of scale.

■ **Tip:** In CAD programs hatching can be scaled in such a way that it makes visual sense for every output scale. In this context, the terms scale- dependent and scale-independent hatching are used. In addition to this, almost all CAD programmes allow the orientation of the cross-hatching to be altered in response to angles. In the case of 45° walls, for instance, the diagonal cross-hatching can be rotated accordingly to create the desired optical effect.

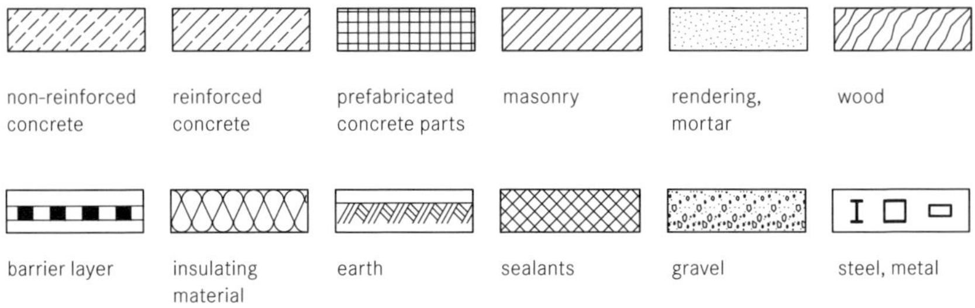

Fig. 13: Typical material-dependent hatching

Fig. 14: Presenting parts of a building in section

The basic hatching for representing a material-independent interface of part of a building is drawn with an unbroken line at an angle of 45°. Narrow sections, such as profile cross sections in steel construction, should be black for greater intelligibility.

LABELLING

Appropriate labelling is needed to produce a complete drawing, as well as lines, areas and hatching. The degree of detail in the labelling is chosen in relation to the scale; it is there to support the technical drawing (e.g. for stating dimensions, numbers of rooms, information about material etc.).

The chosen typeface must be unambiguously intelligible, so a standard typeface is usually chosen. Standard type (also called ISO type) is the name for an internationally used type of labelling using upper and lower case. Standard type is subdivided into four different forms on the basis of type sizes and type angles. Thus, a distinction is made between two type widths:

> Type form **A** - narrow, with a line width of height/ 14
> Type form **B** - medium wide, with a line width of height/ 10

and two type angles:

> Type angle **v** - vertical, with letters placed vertically to the direction of reading
> Type angle **i** - italic, with letters at 75° to the direction of reading

Using type styles

The best-known of the standard type forms used is a combination of type form **B** at the appropriate angle, producing **Bv** (medium wide line, vertical) and **Bi** (medium wide, italic).

Standard type forms are available as stencils for hand drawings in all the usual scales and type widths. Architectural drawings that are still produced by hand use building type. This is restricted only to upper-case letters developed from the shape of a square.

CAD programs can usually use the full range of fonts offered by the operating system. But here, too, it is better to choose a font in common use, as the next user should also have the font installed when data are exchanged.

A B C D E F G H I J K L M N O P R S T U V W X Y Z
a b c d e f g h i j k l m n o p r s t u v w x y z
1 2 3 4 5 6 7 8 9 10 [(! ? : ; - =)]

vertical type form

A B C D E F G H I J K L M N O P R S T U V W X Y Z
a b c d e f g h i j k l m n o p r s t u v w x y z
1 2 3 4 5 6 7 8 9 10 [(! ? : ; - =)]

italic type form

Fig. 15: Standard types Bv and Bi

Lettering is always positioned either horizontally to the direction in which the plan is to be read, or vertically turned anti-clockwise (and thus readable from below or from the right).

DIMENSIONING

Principles for dimensioning

Regardless of whether plans are drawn true to scale, all the relevant dimensions must be defined clearly. This is done with the aid of dimension chains, relative elevations or by indicating specific dimensions. Dimension chains are sections arranged next to each other and provided with individual dimension information. Relative elevations are defined heights for particular points (for example the top edge of a floor slab).

Guidelines for entering dimensions on drawings are laid down in specific national standards.

Dimension chains

Structure of a dimension chain

A dimension chain is made up of the following elements:

- Dimension line
- Auxiliary dimension line
- Dimension limits
- Dimension figure

Dimension limits

Dimension line, dimension limit lines and auxiliary dimension lines are always unbroken lines. The dimension line is placed parallel to the part of the structure to be dimensioned, with the auxiliary dimension line vertical to the dimension line, defining the axis, edge or line being dimensioned.

Dimension limits define the external point of the dimensioned length on the dimension line. Even though in principle the auxiliary dimension line defines this, it is often unclear for intersecting lines on drawings whether the thick line for a wall through which a section has been taken also contains the dimension limit.

Dimension figures in dimension chains

For this reason the dimensions should be clearly demarcated. According to the scale, either a diagonal line or a circle is used (e.g. design with lines, working plans with circles and detail planning with small dimensions chains with closed circles), but in principle a free choice can be made. Dimension limit lines are drawn at 45° from bottom left to top right seen from the direction of reading.

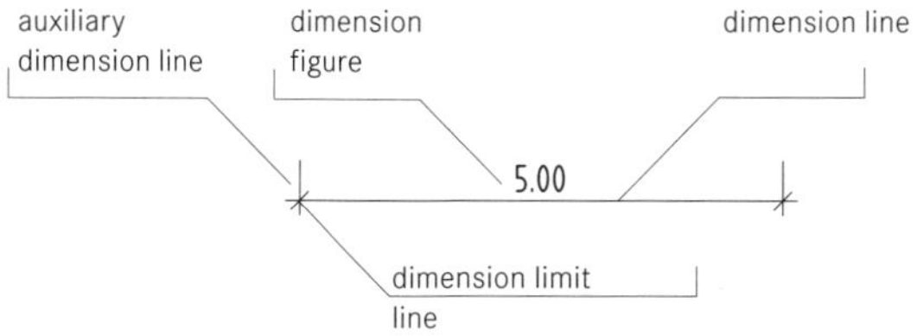

Fig. 16: Elements of a dimension chain

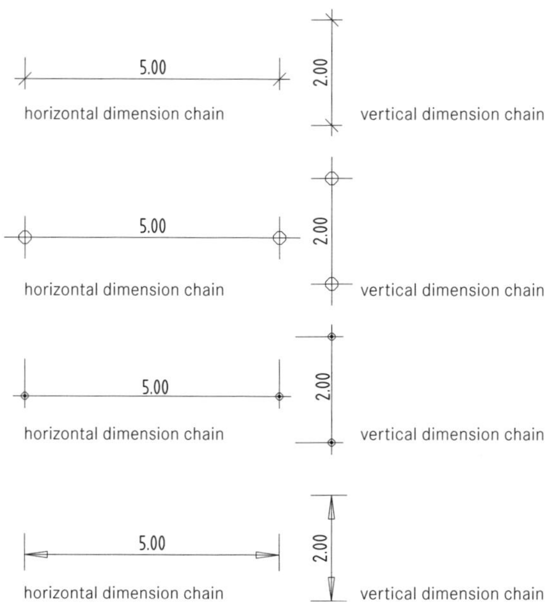

Fig. 17: Example of dimension limits

The dimension figure equals the length of the structural element to be dimensioned and correspondingly also identifies the spacing for the dimension limits. For distances larger than 1 m the figure is given in the meter unit (e.g. 1), for distances smaller than 1 m the unit is the centimeter (e.g. 99 or 25). For millimeters the figures are raised (e.g. 1.25^5 or 36^5). Units such as m or cm are not given.

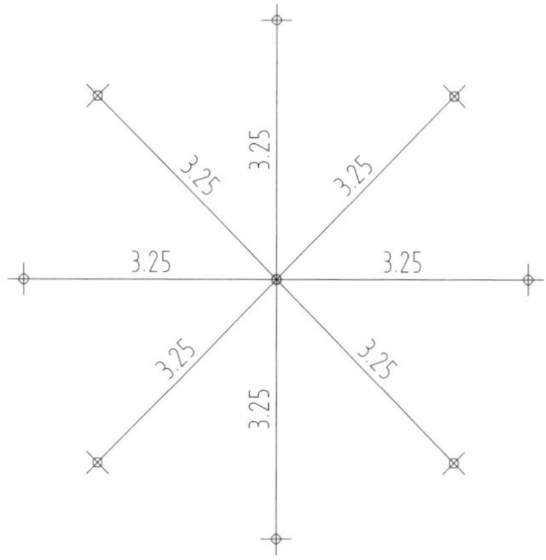

Fig. 18 : Direction of lettering for various angles

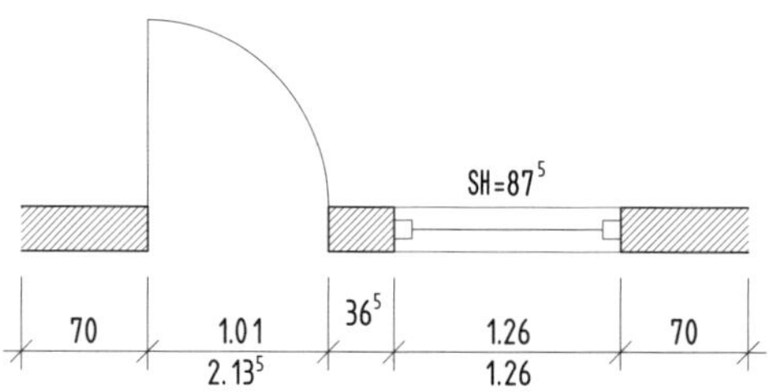

Fig. 19: Dimensioning a door and a window in a wall

Position of the dimension figure

As a rule, the dimension figure is placed above the dimension line and centrally between the dimension limits. For aperture dimensions the height of the aperture is also shown under the dimension line. > Fig. 19 If there is an additional sill (e.g. for windows), the sill height is given directly on the inside of the aperture (e.g. with SH or S = 75).

Dimensioning inside the dimension line is uncommon: as an alternative to dimension figures above the dimension line, the dimension figures may also be inscribed directly into the line, omitting that part of the line.

Problems occur when the distances between the dimension limits are very small, i.e. if there is little room for the figure (e.g. for lightweight walls and installations in front of walls). Here, the figure may be placed directly beside the dimension limit. > Figs. 25-27, pages 124-127 Dimension figures and dimension lines must not overlap, to maintain legibility.

Height dimensions

Height dimensions cover floor, sill and clearance heights and relate to a level ±0.00. This is normally set as the upper edge of the completed floor structure in the entrance area. The surveyor surveys and relates this point to mean sea level or zero level (ZL), so that the building is correctly positioned in terms of height. Hence the reference of ZL and ±0.00 should be defined on every plan. All height indicators then relate to the startingpoint ±0.00 in terms of + and - signs.

A distinction should be made in the drawing between height dimensions of plan or top views and sections or elevations.

Height dimensions in elevations and sections are given by height indicators: the graphic symbol for a height indicator is an equilateral triangle drawn directly with the height figure into the drawing of the structural element or onto an additional dimension limit line (e.g. outside the building).

Height dimensions in elections/sections

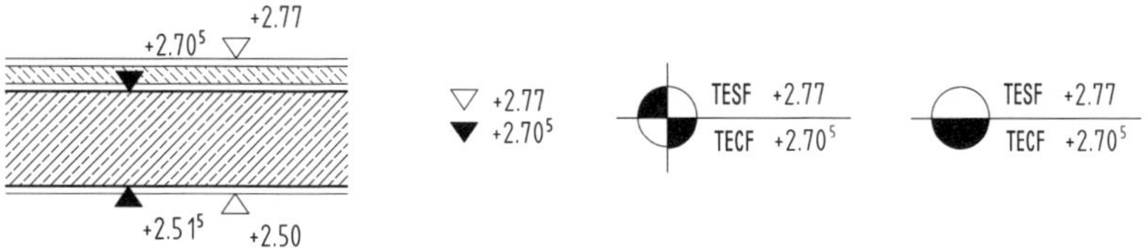

Fig. 20: Typical height dimensions

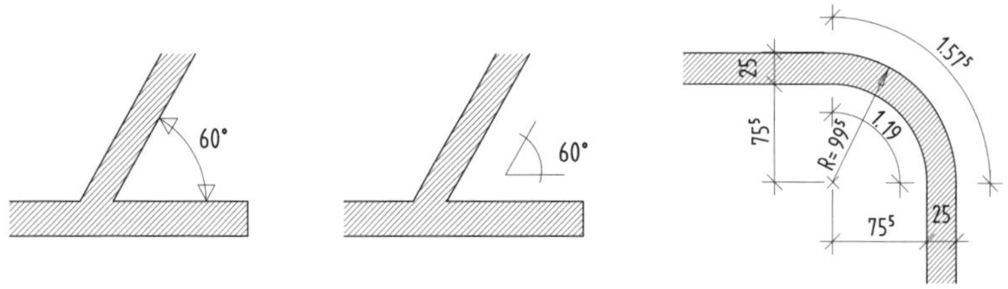

Fig. 21: Example of a circular dimension

Height dimensions on plan views

For shell dimensions the triangle is usually solid black; for completion dimensions it is left as an outline triangle. Thus, the dimensions given can be clearly and correctly allocated even on small drawings.

Height dimensions on plan views and top views are also represented by triangles (solid for shell construction, outline for completion elements), but most commonly, circles with a line passing through them are used, with the completion dimension above the line and the shell dimension below it. Here, too, the dimensions can be directly identified by filling the semicircles appropriately. Another classification option is to use the labelling TECF (top edge complete floor) and TESF (top edge shell floor).

Angle and curve dimensions

Angle dimensions

If structural elements are not at right angles to each other, the relevant angle must be indicated. This is usually done by stating the number of degrees and the typical symbol ∢, but it can also be done by using a segment of a circle with arrows on the ends and the number of degrees in the middle.

Circular dimension

For rounded structural elements, circular dimensions should be given, for example to define the developed length of a curved reinforced concrete wall. This is necessary, among other things, for determining and calculating the dimensions (continuous meters of wall, baseboard etc.). The dimension chain for a circular dimension consists of a circle parallel to the actual curve (i.e. dimension circle and curved wall have the same center). The dimension limits can be used as explained above for circular dimensions, or arrows can be placed at the ends of the dimension circle.

Individual dimension indications

If individual dimensions must be indicated, they are usually written directly onto the particular structural element. They can also be allocated by abbreviations (e.g. SH for sill height), or symbols (e.g. ∅ for diameter or ⊏⊐ for a rectangular section). Radii have a capital R before the dimension figure, screws and threaded rods an M. For simplification, height and width may also be given in abbreviations (e.g. W/H 12/16 for a wooden beam 12 cm wide and 16 cm high).

Planning stages

Construction drawings can be divided into two groups. The first describes the phase in which ideas are established: from design to planning permission.

The second group includes the construction phase with its associated drawings to accompany the building work. Thus, a distinction is made between pre-design, design, drawings with building particulars, and working drawings.

The corresponding planning documents contain specific information for a particular target group. Planning documents can provide a decision-making basis for clients or local authority building departments; specialist planners may use them as a basis for their own plans; and they can contain concrete building instructions for the specialist firms carrying out the work. The scope and precision of a plan derive from the purpose, nature and scale of a drawing. The less it is reduced, the larger the structural elements it shows are, and thus the dimensioning and labelling become more detailed.

DETERMINING BASICS

Land registry plans

Land registry plans (usually on a scale of 1:1,000) of towns and municipalities are available to provide an overview or basis for a design; they may be slightly imprecise in their indications of dimensions.

As-built plans

If an existing building is being converted, its current state must be surveyed and presented in a drawing as a basis for the work. The subsequent planning phases are based on this. The degree of elaboration, and thus the precision, of as-built plans depend considerably on the use for which the building is intended. If a small extension is to be added to an existing home without particular demands on quality of detail, it is usually enough to record the relevant rooms in terms of width, length and height. If monument preservation measures have to be taken in a listed building, the dimensions must be recorded in detail and complemented with precise indications about surfaces and distinctive features.

PRELIMINARY DESIGN DRAWING

Purpose of preliminary design drawing

A concept is turned into an overall presentation in the form of a drawing (a plan) in the preliminary design drawings. A distinction is also made in this phase between construction drawings for future planning and concept drawings to explain an idea to a client. The aim of preliminary design planning is to clarify and explain the idea behind the design.

Fig. 22: Example of a land registry plan

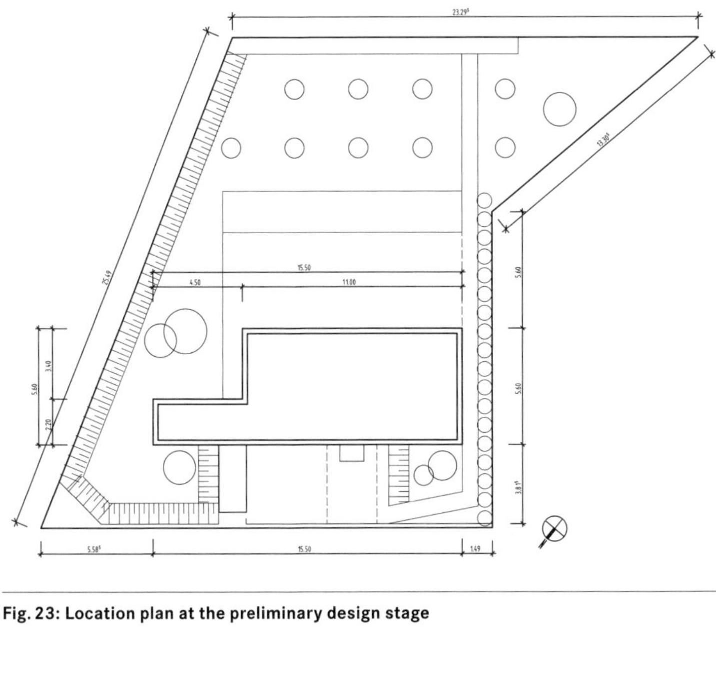

Fig. 23: Location plan at the preliminary design stage

Preliminary design plans thus express the planner's design approach and allow a great deal of latitude in terms of presentation. On the other hand, even a preliminary design plan may be consulted when clarifying information about the building with the relevant authorities. For this reason, it forms the basis for a preliminary decision by the building authorities.

Scale

Preliminary design drawings provide only the most necessary information about the shape and size of the building. These drawings are mainly drawn on a scale of 1:200, or 1:500 for large projects. Location plans are reduced even further (scales 1:500 or 1:1,000).

Location plan

The location plan shows the building on the basis of the plot dimensions in the context of its surroundings. Its location on the plot is defined; hence the term location plan. The information entered gives a general view of the building's size and orientation, the nature of the terrain and its use, and where necessary includes the adjacent plots as well.

Drawing up plan views, sections and elevations

One sensible starting point for drawing up further construction plans is a ground floor plan view matching the location plan. Starting with the ground floor plan view, the best way to develop the floors above is to base them on the plan view that has already been prepared (both at the drawing board and in a CAD program).

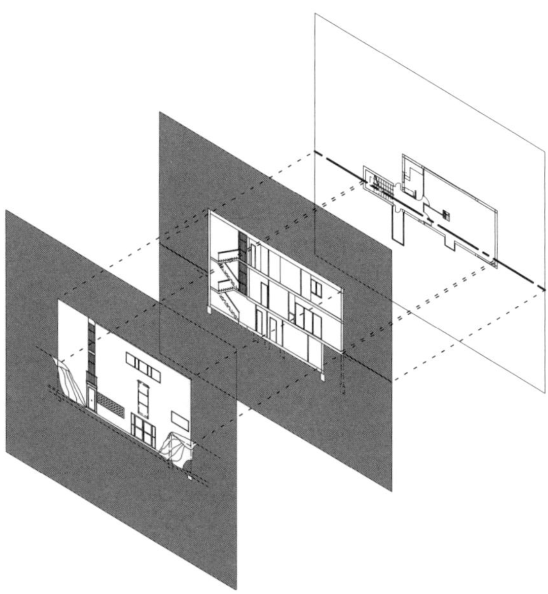

Fig. 24: Constructing sections and elevations

After drawing up the plan views, it is relatively simple to construct the sections. The chosen section line is first drawn into the plan view, and then turned to be horizontal and form the basis for the section. It forms the zero line of the section, i.e. the entrance level for the building. All heights are developed vertically upwards on this line (upper floors) and downwards (basement floors): to do this, the edges of the intersected walls are simply extended to an appropriate level in relation to the zero line. Elevations should be constructed only on the basis of the heights marked in the sections. It is simplest to trace the external outlines of the sections and add windows, doors and ground connections by placing plan views underneath. > Fig. 24

Representing structural elements

The aim of the preliminary planning is to clarify and illustrate the cubature of the building, the distribution of space and the way the building fits in with its surroundings, in terms of a provisional arrangement and provisional dimensions. Structural elements are usually presented without indication of materials, so that at first it is only possible to identify which elements are intersected.

In elevations, all the visible edges are represented by an unbroken line. The thickness of the unbroken line depends on scale, relevance (walls are more important than a door handle, for example) and the degree of detailing in the building. Thus, the outlines of the external walls and their apertures are emphasized most strongly.

Finishing details such as toilets, kitchen or furniture are given in top view and elevation, to illustrate the design. Furnishings are important to inexperienced clients as a yardstick for size ratios in housing construction in particular, so that they can understand proportions and the size of rooms.

Establishing scale

Representing trees, people and the external areas clarifies how the building fits into its surroundings while providing a background that does not conceal information. Proportions and scale can be conveyed better by showing objects whose size or proportions are familiar even to the unpractised eye. This is called establishing scale, and the individual items are scale-establishing objects. These “extras” are mostly used only at the preliminary and design stages, and for competition and presentation drawings.

Dimensioning

Dimensioning is restricted to rough measurements in preliminary design planning. In plan views, external dimensions and important room dimensions are given in order to make room sizes and overall measurements comprehensible. Individual projections and recesses, and door and window apertures, are not usually dimensioned.

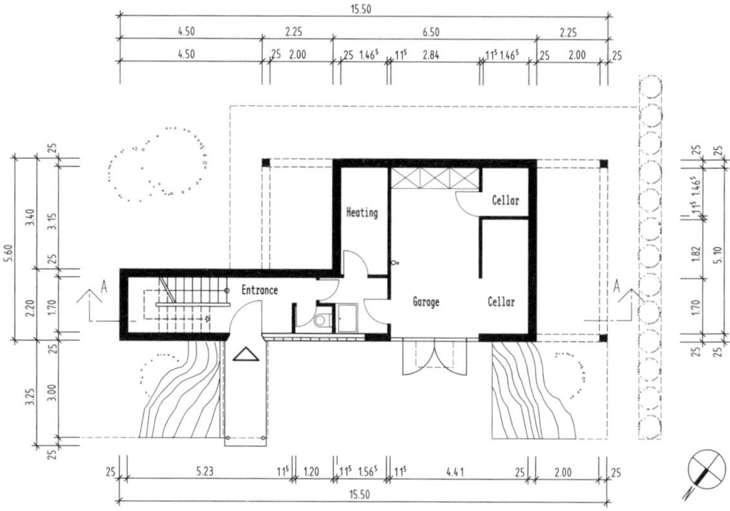

Fig. 25: Preliminary design plan for the cellar floor

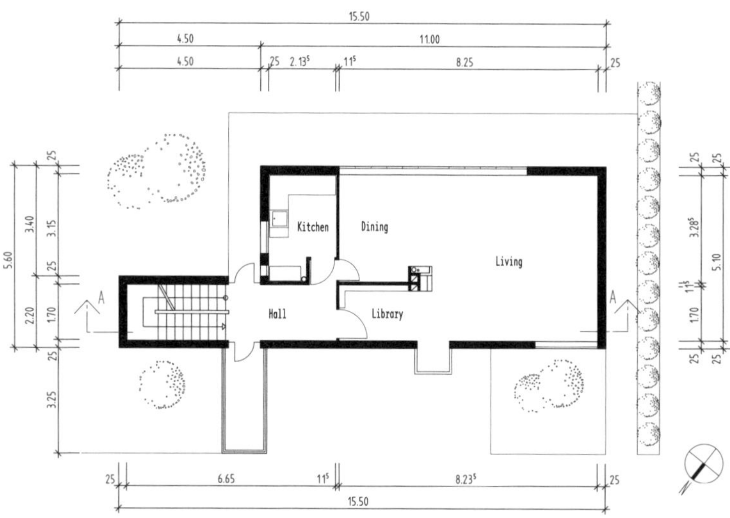

Fig. 26: Preliminary design plan for the ground floor

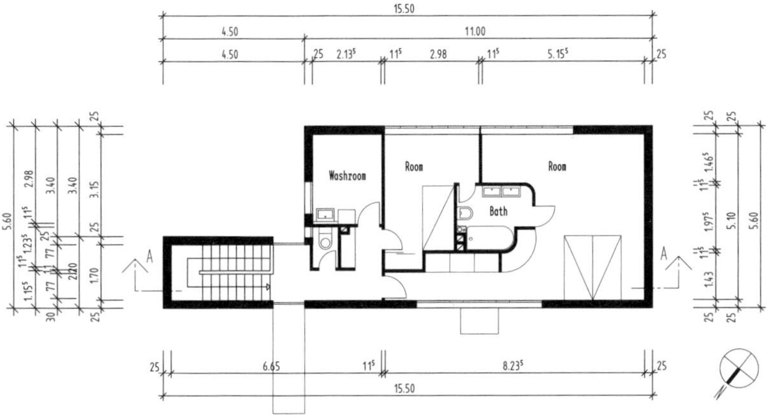

Fig. 27: Preliminary design plan for the upper floor

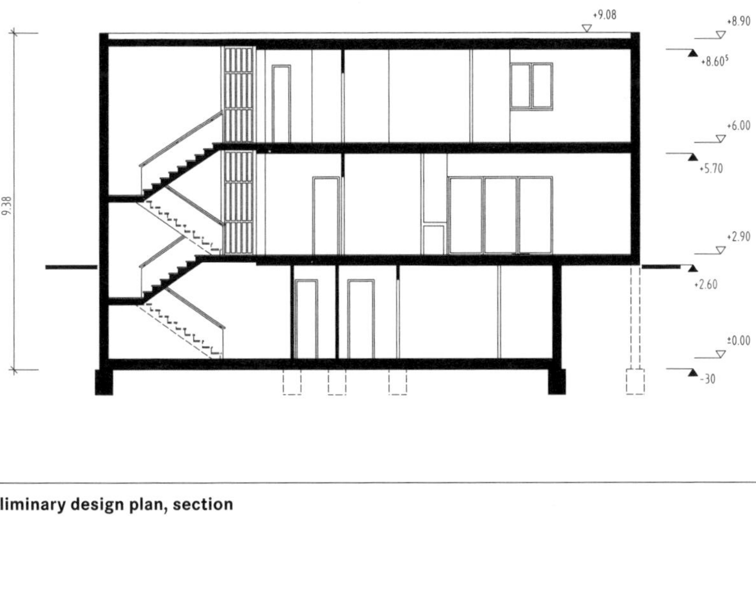

Fig. 28: Preliminary design plan, section

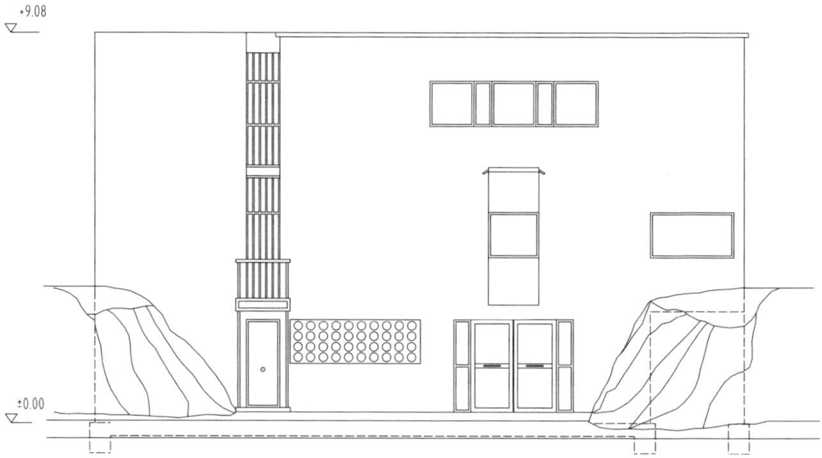

Fig. 29: Preliminary design plan, northwest elevation

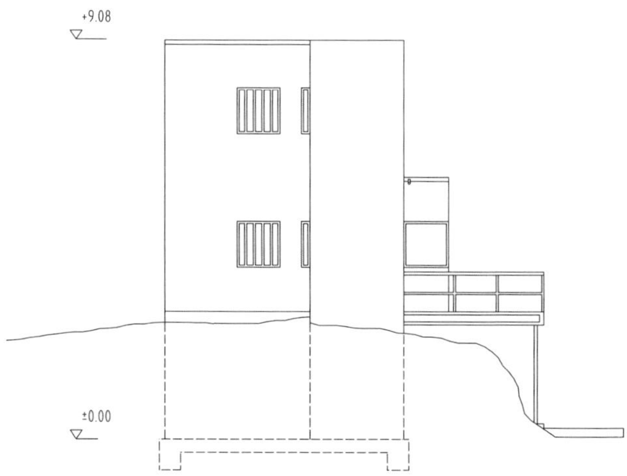

Fig. 30: Preliminary design plan, northeast elevation

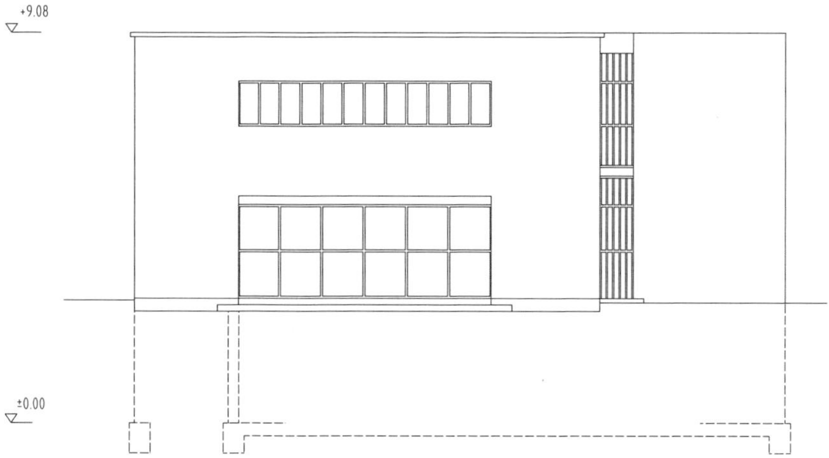

Fig. 31: Preliminary design plan, southeast elevation

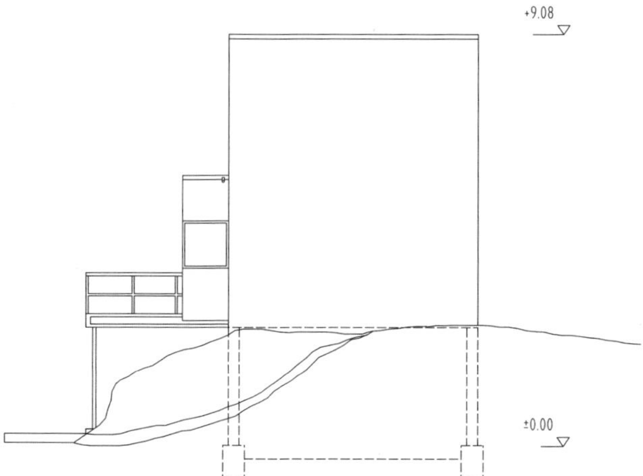

Fig. 32: Preliminary design plan, southwest elevation

○ **Note:** The building presented here is a design for an early residential building in Vaucresson (1922) by Le Corbusier. The plans were copied by the authors on the basis of Le Corbusier's plans, but dimensions and details have been changed and adapted, or measurement chains completed, to illustrate the relevant points here. Some of the dimensions for doors, toilets etc. are no longer admissible under current regulations and should therefore not be used as models for the reader's own construction drawings.

■ **Tip:** It is helpful, particularly in the submission phase for student work or competitions, to draw a short list of headings summing up the key elements of the design idea and translating these into pictograms.

In elevations, only important height dimensions such as eaves and ridge height are given; in sections the room or floor heights appear as well.

Labelling

Labelling is also restricted to simple identification of rooms by function and the estimated areas of the rooms in square meters.

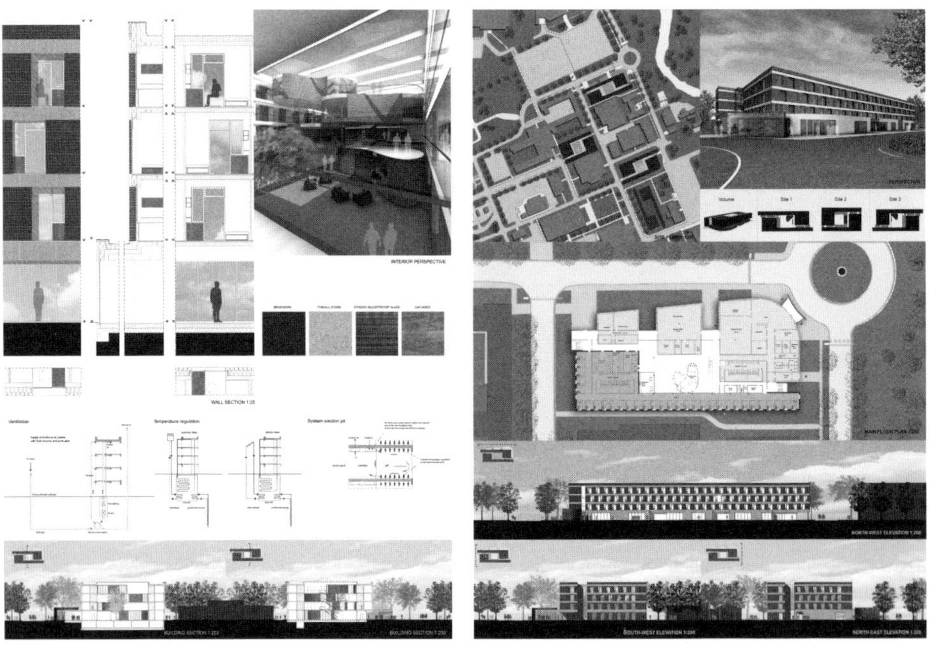

Fig. 33: Example of a competition plan

PRESENTATION PLANS

To present a design, presentation plans are prepared independently of the classical construction drawings. Presentation plans are usually drawn up after a preliminary design has been completed, so that this can then be confirmed for further planning purposes: presentation plans are intended to persuade a particular target group of the design idea and the concept, so they should be devised with this purpose in mind.

Client presentation

If, for example, an inexperienced client is unable to associate a three-dimensional idea with a technical, two-dimensional drawing, then it makes sense to underpin his sense of space with three-dimensional representations or perspective views.

The client may have to present the design to a third party, and may need visual materials to help persuade them. These can be three-dimensional presentations or perspective views, or graphic presentations of

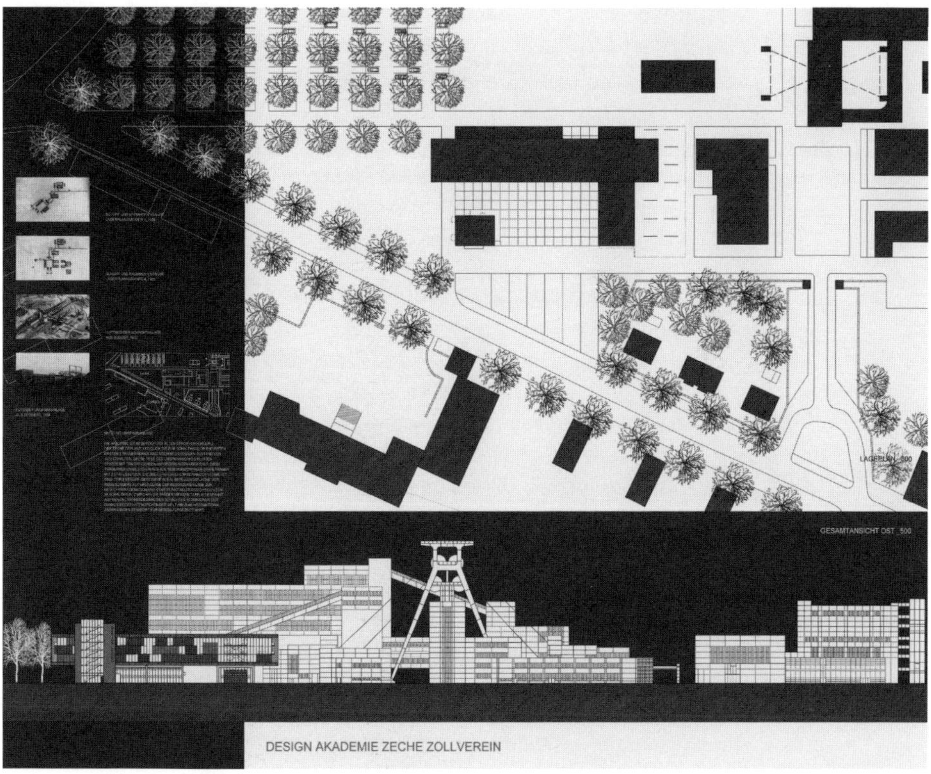

Fig. 34: Example of a student presentation: location plan

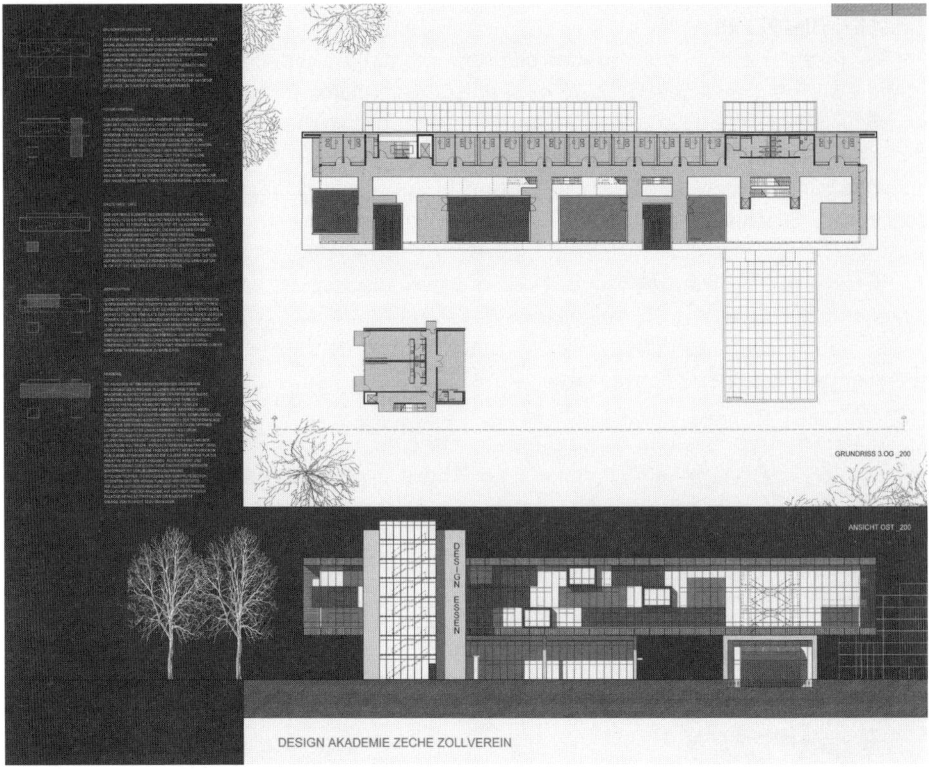

Fig. 35: Example of a student presentation: plan view and elevation

zoning, pathway links, work areas or similar items on the basis of plan views and sections.

Architectural competitions

If planners or students take part in competitions, their own ideas must be presented in such a way that it makes a clear impact on the jury. ■ As juries are usually made up of a mixture of experts and laypeople, the needs of both groups should be taken into consideration. As a rule there is little time available for judging the entries, and so everyone looking at the submissions needs to understand the individual designs quickly. It is also important to make your design stand out from those submitted by the other entrants.

Student presentations

When a student design is presented, the college or university lecturer responsible should be able to understand his or her students' ideas, i.e. the presentation should convince a qualified expert with appropriate skills in terms of abstraction and imagination. For this reason, more conceptual approaches tend to be chosen for student submissions than would

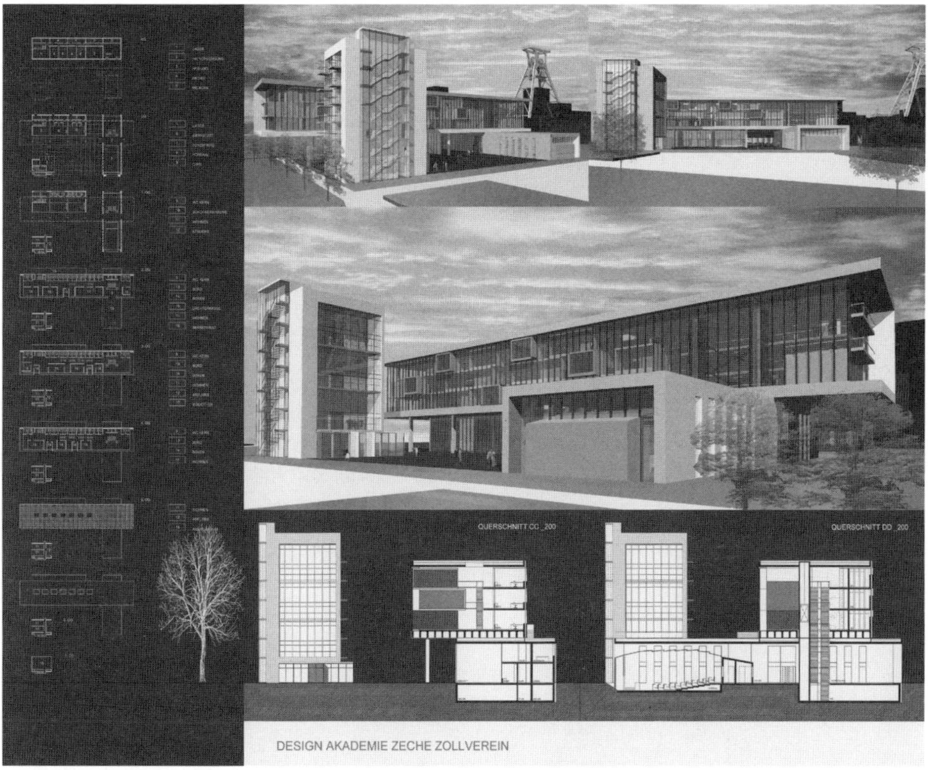

Fig. 36: Example of a student presentation: sections and perspective views

be used for presenting ideas to a client. For example, if this is desirable in graphic terms, it is possible to omit the scale-establishing features that are needed for the layperson.

Content of presentation plans

As well as classical elements such as location plan, plan views, sections and elevations, often contain three-dimensional representations of interiors and exteriors. Pictographic elements may also help to represent the design idea or the functional context of the design.

Devising presentation plans

The plans to be submitted are usually confined to one particular scale. For presentations, there is otherwise a greater degree of freedom than for technical construction drawings. Dimensioning can be reduced to a minimum, structural elements represented graphically or the whole scope of the drawing can be reduced essentially to elements of composition. – There are no limits on creativity. It is important to keep in mind the clarity and accessibility for the person looking at the work, and to devise the presentation appropriately.

DESIGN PLANNING

Purpose of design planning

Design planning is a further development of the preliminary planning stage. Now the architect and the client finally define the geometry and dimensions of the design for the building permission plans that will follow. The design plans must therefore show all the important elements that are relevant for the planning authorities' consideration. This phase also addresses planning in other fields like structural engineering and domestic services, which means that all the fundamental structural information (e.g. loadbearing walls) must be visible.

Scale

Design plan views for housing are usually drawn on a scale of 1:100, and for very large buildings on a scale of 1:200 or 1:500 if necessary. For example, if the plan view of a large industrial hall were presented on a scale of 1:100, a very large number of A0 sheets would be needed, so it would no longer be possible to take in the design as a whole. But, as explained above, since the design plans are intended to provide a comprehensible and useful basis for further discussion, it makes sense to choose a less refined presentation on a higher scale.

Showing walls

Even at the design planning stage, material-dependent hatching can be used for representing walls, in order to define the material, e.g. a reinforced concrete, masonry or dry construction wall. Line widths distinguish between loadbearing and non-loadbearing walls. It is not usual to show wall surfaces (e.g. interior rendering) at the design planning stage. All the doors and windows should be entered on the plan correctly, in such a way that the aperture dimensions and, where applicable, the sills can be seen. The direction in which doors open should also be shown at the design planning stage, to indicate the flow of movement in the building.

Foundations are indicated in consultation with the structural engineers, along with their construction details (individual foundations, ice wall, foundation strip), with their correct depths and widths. If it is necessary to explain the section, invisible parts can be shown as dashed lines.

Showing floors and ceilings

Sectional drawings of floors and ceilings are made up of the shell floor including hatching to show material qualities and the completed floor as an upper edge, in order to define the height of the structure.

Showing invisible elements

Since the horizontal section plane in a plan view lies 1.5 m above floor level (see above), structural elements placed above it are not visible in the plan. But to understand the geometry and the space it is often necessary to show these elements as well. They can be beams or girders,

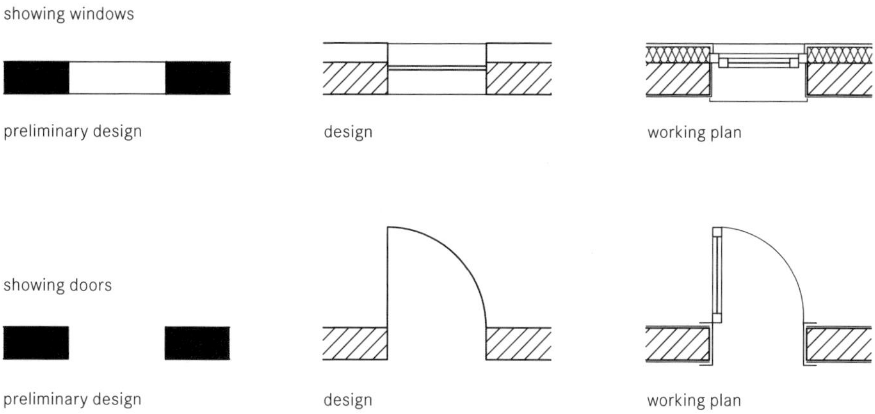

Fig. 37: Scale-dependent representation of walls, doors and windows

which divide a space into several section visually (the dimensions of the beams or girders are shown directly on the plan view drawing, e.g. B43/35); or stairs, whose upper run should be shown, with a junction point to understand the geometry of the steps. The same applies to sections, for example in the case of covered mezzanine floors or invisible stairs. In elevations, the loadbearing walls and floors inside the building envelope can be indicated with a short dashed line.

Additional information in elevations

The following elements can also be shown in the elevations (views): windows with divisions and opening mode, blind cases (BC), height of window apertures, balconies, sills, protrusions and recesses, roof forms.

Site layout

The existing and planned layout of the site before and after building should be drawn in as precisely as possible, as it is relevant for the building's entrances and exits, the necessary earthworks and the building inspection authorities. The building's height systems are also developed from this.

Showing stairs and ramps

Stairs are defined in design plans by stating the number of steps, risers and treads (e.g. 10 risers of 17.5/26). Flights of stairs are also identified by continuous lines, with the starting point (starter) identified with a circle and the end point (exit) with an arrow. Ramps are identified by two lines taken from the start of the ramp to the central point of its upper end.

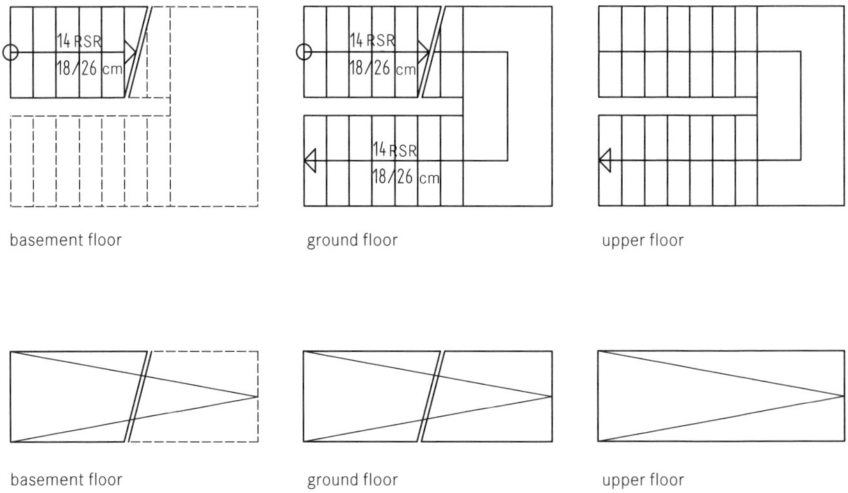

Fig. 38: Showing stairs and ramps

In sections, the stair structure is shown as simply as possible, so that the geometry of the stairs can be understood: a distinction is made between concrete, closed or open steps in wood or metal as stairs with or without landing.

Dimensioning plan views

Dimensioning in design planning is intended to define the geometrical coherence of a building and the rooms it contains. The exterior dimensions of the building are entered first – as in preliminary design planning – including all external cladding and rendering. This makes it easier to determine the gross floor area, the gross space enclosed and the building's position in the location plan or on the plot.

○ The second step dimensions all the external doors and windows, and ideally an additional dimension chain is added for the interior position of the windows. > Fig. 39 Thus, all the apertures can be defined in their geometrical relationship with the elevation of the building and in relation to the spatial impact of the exterior wall. Any possible shifts between interior and exterior axes or possible window rabbets can be seen and planned.

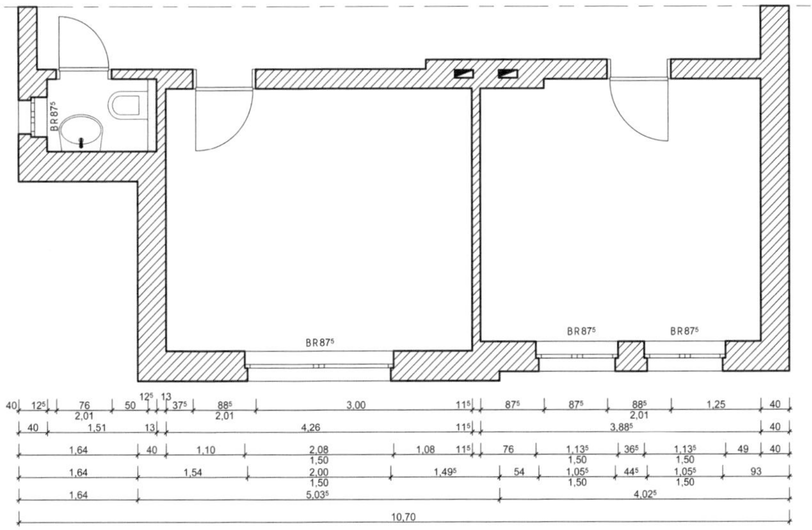

Fig. 39: Example of a horizontal measurement chain package

The next step records the interior spaces with the length and width. This is essential for calculating room and apartment sizes, and is useful for the later user as a basis for furnishing. It thus makes sense to give individual dimension chains for the overall room size and the wall features with door(s). The heights of apertures (doors, sills and windows) are indicated as described above with an additional figure under the dimension line, and sill heights are given for windows. Planners should pay particular attention to arrange dimension chains in a comprehensible order and on clearly distinguishable axes, so that the plan is easily intelligible. A typical sequence for a house works from the outside inwards:

1st dimension chain:	total exterior dimensions (where applicable, additional dimension chain for walls with protrusions or recesses)
2nd dimension chain:	exterior dimensions with all apertures (doors, windows, projections etc.)
3rd dimension chain:	interior dimensions of apertures with all sectioned walls

4th dimension chain:	room dimensions for the rooms behind the exterior wall
5th dimension chain:	interior walls of the rooms with doors, recesses, corners and passageways
6th dimension chain:	room sizes for the interior rooms
7th dimension chain:	etc.

■ If it is relevant to the design (e.g. in industrial buildings) the axis dimensions are placed furthest from the drawing and defined with continuous numbers to the right or left of the plan view and with continuous letters above or below the plan view.

As well as giving lengths and widths, information about heights must be included in a plan view. Only this way can the plan view be clearly built into the height levels on the plot and in the building. If the plan view does not show height gradations, these heights are often defined just once, in the entrance area, and the section is used for detailed heights. For this reason, the height dimensions should be added to the plan views only when the section is complete.

Dimensioning sections

The construction and storey heights are the most important features of sections, as these are needed to complete the plan views. Height indicators are normally used for this > Chapter Principles of representation, Dimensioning, supplemented by dimension chains. The height indicators show absolute heights (related to zero level), and the dimension chains give individual construction and room heights. For example, height indicators

○ **Note:** Octametric dimensions with controlling and working dimensions should be taken into account for masonry buildings. A multiple of bricks 24 cm long including an A joint 1 cm wide, without summit joint, gives the working construction dimensions (11.5 cm; 24 cm; 36.5 cm; 49 cm; ...), and with joint the specified dimension (12.5 cm; 25 cm; 37.5 cm; 50 cm; etc.).

Further information can be found in: Nils Kummer, *Basics Masonry Construction,* Birkhäuser Verlag, Basel 2006.

■ **Tip:** The structure of the dimension chains must be thought through carefully, so that not too much measurement information is defined twice, but also that nothing is forgotten. If there are a lot of small interior rooms, it is often tricky to accommodate all the dimensions in the dimension chain package. If necessary, if individual dimensions cannot be accommodated, an additional dimension chain can be placed directly inside the plan (within a plan view). This is generally more manageable than placing another dimension chain dealing with the whole building on the edge of the drawing, splitting up only a partial section of the measurement chain above it.

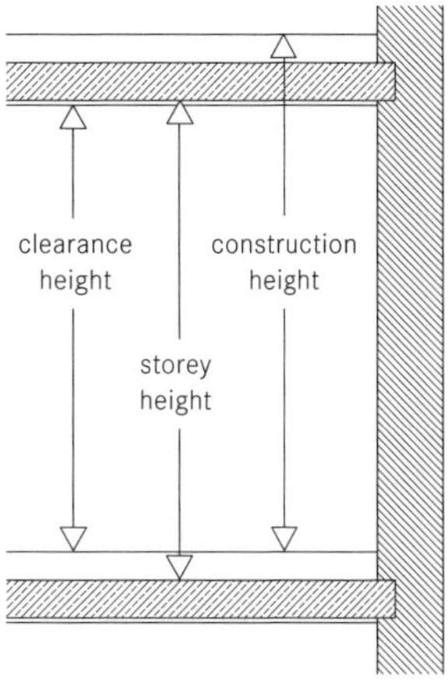

Fig. 40: Height systems in layers

in the roof structure give information about heights in the loadbearing structure and for the overall height of the roof structure (ridge height, attic height). When giving storey heights we distinguish:

- storey height: height from top edge to top edge of storeys in sequence
- clearance height (CH): height between top edge complete floor (TECF) and the lower edge of the complete floor above (where applicable, lower edge of the rendering or suspended ceiling)
- construction height: distance between the top edge of the shell floor (TESF) and the bottom edge of the shell floor above (BESF)

The following sequence should be followed when arranging the dimension chains (as in the plan view):

1st dimension chain:	overall exterior dimensions (where applicable, additional dimension chain for recesses or protrusions)
2nd dimension chain:	external dimensions with all apertures (doors, windows, sill height etc.)
3rd dimension chain:	interior dimensions with all apertures (doors, windows, sill heights etc.)
4th dimension chain:	clearance heights
5th dimension chain:	etc.

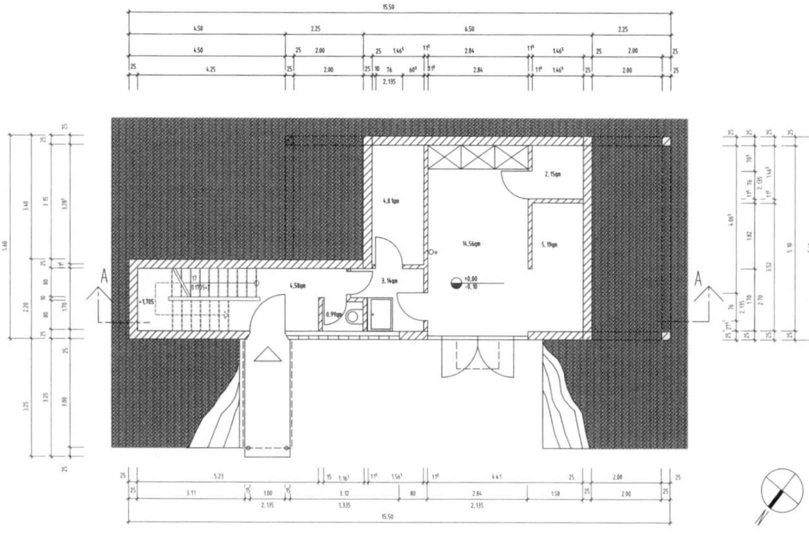

Fig. 41: Design plan, ground floor plan view

Dimensioning elevations

Elevations (views) are dimensioned with height indicators. It may be necessary to use dimension chains for completeness when dealing with larger buildings.

As for a section, the height indicators relate to the zero line at complete floor height on the ground floor, and additional information about height at zero level (ZL) can be appended.

Additional ZL information may be included, particularly to represent street height and the lie of the terrain.

Labelling

As a rule, only distinctive elements, for example the top edge of the land and the roof edge, are given in elevations at the design stage.

■ Additional information on the plan view drawing is given by room identifiers. These contain room numbers and/or room names (WC, living room etc.) and where applicable the room area in square meters. The entrance to the building is often identified by a solid black triangle, to make it easy to find on the plan.

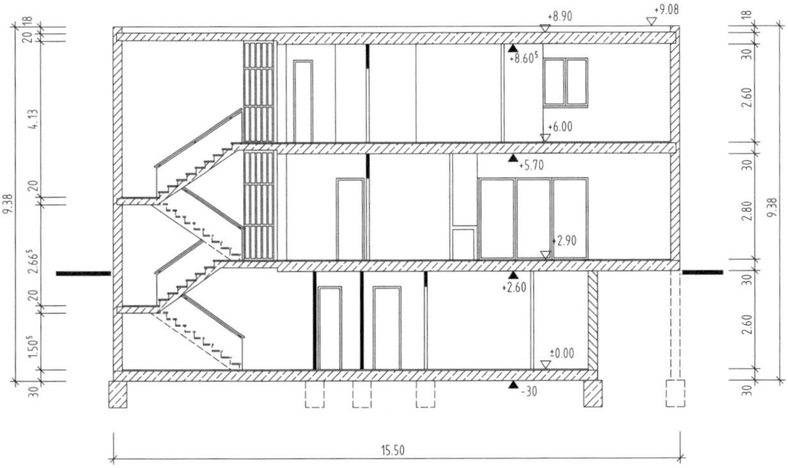

Fig. 42: Design plan, section

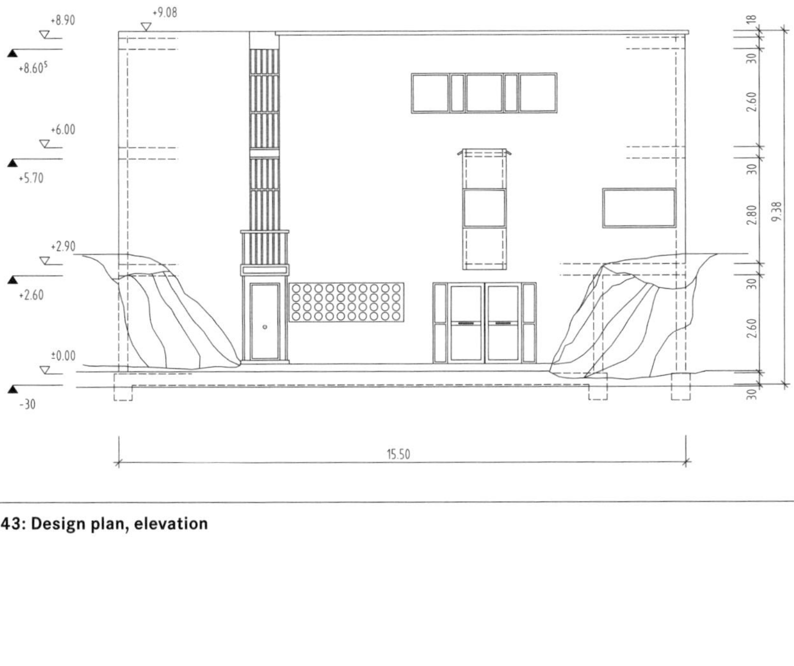

Fig. 43: Design plan, elevation

■ **Tip:** Converting from degrees to percent is simplified if the calculation is done in stages: a slope of x% gives a height difference of x cm over a horizontal distance of 100 cm. If a certain number of degrees is to be converted into a percentage, then the equation tangent angle = opposite leg/adjacent leg is used. For example, 10° gives the following equation: tan 10° = 0.1584. This corresponds to 15.84 cm to 100 cm, in other words 15.84%.

○ **Note:** A detailed introduction to public construction law can be found in: Udo Blecken/Bert Bielefeld, *Bauen in Deutschland,* Birkhäuser Verlag, Basel 2004.

Inclines such as rises and drops are identified by a height dimension and an angle, and in sections the percentage or degree is given, complemented by a directional arrow: e.g. roof pitch to the right, 45°. A north arrow is also drawn in, so that the light quality in the various rooms can be assessed, and so that the elevations can be identified.

PLANNING PERMISSION

In this phase, the location plan and the design drawings are completed by adding information in accordance with the regulations of the relevant planning authorities. Various requirements are imposed according to the nature and size of the planned building. In principle, it is very easy to turn designs plans into planning permission submissions.

Official location plan

Location plans, in particular, must often be drawn up by a publicly appointed surveyor or the local survey office. The responsible authorities should be asked to explain what is required before an application for planning permission is submitted. For an official location plan, written and drawn parts are distinguished. The location plan drawing is usually on a scale of 1:500, but scales 1:1,000 or 1:250 are possible for very large or very small projects. The content of the location plan is usually in black and white, but colors may be used for areas and boundaries where applicable.

○ A location plan should contain the following information:

- Location of the building plot relating to points of the compass, north arrow
- Existing buildings identifying use, number of floors, roof shape (ridge direction)
- The planned building identifying exterior dimensions, heights relating to zero level, number of storeys, roof shape
- Exterior dimensions of existing buildings and new buildings
- Information on type of use for the areas that are not built on, such as garden, parking space, playground, terrace etc.

- Statement and verification of distances from adjacent plots and to public areas (often in a separate plan showing distances apart)
- Marking and demarcation of areas with building restrictions
- Position of supply lines (water, electricity, heat, radio/telephone)

The location plan is supplemented by the following written information:

- Scale
- Details of street name and house number, owner, plot designation (boundaries, open fields, parcels)
- Area dimensions, boundaries relating to land registry
- Information about existing trees, especially if subject to nature conservation or tree protection orders
- Information about areas with building restrictions and their use

If the building plot is part of a development plan its provisions must be complied with; these are usually shown by graphic symbols.

Building in existing stock

If the plan is not for a new building, but an extension or conversion, a clear distinction must be made between demolition and new construction in the plans. As a rule, as-completed plans are drawn at the beginning of the project, to plan conversion and demolition measures. If a great deal of the building is to be dismantled, it is also recommended that separate demolition plans be drawn up, to be developed further as working plans and used as a basis for the demolition work. Demolition is further identified by crosses at an angle of 45° and dashed in on the plan view and section. In addition, existing building, demolition and new construction are colored on the plan:

Black: old, existing sections to be retained
Red: new sections to be added
Yellow: sections to be removed in the course of the building program

Generally speaking, the desired presentation should be discussed with the planning authority.

Drainage drawings

Drainage plans identifying the course of the drainage pipes are drawn to show drainage for sanitary facilities like WCs or kitchens and the exterior drainage of roof surfaces. They show the fall pipes and pipes connecting to the facilities in plan view and section. The pipes are identified by their diameter (e.g. DN 100 = interior diameter 100 mm), according to which wall-mounted installations, plumbing shafts etc. are dimensioned.

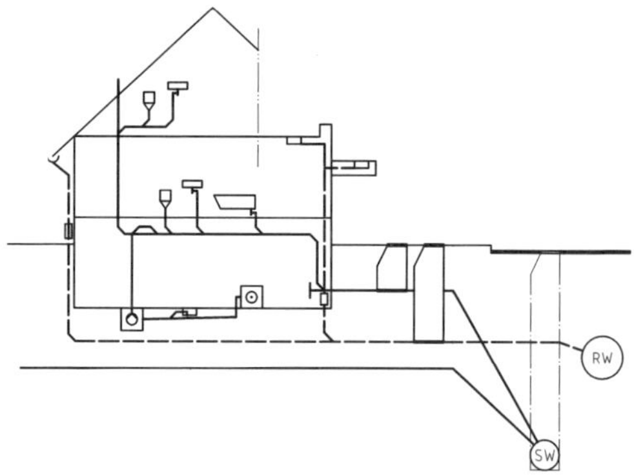

Fig. 44: Drainage system in section

WORKING PLANS

Purpose of working plans

Working plans are intended to provide information that can be used to construct the building precisely. Hence, the working drawings must contain all the individual items of information needed to complete the building. These include the architects' plans, which should also be complemented by plans from other specialists, e.g. heating, sanitary pipework, loadbearing structure, fire protection etc.

The working drawings include two subgroups laying down the scale and degree of detail in the planning. The working plans are on the scale of 1:50 and the detailed plans on scales of 1:20 to 1:1. Fundamentally a distinction can be made between the following working plans – not necessarily a complete list:

- Working plans scale 1:50: these consist of plan views, elevations and sections representing the building as a whole or parts of it.
- Facade sections scale 1:50–1:10: as a rule, the facades are shown in more detail with sections, interior and exterior views, in order to fix the relationship with other parts of the building in structural and geometrical terms.
- Installation drawings scale 1:50–1:20: special installation plans are drawn for individual services. These include screed plans, tiled surfaces, floor covering plans, plans for dry construction and grid ceilings etc.

- Detail plans scale 1:20–1:1: detail plans show individual structural points or connection with every element, in detail.
- Site installation plan, where applicable

Working plan presentation

The planner must translate the design planning into valid and complete working, detail and construction drawings in such a way that the contractor doing the work can understand and implement them without difficulty. The working planning must be so precise that no unintended scope for interpretation or dimensioning is allowed. But it does not have to define every screw in detail, as it can be assumed that the construction specialist will have the necessary expert knowledge. Possible requirements laid down by the planning authorities are also built into the working plans. Working planning must be continued and adapted during the building phase, if changes or confusions arise.

Representing intersected structural elements

As a rule, the intersected structural elements are presented on a scale of 1:50 so that they can contain direct structural statements about the wall structure (e.g. masonry rendered on both sides or reinforced concrete ceiling with floating screed). Openings and slits in walls and ceilings must also be shown. These are often needed for service installations (e.g. fireplace, ducts for heating, sanitary, ventilation and electrical services) and should be agreed with the planner responsible. Slits are shown by a diagonal line; as soon as the structural element is cut through completely, the opening is crossed through. Triangles can be solid black for emphasis.

Axes in working plans

For buildings with repeating loadbearing systems, such as industrial or office buildings, the longitudinal and lateral axes of the loadbearing frame should be identified by numbers or letters. Thus, individual areas can be categorized directly in such a way that the structural engineer can relate to the system and work with the axis definitions. Axes are drawn with dash-dot lines, either throughout the drawing or outside the building only.

Dimensioning working plans

All the dimensions needed for correct execution of the plans must be included at this stage. They include all the dimension chains already shown in the design plans; but also the height, width and depth of every relevant structural element, without any omissions, and each element must be attached to a part of the building that can be used for on-site measuring. First, the general dimension chains are placed outside the building in the design plans; the detailed measurement chains are given inside the plan view or section.

■

elevation | plan view

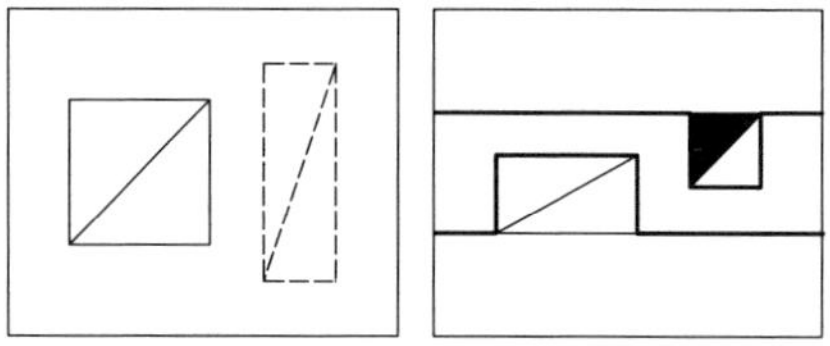

recesses that are not as deep as the structural element

elevation | plan view

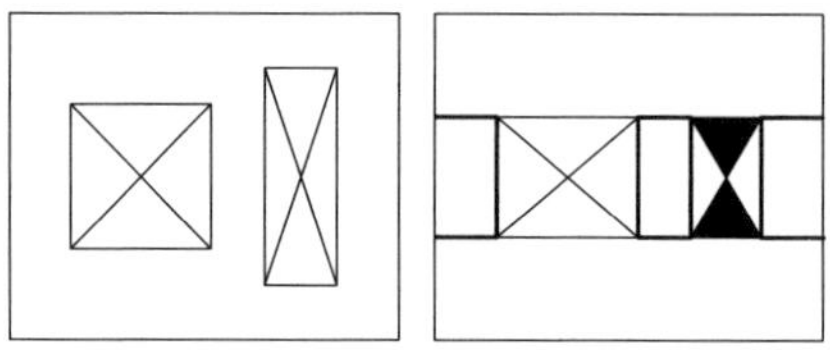

recesses that are as deep as the structural element

Fig. 45: Representing slits and openings

Room labels

The room labels contain much more information in the working plan than in the design plan. In addition to room numbers and room designations, we include:

- the room area (A) in square meters
- information about the surrounding walls (S), for example measurements of skirting boards
- clearance height (CH), which is needed in turn for wall developments, e.g. measuring up for painting

It is generally also possible to specify floor, wall and ceiling fittings. As they cannot usually be accommodated inside a room, the fittings can be named in the plan header > Chapter Plan presentation and allocated to the rooms by means of abbreviations (e.g. W1, W2 for wall fitting etc.).

■ **Tip:** When dimensioning, you should imagine yourself in the role of the construction specialist carrying out the work on the building site, who has to implement the plans on the spot. For example, if a door is to be set with its outer edge flush with the jamb, it makes little sense to dimension the center axis of the door. Double dimensioning should also be avoided as far as possible, because it increases the amount of work needed to make a change made, and double dimension chains are easily overlooked, which can lead to inconsistencies within the plan.

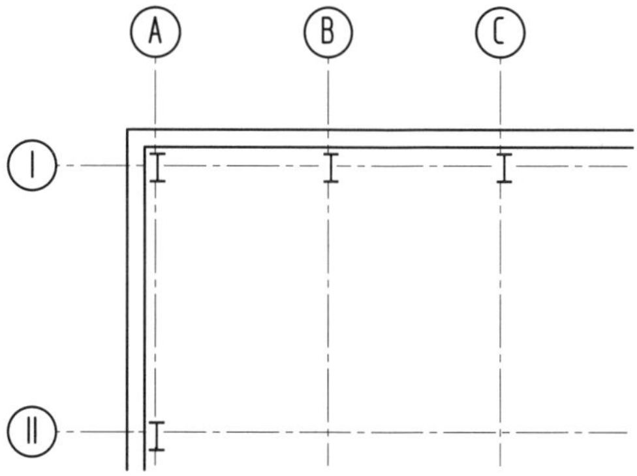

Fig. 46: Defining axes

Working drawings

Plan views should give the following information:

Content of plan views

- The nature, qualities and dimensions of structural elements
- Material-related presentation of wall, ceiling and floor fittings
- Representation of the sealing and insulation levels
- Door and window apertures with direction of opening, aperture and sill heights
- Stairs and ramps with walking line, details on number and relation of steps and oversteps where applicable
- Structural element qualities such as fire protection and sound insulation
- Structural joints such as expansion joints or changes of covering
- Wall and ceiling apertures, slits, shafts etc.
- Technical fittings, channels, chimneys, drainage systems, underdrainage etc.
- Fixed fitting and furnishings, sanitary and kitchen equipment
- All dimensions of structural elements needed for the correct construction of the building (every protrusion or recess must have a dimension)
- All the dimensions needed to establish room sizes and for quantity calculations

- Room labels (see above)
- Height related to ZL, so that the storey height can be assigned unambiguously
- Detail references

Content of elevations and sections

Elevations and sections will contain the following additional information:

- Storey heights, clearance heights, shell heights
- Height markers for shell and finished floor, foundations, roof edges etc.
- Floor and roof structures
- Presentation of the existing and planned organization of the terrain surface
- Windows and doors with graphic representation of divisions and modes of opening
- Gutters, downpipes, chimneys, roof structures
- Covered intermediate floors, loadbearing walls and foundations as dashed lines
- Course of foundation pit drawn in
- Structural ceiling, roof and floor details
- Glass specifications in elevations, if different

Facade section

It can make sense to draw a facade section in order to show the entire facade in detail and not take out individual points of detail. This will show the complete height development in section, interior view, exterior view and where applicable complemented with a plan view detail with all connection points and height relations between interior and facade.

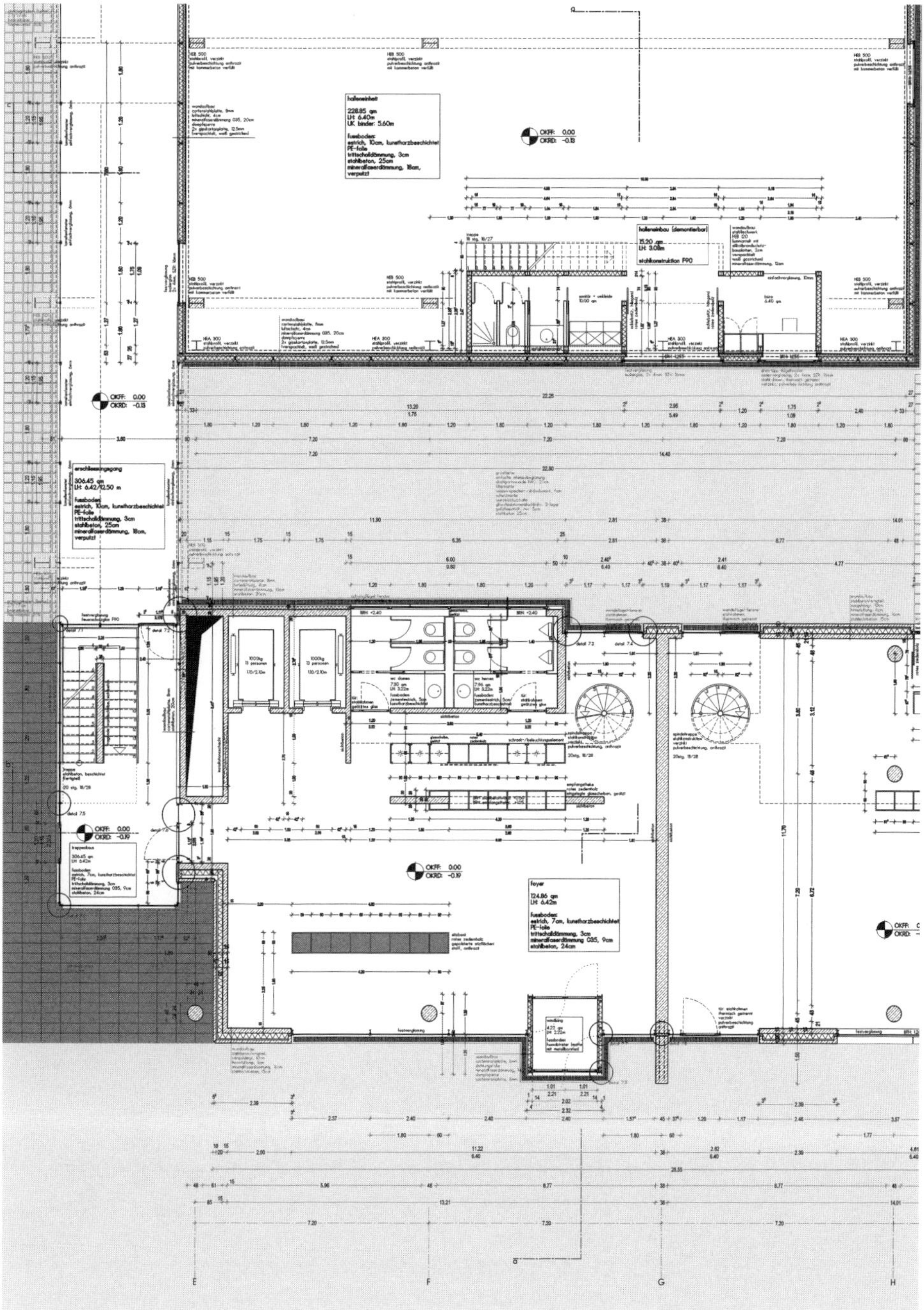

Fig. 47: Details from working plans, scale 1:50

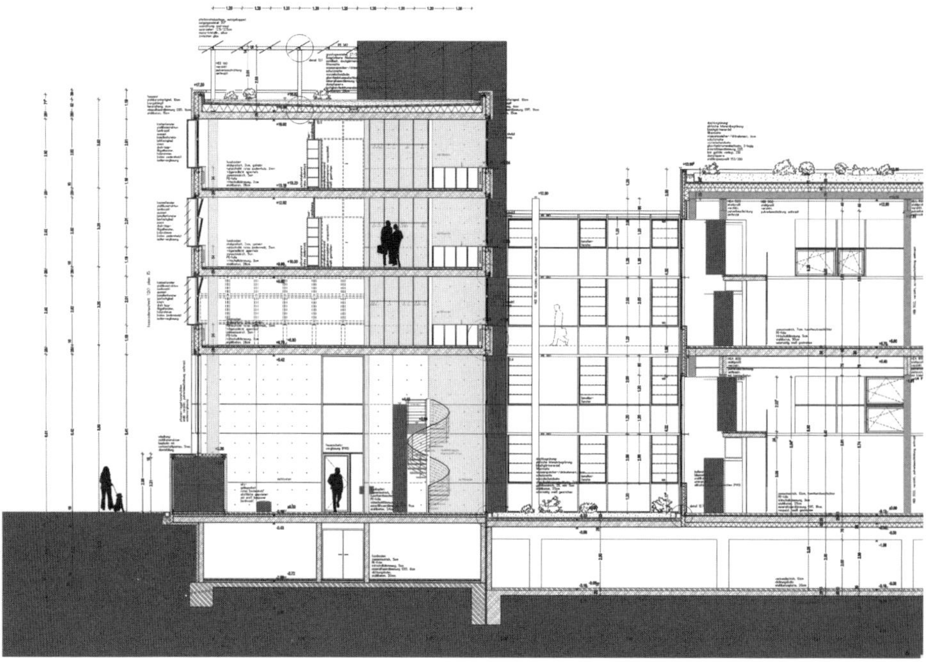

Fig. 48: Detail from an elevation, scale 1:50

Installation plans for service areas

Installation plans are construction drawings that show the way particular structural elements are to be fitted. They may include fitting information for the following structural elements:

- Prefabricated reinforced concrete parts
- Steel parts
- Wooden beams or roof trusses
- Areas of screed (showing expansion joints and conduits)
- Laying stones (with layout grid, intersections and expansion joints)
- Tiled surfaces (with layout grid, fittings and expansion joints)
- Suspended ceilings (layout grids, fittings, acoustically effective areas etc.)
- Double or cavity floors (layout grid, fittings under the floor)
- Floor covering (layout grid or axes, change of floor covering etc.)

Installation plans are often drawn up on the basis of existing working plans, with the appropriate additional information entered, e.g. through grid lines, colors or hatching. Installation plans cover a specific

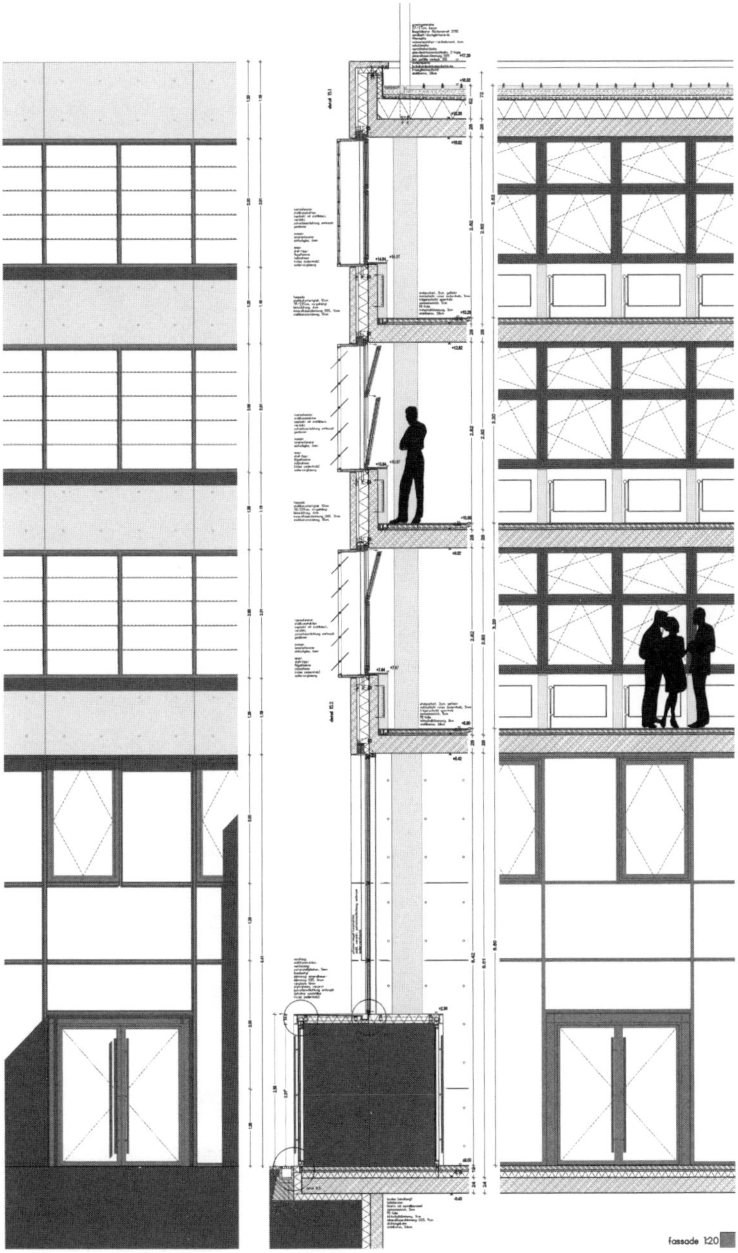

Fig. 49: Example of a facade section, scale 1:20

service area and are usually drawn up before tenders are invited for the particular field, so that the plans can be enclosed with the tender information.

Detailed plans

Detailed plans include all sorts of connections, system structures and transitions. As well as fixing control equipment in the drawing, there are particularly important points at which various control systems coincide or merge with each other. It is impossible to make a general statement about the detailed plans needed for a project, as they depend strongly on the individual project, the depth of detail required, the planning demands, and questions and uncertainties within the firms doing the work. Typical areas where detail is needed are:

- Facade: window joints and systems, transition between ground and rising walls, connections between facade and roof, corner situations, external doors, balconies, sills and parapets, shades against sun and glare
- Footings: foundations, drainage, sealing, insulation at ground level
- Roof: attic, eaves, ridge, verge, gable, roof apertures such as chimneys, ventilators, skylights and roof windows
- Stairs: system section, upper and lower connection, landings, banisters, handrails
- Floor and ceiling fittings: system sketches for all ceiling fittings used, transitions between different floor types, connections to rising building sections, fixtures, conduits
- Doors: system doors, frame systems, steel-framed doors, lift doors, shaft caps
- Dry construction: connections of walls to facade, shell structure, floor and ceiling, suspended ceilings
- WCs, kitchens, fitted furniture: structural details, connections, WC dividing walls etc.

Site installation plans

Site installation and organization plans coordinate the site and the construction firms involved. It is often unnecessary to draw up a separate site installation plan for small projects. But if there is only a small amount of room on site, it makes sense to do so, to avoid getting in each other's way and using the plot inefficiently. Hence, the following should be recorded in a site installation plan:

- Storage areas and working areas/site road
- Site management containers

- Accommodation and sanitary facilities
- Working areas around the building
- Excavation pit
- Lifting equipment (e.g. cranes) with radius and operational area
- Building fences, entrances, signs etc.
- Areas for individual trades (e.g. bending and cutting areas for concrete construction)
- Soil storage areas where applicable
- Power and water supplies, disposal facilities, rubbish management etc.

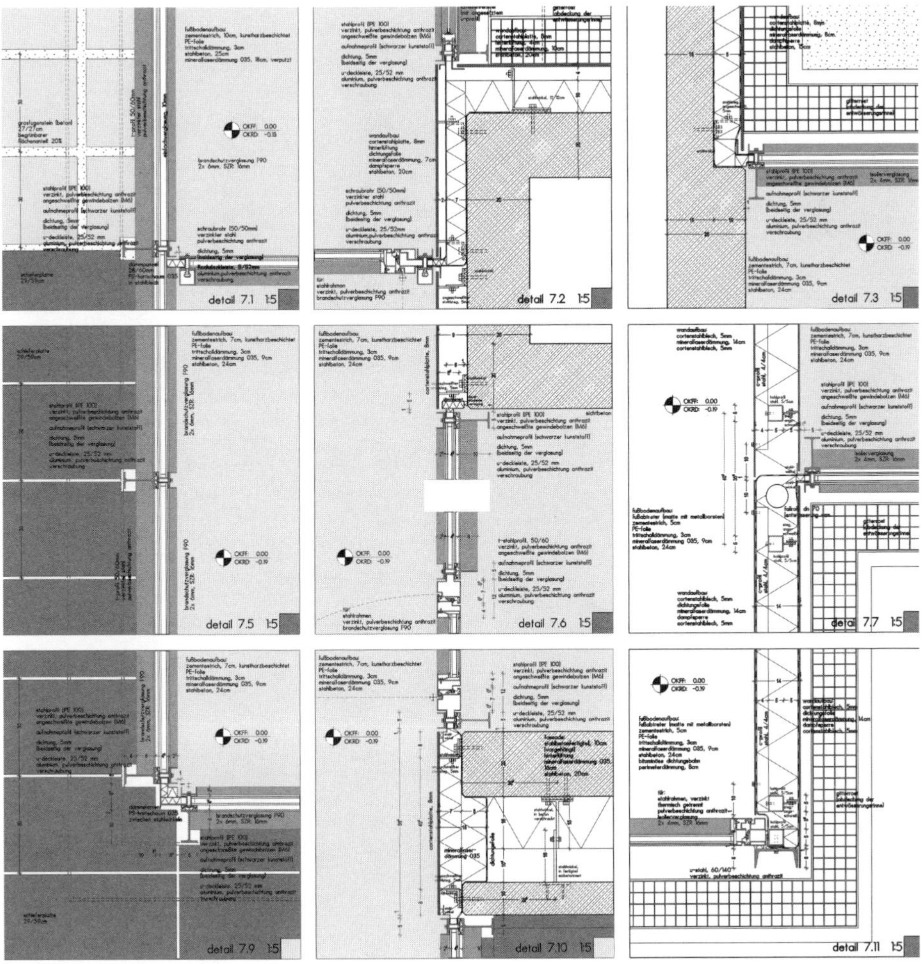

Fig. 50: Examples of detailed plans

Workshop drawings by firms involved in the project

Construction firms in different service areas involved in the project make their own workshop drawings on the basis of the working plans (sometimes also called works drawings). These are submitted to the planners before building starts and must be examined and signed off by them. Typical specialist firms who make their own workshop drawings include the following service fields:

- Metal or steel construction work (windows, steel constructions, railings etc.)
- Timber or carpentry work (wooden structures, roof trusses, windows etc.)
- Ventilation construction work
- Lift construction work

SPECIALIST PLANNING

Loadbearing structures

Structural engineers draw their own working plans, placing particular emphasis on statically relevant elements. Which plans are drawn depends primarily on the choice of building materials. If the building is to be in reinforced concrete, encasement and reinforcement plans should be prepared; for wood or steel construction, plans for the appropriate rafters, timber and steel construction.

Working plans for structural engineers

Position plans show individual positions to clarify the statical calculations. The positions are numbered on the basis of the design drawings, and these numbers are also found in the statical calculation.

Position plan

○ ●

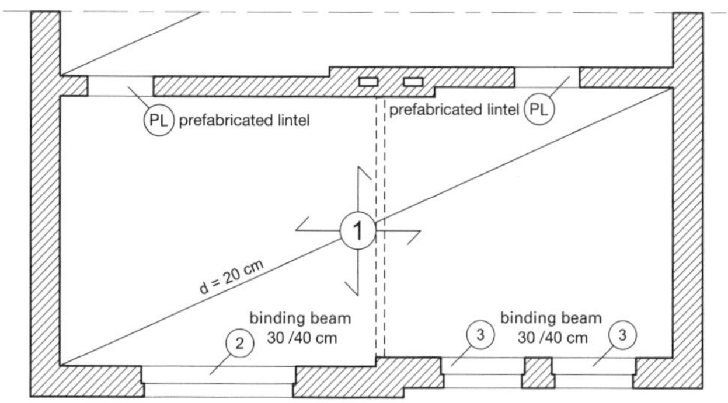

Fig. 51: Example of a position plan

○ **Note:** Plan views for structural engineering planning do not usually present a top view of the floor below, but of the ceiling above it. A structural engineer's plan view for the 2nd floor shows, as well as the identically intersected structural elements, a different view from the architects' plans. For clarification you should imagine a mirror floor showing all the outlines of the ceiling.

● **Example:** A reinforced concrete beam is calculated statically and allotted the number 21. This beam is then also given the number 21 on the position plan, to make it clear to which beam in the building the statical calculation applies. If applicable, all the beams that are the same can be allotted the same number.

Encasement and reinforcement plan

Encasement and reinforcement plans are drawn up for reinforced concrete buildings. Here, shell plans show the structural elements to be encased (e.g. a reinforced concrete ceiling or wall). Encasement plans are particularly important if the subsequent surface is to be important visually (e.g. for fair-face concrete walls).

Encasement plans show the ceiling above the storey shown with:

- axis, mass and height
- supported or loadbearing construction elements
- cavities relevant to loadbearing
- types and strength classes
- directions of span

Reinforcement plans contain information about reinforcement mats and bars to be built into a reinforced concrete section. A mat is usually shown as a rectangular area with a diagonal line marked with the mat type. Additional information for reinforcement plans:

- Concrete steel types
- Number, diameter, shape and length of steel bars and welds
- Concrete strength classes, concrete covering
- Apertures and special structures
- Precise steel or item lists for construction to complement the drawing

Timber construction plan

Timber construction plans are drawn up for wooden structures, showing the precise position and dimensions of the individual timber construction elements (beams, supports, purlins etc.). As a rule, axes are dimensioned and connection points shown separately in detail. For example, if a pitched roof is to be built, the position and dimensions of the purlins and rafters must be shown in a rafter plan. ○

○ **Note:** Timber constructions and rafter plans are described in detail in: Tanja Brotruck, *Basics Roof Construction*, Birkhäuser Verlag, Basel 2007.

Building services

Special plans are also drawn up for building or domestic service installations, providing a basis for the installing the service equipment. Separate plans are usually made for each service. Particular services include:

- heating installation
- water supply and sewerage installations
- ventilation installation
- electrical installations
- fire technology and alarms
- data technology
- lift technology

As well as the actual rooms for services, such as a utilities room, boiler room or similar, the pipe runs, holes and cable runs are the most important features. A plan showing slits and holes is often prepared to be included in the architects' plans, giving precise details of interventions in the shell.

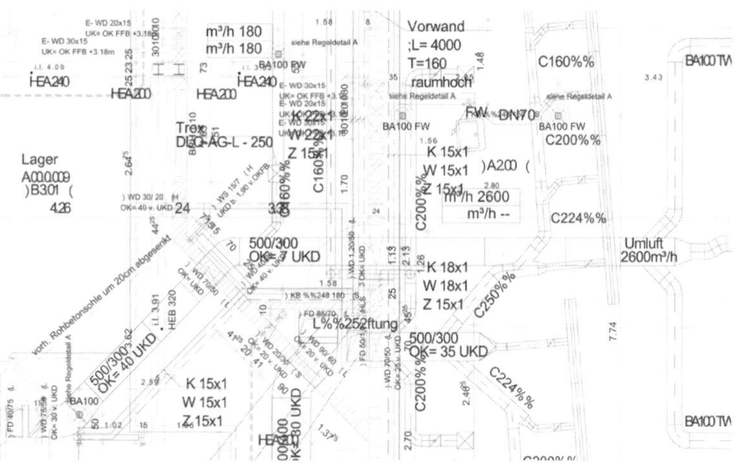

Fig. 52: Extract from an implementation plan for the areas of heating, ventilation and sanitation

Plan presentation

If a drawing is to be issued in paper form, the paper format must be established to meet the demands of modern reproduction, and given a plan header.

PLAN COMPOSITION

Drawing area

Once the size of the building or section of a building to be shown and the scale of the drawing are fixed, the necessary amount of drawing space can be calculated. Then an appropriate area is added to the building dimensions on both sides to allow space for the dimension chains, and the drawing area needed is calculated on the basis of the scale. A plan header must be accommodated next to the drawing area (see below) and where applicable a frame, allowing for the intersecting edges.

Choice of paper format

All kinds of plan formats with different side measurements are possible for presentation purposes (competitions, student assignments). For example, a long, narrow building could be presented on paper with the same proportions, which would enhance the effect of the building's shape.

It generally makes sense to choose a common paper format for construction drawings (e.g. the DIN A series), as this can be reproduced easily. Large-format paper is needed for working plans, while for detailed drawings it is usually advantageous to use a format such as DIN-A3, which can be duplicated on most photocopiers. > Chapter Principles of representation

Different scales

Drawings can also appear on different scales on a single plan: for example, it can make sense to show appropriate details of individual anchor points alongside a facade section. Care should be taken so that the scale for the individual drawing can be identified precisely through clear labelling.

PLAN HEADER

Each plan contains a plan header, showing clearly which project and what details this particular plan shows. The header is usually placed in the bottom right-hand corner of the plan. Plan headers for presentation and construction drawings are organized differently.

Presentation plan header

If the plans are intended for presentation purposes, they should have a corresponding plan header. The overall graphic design of the plan usually includes the header. As well as the project name, it gives details of scale, plan contents, (e.g. ground floor) and author. Supporting design

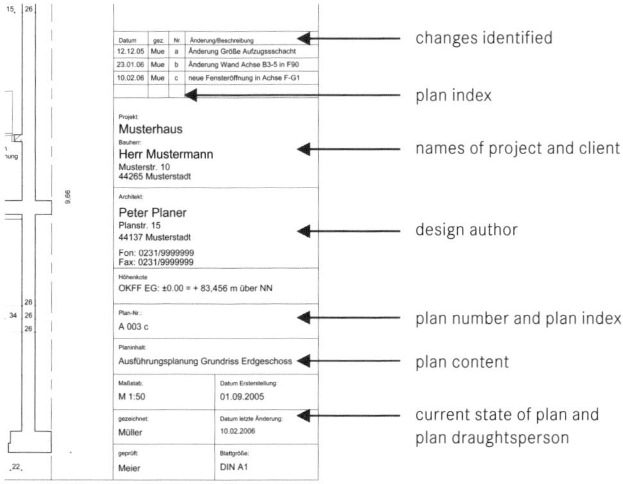

Fig. 53: Example of a plan header

pictograms, explanatory sketches on the section, or plan view level and north arrows can also be included in plan headers.

For university and college projects, the student's matriculation number should be included, as well as his or her name, department or professor. For competitions, names or attributions do not usually feature on the plans. Instead, a camouflage number is often provided in the competition documents, and is placed in a particular corner of the plan. It is submitted with the competition plans in a sealed envelope, which will be opened only after the competition has been judged, to reveal the author of the design.

Construction drawing plan header

For construction drawings, the plan header first names the client, the author of the design, the plan draughtsperson and the scale. The current status of the plan is indicated. As new developments or specialist planning material have to be worked in regularly, the precise date of the current plan must be recorded. It is also a good idea to give the dates of the first version and the current revision. It is also helpful for understanding the additional data to include a summary of the plan changes to date. Building permission plans usually have plan numbers, which define them unambiguously. For simplicity, the current position expressed by the plan can be incorporated in the plan number: Plan A34d then means: working plan no. 34, fourth revision (d). Of course plan numbers can be allotted as wished; it is easier to administer the plans if a system is established at the beginning of the project and agreed with all concerned.

PLAN DISTRIBUTION

It is rare nowadays for plans to be drawn by hand, and CAD programs are generally used, making it easier to duplicate and distribute plans than when they are drawn by hand.

Plotting

CAD files are printed on plotters; smaller formats can be produced on standard commercial printers. Plotters are large-format printers, usually in the A1 or AO format, and plans are printed on them from paper rolls. The roll widths are generally 61.5 cm for A1 rolls and 91.5 cm for AO. The size of the plan can be input individually in most CAD programs, so that any plan format compatible with the width of the roll can be used.

Copying

If a plan that already exists on paper is to be copied, large-format copiers are available. These usually operate with the same roll widths as ■ plotters. Color copies of large-format plans are generally very expensive, so a plan should be reproduced by multiple plotting. It is worth choosing a plan format for detail drawings that can be duplicated on standard commercial copiers.

Blueprints

If hand drawings are produced on tracing paper, it is possible to make blueprints of them, rather than large-format copies. Here, blueprint paper is placed on top of the original tracing paper, and exposed to ultraviolet light in a blueprint machine. Blueprint papers exist in various color shades, and can then be called black-, red- or blueprints.

Blueprints are rarely used today because they have been replaced by CAD drawings, but they offer a reasonably priced possibility for reproducing hand drawings.

■ **Tip:** Copy-shops often have mechanical folding machines that make it easier to fold a lot of plans. If you have to fold the plans yourself, it is best to use a sheet of A4 paper and a set square. First, take the left-hand side of the plan and fold it upwards to the width of the A4 sheet. The fold can be smoothed down with the help of the set square. Then the right-hand side is folded to a width of about 19 cm, until the remainder can be folded in the middle if necessary. Now fold the remaining strip back to the height of the A4 sheet (several times for larger formats). The inner corner, as shown on the diagram, is then folded inwards, so that is not perforated at the subsequent hole-punching stage. If you use the plan header and plan frame frequently on a CAD plotter, it is possible to draw in little lines on the plan frame, so that there is no need to measure, and the plan can be folded directly along the lines.

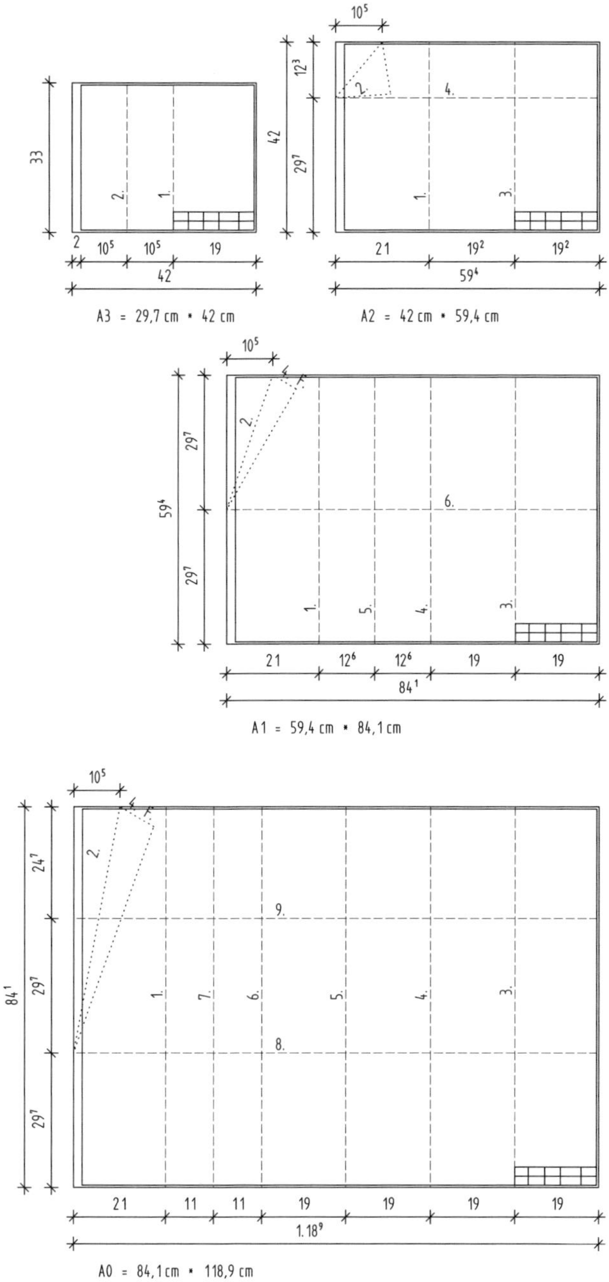

Fig. 54: Folding plans

Folding

In many cases, plans are circulated not in their original size, but in A4 format, which means that larger formats have to be folded to A4 size. It is important here to ensure that the plan header is visible in the bottom right-hand corner even when the plan is folded. It should also be possible to unfold the plan even when it is filed away, so holes should be punched in the lower left-hand area only.

Jan Krebs

CAD

CAD: Meaning and fields of application

CAD – short for computer-aided design – is the catchword for drawing and designing with the help of a computer. A wide selection of both simple and complex CAD computer programs (software) makes it possible to create two- and three-dimensional drawings using input devices such as the keyboard, mouse and other tools. These drawings are displayed by output devices such as monitors and printers. The CAD field of IT plays an important role in many areas including engineering. It is used in automotive and plant engineering, as well as in structural engineering and architecture – the focus of this book. Aside from creating technical drawings, CAD programs can be used to develop powerful virtual models that provide a basis for a wide range of simulations. CAD programs can generate photorealistic visualizations of buildings, as well as climate and light simulations. With the right CAD software, users can also design load and fluid flow simulations in addition to simplifying development and production processes.

The first CAD programs were developed in the 1960s and were used primarily in aeroplane construction. With the breakthrough of personal computing and the lower costs of computer workstations in the 1980s, these programs became available to a larger number of users. The powerful, standardized computing systems developed in the early twenty-first century has led to efficient, relatively inexpensive CAD systems that meet a wide range of requirements.

○ **Note:** In order to establish a practical relationship to application software, *Basics CAD* includes a selection of sample functions from leading CAD software providers in the CAAD (computer-aided architectural design) field. You can find an extensive list of the diverse CAD programs on offer in the appendix of this book.

Although nearly all the programs have a similar foundation, they differ significantly at times in terms of operation and use. There is a great deal of literature on CAD on the market – so much that it is nearly impossible to keep track of – but most of it deals with particular CAD systems. By contrast, the book *Basics CAD* offers a general approach to learning CAD. It contains basic, application-oriented knowledge and is designed to assist the novice in selecting a suitable CAD system. ○

The virtual drawing board

When you draw with CAD, the sheet of paper is replaced by the computer monitor, the pencil by the mouse and keyboard. Lines and shapes are created by mouse clicks and keyboard entries, and the whole process is supported by functions that simplify drawing. > Chapter Drawing functions, Drawing elements

Screen scale

The objects in CAD drawings are usually created on a scale of 1:1 – that is, at their real size. This means that a 10 m wall is drawn with a length of 10 m. To display the entire length of the wall on the screen, you must choose a smaller scale since the space would otherwise not be sufficient to show it. Screen scale describes the ratio between the real size of drawn objects and their depiction on the computer monitor. It changes automatically when the size of the screenshot changes. The actual representational scale that you follow when drawing on paper is created only in the output process in CAD (e.g. printing), but you must always bear it in mind when doing your drawing.

Reference scale

In a CAD drawing on the monitor, this representational scale is referred to as the reference scale. It describes the scale in which the drawn object is likely to be printed (e.g. 1:20, 1:100 or 1:500). Since some of the elements in a drawing, such as lettering, are independent of building components and must be displayed in an appropriate size in subsequent prints, they are not based on a drawing scale of 1:1, but on the probable scale of the printout. This means that, in the drawing operation, the software illustrates on screen the size ratio between the typeface and other ■ elements, including the actual drawn object. > Chapter Data flow, Printing and plotting

■ **Tip:** Screen scale must be the same as the reference scale if you wish to view and evaluate the real size of the printout on the screen. Some CAD programs show the screen scale as a percentage of the reference scale: when set at 100% it thus shows the real size of the print. It is also advisable to create sample prints during the work process in order to evaluate the effects of the scale drawing.

○ **Note:** In addition to the mouse and keyboard, you can use a variety of other input devices, including sketchpad and SpaceMouse. However, these play a minor role in architecture-related CAD (see Chapter System requirements, Hardware).

When technical drawings are made, architects use common units of length so that their work is comprehensible to everyone. In Central Europe, these units are millimetres, centimetres and metres. Some English-speaking countries continue to use feet and inches as units of length, but due to the need for standardization in managing international projects, even these countries are increasingly using the more easily convertible units favoured in Central Europe. You are free to select the units on which you wish to base your CAD drawing. The smallest units can be millimetres, centimetres or metres, or inches or feet.

Measurement units

USER INTERFACE

CAD user interfaces consist of special building blocks that we will explain briefly below by elucidating their underlying concepts.

The various tools of the CAD program are displayed by symbols and menus on the user interface. > Fig. 1 You can generate a drawing on the computer using the usual entry devices such as the mouse and the keyboard.

○

Drawing area

The drawing area is the most important part of the user interface. It allows you to draw and modify objects in either a two-dimensional field or in a space defined in three dimensions. Generally speaking, the CAD drawing area is comparable to a piece of paper. The main difference is that it is a virtual workspace that offers far-ranging options and various virtual tools.

Selection and drawing tools

The computer mouse is a commonly used <u>pointing device</u>. A pointing device controls the cursor on the user interface and functions as a virtual selection and drawing tool. It is represented by an arrow, crosshairs or some other symbol, according to the CAD program in question. This symbol generally changes when you use different selection and drawing options in the drawing operation to indicate the function you are currently using.

Electronic pens

CAD programs allow you to customize electronic pens and specify various line widths, line types and colours. > Fig. 2 You can define line properties before you begin to draw a line, or you can modify them retroactively. This brings greater clarity to both the drawing process and the methodology, since different lines emphasize and illustrate different elements of a drawing. Since many CAD programs link line colours to specific line widths, you can immediately see which elements have been drawn with a specific line width even in complex drawings. In this way, the different elements of a drawing are prepared for subsequent printing

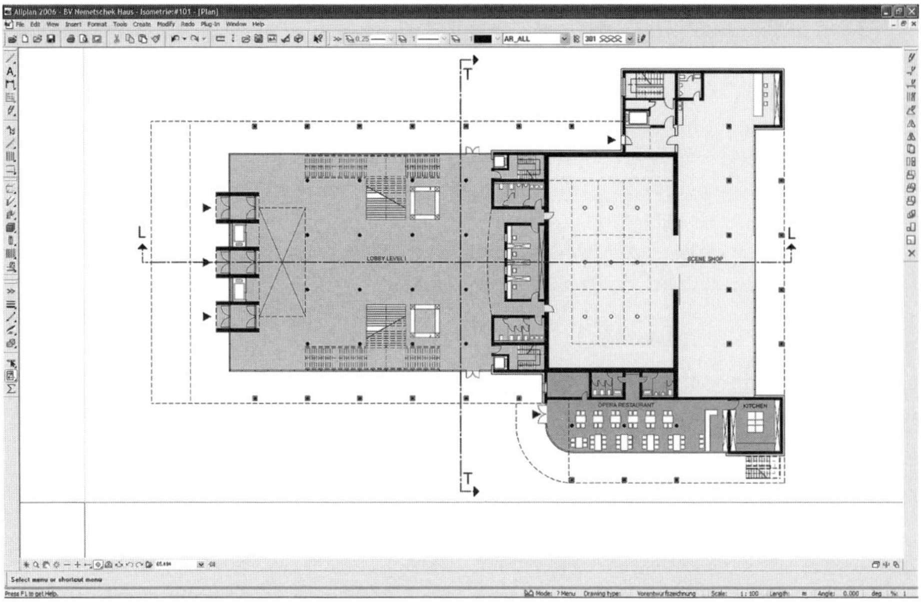

Fig. 1: Example of a CAD interface (Nemetschek Allplan)

based on their screen depiction. > Chapter Data flow, Printing and plotting The depiction of the pen line represents the subsequent result in the printout.

In addition, many CAD programs allow you to show true-to-scale line widths on the screen. In the corresponding screen scale, the line widths are shown just as they appear in a printout and give an impression of what the print will actually look like. Electronic pens can also be assigned other virtual properties that are important for the visualization of structures. > Chapter Visualization

Menu bar

The menu bar is located above the drawing area and displays the software options in interactive lists. For instance, as is generally the case with Windows-based applications, you can use the "File" menu to create new drawings, open existing ones or store drawing files. Via the menu bar, you can also custom-configure the user interface and activate all software commands and functions by means of the mouse and the keyboard.

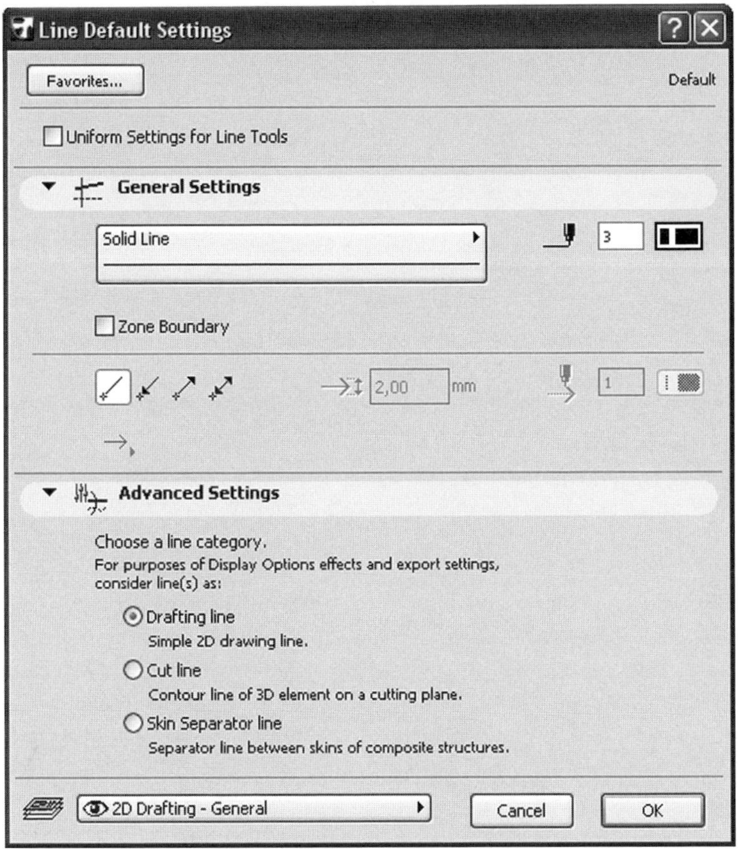

Fig. 2: You can customize the width, type and colour of the lines drawn by electronic pens (Graphisoft ArchiCAD).

The toolbox buttons display symbols of the drawing and tool functions available. They are activated by selection with the virtual selection tool. > Fig. 3 If you move the selection tool to a symbol, the software will usually display the name of the corresponding function. When you use a CAD program for the first time, the user interface will contain default functions that can be configured individually and shown or hidden according to your needs. Toolbox

■

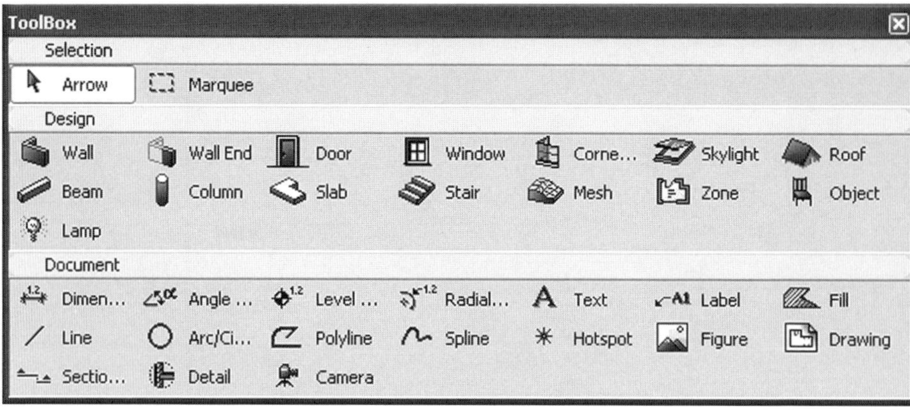

Fig. 3: Example of a toolbox with various functions (Graphisoft ArchiCAD)

Context menu

Context menus are related to the function you are currently using and contain commands relevant to each drawing operation. In default mode, they can be displayed by right-clicking the mouse, which will make them appear near the drawing and selection tool. Context menus allow you to repeat or cancel commands quickly, and to activate other drawing tools.

Dialogue boxes

A dialogue box allows you to engage in a "dialogue" with the CAD program on a specific function. Dialogue boxes often provide a more detailed description of a selected command, or explain the steps necessary to perform this command. They also make it possible to select special options or to enter numerical values via the keyboard. The boxes are part of the various drawing and tool functions, and they open automatically on the user interface when you activate the commands. > Fig. 4

■ **Tip:** The toolboxes can be displayed in a vertical or horizontal column on the edge of the user interface, or they can be positioned alongside or within the drawing area. An intelligent setup will enlarge the working area and allow you to work more efficiently. Once you have gained some experience of drawing with CAD, you will learn which functions you use frequently, and can then arrange the required toolboxes on the interface so that you can access them quickly.

○ **Note:** Cartesian coordinates are not the only available system. One alternative is the polar coordinate system, in which a point is described by a radius and an angle instead of by X and Y axes.

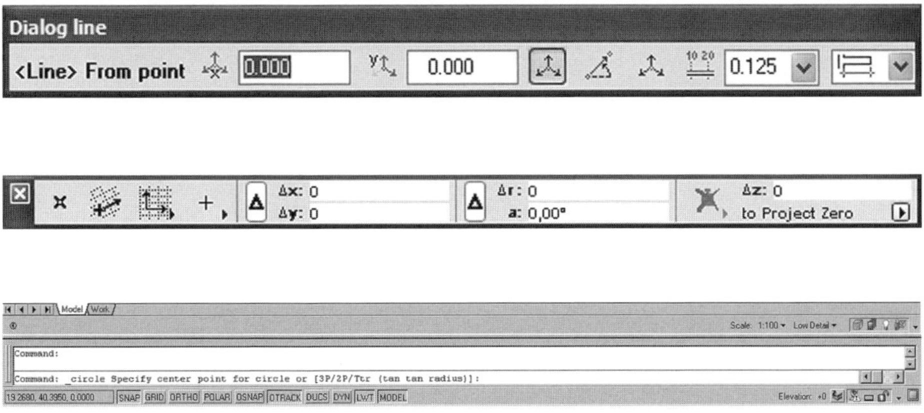

Fig. 4: Communicating with CAD software through dialogue boxes (Nemetschek Allplan, Graphisoft ArchiCAD, Autodesk Architectural Desktop)

COORDINATE SYSTEMS

The basic geometric reference system in CAD software is a coordinate system that defines the virtual drawing area as a construction plane. This construction plane can be thought of as a piece of graph paper divided by horizontal and vertical lines. Points on a plane, which are specified as coordinates, are thus clearly mapped out within the CAD system and can be used to define the location and shape of drawing elements.

> Chapter Drawing functions, Drawing elements

The Cartesian coordinate system, which is used most commonly, is based on two perpendicular axes (X and Y) in two-dimensional space. These axes describe the distance between any given point and the zero point of the system. > Fig. 5

Imaginary lines parallel to the X and Y axes intersect within the coordinate system and define the position of any given point.

Going one step further, we can define a line in geometric terms as the connection between two points. This is also how both endpoints of a line are specified in the Cartesian coordinate system. > Fig. 6

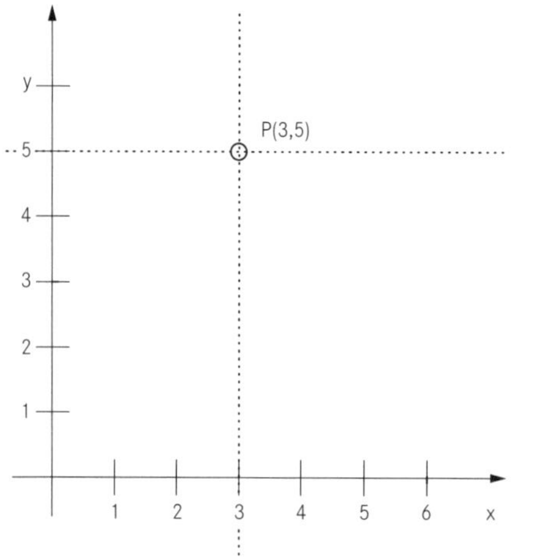

Fig. 5: The point P(3,5) is described by lines parallel to the X and Y axes.

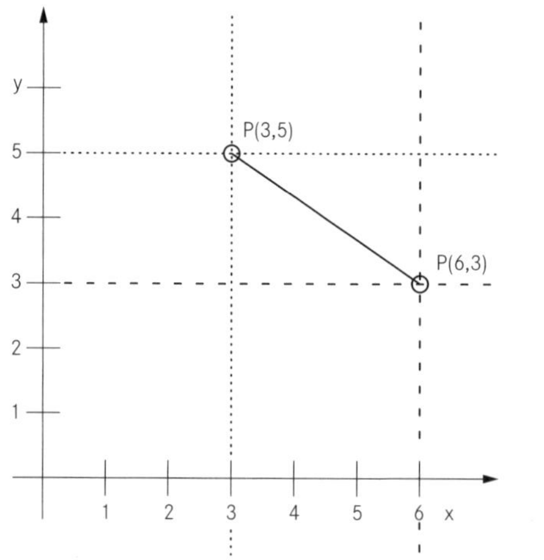

Fig. 6: Both endpoints of a line are defined as two individual points.

Absolute coordinates

Absolute coordinates are based on the above-mentioned zero point of the drawing, at which the X and Y axes intersect. It makes sense to use absolute coordinates when the exact X and Y values of the coordinates you wish to define are known.

User-defined coordinate system

It would be disadvantageous to enter only absolute coordinates together with an absolute, fixed zero point since this would make large drawings particularly difficult to generate using the keyboard.

This is one of the main reasons that most CAD programs allow you to move and thus redefine the point of origin within the coordinate system any time you draw new elements. You may also rotate the coor-

○ **Note:** A coordinate system like the one introduced in Figs. 5 and 6 is not usually visible on the screen and serves only as an imagined or virtual basis for drawing. In some CAD programs, symbols appear in one corner of the drawing area for orientation purposes and to show the directions of the coordinate axes. They are, however, an exception.

● **Example:** Apartment walls can be drawn on one layer of a floor plan, the interior furnishings on another. Both levels can be viewed separately, edited or, if necessary, combined (see Fig. 8).

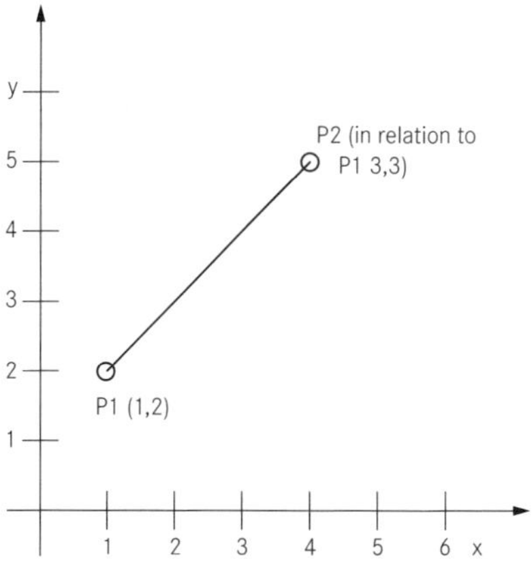

Fig. 7: Point P2 is described in relation to Point P1.

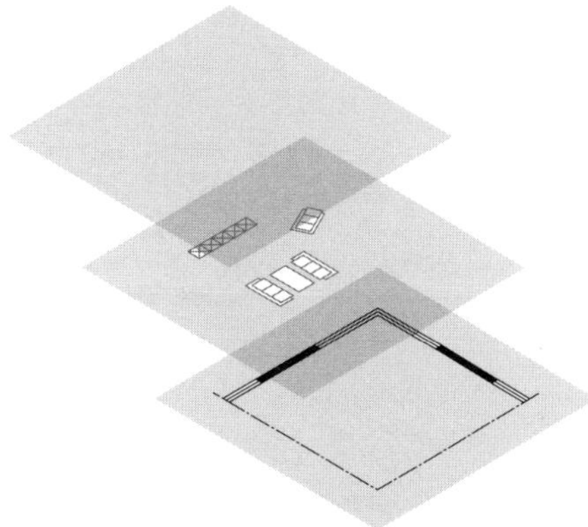

Fig. 8: You can stack different drawings.

dinate system and thus the entire construction plane by any angle of your choosing. This makes it easy to design linear objects that are not perpendicular to the original coordinate system. Below, we refer to such user-defined coordinate systems as UCS.

Relative coordinates

A flexible, alternative method for specifying coordinates incorporates so-called relative coordinates. These are based on the point last defined in the drawing process, which then becomes the temporary reference point for new coordinates. > Fig. 7

TRANSPARENT PLANES – THE LAYERING PRINCIPLE

CAD drawings often contain large amounts of information. As the scope of a drawing expands, so does its complexity, and you might find it increasingly difficult to work on or change elements. This is particularly problematic when many different objects are positioned right next to or on top of one another. CAD programs solve this problem by using variable drawing layers that, like transparent drawing paper, are placed on top of one another as needed. > Fig. 8 These layers may have different names in the various CAD programs. In Nemetschek Allplan, for example, they are called DRAWING FILES.

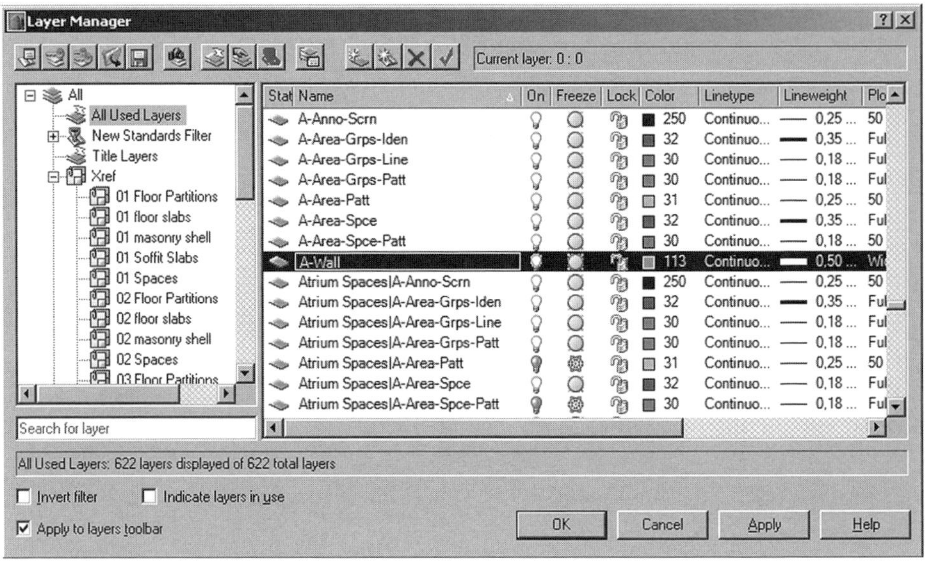

Fig. 9: Example of a CAD layer structure, which enables users to manage different layers and pen properties in a dialogue box (Autodesk Architectural Desktop).

■ **Tip:** At the outset of a project, it is worthwhile to give some thought to the way layers – and thus the entire project – need to be organized. For instance, layers can be predefined for different drawing content, even if the layers are used only at a later stage in the project. In addition, if a component consists of several layers, they can be systematically combined to form meaningful overarching layer groups. This approach will allow you to create a hierarchy within a drawing, one that brings the requisite clarity even to complex projects (see Fig. 10).

● **Example:** If two layers are stacked on top of each other, it is possible to see both, but it makes sense to lock one while you continue to work on the other so that you do not inadvertently alter the first one. This is particularly important for complex, multi-layered drawings.

○ **Note:** With many CAD programs (e.g. Graphisoft ArchiCAD), you can structure a drawing not only by layers but also by floors, a feature that is especially useful when designing buildings. The floors are linked to specific elevations and permit a vertical organization of floor plans (based on ground floor, first floor, second floor etc.).

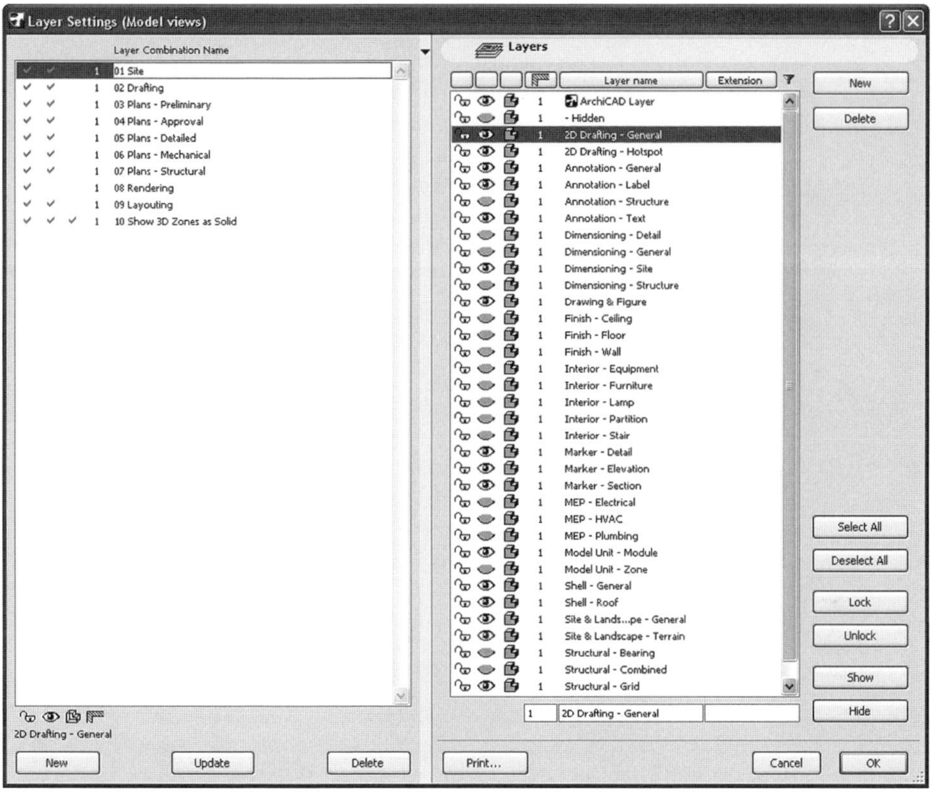

Fig. 10: Creating a hierarchy for drawing content within the layer structure. This brings clarity to the project (Graphisoft ArchiCAD).

In addition, layer structure plays an important role in organizing a drawing. Using a special dialogue box, you can create any number of layers and manage different drawing content easily. If a structure has many different design elements, this considerably simplifies the design process: independent layers can be created for exterior and interior walls, dimension lines, text, hatching and so on. You can organize drawing contents and retrieve drawings easily. > Fig. 9 and Appendix, page 395

Further, by creating specific layers, you can show or hide drawing content, or you can "lock" a drawing, making it impossible to alter for a defined period.

Filter function

The layer system described above not only creates clarity in drawing operations but also allows you to retrieve specific drawing components or general elements quickly and easily when needed. That said, all categorization systems have logical limits or, in certain situations, are not consistently followed. For this reason, many CAD programs also offer a special function that permits users to search for special properties of drawing elements, by either filtering these elements out or activating them. > Fig. 11 This filter function goes by different names in current CAD ● systems and is sometimes referred to as the FILTER ASSISTANT, or by the more pragmatic term SEARCH AND ACTIVATE. It is normally selected from ■ the menu bar.

● **Example:** If you have drawn all the exterior walls in a complex floor plan using a special line type, which then proves to be too thick or too thin on a sample print, you can filter out the walls based on their line properties and redefine all of them in just a few short steps. They do not have to be selected individually.

■ **Tip:** The filter function can be used for a great variety of CAD elements. Search criteria include line colour and type, and component specifications (see Chapter The third dimension, Architectural elements). It is useful to draw certain elements or entire components using a specific line colour so that they can easily be filtered out and edited later on.

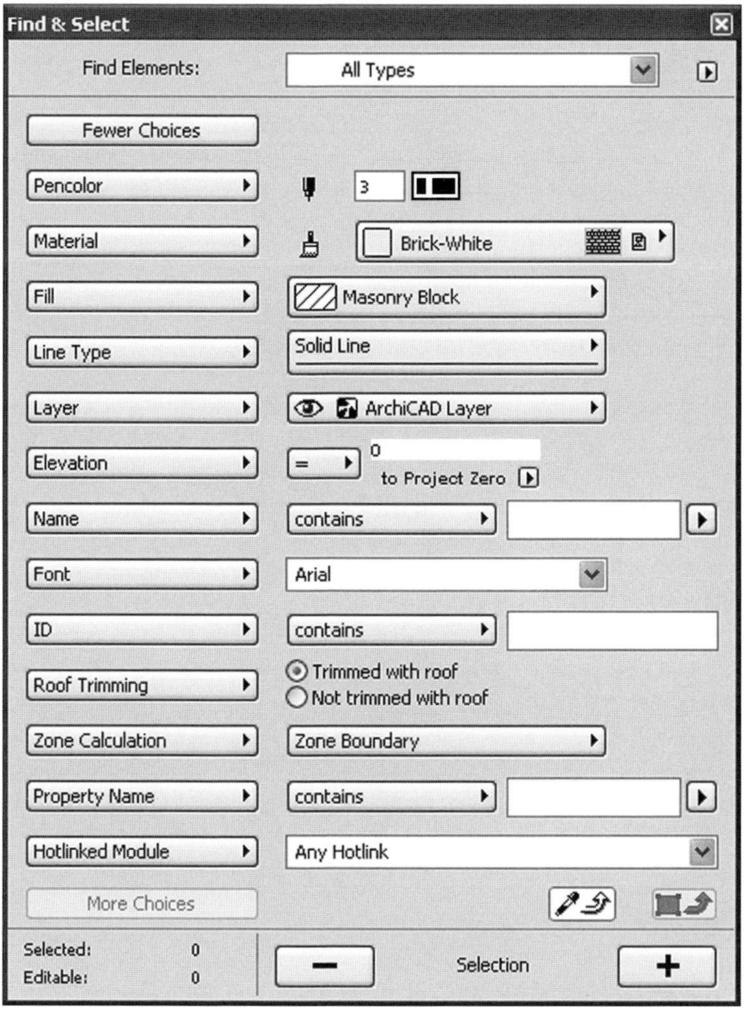

Fig. 11: Various filter criteria can be used to search for and activate drawing elements (Graphisoft ArchiCAD).

Drawing functions

The design methods introduced in this chapter are basic approaches to drawing sample forms using the related drawing functions. They are popular, simple methods, and we will not treat them exhaustively or touch upon all their variations. Other approaches are possible, depending on the specific features of the program. In CAD there are almost always several ways to reach a destination, and it is important for you to find the quickest, simplest method for your own drawing.

Drawing is supported by CAD commands that make it possible to create the most common geometric elements (points, lines, squares and circles) in an easy, direct process. The various functions can be selected via the symbols displayed in the toolboxes on the user interface. > Fig. 12 and Chapter The virtual drawing board, User interface

DRAWING ELEMENTS

Points

As in a hand drawing, the most basic element in a CAD drawing is a point. In geometric terms, a point is a zero-dimensional object that does not extend into space. All other geometric objects can be described by points and incorporate a particular number of them. For example, two points define a line, three points a triangle, four points a rectangle, eight points a cube and so on. Points are depicted through different symbols in the various CAD programs. > Fig. 13

■

To draw a point, you must first activate the corresponding drawing function using the POINT command.

Fig. 12: A sample toolbox used to create simple drawing elements such as lines, points, rectangles and circles (Nemetschek Allplan)

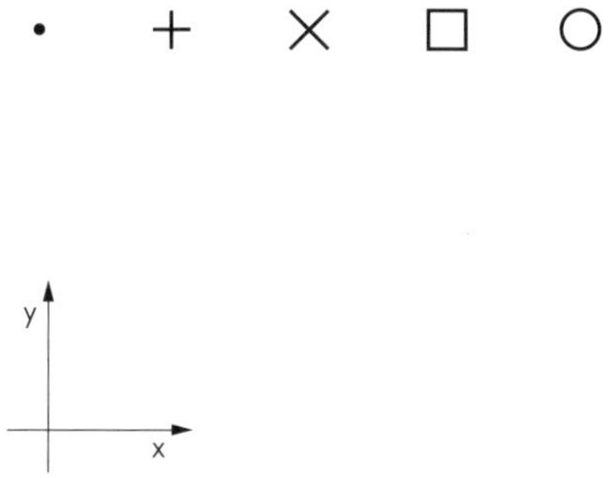

Fig. 13: Ways of depicting points

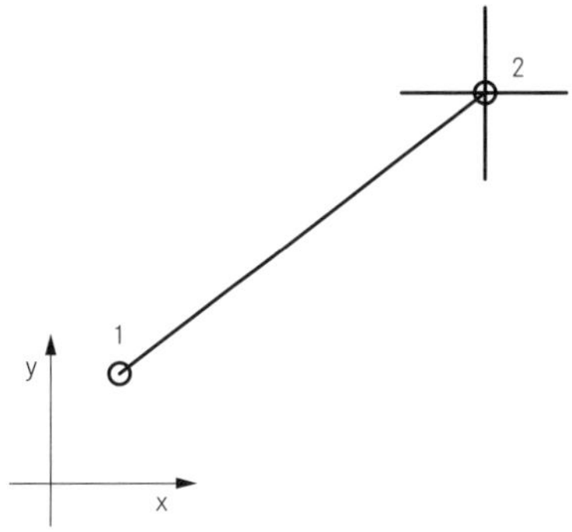

Fig. 14: A line is described by its two endpoints.

With a simple click of the mouse, you can define the position of a point on the construction plane, or you can use the keyboard to enter the X and Y coordinates into the dialogue box. These drawing and entry principles provide a foundation for all the drawing functions described below, and they make it possible to create any desired shape – though at times a number of intermediate steps may be involved.

Lines

A simple straight line is described by two points. After you fix a point on the construction plane using the LINE command, you need to specify a second point as the endpoint. The CAD program then creates the line in the desired position. > Fig. 14

Polylines ○

A polyline consists of several line segments connected to create a coherent object. > Fig. 15

■ **Tip:** In addition to toolboxes and interactive menus, it is more efficient to use shortcuts to activate drawing and tool functions. Shortcuts are special keyboard combinations linked to specific functions. A well-known shortcut in the Windows operating system is CTRL+C, which copies a file onto the clipboard. The various CAD systems feature a number of default shortcuts that can be quickly adapted to individual needs via the menu bar.

○ **Note:** A polygon is a many-sided object that consists of an enclosed area and a specific number of edges. A polyline is a series of lines and vertices.

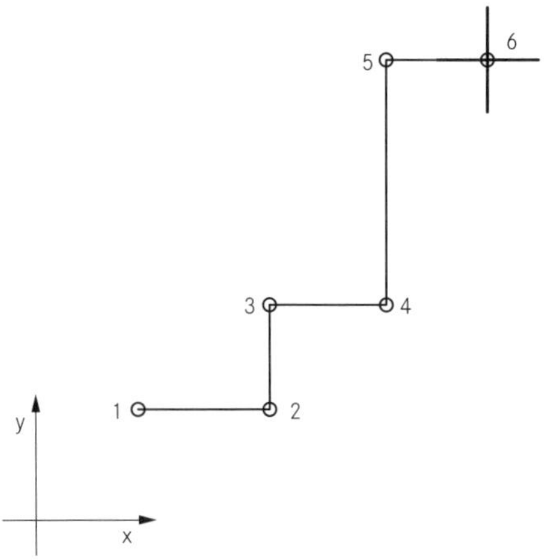

Fig. 15: A polyline joins several line segments to form an object.

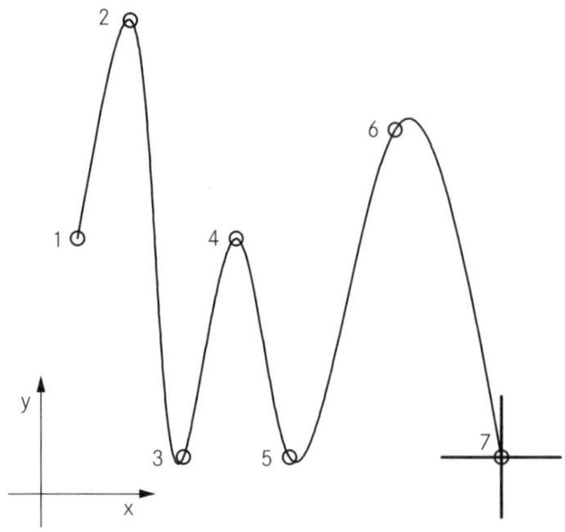

Fig. 16: The SPLINE function adapts the connection between any points you choose.

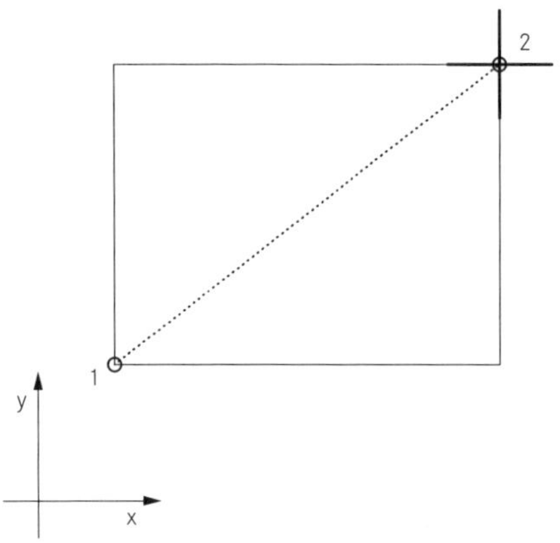

Fig. 17: In CAD, a rectangle can be dragged open with the mouse.

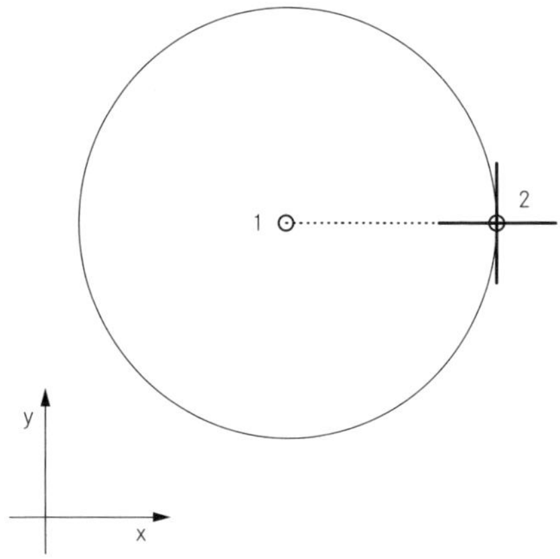

Fig. 18: Using a radius to draw a circle

Splines

The term "spline" comes from shipbuilding, where it is used to describe a pliant board that is anchored at several points and bent to fit the curvature of a ship's hull. The corresponding drawing function works in the same way. It interpolates curves between arbitrary points, creating soft, flowing shapes. > Fig. 16

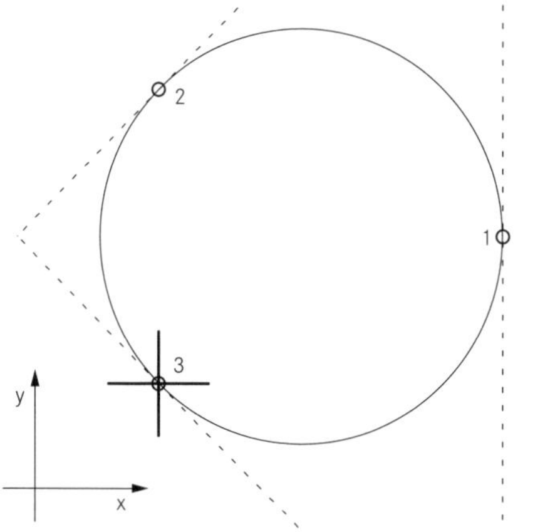

Fig. 19: A circle can also be defined using three points.

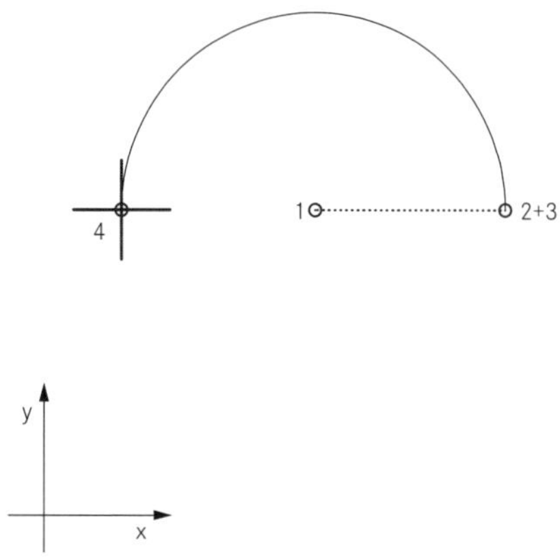

Fig. 20: Drawing arcs

Squares and rectangles

A rectangle does not need to be drawn in a complicated fashion using four individual lines. It can be created much more easily via a single function. One method is to draw the rectangle using its diagonal. > Fig. 17 You can either drag it open with the mouse or enter its parameters with the keyboard.

Circles

There are various ways to define a circle. To begin with, you can describe it by its radius. In this case, you enter its centre into the dialogue box of the CIRCLE command. Then you specify the desired radius with the mouse-controlled drawing tool or enter a numerical value into the dialogue line using the keyboard. > Fig. 18 In other CAD programs, you can draw a circle by defining its diameter or three points on its perimeter, by using tangents, or by combining these methods of specifying points on a plane. > Fig. 19

Circular arcs

The arc is another important drawing element. Using the CIRCLE command, you can create either an entire circle or a section of it. If you wish to draw an arc, first define the centre and radius, then specify the arc's beginning and endpoint. > Fig. 20

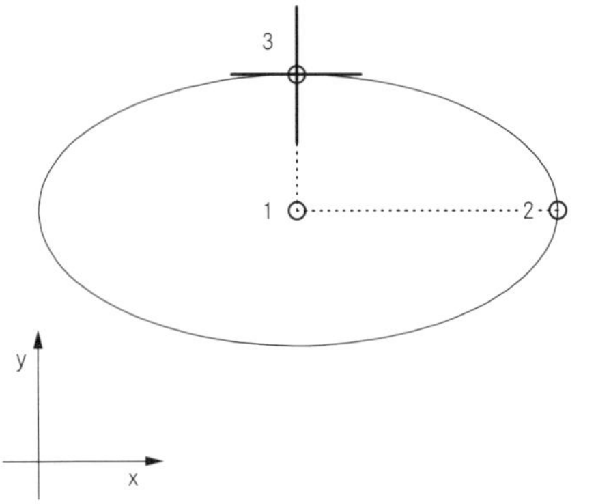

Fig. 21: An ellipse is drawn using its two radii (Point 2 and Point 3).

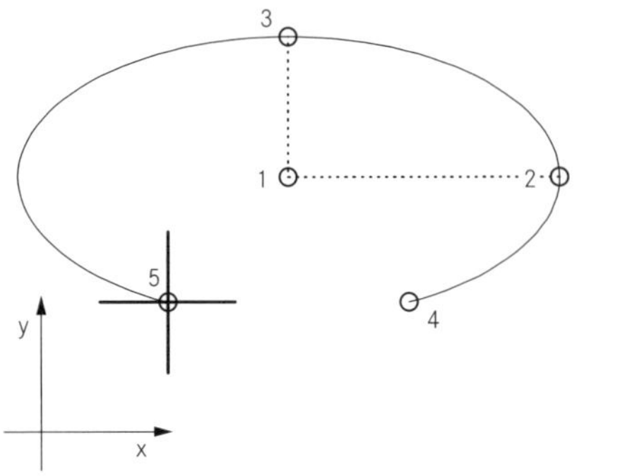

Fig. 22: Drawing an elliptical arc

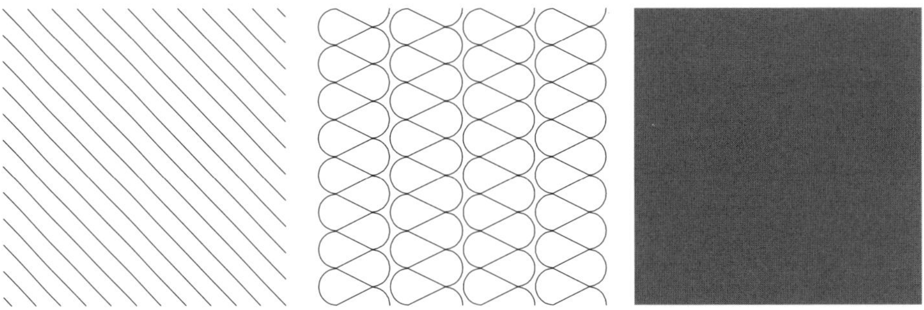

Fig. 23: Hatching, patterns and fillings identify different materials

Ellipses

Ellipses are drawn in the same way as circles. The only difference is that both radii must be specified after the centre is defined. > Fig. 21

Elliptical arcs

An elliptical arc is created in the same way as an ellipse, but requires a beginning and an endpoint as well. > Fig. 22

Hatching, patterns and fillings

Using hatching, patterns and fillings makes it easy to represent surfaces and enhances the legibility of individual drawing elements. > Fig. 23 Hatching provides information on the properties of both the materials and building components used in the design. Patterns and fillings allow an abstract depiction of surfaces and can also be used for the graphical

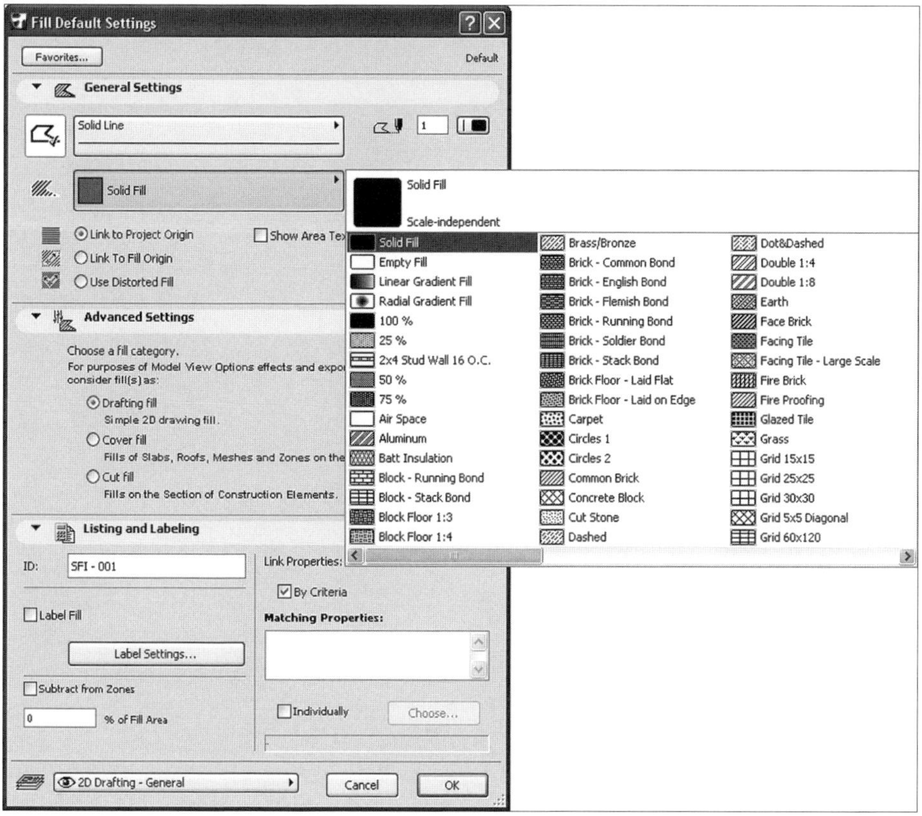

Fig. 24: A toolbox for creating hatches, patterns and fillings (Graphisoft ArchiCAD)

presentation of drawings. Not all CAD programs distinguish between hatching, patterns and fillings. Many display all these functions in a single toolbox. > Fig. 24

After selecting the desired surface by clicking the matching symbol, it can be "drawn" in a number of ways. You can enter each corner point of the depicted surface one after the other, or generate a rectangular surface using its diagonal, as in the process of creating a square. > Page 181

Automatic boundary detection

Many CAD programs offer an alternative method for enclosed figures: if the outer perimeter of an object completely surrounds its inner

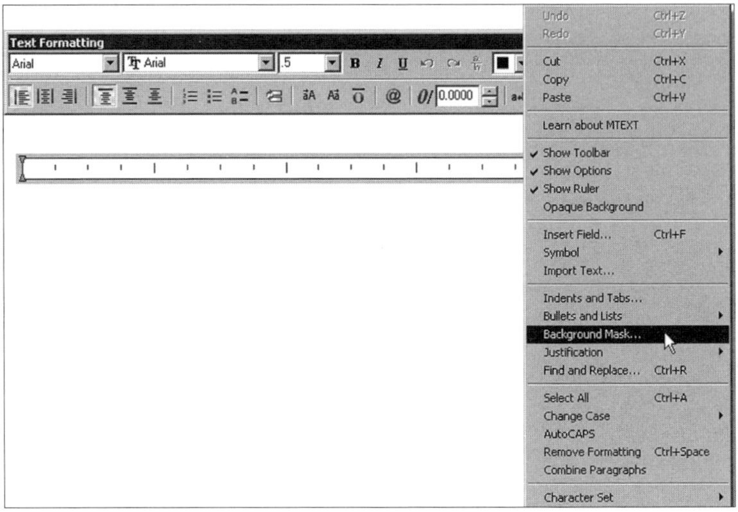

Fig. 25: A sample CAD text editor (Autodesk Architectural Desktop)

area, you can activate the automatic boundary detection function, which ■ is usually located on the menu bar.

After this function is activated, the software inspects the surrounding contour line and fills in the selected surface. This saves a great deal of time, particularly when objects have complex geometries or a large number of corners.

Text elements

In many CAD programs, you can add text to drawings using a text editor. Like the common word-processing programs, this editor can be used to change various parameters, including font type and character

■ **Tip:** Automatic boundary detection works only for completely enclosed areas. If a drawing is imprecise, the contour lines may have small gaps that might not be visible when displayed on the screen in a normal size. Subsequent attempts to find the error can be timeconsuming. For this reason – and for other drawing functions that build on one another – it is important to create precise drawings if you want to efficiently exploit the benefits of CAD.

○ **Note:** A precisely defined reference elevation, on which all higher or lower elevation points are based, is essential to ensure the correct relationship between the elevation points. This reference elevation is normally represented by the finished floor level (FFL) of the building's ground floor, and it equals ±0.00 m.

Additional information on dimension lines in particular and technical drawing in general can be found in *Basics Technical Drawing*, page 97 ff.

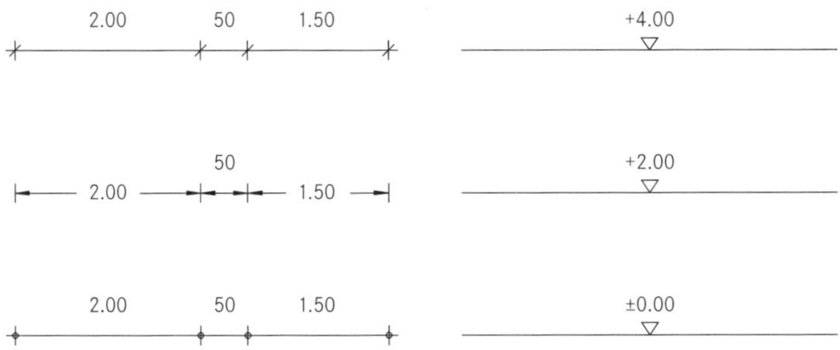

Fig. 26: Examples of linear dimensioning and elevation dimensioning

size. > Fig. 25 After activating the editor, you enter text word by word or copy it from other programs (e.g. Microsoft Word) using the standard copy function. However, some CAD programs do not have a text editor with a special entry window. In this case, you enter text directly into the drawing area and select it there for subsequent editing.

Dimension lines

Even though technical drawings are usually drawn to a particular scale, you should define all the relevant dimensions of a drawing. This can be done with dimension chains, elevation points and individual dimensions.

Linear dimensioning

The linear dimensioning function allows you to add dimension lines to horizontal, vertical and diagonal elements. First, you select, in any order, the points that need to be dimensioned. After you execute the function, the CAD program automatically generates the dimension lines and positions them in the desired location with the matching arrowheads, numbers and, if necessary, text. > Fig. 26 left These parameters can be set and subsequently edited in a dialogue box. Dimension points can also be entered into or deleted from existing dimension chains. The software independently computes all new distances.

Elevation dimensioning

Elevations in views and sections are also defined by elevation points. These are represented by an equilateral triangle and displayed directly in the drawing along with numerals. This dimensioning method is intended to measure and display height differences only. > Fig. 26 right The important points are simply clicked with the mouse, and a reference elevation is selected. Afterward the CAD program calculates the elevation and displays it at the chosen spot.

DESIGN TOOLS

The design tools introduced in this chapter are stand-ins for the large number of available options in CAD programs, where they depend on the individual software configurations. They are not necessarily identical in these different CAD programs, nor do they work in the same way. You will need to learn the special functions of the CAD program you choose and familiarize yourself with its special features. Ultimately, choosing a suitable CAD system depends not only on product quality but also on your own particular way of drawing.

Grids

Grids play an important role in the design of structures. They bring clarity to the work, particularly when large objects are involved, and provide critical support for the design process. For instance, a support grid can simplify the process of designing a building's loadbearing structure, and an axis grid can make it easier to design facades. Grids can be used for these same purposes in CAD and are a constructive drawing tool as ■ well. > Fig. 27

Snap functions

To create accurate drawings, you must draw objects using precisely defined points. Using coordinates > Chapter The virtual drawing board, Coordinate systems you can enter these points via the keyboard. Even so, the mouse is a much quicker and more intuitive entry tool for CAD drawings. The snap function, accessed via the menu bar or special toolboxes, allows you to select a point precisely with the virtual drawing and marking tool and prevents you from erring by a few millimetres within the drawing. It "snaps" onto drawing elements – that is, it selects them with great precision. The above-mentioned grid points can also serve as snap points: if you move the drawing tool close to one of these points on the screen, the CAD software marks it with a symbol. If you then execute the LINE command, specifying the starting point of a line with a mouse click, it will become the ○ snap point. > Fig. 28 This ensures the necessary precision for drawing.

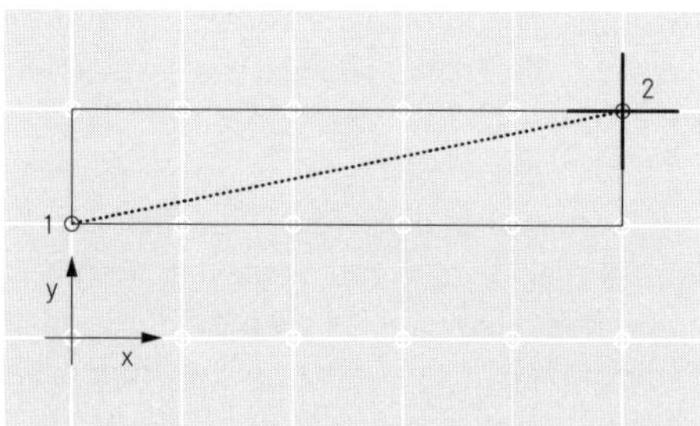

Fig. 27: Axis grids define point spacings along the X and Y axes.

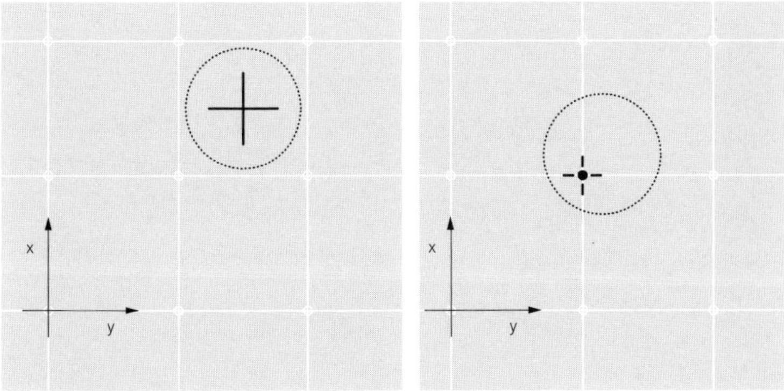

Fig. 28: When the drawing tool is dragged to the grid point, it is displayed as a snap point by the CAD software.

The snap function usually works only in conjunction with other drawing commands. The required command must first be selected if you want the CAD software to activate the snap points automatically once they are within the drawing tool's snap radius.

Object snap

Snap points may be used in various ways. They may incorporate the end and mid points of lines, the corners of squares, the centres of circles, the intersection points of two objects and so on. > Figs. 29–31 A symbol, displayed temporarily, illustrates the proximity of a potential snap point to the drawing tool – similar to the process of snapping onto grid points. The snap radius defines the maximum distance within which the drawing tool activates the snap point. Hence, the required snap point is temporarily activated once it is enclosed by an imaginary circle around a specific point whose radius usually measures a few millimetres on the screen.

■ **Tip:** A grid consists of points, at user-defined distances, which can be connected with lines. For instance, a grid can be formed by the same sized spaces corresponding to 1 m on the X and Y axes. In CAD, grids can be arbitrarily moved within a drawing, just like the zero point of the underlying user-defined coordinate system (UCS).

○ **Note:** Precision is crucial when drawing with CAD, since coordinates and drawing elements are usually linked, and even small mistakes made at the beginning of a drawing can quickly become magnified as the work continues.

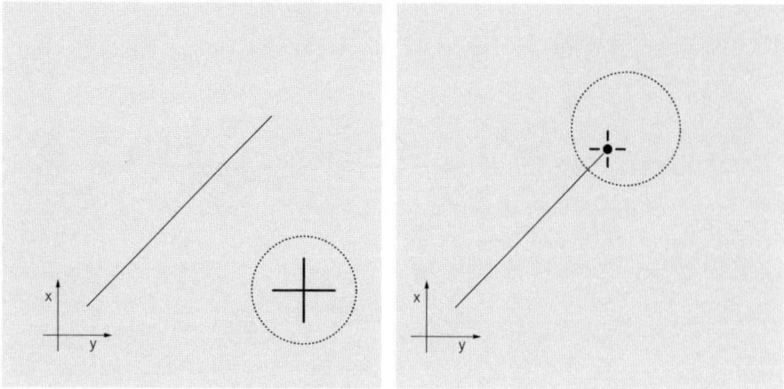

Fig. 29: Object snap with an endpoint

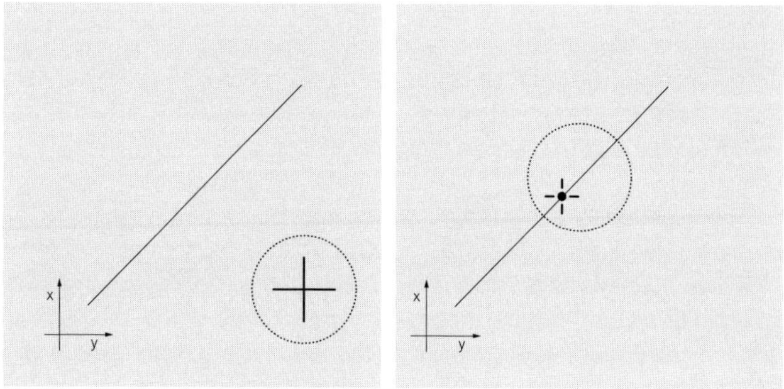

Fig. 30: Object snap with a middle point

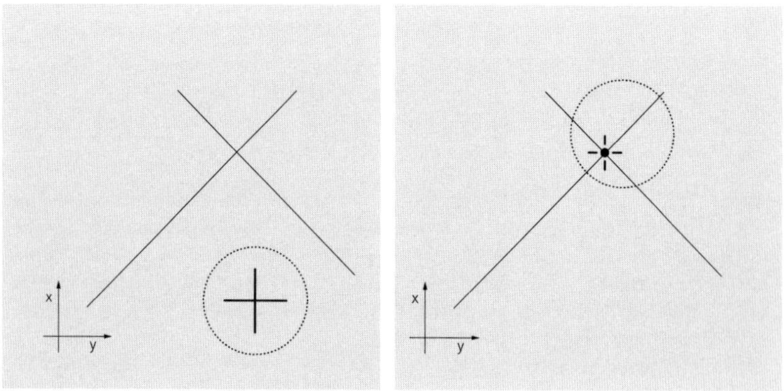

Fig. 31: Object snap with an intersection point

Precise angle specifications are one of the most important criteria for creating precise technical drawings. CAD programs create precise angles in different ways. They usually allow you to specify the desired angle in a dialogue box via the keyboard or an interactive angle-degree selector. In many CAD programs, you are also given the option of an angle snap command with predefined angle increments if you hold down the shift key while drawing. Additional tool functions can normally be used as drawing aids and are available in toolboxes. > Figs. 32–35

Angle specifications

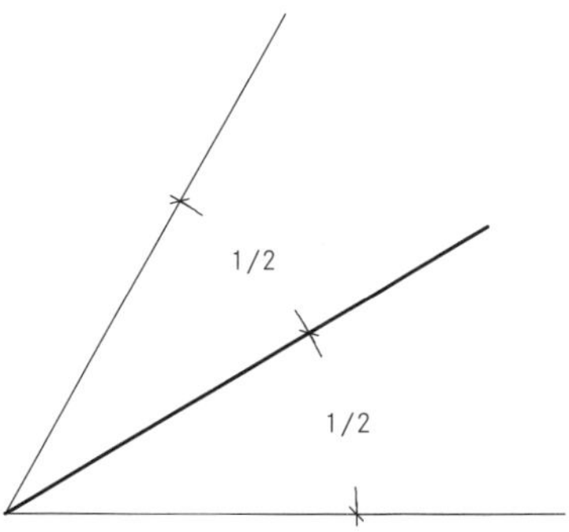

Fig. 32: The BISECTOR function bisects an angle enclosed by two lines, even if its exact degree is unknown.

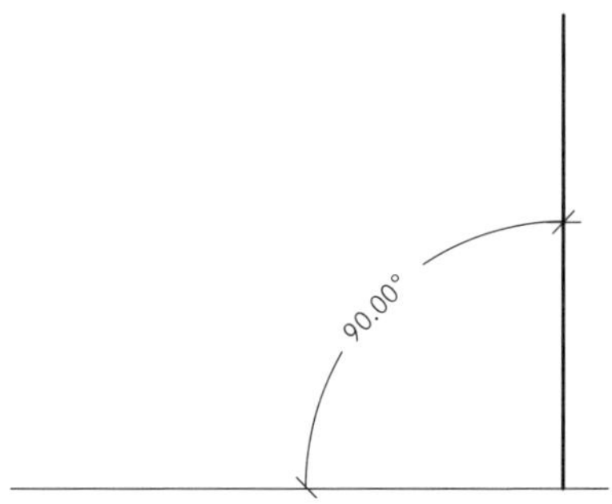

Fig. 33: With the PERPENDICULAR snap function, you can position a line perpendicular to a point on a circle or on another line.

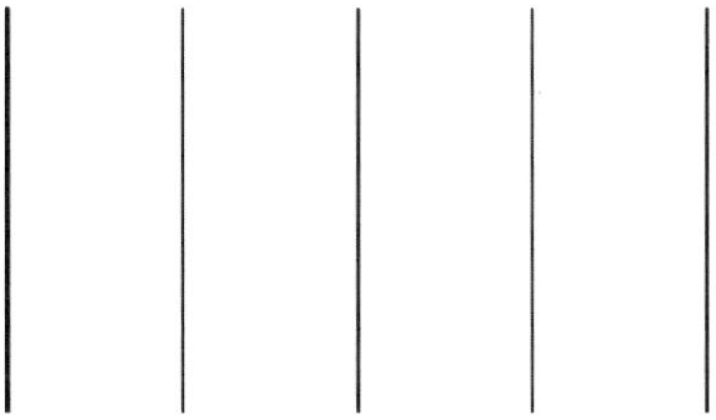

Fig. 34: With the PARALLEL function, you can create parallel lines and position them to the right or left of the original line.

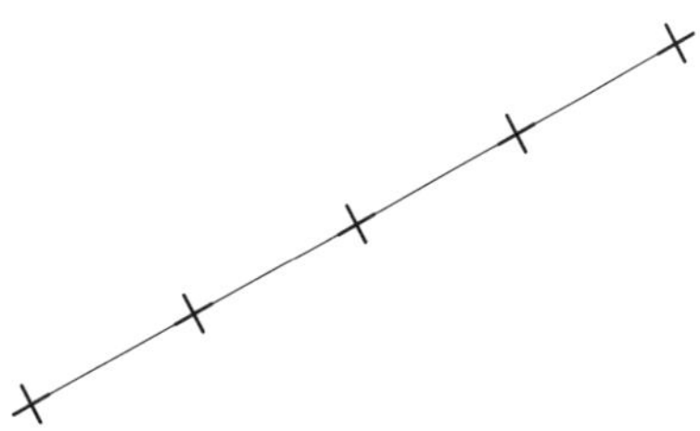

Fig. 35: Lines can be divided into varying or equal-sized segments using points.

MODIFICATIONS

One of the great advantages of CAD is that it allows you to edit and change objects after they have been drawn. This means that, in the design process, you can execute modifications and optimizations with relatively little effort. You can also, if necessary, modify templates and adjust them to meet a variety of requirements. There is no need to re-create every drawing from scratch, and it is possible to streamline the generation of standard objects. > Chapter Data flow, Program libraries

Associativity

CAD elements can be "associatively" modified. For instance, if you fill a square with hatching and subsequently change its shape, the hatching automatically follows its new perimeter. > Fig. 36 The square and its filling are linked and geometrically dependent on each other. Another example of associativity is a component that is altered in combination with dimensioning lines: if the length of the component is modified, the corresponding dimension chains automatically change too - provided there is an associative link between the two. This means that it is not necessary to create new dimension lines for an edited component that has already been dimensioned.

Grouping

In CAD, objects are often made up of various elements that form a unit in the drawing but are not necessarily linked. For instance, the drawing of a bed may consist of several lines, which must be individually selected if they are modified. Here, it is possible to group together several elements so that you do not need to activate all of them when you select an object. Depending on the CAD system used, they are combined to create GROUPS, BLOCKS or SEGMENTS. Defined as such, they form units that can be broken up again if necessary. This normally makes the work much easier.

Modifying points

The process of drawing objects becomes much more flexible because users are able to modify individual points or several points at the same time. Simple changes in line length can be made with the mouse, and surfaces and three-dimensional objects can also be altered easily. > Chapter The third dimension ■

■ **Tip:** An existing building layout can easily be modified by selecting all the points on one side of the building and moving them in the desired direction within the UCS. All the selected points will move as well, and the lines and components will automatically be lengthened.

○ **Note:** When you make other types of modifications, it is also helpful to use a selection window to activate elements because this tool provides greater control in selecting and changing elements.

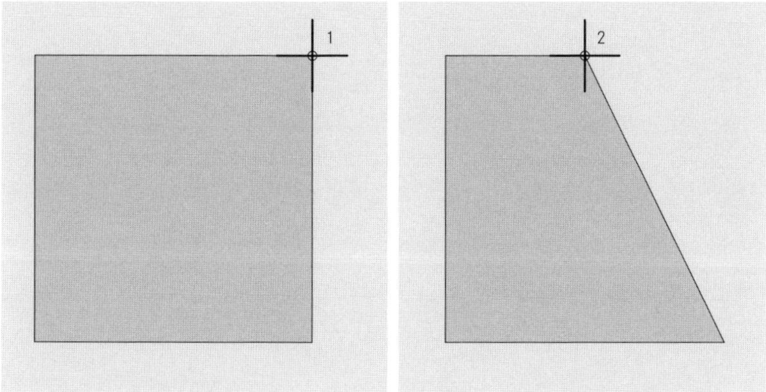

Fig. 36: An individual point is changed in a square. The filling "associatively" follows the modified contour line.

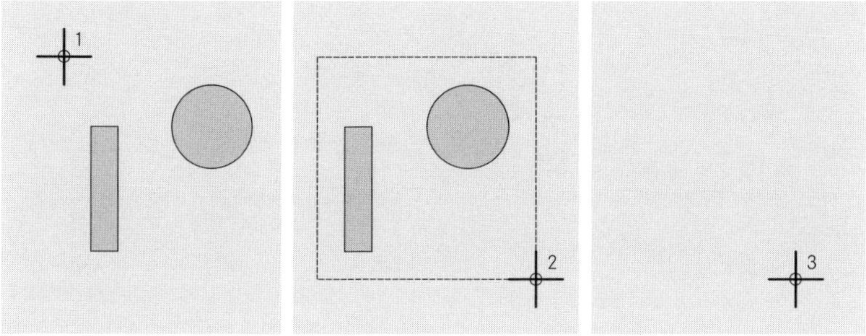

Fig. 37: A selection window is dragged open to erase two components.

After activating the command, you can, for instance, grasp the corner of a rectangle using the snap function and move it to the desired position within the virtual drawing area. > Fig. 36

The erase function is executed using the selection tool. It can be used to remove any element in the drawing completely, or to erase several elements at once. After activating the erase function, you simply drag open a window with the mouse. Depending on the basic settings, you can erase all objects that are located within the selection window or that are intersected by it. > Fig. 37

Erase

○

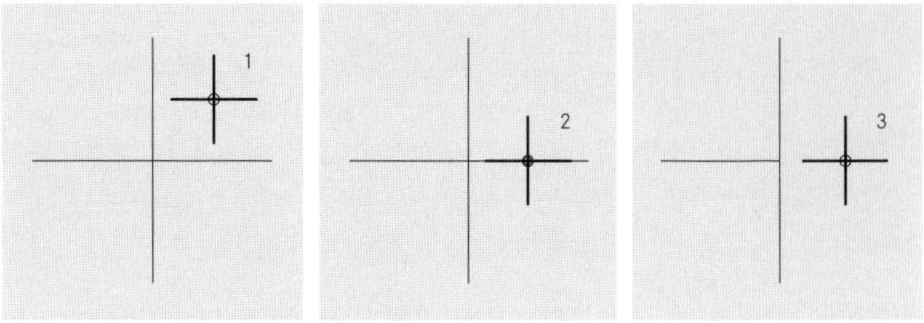

Fig. 38: Erasing a projecting line with the TRIM function

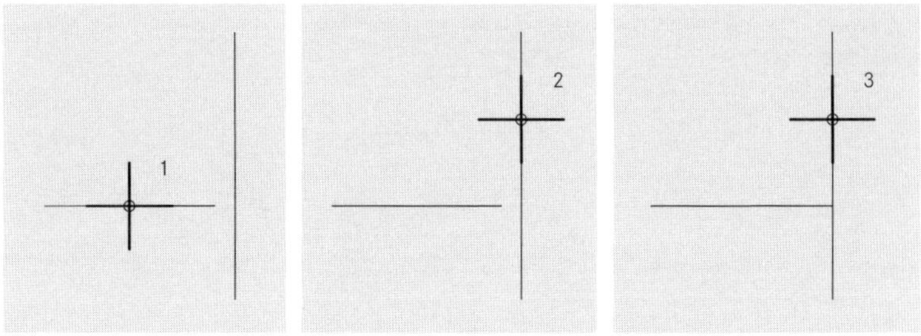

Fig. 39: The EXTEND function extends one line to its intersection point with another line.

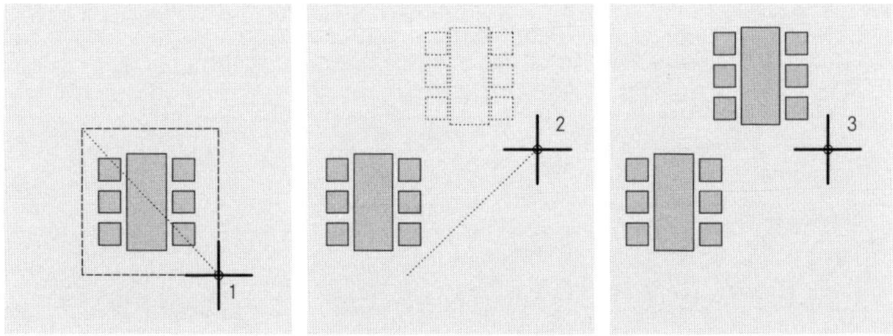

Fig. 40: The symbol of a dining table is selected and copied using the mouse.

■ **Tip:** You can usually use the TRIM and EXTEND functions for either a single line or for several lines. Hence, any number of lines can be selected, trimmed and extended at the same time.

■ **Tip:** Snap points can also be used to grasp an object. They allow you to snap onto the object and move it to another location with great accuracy. Snap points can also be used to position it there.

Trim

It is also possible to trim or remove parts of elements. With the trim function (also called SHORTEN or DELETE ELEMENT BETWEEN POINTS in some CAD systems), a line segment running between two points or extending beyond a single point can be erased by activating the function and clicking the line segment with the selection and drawing tool. > Fig. 38

Extend

The opposite command, EXTEND (also called LENGTHEN or CONNECT TWO ELEMENTS), extends a line to its intersection point with another line. > Fig. 39 ■

Copy

The COPY function is one of the most important drawing commands and forms the basis of an efficient work process. Generally speaking, before redrawing an object, you should always consider whether a drawn object can first be copied and then changed. This is especially true of complex objects that are time-consuming to create, whether these are objects you draw yourself or library elements. > Chapter Data flow, Program libraries

To copy an object, first select it and then drag it to the desired location by holding down the selection and drawing tool. The original object will remain in its initial position. > Fig. 40 ■

Mirror

You can use the MIRROR function to create mirror-images of objects along any axis you choose. You can also create a copy – which is naturally inverted – and continue to use the original. After activating the command and selecting the object, you specify a mirror axis at the desired distance and angle to the original and then mirror the object across the chosen axis. You can also use lines and edges of existing elements as mirror axes.

In combination with the copy function, this command makes it possible to draw symmetrical objects efficiently: only one half must be drawn, and the other half can be mirrored across the middle axis. > Fig. 41 ●

● **Example:** If you are drawing the floor plan of a twin house, you can mirror either all or a part of the layout across the middle axis before continuing with your work. The same approach lends itself well to drawing facades and other building components quickly and efficiently.

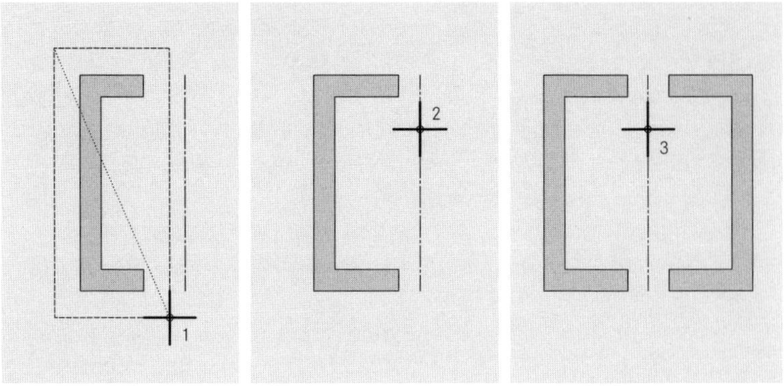

Fig. 41: After an object is selected, the mirror axis is chosen and the mirror-image created.

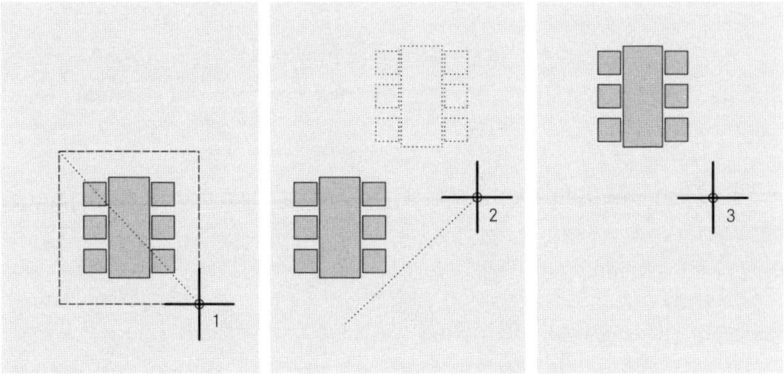

Fig. 42: The MOVE function allows you to change the position of either one object or several objects at the same time.

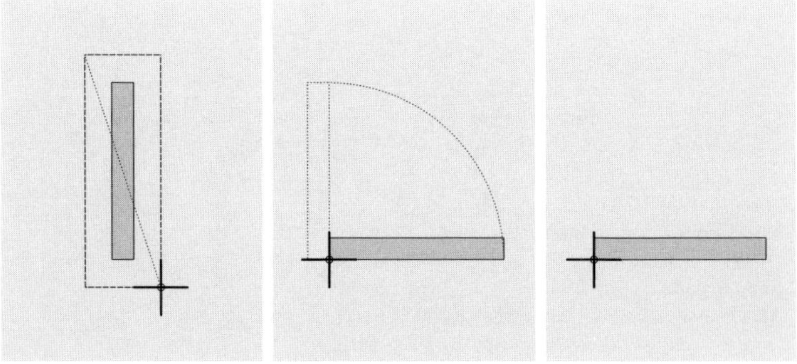

Fig. 43: An object is selected and rotated by 90°.

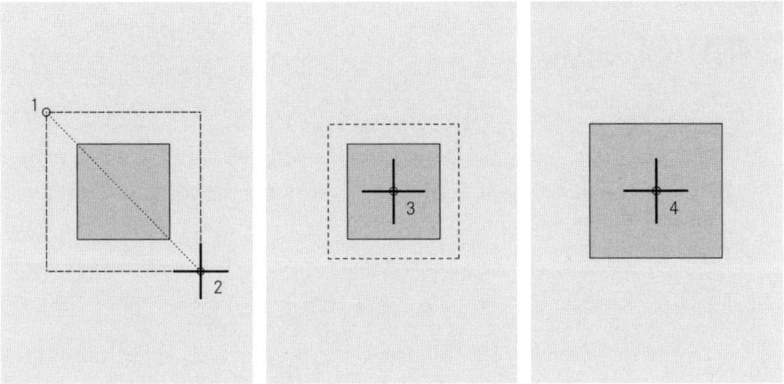

Fig. 44: A square component is selected and scaled by a factor of 1.41 along the X and Y axes of the UCS, doubling its surface area.

Move

The MOVE function is quite similar to the copy function. The only difference is that the object is moved and no copy is made. > Fig. 42

Rotate

With the ROTATE function, drawn objects can be rotated an arbitrary distance around an arbitrarily selected point. If all that is needed is to change the object's orientation, its middle point represents an ideal snap point. With the mouse, you specify the original angle – normally the positive X axis in the UCS. Starting here, the object is then rotated around its centre. Alternatively, you can use the keyboard to enter the rotation angle after determining its pivot point. This method can be employed to rotate a vertical structure by 90°. > Fig. 43

Scale and stretch

The size, length and shape of all drawn objects can be changed with great accuracy. The SCALE or STRETCH function allows you to scale an object in all directions of the coordinate system. > Fig. 44

The third dimension

The preceding chapters dealt primarily with drawing functions on the construction plane, which, from a geometric perspective, is the equivalent of a two-dimensional sheet of drawing paper. One great advantage of CAD systems is that they allow you to work in space, that is, in three dimensions.

Whereas a drawing only reproduces a view of a 2D structure, three-dimensional design in CAD allows the designer to give shape to the 3D object. A Z axis must be added to the basic CAD reference system – the coordinate system – in order to transform a two-dimensional plane into three-dimensional space. The most commonly used coordinate system is the Cartesian system discussed above, which is merely expanded to include the Z axis. The Z axis rises perpendicularly from the zero point of the plane defined by the X and Y axes and makes it possible to define the point P(3,5) from Fig. 5, page 172, in three-dimensional space. > Fig. 45

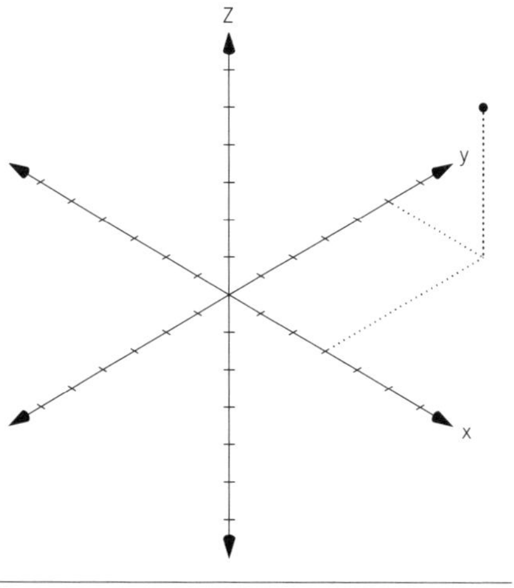

Fig. 45: The point P(3,5) is also defined in three dimensional space through the coordinates P(3,5,4).

Fig. 46: Using the right-hand rule, you can determine the direction of the positive Z axis.

THREE-DIMENSIONAL DESIGN

In the third dimension, the two-dimensional construction plane becomes an element of the three-dimensional workspace. However, as a rule, use of this workspace normally relies on two-dimensional pointing and output devices such as a mouse and a screen. This can take some getting used to when complicated, three-dimensional drawings are involved. ■

Projections

Whereas two-dimensional drawings generally only involve the projection of a plane (e.g. floor plan or view), three-dimensional representations allow you to alternate between the top or bottom view, the four different elevations and the isometric representations. > Fig. 47 All these presentation methods create projections of the same three-dimensional

■ **Tip:** The "right-hand-rule" can help you get your bearings within the Cartesian coordinate system. If the directions of the X and Y axes in a three-dimensional coordinate system are known, this rule shows the direction of the positive Z axis. If the thumb and index finger of your right hand point in the positive X and Y directions, your extended middle finger represents the positive Z axis (see Fig. 46).

■ **Tip:** When designing, you should start thinking and working in three dimensions as early as possible, since many of the links and relationships within a structure are best checked in spatial terms. Along with simple cardboard models, abstract virtual 3D mass models are particularly useful, since they can be constructed relatively easily and provide quick results (see Chapters The third dimension, Construction methods, and Visualization).

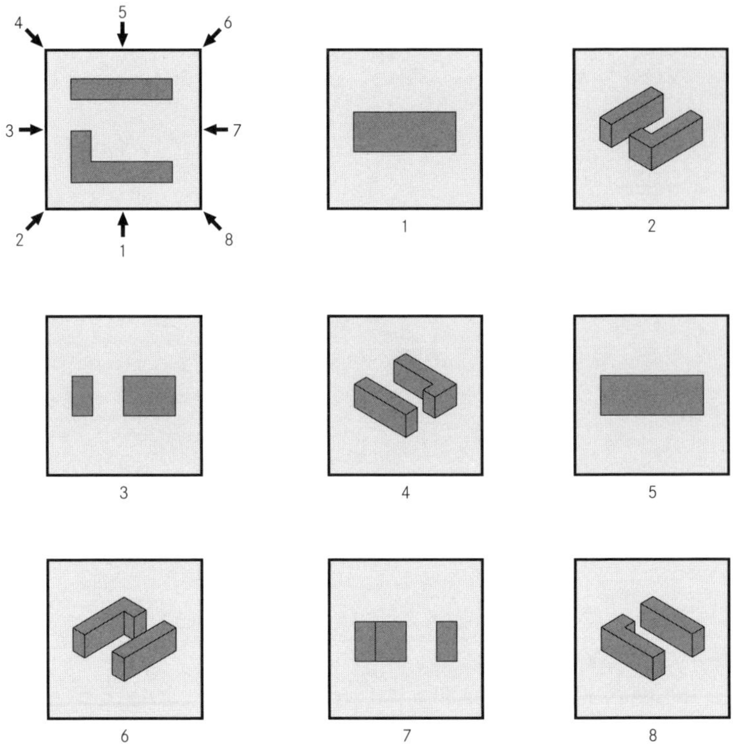

Fig. 47: The virtual space allows you to view the same object from different angles.

objects and facilitate both clear spatial presentation in the respective viewing mode and the editing of particular points of a 3D design. Most CAD programs allow you to view several projections simultaneously in different windows on the screen. You are thus able to see the object from all directions.

Models

Three-dimensionally defined objects have different qualities and, depending on the design method used, can be categorized as volume models, plane models or edge models.

Volume models

A volume body is a solid object that contains a great deal of information within the CAD system. > Fig. 48 As well as providing volumes and the information derived from them such as mass and centre of gravity, volume models can be used to define surface characteristics and specific

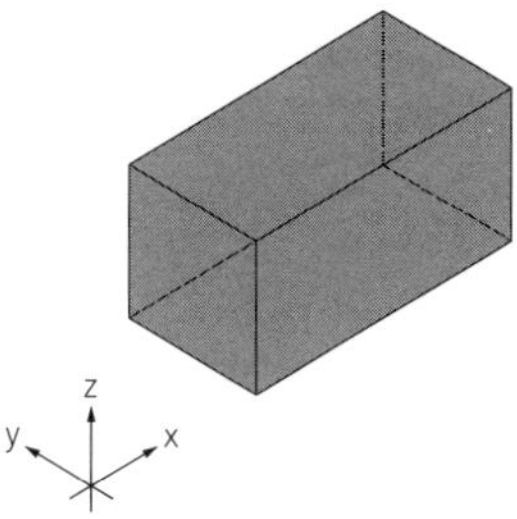

Fig. 48: Isometric diagram of a solid body in a volume model

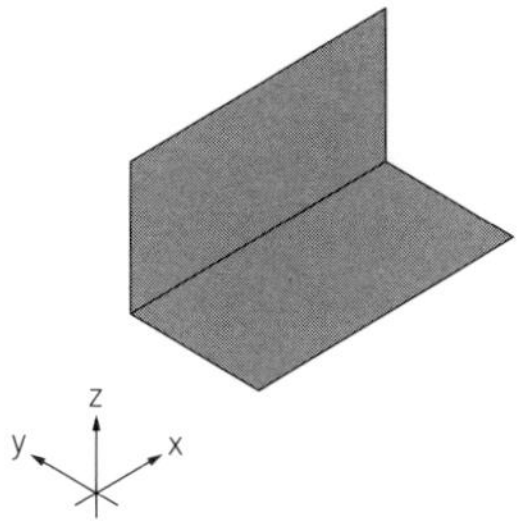

Fig. 49: Example of a plane model

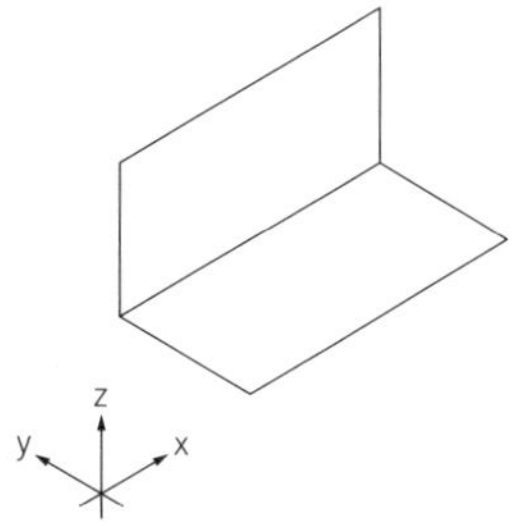

Fig. 50: Edge model. No information is provided on volumes and planes.

materials. > Chapter Visualization This enables the production of a virtual image of a structural component that exhibits the same characteristics under programmable virtual conditions as its real counterpart. Moreover, the image allows for interpolations, which can be geometrically defined within the volume. This makes it possible for bodies to be geometrically combined, subtracted from one another or positioned to form intersections. > Chapter The third dimension, Modelling

Plane models

As their name suggests, plane models consist exclusively of planes and do not have any defined volume. In the CAD program planes can be defined in terms of the visual characteristics of their surfaces, and they can be rotated and inclined at any angle within the virtual workspace. > Fig. 49 ○

Edge model

An edge model uses three-dimensional lines to simulate only the edges of a body. No information is provided concerning surfaces or

○ **Note:** Plane models can enclose a volume without the latter being geometrically defined like a volume model. This produces objects whose shell provides information on surface characteristics and may resemble a volume model. Nevertheless, this shell consists exclusively of two-dimensional planes without material thickness. The object is just a hollow body.

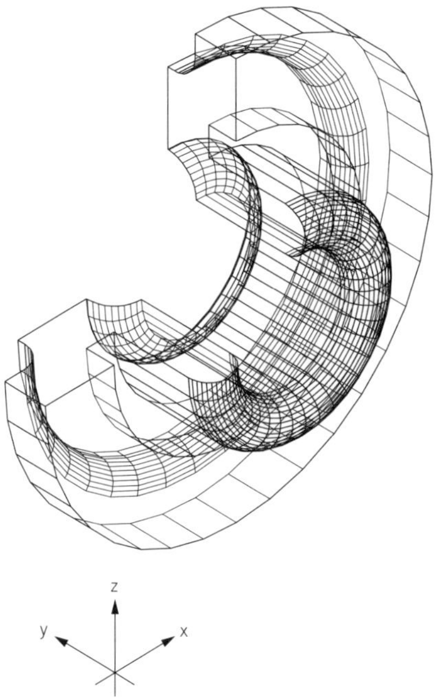

Fig. 51: A complex volume body depicted as a wire frame model in design mode

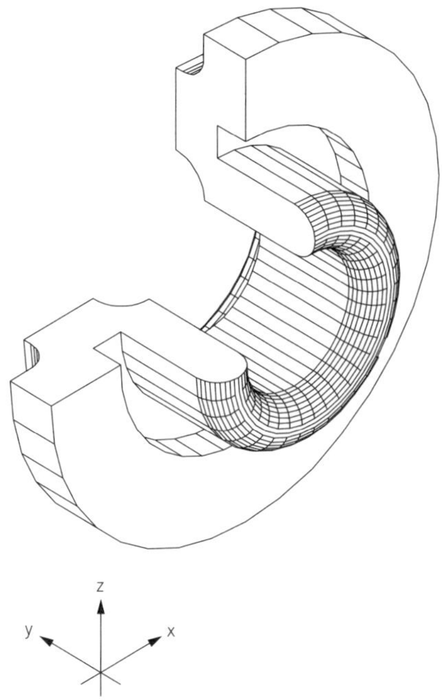

Fig. 52: The wire frame model from Fig. 51 with hidden edges. Only the surfaces and edges facing the viewer can be seen.

volumes, which are thus not geometrically defined. Edge models play only a minor role in architectural CAD since they are highly abstract representations. > Fig. 50

Wire frame model

In the 3D design mode of most CAD programs it is standard for all spatial objects to be depicted as wire frame models in order to take all point coordinates into account.

A wire frame model – which should not be confused with the edge model described above – is a skeletal depiction of a 3D object using three-dimensionally defined lines. In the design mode, both volume and plane models are shown as wire frame models, although in this special type of constructive representation information about volumes and planes is not included. In the virtual workspace a wire frame representation can be observed from any chosen point, allowing you to check spatial relationships such as the distances between structural components and overlaps. Some practice is required to be able to differentiate between "front" and "back" in a complex wire frame model, because the model shows spatial depth even though a two-dimensional representation appears on the monitor. > Fig. 51 Some CAD programs function without the depiction of wire frame models and visualize three-dimensional objects directly with shaded or coloured surfaces.

Hidden edges

If required, all edges located behind three-dimensional objects and planes can be concealed to provide better orientation within the drawing. This makes the representation much more comprehensible and is a preliminary stage in computer rendering, although in contrast to a completed visualization it can still be modified. > Fig. 52 and Chapter Visualization ■ Other CAD programs give the command for this representation option as HIDE or HIDDEN LINE. ○

Generating floor plans, views and sections

Technical drawings typically depict floor plans, views and sections of entire structures or structural components as detail drawings. However, in three-dimensional design mode you can produce complete virtual models that, if necessary, can provide a basis for generating the two-dimensional figures of a technical drawing.

Floor plans and horizontal sections

In default mode, the construction plane of a CAD system is represented as a top view, i.e. the user looks down on the XY plane of the UCS and thus onto a virtual model. In order to represent a particular floor of a virtual building as a floor plan, a horizontal section plane is generated

■ **Tip:** Calculating the dimensions of hidden lines can be time-consuming. Where the scale and detail of a 3D representation has been clearly specified prior to the construction of the 3D model, you should, where applicable, avoid irrelevant elements and unnecessary depth of detail. If you require a 3D model for both a rough representation and a detailed depiction, details such as doorknobs should be represented on an additional layer so that they can be excluded from the calculations relevant to the rough model (see Chapters The virtual drawing board, Transparent planes – the layering principle, and Visualization).

○ **Note:** Along with a design mode window, many CAD programs also offer an optional 3D depiction. This can be activated as an additional window and can show three-dimensional objects with hidden edges and shaded or coloured surfaces. Objects depicted in this way can usually be rotated and examined from all sides.

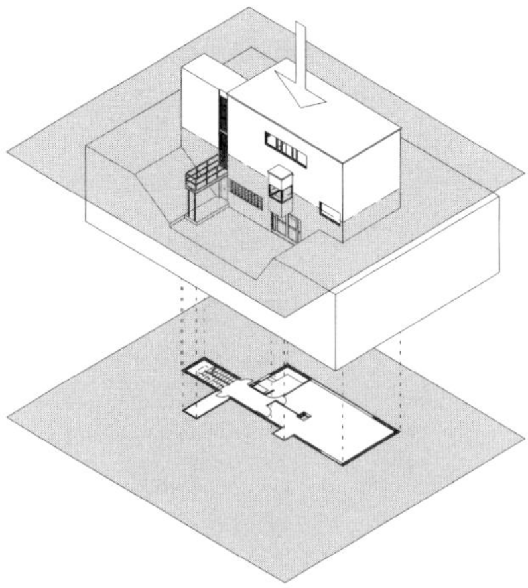

Fig. 53: In order to produce a floor plan using a virtual model, a section plane is generated.

○ ■ which slices through all walls and objects within the building at a particular height and thus depicts them as elements of a floor plan. > Fig. 53

Views and vertical sections

Most CAD programs employ the same tool functions to generate views and sections. In technical drawing, a section is also a view: one that cuts through a building or component, thus allowing you to see the interior of the object. In contrast to the generation of a floor plan, longitudinal and lateral cuts produce vertical sections, which slice through an

○ **Note:** The drawings in Figs. 53–55 are based on a design by Le Corbusier for an apartment block in Vaucresson (1922), although the dimensions and details do not correspond exactly to the original.

■ **Tip:** A horizontal section cuts through objects parallel to the XY plane of the UCS. It follows that a vertical section bisects objects parallel to the Z axis. Some CAD programs provide predefined horizontal section planes as floor levels (e.g. Graphisoft ArchiCAD), and you can alternate between these while working on the different floor plans of a building (see Chapter The virtual drawing board, Transparent planes – the layering principle).

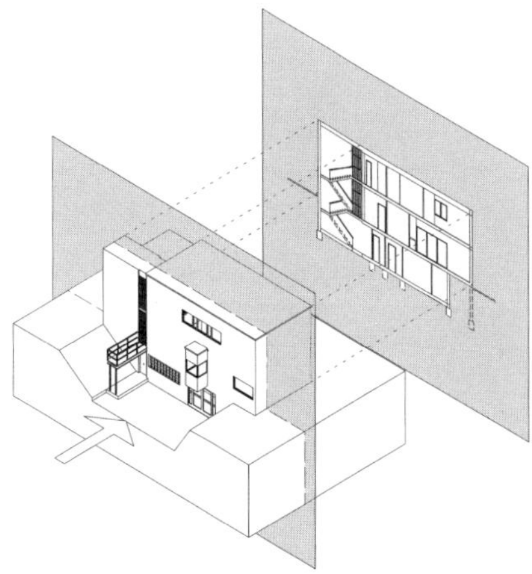

Fig. 54: A sectional plane is created with a vertical orientation to draw a vertical section.

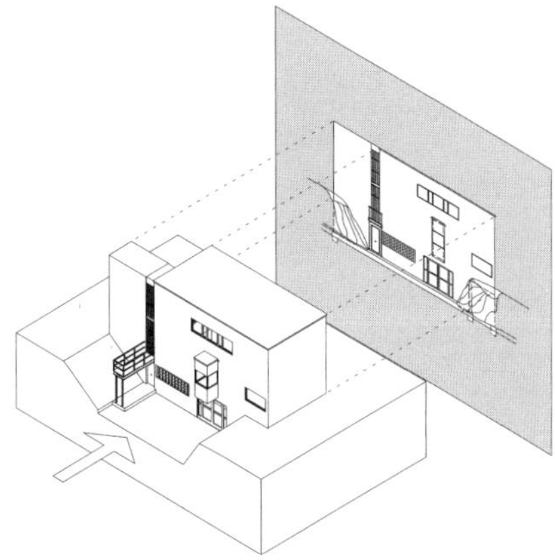

Fig. 55: In order to produce a view of a virtual model, the section plane is positioned in front of or behind the structure.

object in a longitudinal or lateral direction. The first step is to establish the length as well as the line and depth of vision of the section plane. (In the case of a view, this section plane is located in front of or behind an object.) Within the top view, the CAD software then generates the symbol for a section boundary, which you can select to access a depiction of the defined section or view. Depending on the CAD system used, this depiction is shown in a special section-view window or is generated as a two-dimensional drawing, which you can then work on. > Figs. 54 and 55 ○

○ **Note:** Some programs allow you to create and label a view or section and assign it a separate window even though the relevant virtual model is still linked with 3D data (e.g. Graphisoft ArchiCAD). As a result, when you work on elements in construction mode, any changes you make are automatically reflected associatively in the projection. Alternatively, the projection can be generated on an additional layer consisting only of two-dimensional lines.

CONSTRUCTION METHODS

Three-dimensional construction methods function similarly to two-dimensional drawing commands. That said, there is a fundamental difference: coordinates are not only defined via the X and Y axes but are also positioned in space using the Z axis. > Chapter The third dimension, Three-dimensional design

Points, lines and planes in space

As when drawing points, lines and planes in the construction plane of the UCS, you use a drawing function to draw them in three-dimensional space. Working within a spatial projection takes some getting used to, since you are often unable to see the real lengths of spatial representations, because not all objects are shown parallel to the coordinate axes and thus appear shortened or elongated in different projections. > Fig. 56

Cuboids

Simple bodies can be generated as volume models with the drawing functions. For example, a cuboid is initially defined by its base or base area by using its diagonal and then assigned a height. > Fig. 57 The base is always positioned on the construction plane and is parallel to the XY plane of the UCS.

Cylinders

A cylinder can have either a circular or an elliptical base. Once this has been defined, the height of the cylinder is determined using the Z axis. > Fig. 58

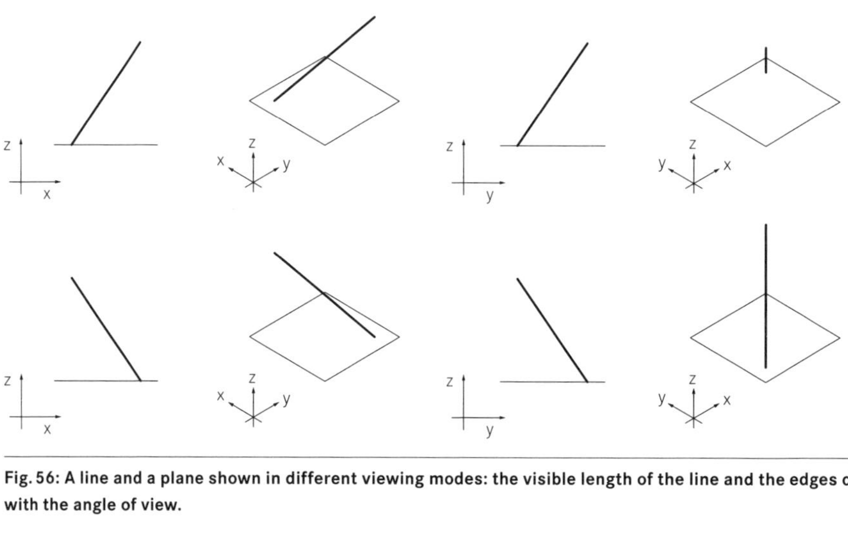

Fig. 56: A line and a plane shown in different viewing modes: the visible length of the line and the edges changes with the angle of view.

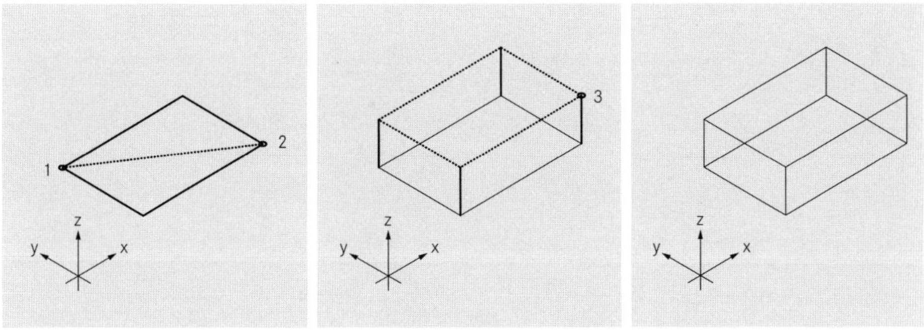

Fig. 57: Generating a cuboid in isometric construction mode

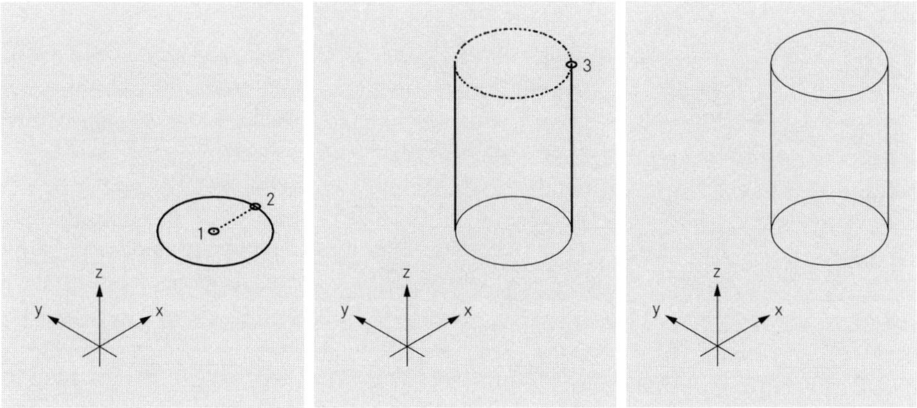

Fig. 58: Constructing a cylinder using CAD is similar to constructing a cuboid. The only difference is that a cylinder has a round base.

■ **Tip:** In three-dimensional space, planes can be generated as polygon planes. In this case, you can use not only simple horizontal and vertical orientations but also any angle of inclination you require. If a plane is supposed to have a certain inclination, the simplest method is first to generate it in two dimensions in the top view and then to rotate it in three dimensions.

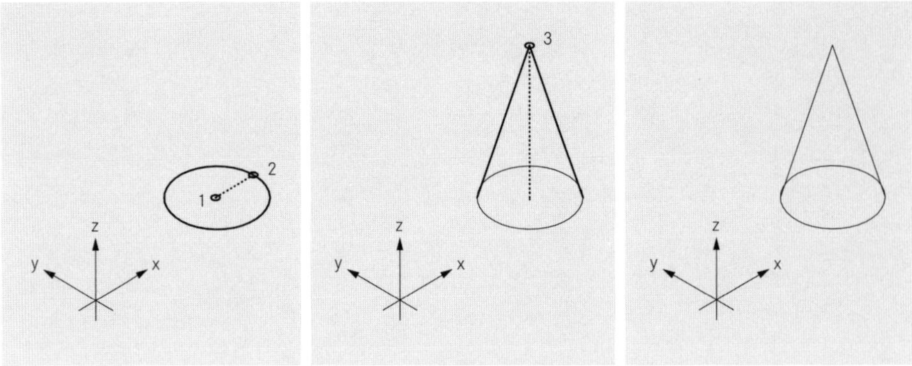

Fig. 59: A cone is defined by the height of the apex above the round base.

Cones

A cone is defined by a circular or elliptical base and narrows vertically to a point. When generating a cone, first define the base in terms of the base area and then determine the apex as a point using the Z axis. > Fig. 59

Spheres

In CAD a sphere is defined using a midpoint in the base and a radius or diameter. The sphere's lines of latitude are positioned parallel to the XY plane of the UCS, and the vertical middle axis is congruent with the Z axis. > Fig. 60

Extruded volume bodies and planes

The 3D drawing functions described above make it very easy to generate simple geometric bodies with a single drawing command. Not all CAD programs offer these functions and in such cases the possibilities of geometric design are limited by preset form definitions. Another method of generating volume bodies is extrusion, which involves raising the body out of the ground plan sketch. This function allows you to transform two-dimensional objects consisting of lines, polylines and splines into volume bodies and planes.

This method is useful above all when working on objects that include rounded edges, bevels and other geometric peculiarities, since they are difficult to define without a preset basic shape. It is important that the figure consisting of line segments is closed and does not overlap with other figures. If the basic form is not closed, a plane is generated rather than a volume body.

Different CAD programs use different terms for extrusion, such as RAISE, TRANSLATION and TRAJECTION. Extrusion is carried out along a

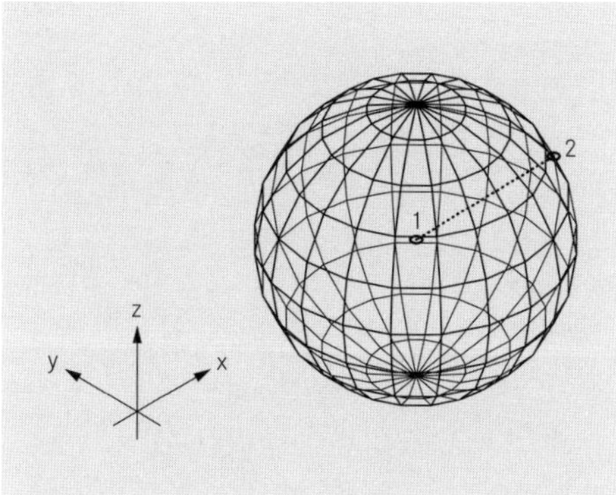

Fig. 60: A sphere as a wire frame model in construction mode

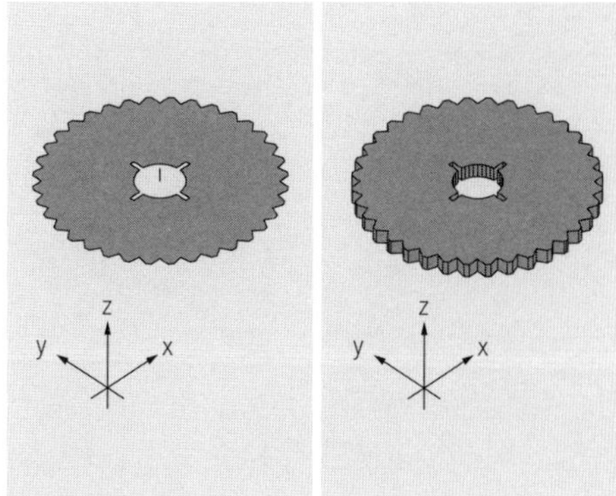

Fig. 61: Extrusion of the outline of a cog. In the middle of the left-hand figure the path is marked to define the height and direction of the extrusion.

construction line or through entry of a height value. In the process of extrusion, the two-dimensional basic shape that is to be transformed into a volume body is usually shown as an OUTLINE. The construction line along which the outline is to be extruded is often labelled PATH. Some CAD programs require both the basic shape and the three-dimensionally defined path in order to carry out the extrusion operation (e.g. Nemetschek Allplan). Others (e.g. Autodesk Architectural Desktop) need only a basic shape and a particular height, width and length entered as coordinates along the coordinate system axis in order to extrude a model from the outline. > Fig. 61 ■

Rotational solids

The ROTATION command enables you to rotate and generate a two-dimensional basic shape around the X or Y axis of the underlying UCS – or around any other axis defined by two points. As with the EXTRUSION command, ROTATION is particularly useful when dealing with objects with rounded edges and other details that are difficult or impossible to form using simple 3D drawing commands. Here, too, the outline of the underlying profile must be closed and cannot have any lines overlapping. In the

■ **Tip:** Extruded volume bodies are very useful when generating terrain models. As in a cardboard model, where the terrain profile is reproduced in different layers, you can construct similar layers on the computer for every basic shape and extruded height and place them on top of one another.

Further information on manual modelbuilding can be found in *Basics Modelbuilding*, page 247 ff.

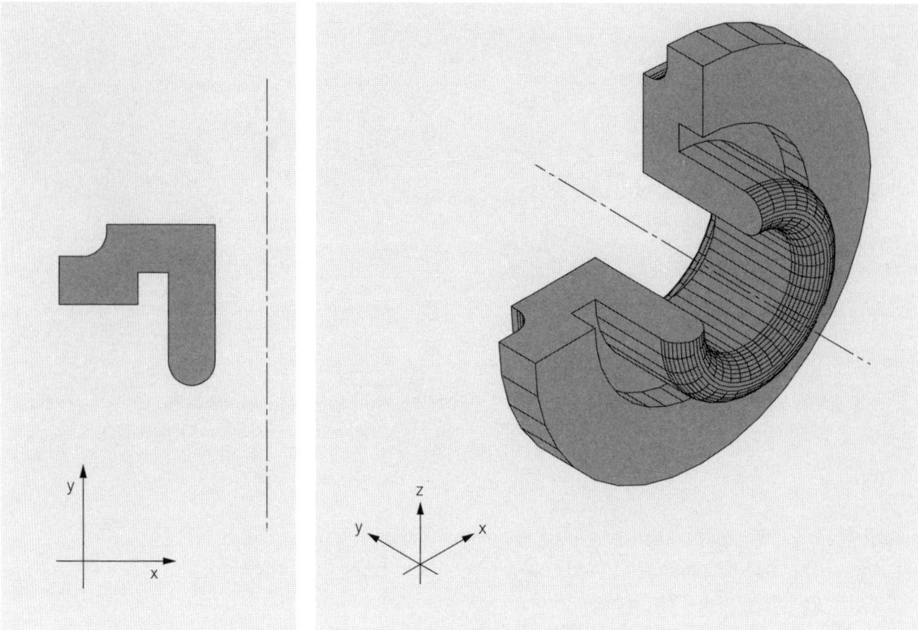

Fig. 62: The outline of a complex profile is rotated around an axis, thereby producing a rotational solid.

example provided in Figure 62, the profile positioned in the XY plane is rotated around an axis that is parallel to the Y axis of the UCS. The process is comparable to using a potting wheel that is spinning around a vertical axis, where the rotation makes it possible to form the modelling material to any shape you wish.

MODELLING

The previous chapters have presented construction methods that involve using a drawing function or deriving an outline to generate simple and complex volume bodies. Volume bodies can also be modelled, i.e. their fundamental shape can be altered. Depending on the geometry involved, one or more points of a body can be modified and moved in the directions prescribed by the axes of the UCS. For example, in only a few steps you can shape a cuboid into a wedge. > Fig. 63 Or – if you need to tackle a more complex operation – you can change the overall height of a building.

Construction with volume bodies

However, modelling is not restricted to simple manipulations of points. It can also be carried out in a large number of ways using com-

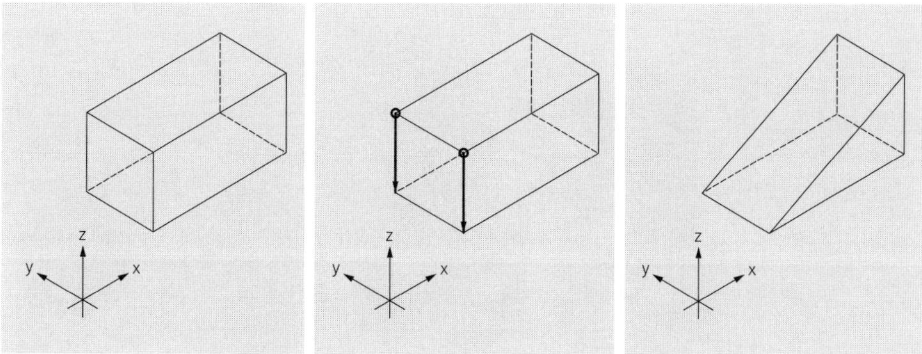

Fig. 63: By simply moving two points in the direction of the Z axis, you can shape a cuboid into a wedge.

mands that are at times more complex and at others quite simple. For example, the fact that volume bodies can be added to and subtracted from one another opens up a wide range of options. As with many drawing functions, these geometric operations go by different names in the various software packages, e.g. COMBINATION, CSG (short for Constructive Solid Geometry) and BOOLEAN OPERATIONS. The basic functions of these construction methods are based on addition, subtraction and intersection.

Addition

Addition allows you to combine two or more volume bodies into a single object. Here, the order in which the objects are selected for addition is unimportant. After they have been combined they can be selected and worked on only as a group, since they now constitute a newly defined object. This operation is particularly useful when separate building components need to be combined into a single structure. > Fig. 64b

Subtraction

Subtraction allows you to separate bodies from one another and to form different objects. In this operation the order of object activation is decisive, since only the first object to be activated remains intact while the second is erased along with the intersection volume. The second object thus determines the negative shape of the interpolation in the first. > Fig. 64c This operation makes it very easy, for example, to generate recesses for windows in wall components.

Intersections

When generating intersections, the intersection volume of two bodies is formed as a new object. The form of the object to be generated is determined by the way in which the two bodies are interpolated and is then shown as a positive shape. Areas that do not overlap are removed. > Fig. 64d

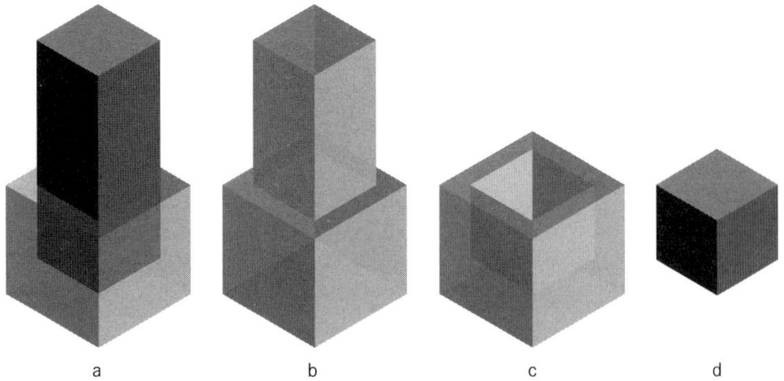

Fig. 64: Drawing with volume bodies: ADDITION, SUBTRACTION and INTERSECTION

ARCHITECTURAL ELEMENTS

Generally, CAD elements are defined geometrically or via the coordinates of their points. This geometric information allows the calculation of lengths, widths and heights and thus determines planes and volumes. In addition, it is possible to link this information to other specifications and to define general and specific characteristics. CAD programs that specialize in architectural drawing and visualization employ these associative possibilities for the efficient generation of typical architectural components. As a result, complex building components such as multilayered walls, windows and stairs can largely be predefined and thus drawn with optimum accuracy. These components therefore no longer need to be constructed in many individual steps and subsequently combined; instead, they are predefined in a dialogue box. Moreover, depiction parameters for pens, hatching and the surfaces of a building component can be defined in terms of colour and transparency. > Chapter Visualization Furthermore, it is possible to prepare and categorize different building components for the subsequent calculation of planes and volumes. > Chapter Data flow, TAI In this way an entire building can be efficiently constructed, visualized and quantified in virtual form.

Drawing architectural elements

Similarly to two-dimensional objects, architectural elements are usually constructed in the ground plan from the top view. The fundamental difference from 2D drawing is that you draw not simply a single line, but the entire component, creating several layers to record structure, height and the parameters for representing materials. ○

Walls

If you are drawing a wall as a complex component with a wall tool, a dialogue box linked to the drawing function allows you to define

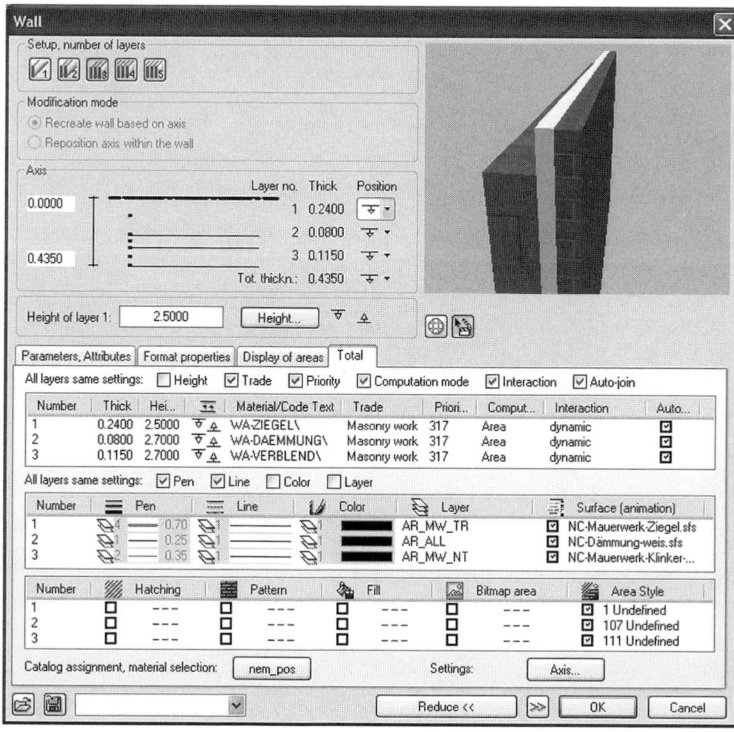

Fig. 65: Dialogue box for the WALL tool (Nemetschek Allplan)

the characteristics of this component prior to the actual drawing process. > Fig. 65

This means that you can set the default setting for wall height and structure to generate single or multi-layered elements. The layers are defined as lines with different pens and, if necessary, given additional attributes that can be used for subsequent visualization or calculation

> ○ **Note:** An advantage of this type of design is the capacity to combine certain building components that associatively influence one another. For example, the material connections between two overlapping, multi-layered walls form automatically and do not require laborious design work.

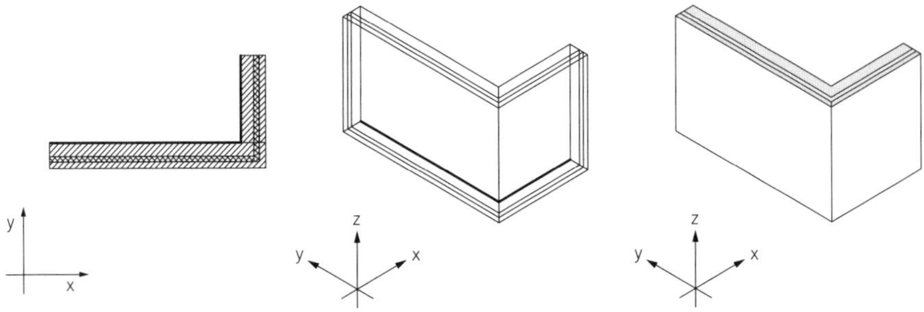

Fig. 66: A multi-layered wall element in a ground plan projection, generated as an isometric wire plan model and as an isometric surface model

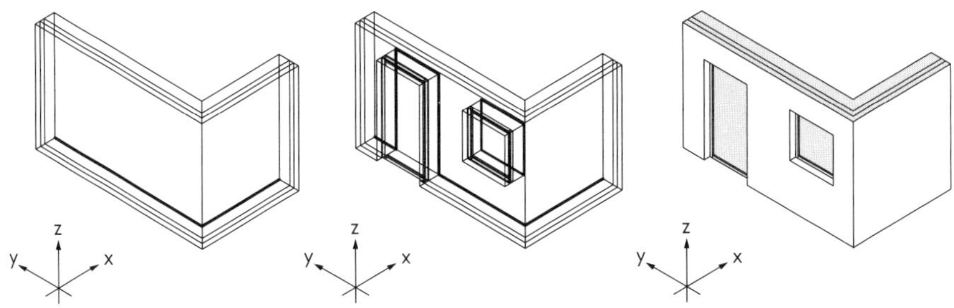

Fig. 67: In construction mode, apertures and window elements are set into an existing wall.

of quantities. When you now draw the wall, the depiction will include all predefined information and the result will be a complex component. > Fig. 66 In this way a whole series of steps which are required when drawing 2D or even simple 3D elements are combined in a single drawing function.

Apertures, windows and doors

After you have drawn the walls as components, you can generate windows and doors in the wall planes in any format you choose. Rather than merely defining the width and height of an aperture, you can also insert and fit windows and doors as finished components with frames, partitions and panels. > Fig. 67

O

Ceilings

As in the automatic generation of walls, ceilings are defined geometrically in terms of shape, panel thickness and position, and are predefined in the depiction by means of hatching and surface characteristics. If

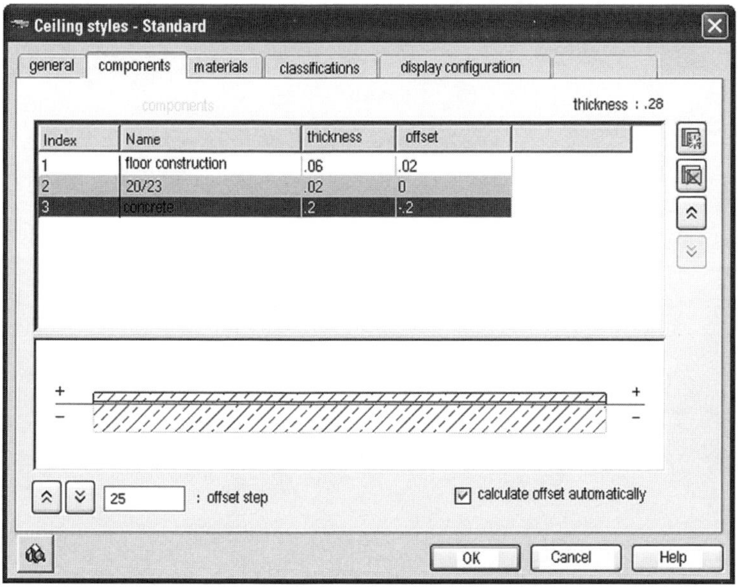

Fig. 68: Dialogue box for CEILING tool (Autodesk Architectural Desktop)

required, other attributes relating to the calculation of quantities and visualization can also be indicated. > Fig. 68

Once you have predefined the ceiling in this way, you can draw it with a base area of your choosing using a polyline and portray it as a completed component. Ceiling recesses such as stair openings can be constructed subsequently as polylines and recessed into the ceiling plane.

Stairs

When drawn by hand, stairs require laborious construction and calculation. CAD software combines the height and width of the stairs with the stair ground plan and the height between floors to construct the stair

> O **Note:** Wall openings and inserted components such as doors and windows are associatively linked. The building components are automatically adapted to the structure of the wall with an appropriate embrasure.

Fig. 69: Dialogue box for STAIR tool: different stair types can be selected (Graphisoft ArchiCAD).

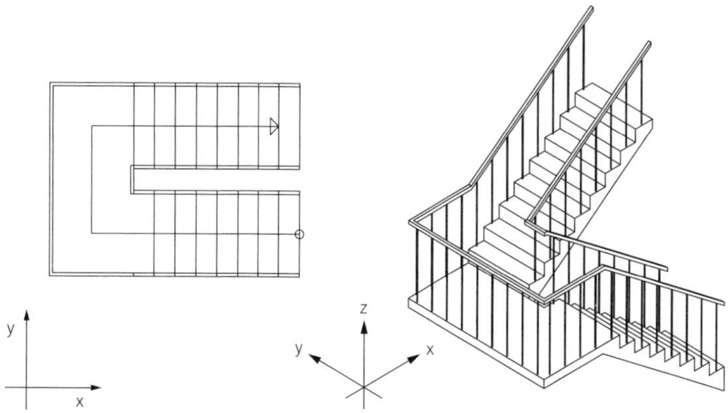

Fig. 70: An automatically generated double-flight, dog-leg podium stairway in a ground-plan projection and in an isometric diagram

geometry, all of which parameters can be altered during or even after the construction phase. Once you have selected the shape of the stairs, a dialogue box allows you to select and set their geometry and construction details. > Fig. 69

The stairway and all its construction characteristics are automatically calculated and generated. They can then be checked in the three-dimensional view and if necessary altered again. > Fig. 70 ○

○ **Note:** Some of the CAD programs that provide a stair tool initially predefine the stairway as a complete component in a dialogue box and allow you to save it as a library element before you place it within the virtual drawing area (e.g. Graphisoft ArchiCAD.) Other programs use a predefined 2D ground plan as their basis, to which you add geometric, constructive characteristics by selecting polygonal points (e.g. Nemetschek Allplan).

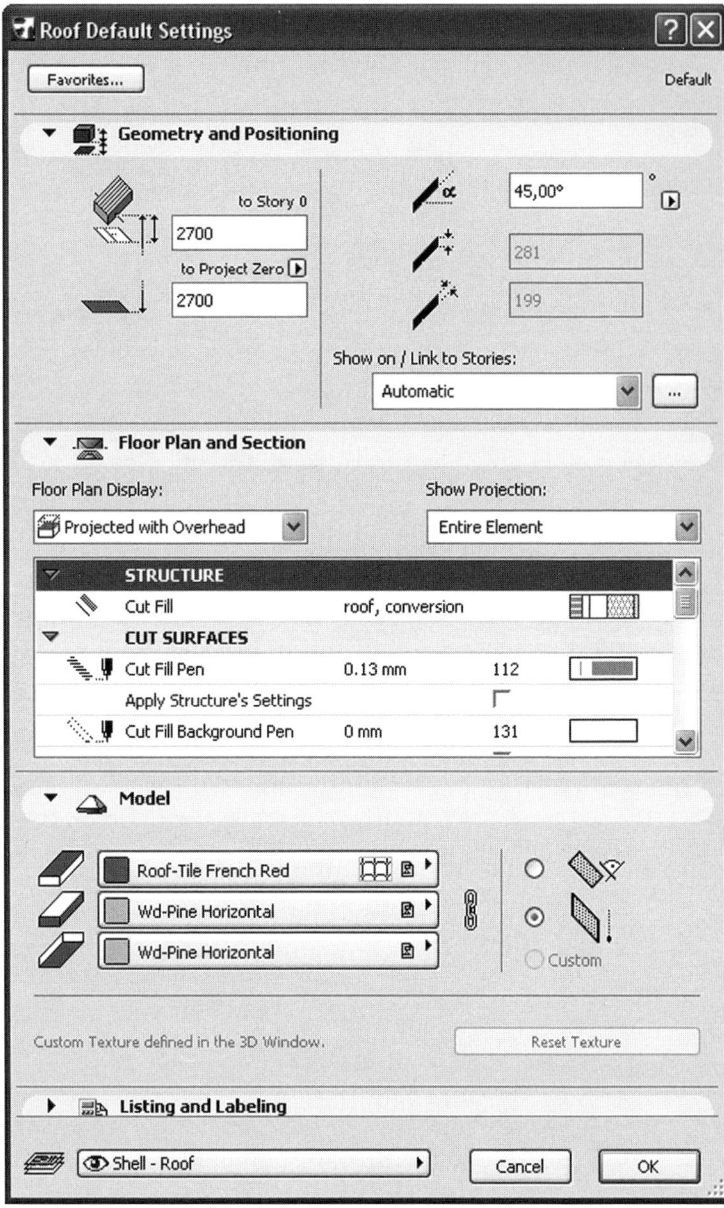

Fig. 71: Dialogue box for ROOF tool: along with line attributes, parameters can also be defined for storey height, roof inclination etc. (Graphisoft ArchiCAD).

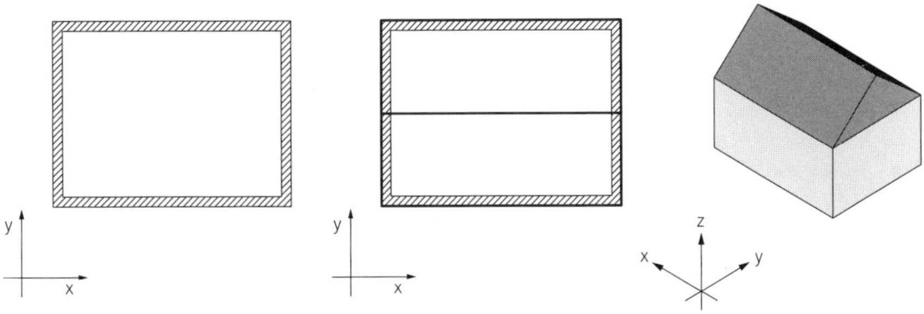

Fig. 72: Using an existing exterior wall plan, you can calculate edge lines, pitch and the orientation of the ridge of a saddle roof.

Roofs

Roofs are geometrically determined by the shape of the base area, the roof profile and inclination, the ridge, the edge height, and in some cases by the overhang. In many CAD systems, simple roofs can be designed with a ROOF tool by drawing the base area of the roof as a polyline and entering all desired parameters of the roof profile using the corresponding dialogue box. > Figs. 71 and 72 ■

■ **Tip:** Once the shape of the roof has been generated, many CAD programs allow you almost automatically to generate a rafter plan and definitions of the roof structure. These programs are thus able to take a virtual model from the design stage to the construction planning stage in only a few steps.

Visualization

In architecture, the term visualization refers to the pictorial representation of a detail or a planned building. One of the advantages of computer simulation over technical drawing as a means of visualization is that computer imaging is easier for non-professionals – including many building clients – to comprehend, because it provides a visual translation of the technical information contained in a construction drawing.

Visualization – a design tool

Computer visualizations serve different purposes. Planners can use them as a design tool to check the proportions of structural elements and spatial relationships between components and their surroundings.

Fig. 73: Visualization as a design tool: cubatures, lighting and materials can be examined in different phases of the design process.

In addition, visualizations can be used to evaluate the effects of various materials and lighting conditions when planning building projects. Using simple and relatively abstract virtual models at an early stage in the design process, you can check many aspects of the design, such as the suitability of materials and structural proportions. You can thus generate detailed computer simulations that, depending on the stage of the design and the degree of differentiation incorporated into the original virtual model, can help you make decisions during the planning process. The possibilities open to you range from simple mass models to virtual buildings, which reflect the current stage of planning. > Fig. 73

Computer visualizations also enable you to evaluate the advantages and disadvantages of different design approaches in the context of the planned location. While the exterior space remains unchanged, you can examine the relationship between the different architectural languages of alternative structures and the location. > Fig. 74 ■

Visualization for presentation

Architectural visualizations – like other methods of representation such as drawings and scale models – can also be used for the final presentation of a design. Depending on the requirements of the specific design and the target group, a visualization can be photorealistic or abstract. A successful presentation need not necessarily use photorealistic depictions: simple cubatures and abstracted surfaces can be non-realistic yet still communicate many aspects of the envisioned architectural effect. > Fig. 75

If possible, virtual models should be constructed to reflect subsequent visualizations. It is an advantage to adapt the degree of detail in a model to the possibilities of the visual presentation in order to use time efficiently in both the design and computation of a visualization. > Chapters The third dimension, Three-dimensional design, and Visualization, Rendering parameters

○ **Note:** In order to generate a visualization you need appropriate software, called rendering software (see Chapter Visualization, Rendering parameters, and Appendix, page 397). A number of CAD programs include an integrated rendering module that executes at least the initial steps in the visualization process. To achieve good, detailed results, you will often need special software, referred to as a renderer.

■ **Tip:** Many rendering programs allow you to position a pixel image in the background of a virtual object and thus to create a real backdrop in a virtual situation. For example, by using a digital photo of surrounding structures as a background image, you can depict a planned building in its actual future surroundings.

Fig. 74: Different architectural approaches in the same urban-planning context

For instance, details such as protuberances, recesses, window allocations and the exact differentiation of materials are not necessary for the simulated aerial view of an urban design, because they cannot be seen from a great distance. > Fig. 76

It is only at closer distances that details of the building cubatures and the structure of materials become visible and thereby important for the visualization. Features of the external space such as trees, cars and people can also fill a visualization with life, creating – as in a photo –

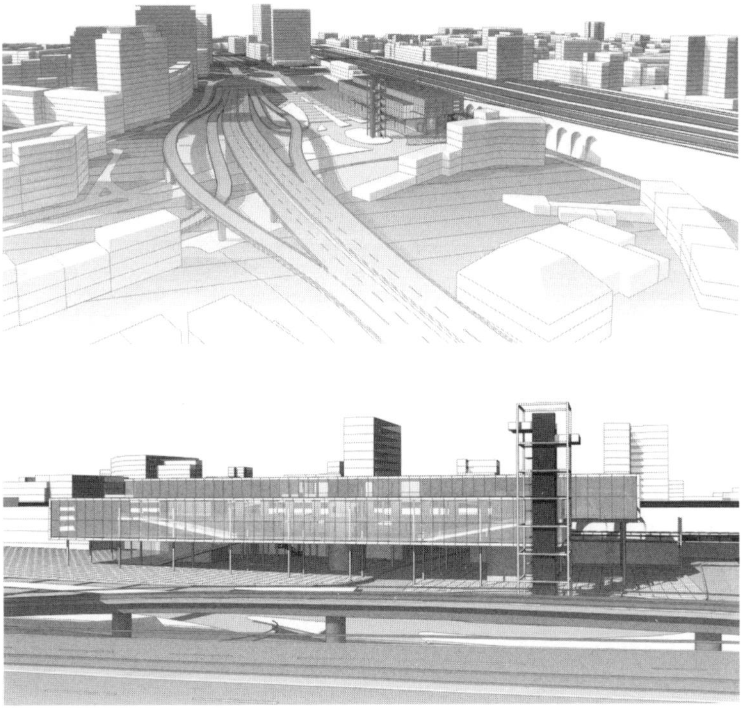

Fig. 75: Abstract visualizations can clarify many aspects of a design.

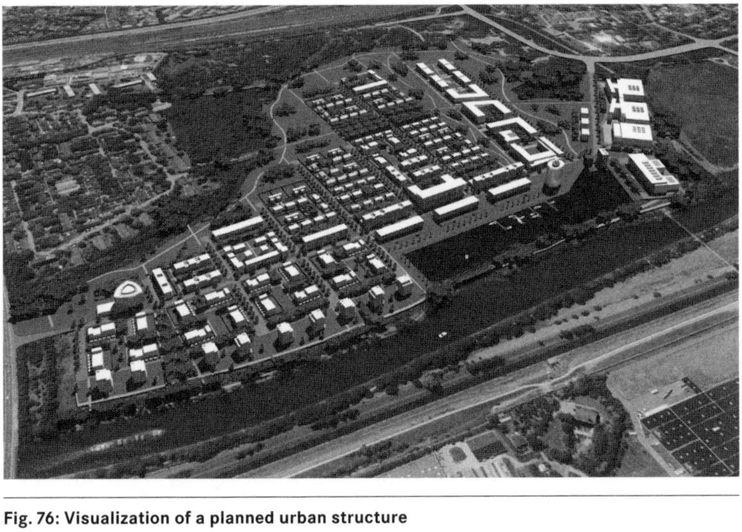

Fig. 76: Visualization of a planned urban structure

Fig. 77: The details of a building and its surrounding become more important as the viewer draws closer.

familiar references to everyday life and providing the viewer with a means to grasp the scale of the objects being depicted. > Fig. 77

Interior space also plays an important role in architectural visualizations. When creating a realistic interior visualization, you should pay attention to structural details and surface qualities, since interior views are often presented in close-up. > Fig. 78

SURFACES

An important part of a computer visualization is the optical effect of surfaces, which are given their material quality by colours, textures and lighting effects.

■ **Tip:** In a visualization of a high technical quality, virtual worlds seem perfect – and precisely for this reason unrealistic. The real world contains many "mistakes" that are significant for a computer visualization. Creating virtual facades with slightly uneven surfaces and colour nuances, for example, produces a better visualization with a much more realistic effect.

Fig. 78: Different depictions of an interior view in the visualization process

In the real world, it is the colour spectrum that allows us to perceive surfaces visually. The light that hits a surface is absorbed or reflected. If the entire colour spectrum is reflected by an object it appears white; if the entire colour spectrum is absorbed it appears black. Thus, our Colours

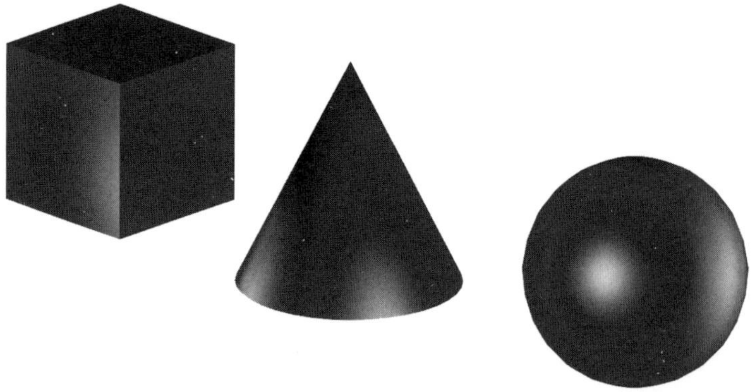

Fig. 79: Brightness gradations enhance the realistic effect of virtual surfaces.

perception of a colour depends on whether it is reflected or absorbed by the surface. For example, a blue surface reflects the colour blue while absorbing all other colour values.

An important method for creating realistic simulations of surfaces is selectively to change their colours. To have a realistic effect, the colour values of objects need to show nuances that are produced by differences in the way they reflect light. > Fig. 79

The sides that are turned away from the light source appear darker than those directly exposed to it. Moreover, highlights on strongly reflective surfaces appear white, irrespective of the colour of the object. As a rule, the possibilities for defining the rendered objects offered by the rendering software allow you to introduce variations in both the surface colour and the reflected colour, as well as in specific mirroring and transparency characteristics. If required, these can be set as percentages in a dialogue box.

You can use the electronic pen with which you drew the object to define its colour properties and reflective and transparency characteristics. Within the CAD system, the pen, or pen colour, is associated with the corresponding virtual information that is represented in the computer

● visualization as visible characteristics. > Chapter The virtual drawing board

Textures

Textures can be applied to the surfaces of a virtual object in order to represent a wide range of materials. This usually involves using a detail

Fig. 80: Textures can be used for the visualization of surfaces in a rendering.

of a pixel image – e.g. a photographic close-up of a brick wall. > Chapter Visualization, Rendering parameters With the help of the so-called MAPPING function, you can place this pixel image on the virtual surface and adapt the textured area to the size you require. Finally, when the view of the texture – in this case, a virtual brick wall – is rendered, it has the same surface of its real correlate. This is how a piece of the real world is imported via a photo to the virtual model and used for the visualization. > Fig. 80 ■

LIGHT AND SHADE

Well-placed light sources and selectively applied shadow effects are important for creating realistic surfaces and a particular atmosphere. Rendering software enables you to position and adjust different virtual light sources to simulate lighting conditions in exterior and interior space.

Virtual light sources

Virtual light sources can be used with differing intensities and colours. Moreover, it is possible to make light visible that under normal conditions is invisible until it falls on a surface – an effect that is similar to the light from a torch shining through fog.

● **Example:** While a normal window glass is transparent, it also reflects the surroundings to a certain degree. As a rule, you can check the effect of the settings for the respective surface materials in a renderer preview. Given a little practice with the software, you will thus be able to carry out the initial stages of simulating the object you have in mind.

■ **Tip:** As a rule, a selection of standardized textures is provided by the rendering software. This means that you can try out some initial textures without having to photograph the environment you are dealing with. In addition, you can find a large selection by running a search on the keyword "texture" on the Internet.

Fig. 81: Light sources have a great influence on the atmosphere of a visualization.

Fig. 82: A spotlight is a directional light source emitting light that spreads out in a cone. Depending on the angle at which the light falls on the surface, the target point is enclosed by a circle or an ellipse.

Fig. 83: A parallel light emits a directional shaft of light that does not form a cone.

Fig. 84: A point light emits non-directional light that spreads out in the space like the illumination from a light bulb.

○ Spotlight, parallel light and point light are different virtual light sources that create distinctive light distributions and effects. > Figs. 81–84

Ambient light

Apart from local light sources, ambient light can also be used in a design. This non-directional light is distributed equally throughout a space and constantly illuminates and colours the objects within this space. The brighter this light, the weaker the influence of other sources of illumination. You should use ambient light to fine-tune lighting and to avoid saturation or clouding in the visualization.

Intensity of illumination

The intensity of illumination is controlled via the colour of light, which is set individually for each light source in a scene. The brighter the colour, the stronger the luminosity of the light source. Pure white has the greatest luminosity. If you find that the luminosity of a light source is not sufficient, you can activate additional light sources. Since light colours can have all the colour values of the light colour spectrum, they can illuminate the space in every possible colour.

Shadows

Like real light sources, virtual light sources can produce shadows, thereby enhancing the realism of a virtual scene. Different methods of computing shadows can be used to produce hard, soft and area shadows. > Figs. 85–87 ■

PERSPECTIVE AND VIRTUAL CAMERA

The choice of the right perspective is key to computer visualization. > Figs. 73–78 All factors relevant to the image should be taken up in an appealing image format, if necessary with striking details. Image content should also be shown at a normal angle so that viewers will find parallels to the real world in the use of perspective. During the visualization process, you can arrange elements of a virtual model in combination with virtual light sources from an advantageous perspective. These form the render scene.

○ **Note:** Although sunlight should generally be understood as point light, it has an effect similar to parallel light when it strikes the Earth's surface due to the sun's enormous size.

■ **Tip:** Some CAD programs include sun and shadow studies as a design aid (e. g. Graphisoft ArchiCAD and Nemetschek Allplan). To set the position of the sun, you enter into a dialogue box the desired latitude, longitude, time of day and time of the year. This allows you to simulate the lighting conditions in any place on Earth at any time and thus provides you with valuable information on the effects of building orientation.

Fig. 85: The light source produces a hard shadow which, while not geometrically precise, requires little computation time.

Fig. 86: This soft shadow appears more realistic than the hard shadow in Fig. 85 and can be computed as a greyscale graphic in a relatively short time.

Fig. 87: The area shadow produces a geometrically correct shadow, but it requires considerably more computation time than hard and soft shadows.

The use of scenes often saves time because they can be stored as a template and thus do not have to be recreated for every visualization computation. As a rule, the render scene is visualized using a virtual camera, which can be used and adjusted within the application parameters like a real camera and defines eyepoint, aiming point, focal distance and camera angle. > Fig. 88 The eyepoint corresponds to the "eye level" of the observer in the virtual space. Like the aiming point of the view, it can be defined via coordinates in three dimensions. > Chapter The virtual drawing board, Coordinate systems

> ○ **Note:** When using rendering software, you can generally store scenes and retrieve them at a later point. A scene is an arrangement of virtual objects and light sources shown from a selected perspective that can normally be adjusted by means of virtual cameras (see Chapter Visualization, Perspective and virtual camera).

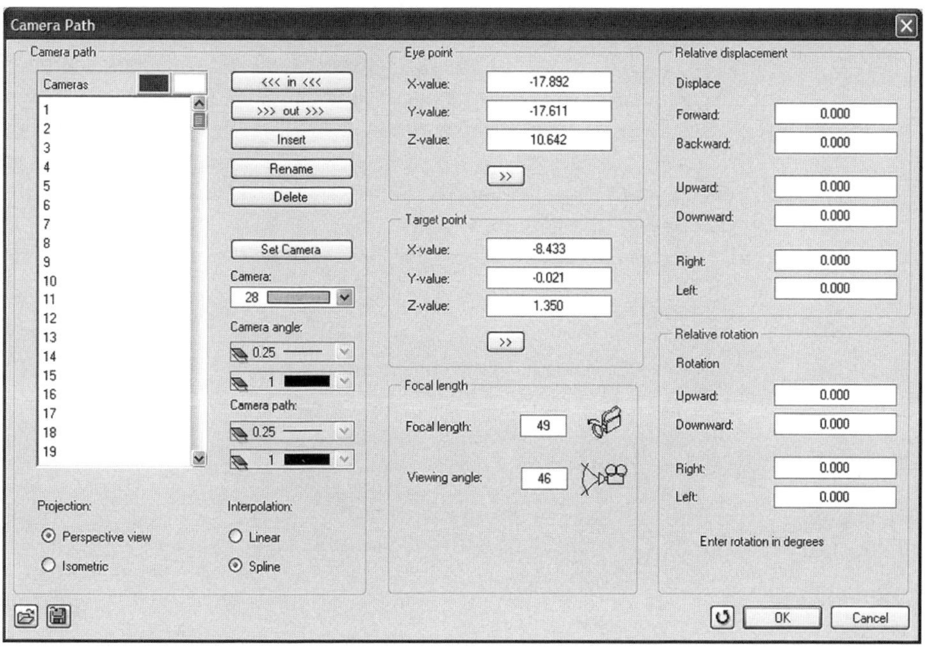

Fig. 88: Setting options for the parameters of a virtual camera (Nemetschek Allplan)

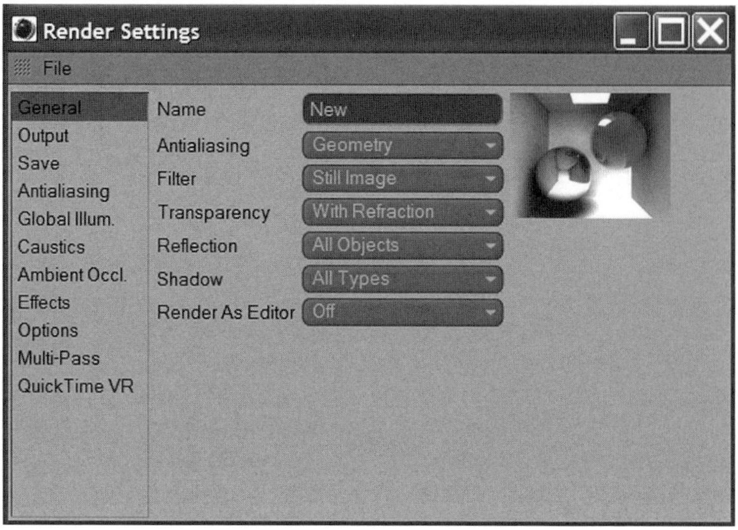

Fig. 89: Example of a dialogue box for rendering presettings (Cinema 4D)

The camera angle and the focal distance are geometrically dependent on each other and determine the visible field of the camera perspective: reducing the focal distance allows you to extend the visible field even in cramped spatial situations. However, to avoid the "fisheye" effect, you should not reduce the focal distance too much. If possible, eyepoint and aiming point should be located at the same height so that vertical edges can be depicted parallel to one another.

○ **Note:** Many rendering programs offer a variety of rendering engines (rendering types) that differ in terms of their basic computational methods. They include Raytracing, Phong Shading, Gouraud Shading, OpenGL and Z-Buffer. A simple way to compare image quality, calculation times and the advantages/disadvantages of each engine is to generate renderings of the same object.

RENDERING PARAMETERS

The quality of a visualization is based not only on an optimum arrangement of objects, surfaces and light sources, but also on the technical quality of the image. This quality depends on a wide variety of parameters, which must be properly harmonized. One method of defining parameters is by the presettings of the rendering software. We provide a basic explanation of these parameters below. > Fig. 89 ○

Generally speaking, the term "rendering" refers to the generation of new data from suitable "raw" or source data. In the specialized field of computer visualization, it describes the process of converting a vector graphic ○ into a bit-mapped graphic ○.

Resolution

The resolution of a pixel graphic is based on the number of pixels in a given area and determines the quality of the image. Normally, resolution is expressed by the abbreviation dpi (dots per inch) as the width × height of the image. The more pixels there are in an image, the finer the resolution. Conversely, an image with fewer pixels looks grainier and the depiction of finer details is not as crisp. > Fig. 90

In conjunction with the total number of pixels, the resolution determines the effective size of a pixel graphic as expressed in centimetres. At a resolution of 300 dpi, a 1000 × 1000 pixel rendering has a square shape measuring 8.47 cm × 8.47 cm. If the resolution is reduced to 150 dpi, the size of the image increases significantly to 16.94 cm × 16.94 cm, and the same number of pixels is distributed over an area that is four times as large. This is why, in contrast to a vector graphic, a pixel graphic cannot be enlarged without a loss of quality, since only the size of the individual dots increases. This affects the quality of the image, which becomes "pixelated" and has a coarser resolution.

○ **Note:** A vector graphic is a two- or three-dimensional computer image composed of different drawn elements, each of which is defined by coordinates. In contrast to bit-mapped graphics (see below), vector graphics can be enlarged to any desired size without a loss of quality. Compared to other graphics formats, they also require little memory volume.

○ **Note:** Bit-mapped graphics (also called pixel graphics) consist of an arrangement of individual pixels. A pixel is the smallest unit of a pixel graphic and contains a particular colour value as graphic information. Put differently, a pixel graphic is a combination of many pixels that is comparable to a mosaic of many small elements.

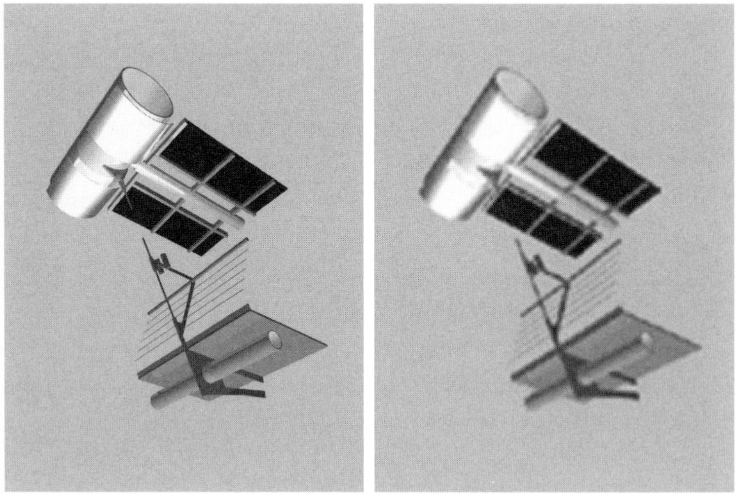

Fig. 90: The same rendered object shown at different resolutions

You need only a little experience to determine the required computational times based on the planned resolution of a rendering. If a larger number of pixels need to be calculated for a computer graphic, the calculation will require more time and effort. Renderings that represent intermediary stages of the design generally require a lower resolution than final presentations and their rendering times will be shorter too.

Anti-aliasing

When converting a vector graphic to a pixel graphic, you can use anti-aliasing to avoid a jagged depiction of diagonal lines (the so-called stair effect). A pixel graphic is only capable of portraying horizontal and vertical lines without great difficulty. If a line is slanted, "stairs" appear because slanted lines are portrayed by offset square pixels in a pixel graphic. > Fig. 91

The same effect can be seen in all kinds of round shapes and even in typefaces. The grainier the resolution, the larger will be the individual pixels – and the more pronounced the stair effect. Anti-aliasing interpolates and partially weakens the colour values of the individual "steps" so that they are not as distinct. The level of anti-aliasing has a substantial effect on the time needed to compute a rendering: if the round shapes and diagonal lines need to be portrayed crisply, the calculation will take longer. This is why maximum anti-aliasing should only be used for final presentations. ■

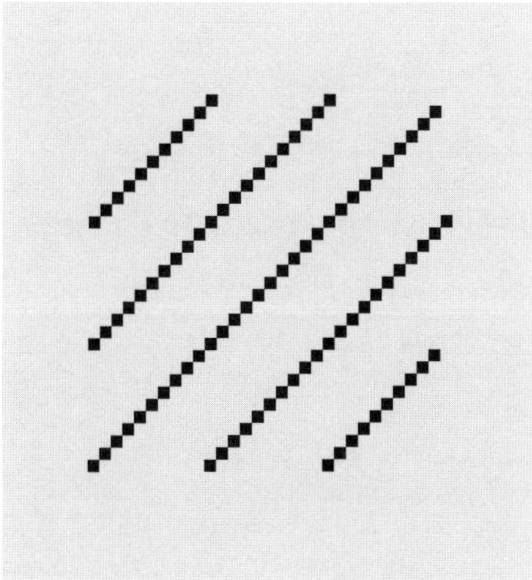

Fig. 91: Diagonal lines in a bit-mapped graphic are frequently marred by the so-called stair effect.

Aside from the wealth of geometric information required for a virtual model, the rendering settings, in particular, exert a great influence on the time needed to compute a visualization. For this reason you should, if possible, consider the purpose and the intended quality of a visualization or rendering result before you begin the rendering process.

> Appendix, page 396 ■

■ **Tip:** You can also increase resolution to diminish the stair effect. In this case, the diagonal lines and edges are calculated using an especially large number of pixels and there is a finer depiction of the inevitable jagged patterns.

■ **Tip:** You should first test the rendering settings on a detail from the virtual scene in order to examine, in advance, the effects of light and materials. Complex models, in particular, may require a rendering time of several hours.

Data flow

PROGRAM LIBRARIES

CAD programs normally feature integrated program libraries with an array of symbols, document templates and predefined building components. Architectural CAD programs include sundry objects that can serve as standard drawing elements or that can be changed to reflect your own style and ideas. > Fig. 92

You can also create templates from objects you have drawn yourself and use them in more than one project. It will save you a great deal of time to use objects defined in this way since no intensive research is required; and you can integrate objects into drawings, and copy and edit them as you require, instead of drawing them from scratch in the future.

Symbols

There are symbols to represent both interior furnishings (furniture, bathroom fittings, kitchen elements etc.) and elements of landscape design (trees, plants, cars, people etc.). Additional icons depict objects in the field of structural engineering, building services technology and the planning disciplines linked to architecture.

Building components

The use of standardized components saves a great deal of work, particularly when you create working drawings, because you can then select drawing elements like steel components (beams, pipes etc.) and connectors (screws, bolts etc.) from a catalogue, incorporate them directly into the drawing and edit them there. Even complex components such as stairways, windows and doors can be stored and used in this way. > Chapter The third dimension, Architectural elements

■ **Tip:** Using a scanner, you can scan both freehand sketches and other hand-drawn technical drawings, and then import them as pixel graphics into CAD drawings. Conversely, you may also print out mid-project CAD drawings, modify them by hand using transparent paper, and then transpose the results to CAD. This is one way to combine the advantages of CAD and hand drawings.

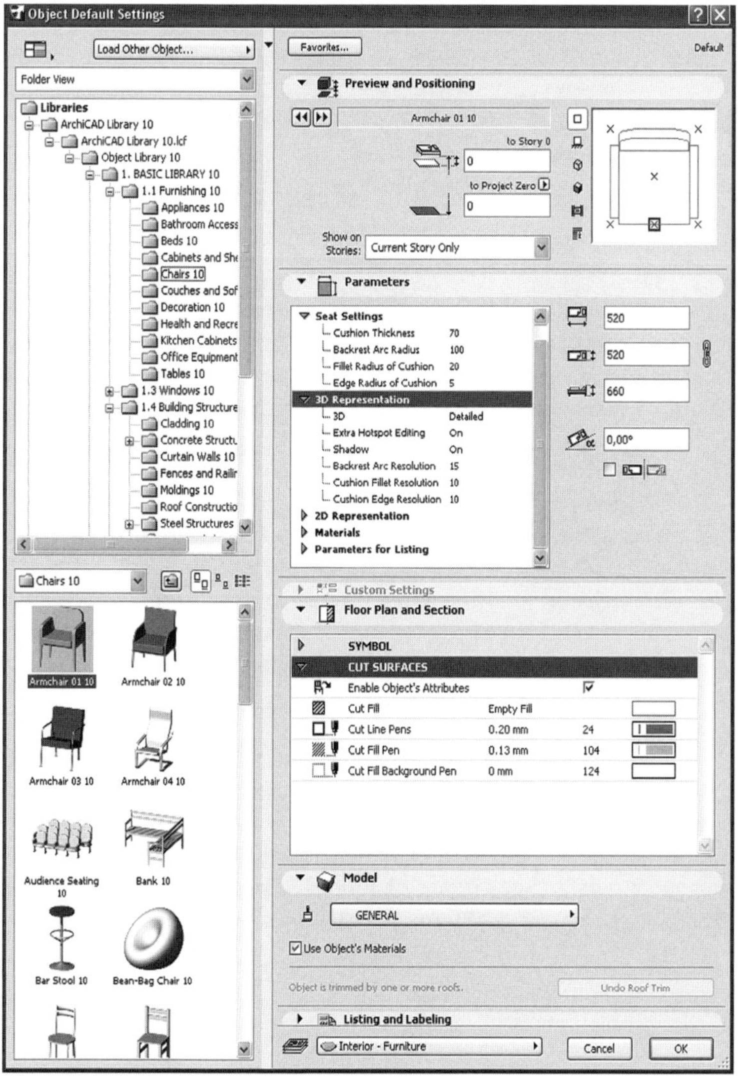

Fig. 92: Example of a program library (Graphisoft ArchiCAD)

In addition to elements in vector graphics, pixel images can also be incorporated into libraries and administered there. These images may include digital photographs, scans and renderings that are systematically imported, stored, and – if needed – integrated into a drawing. ■

Pixel images

Document templates

Drawing frames can also be imported and edited, and the same applies to standardized lettering and drawing headers in the respective scale. This means you need to create customized document and printing templates only once. These are then stored for later use in the program library. > Chapter Data flow, Printing and plotting

CAD INTERFACES

CAD interfaces facilitate the exchange of data between different programs. Although all CAD systems generally work with vector graphic information, most programs employ their own file formats, which are often incompatible and impede data exchange between different CAD programs. DXF has largely caught on as the standard data exchange format for architectural drawings, as it can be read and written by nearly all CAD software and even by a few graphics programs.

DXF is short for drawing interchange format (or drawing exchange format) and was developed by the company Autodesk to exchange CAD data.

If a DXF file is imported into a CAD program, different options can be chosen to adapt specific properties of the vector graphic data. These include unit, scale and the two- or three-dimensional mode of transmission. > Fig. 93

○ ○

A number of architectural CAD programs not only use DXF and their own data formats, but also provide interfaces to select programs in order to ensure trouble-free data exchanges. This is particularly true in the field of rendering programs – the additional software necessary to guarantee outstanding visualization results. For instance, Nemetschek Allplan uses a special data format to export three-dimensional models to

○ **Note:** Exchanging different CAD data is not unproblematic and rarely goes off perfectly. Important details specific to a CAD system are often lost or may not be displayed in the same way as the original exported information. This can become glaringly evident in the case of typefaces, program-specific symbols and dimensioning data, since they rarely have an equivalent in the target system.

○ **Note:** Special programs that read and write data in several file formats and thus facilitate imports and exports between different CAD programs provide an alternative to DXF-based data exchanges. That said, you may have difficulty transmitting data if you lack the necessary experience.

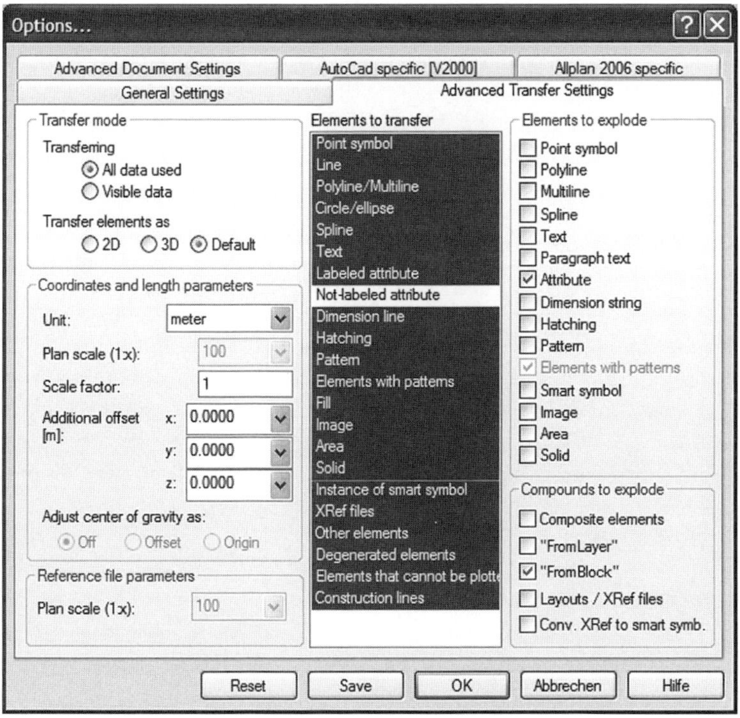

Fig. 93: Example of a dialogue box for exporting and importing DXF files (Nemetschek Allplan)

Cinema 4D rendering software, Autodesk Architectural Desktop offers a comparable interface to 3D STUDIO MAX/VIZ, and Graphisoft ArchiCAD has developed an interface for Artlantis.

TAI

TAI, short for tendering, awarding and invoicing, represents an important area of building construction. After architects create the design and construction documentation for an architectural object, bids or tenders are invited for the individual construction jobs – in other words, this work is described in written form, its scope is specified, and this information is made available to construction companies together with relevant drawings so they can submit a tender. After a quotation is received, the construction company is selected based on the specified prices and quality standards, and the construction work is commissioned. Finally, after the construction work is completed, accounts must be settled for the costs incurred.

Special tendering, awarding and invoicing programs make it easier to manage quantities and costs in building construction. When architects create a structure as a complete virtual model using CAD, they can categorize the quantities of the individual building components according to materials and skilled trades. > Chapter The third dimension, Architectural elements This information can be imported directly to the TAI programs and edited there, eliminating the need for time-consuming calculations of quantities by hand.

From the CAD system to TAI software to the construction site and back again

Ideally, data will flow from the CAD drawing to the tendering program. Setting quantities links components from the CAD drawing directly to the TAI program, allowing users to check the allocation, quantities and dimensions of components and items in both the CAD and the TAI system. This allows you to compile a list of contract specifications efficiently and monitor their completion effectively. Information from the CAD program (attributes, quantities etc.) can be calculated and organized in corresponding lists.

PRINTING AND PLOTTING

○ ■ After a drawing is completed in design mode, it can be printed or plotted. While large-size CAD drawings are printed on plotters, small formats are printed on standard DIN A4 and A3 printers.

Drawings and plans are usually prepared for printing in special windows that allow you to arrange different drawing content and pixel images on a page, as well as subsequently labelling them and making other settings relevant to printing.

Print scale

Here you make the final specifications regarding the printing scale and the required paper size. You also have an additional opportunity to examine, prior to printing, the effect of scale-related settings such as line width and font size. In this context it is important to make sure that the reference scale matches the printing scale, since characters and other

○ **Note:** Plotters are large-format printers, usually DIN A1 or A0, on which plans are printed on roll paper. Roll widths normally measure 61.5 cm for A1 rolls and 91.5 cm for A0 rolls. Plan sizes can be entered individually into the CAD programs so that every plan format can be used inside the given roll width.

■ **Tip:** When printing on a plotter, you can usually choose from three different quality settings. A low quality level will print much more quickly than a higher setting, but the print will have a lower resolution and not be as sharp. Lower settings also use less ink.

scale-dependent features of a drawing might otherwise be too small or too large. > Chapter The virtual drawing board

For instance, if a plan is supposed to show a facade section together with corresponding detail views, it is possible to present drawings in different scales on a single architectural plan. In this case, each individual drawing is depicted in the required scale. ○

Paper formats

Plan formats with different aspect ratios are available for presentation purposes. It usually makes sense to choose a common paper format for architectural drawings (e.g. the ISO/DIN A series), since it is easy to produce them. Large formats are needed for construction drawings, while for case of detail drawings, it is generally better to use a format that can be copied on most copy machines, such as DIN A3 or A4.

A drawing frame created for the selected paper format generally defines the area taken up by the drawing, and shows the edge that can be used to subsequently cut the drawing. The drawing header contains technical information such as a precise description of the content (floor plan, section, view etc.), the scale (M 1:50, 1:100, 1:100 etc.), as well as printing date, author and other supplementary data. > Fig. 94

The drawing frame and header can be created as templates in the required scale, making it possible to use the basic settings for other projects as well. > Chapter Data flow, Program libraries

Virtual print

You can also print drawings and plans "virtually" in the form of files. In this case, you do not transmit the vector graphic information in a drawing to a real printer or plotter but store it as a plot file using the printer software. A plot file contains all the drawing information that is required by a specific printer or plotter to print out the drawing at a subsequent point in time without using the CAD software's printing environment. ■

○ **Note:** There are sometimes significant differences in the plan design options provided by CAD programs, and their ease of use can differ too. A few providers offer supplementary modules specially developed for plan design and printout (e.g. Nemetschek Plandesign).

■ **Tip:** This method can be employed in a number of situations – for example, if a student does not own a plotter and needs to make a print on the university's plotter or at a professional copy shop. Data can be printed on the plotter without installing the corresponding CAD program on the attached computer.

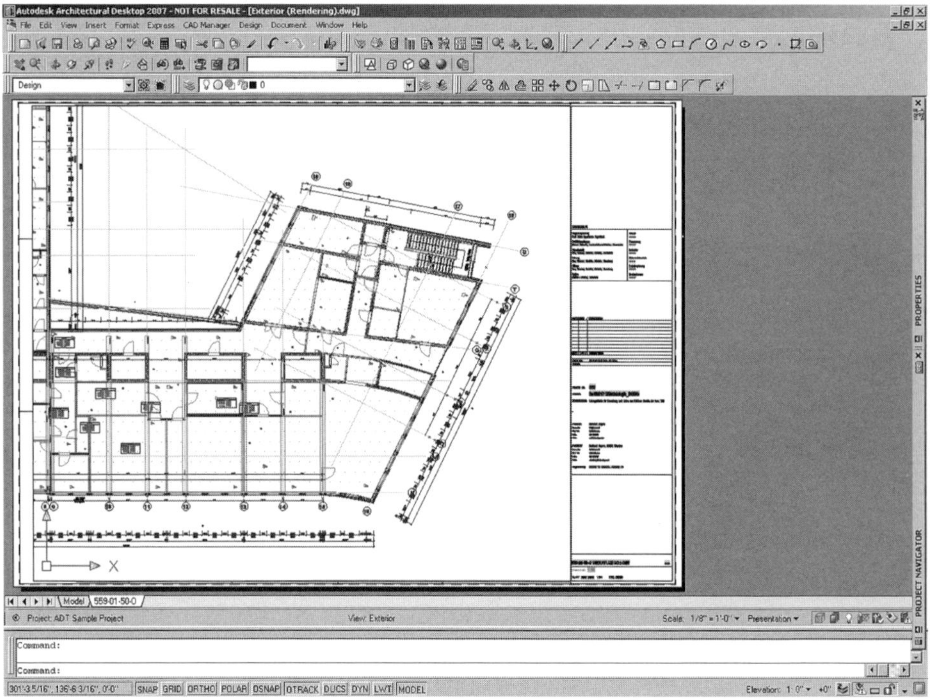

Fig. 94: Example of drawing window (Autodesk Autocad)

PDF — PDF stands for "portable document format" and is a common data exchange format developed by Adobe Systems that can contain both vector graphic and bit-mapped information. Many CAD systems allow you to create PDF files as an export function. Alternatively, you can install a virtual printer (e.g. Adobe Acrobat Distiller) in much the same way as a real printer and then select it for printing. It will create a PDF document containing all the graphic information of the virtually printed drawing.

Pixel graphics — A few CAD systems allow you to export drawing content as pixel graphics. These can be stored both in different file formats and, if required, in user-defined resolutions, two examples being the JPEG or/and TIFF formats. A distinguishing feature of the JPEG format is that the bit-mapped graphic information is mostly stored in compressed form so the file sizes are accordingly small and easy to manage. The TIFF format requires much more memory, but it contains a great deal more graphic information and is better suited for additional editing steps (e.g. image-editing programs).

System requirements

HARDWARE

Even though, as the user of a computer, you do not necessarily need to know much about its inner workings, we are including the following sections to provide some basic information about a number of hardware components.

Central processing unit

The central processing unit, or CPU, is the heart of the computer and controls all its other components.

Mainboard

The mainboard (also known as "motherboard") is the central circuit board of the computer and has attachment points for its processor and memory modules as well as for supplementary cards such as graphics, sound and network cards. These components can also be integrated directly into the mainboard, in which case they are said to be "onboard."

RAM – working memory

RAM, short for random access memory, is your computer's working memory.

Graphics card

The graphics card in a PC controls the screen display, ensuring, among other things, that data are computed quickly for visualizations. For CAD systems, it is advisable not to have an onboard graphics card since the relatively slow RAM will be used for graphics processing and the other processes may be slowed down.

Hard drive

A hard drive is a storage medium that writes data on the magnetic surface of a rotating disc. The surface is magnetized based on the information being recorded. Even if a hard drive has sufficient memory capacity for all CAD data and is a relatively secure storage device, you should regularly secure CAD data on external media such as CDs and DVDs to protect against possible data loss.

Monitor

The screen size of a monitor is normally indicated in inches and is based on the screen diagonal. The screen should not be too small since it is used to display the virtual workspace. Alternatively, you can use two screens: if you display all the interface's control functions on one, you can use the virtual drawing area on the other without restriction. Please keep in mind, though, that your graphics card must support this setup.

Special input devices

Aside from the keyboard and the mouse, other input devices have been specially designed for the virtual workspace. The best-known are the joysticks used to play three-dimensional computer games.

SpaceMouse

The SpaceMouse functions like a joystick and can efficiently control virtual views. Additional keys can be programmed to execute drawing and tool commands.

Sketchpad

The sketchpad, also called a "digitizing board," digitizes data entered with a pen-like pointing device. Since the sketchpad provides a much higher resolution than a standard computer mouse, you can use it to draw an object in much the same way as you would draw on a piece of paper with a pencil. When assigned the appropriate scale, the drawing area of the user interface will correspond to that of the sketchpad.

Touchscreen

New touchscreens can also be used for drawing, like sketchpads. The touchscreen is not set up vertically like a monitor in front of the user, but is used as a horizontal work surface to create and display drawings.

SOFTWARE

If at all possible, you should choose CAD software to match existing hardware. The use of modern software on old computing systems can be problematic, since these may not provide the computational capacity required to execute the software operations adequately. You must also have a suitable operating system, which controls the computer's fundamental processes. This is a basic requirement for running all application software. The most popular operating systems are Windows (Microsoft), Mac OS (Apple) and, increasingly, LINUX, which you can largely use without a license. Not all operating systems are suitable for all CAD systems, and you should pay close attention to the software providers' specifications.

There is a large selection of CAD software on the market, and the various CAD programs often function differently and have significant price differences. From freeware and shareware to costly specialized programs, the offerings are immense. > Appendix, page 397

An alternative to the expensive complete versions of CAD software are the demo and student versions that a few providers make available to consumers. The student versions are inexpensive compared to the normal versions, and you can even use the demo versions for free for a limited period. Even so, it is prohibited to use them professionally. A demo version may make sense to take the first few steps with CAD since it allows you to try out the software and evaluate its strengths and weaknesses.

Selecting software

Selecting a CAD system depends on a number of factors: the (architecturally relevant) functions, the special properties of operation and use, the cost and the required hardware. An additional criterion is the CAD user's personal or professional environment since data exchange with project partners – to name just one example – should be as trouble-free as possible and is best ensured by exchanging data from one and the same software program.

Program-specific literature is available for the various CAD programs in addition to training courses at universities, adult education centres and private institutions. If you do not want to learn CAD on your own – which is, of course, entirely possible – you can take a course that suits your particular level of expertise.

It is advantageous to learn not just a single CAD system, but to master at least the basic principles of other programs so that you are not restricted to particular system requirements and remain flexible in your work. Although the operation of many CAD programs differs, they all have the same underlying foundations. Once you have a good command of these basics, you can apply this knowledge to other programs and learn them more easily.

○ **Note:** Different software providers will make recommendations concerning hardware configurations. These should be regarded as minimum requirements when you purchase your CAD system. The software may function on the recommended hardware, but it may not be able to carry out work processes involving large volumes of data. This is why it is worthwhile to get advice from a specialized vendor on which computer system to buy.

■ **Tip:** Freeware and shareware can be downloaded from the Internet but in most cases only offer limited basic functionality.

Designing in dialogue with the computer

The computer in general and drawing with CAD in particular streamline work processes and provide a basis for efficient and exact approaches to creating and managing digital drawings and other data. Associative components and virtual models not only simulate reality, but also influence it directly by offering a new manner of designing and systematized planning process. But even with all its benefits, this working method has a few drawbacks. Designing with CAD usually entails drawing with a mouse, which cannot be guided as precisely as a pencil. Also, you only have indirect contact with the drawn object via the entry and output devices—an aspect of the work that should never be underestimated. When drawing with CAD, beginners, in particular, are confronted with many operations that may initially seem complicated and can influence their mental processes, particularly when they engage in creative design.

By contrast, drawing by hand is often an intuitive process in which personal ideas are implemented directly and sometimes even largely unconsciously. The results on paper are continually influenced while you draw, and the representational method, which is, not least, dependent on experience and feel, is aligned with the drawing material and the represented object. This is another reason that you should incorporate hand drawings into the design process and, if possible, enhance the use of the CAD application with hand sketches.

Outlook

CAD has become a firm feature of the day-to-day work of designers, and it will continue to grow in importance in the future. In the field of architecture, the developments playing an especially important role are those that allow all project participants to have direct access to an object as a virtual model - from the creation of the design and working drawings to the construction of the object. This makes it possible to evaluate, print and even modify the data and drawings that are relevant to planning and construction directly. It lays a foundation for virtual planning that is always up to date and, if need be, reflects the architectural object down to the finest detail. In addition, even when it accompanies an ongoing development process, CAD influences the development of new approaches to planning and allows for the design of architectural structures that could not completely be depicted by hand drawings, including amorphous and other free forms. In this context, complex structural calculations or the computation of complicated component geometries are an important basis for the design and construction process. CAD represents much more than an easy-to-use drawing tool. It is both a comprehensive instrument and an important building block in the development and future of architecture.

Alexander Schilling

Modelbuilding

The architectural model as a means of representation

What is modelmaking?

In the early Renaissance in Italy, modelmaking evolved into the most important means of architectural representation. It not only supplemented architectural drawings, but was often the primary method used to convey ideas and depict spaces. Ever since then, architects, engineers and clients have used models to represent designed buildings.

Plans (design sketches such as technical plans) and architectural models are both means of depicting buildings and spaces, yet plans convey only two dimensions. Once the design and the project have been thought out and sketches and details drawn, it is time to tackle the object in space. While it is true that only the finished building can communicate a complete understanding of three-dimensional effects, models anticipate the subsequent construction process. Seen this way, models represent architecture on a smaller scale. Work on models is of great importance, particularly in architectural studies, since students do not usually have the opportunity to build their own designs.

Motivation: why build models?

A model is not absolutely necessary to complete a design or architectural assignment successfully, yet it can be a useful tool in many ways: the model's scaled-down size makes it possible to examine the quality of the design and allows designers to develop a feel for space, aesthetics and materials. The additional advantages of a model include its communicative and persuasive potential: a model helps designers to demonstrate to themselves and others the quality of their ideas or projects. In addition, the model can serve as a control mechanism for assessing the building before it is built.

Working models – three-dimensional sketches

Architectural students are often confronted with the challenges of modelmaking in their first year at college. They quickly see that the models they built as children – trains, planes and ships – have nothing to do with the demands made on them in their studies. The green lawn from their train set is of no interest to professors or lecturers. The toys of childhood are now professional reality.

So how should students proceed? Let us assume they have been given a design assignment and require a model, on a pre-defined scale, that will play an important role in the way their proposed solution is evaluated. Whether they use a model in their design work will largely depend on both how they design and how the design evolves. If the spatial structure is of greater complexity than a two-dimensional drawing can repre-

Fig. 1: Architectural models create an impression of spatiality (three-dimensionality), convey an idea of a building structure and the effects of interior and exterior space.

sent, a model may be the only way to depict it. Simple models, so-called working models, enable designers to find solutions and test ideas. The ideas that do not work on the model can be rejected. ○

The working model accompanies the entire design process. Once this process is complete, the goal is then to illustrate the ideas and concepts that are essential for the design. The viewer must be convinced of the feasibility of both the concept and the proposed solution. ■

○ **Note:** Working models have earned their name because designers can "work" with them. They can, and should, be modified even if that harms their quality. It is therefore best to build a model that is easy to take apart and reassemble. Students can join parts with pins or easily removable rubber cement. Once two parts are glued together, they are committed to a particular form, which is not the purpose of a working model.

■ **Tip:** Working models, which support the design process experimentally, can also be used effectively for presentational purposes if they are sufficiently refined. Elements such as building sections and topographic layers should be assembled temporarily both to ensure that the model can be modified and to avoid unnecessary stains and damage during work. Painting at a later stage in the process is an excellent way of enhancing a working model.

Presentation models – portraying and persuading

The presentation model, built with a great deal of effort to be almost perfect, marks the completion of the design process. At universities, this type of model is used to present a design idea – the concept. In architectural competitions, it depicts the proposed solution and competes with the designs of other participants. In both cases, the model supplements the architectural plans submitted. New media are often used to present drawings: three-dimensional computer-generated images provide a very realistic rendering of how the future structure will look. Photo-realistic representations are another modern way of simulating a spatial experience. A model cannot perform all these functions. It always remains an abstraction of the reality it portrays. Its only true function is to translate the sketched idea into three-dimensional form. ■

■ **Tip:** It is always difficult to build a presentation model when under pressure to submit a design. It is often more efficient to make parts of the model in advance or use a site model as both working and presentation model. A presentation model does not need to be perfect or to be made of the very best materials. All that is needed is a very convincing model.

Types of models

A model is a more or less abstract, miniaturized representation of reality. But what does abstraction mean in modelmaking?

Abstraction – the trick of miniaturization

The opposite of abstract is concrete. In painting, "concrete" refers to an object that is portrayed as accurately as possible. In contrast, abstraction as applied to architectural models shifts the focus onto the subject matter, the informational value of the object portrayed and the spatial framework. What is at stake is not an accurate portrayal of reality but a process of simplification, which guides the eye to the model's essential features. It is crucial to find a suitable form of abstraction, one that reflects the selected scale. This point can be illustrated using the example of windows: on a scale of 1:200, a window is usually portrayed as a precisely cut-out aperture in the surface of the chosen material. On a scale of 1:50, a window is much easier to see. Glass is reproduced using a transparent material, and the window frame is built of small bars. Another example is facade cladding: on a very small scale, it cannot be depicted at all, but in larger models this element has greater relevance and is included in the design. The facade can be simulated very realistically using the right material.

Relationship between scale and representation

At the very start of a project, modellers must select the scale of their models. The dimensions in which an architectural object can be represented illustrate the role that scale plays. Depending on the scale and level of abstraction, there exist a number of model types, which will be explained below.

Fig. 2: Windows shown at different scales

● **Example:** Try to reproduce the character and feel of surfaces in miniature. Rough or grainy surfaces can be simulated by sanding or "keying" cardboard and wood. Structures can be simulated as follows:
- Wooden cladding can be reproduced using small pieces of wood that imitate the real design.
- Brick facades are simulated by cutting joints in the surface of the material.
- Supports and beams can have the same shape as in reality.

CONCEPTUAL MODELS (WITHOUT A CONCRETE SCALE)

A spatial pictogram can generally be described as a conceptual model. Here, the underlying idea of a design or a creative concept is depicted in an entirely abstract manner as a three-dimensional object (e.g. using a metaphor as a basis). Material, form and color highlight structures and create compositions. The model can, for instance, be used to visualize the results of urban space analyses at the start of the design process. By exploring a theme or place on a spatial yet abstract level, architects can alter or improve the view of that place. A model can support this approach.

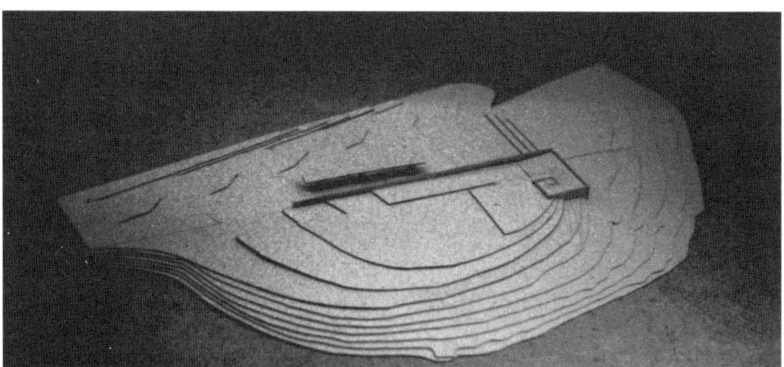

Fig. 3: Conceptual model

URBAN DESIGN AND LANDSCAPE MODELS, SITE AND TOPOGRAPHY (SCALE 1:1,000, 1:500)

This type of model represents urban or natural environments. It is the first step in the representation process, since it shows the relationship with the existing environment. In urban space, it is important to show how the context changes with the addition of a new structure.

This type of model is characterized by the highest level of abstraction. Buildings are reduced to "building blocks" - to abstract structures that reproduce building form and three-dimensionality in a highly simplified manner. Even so, the model includes the characteristic features of buildings such as recessions, projections, bay windows and roof designs. In its abstract form, the site - the scaled-down landscape - is simplified

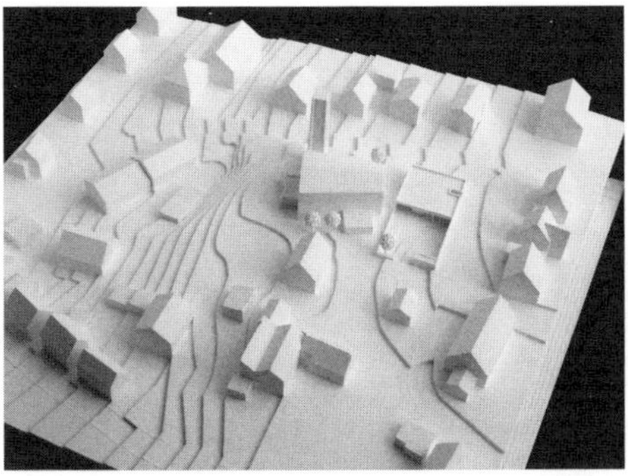

Fig. 4: Urban design model showing the surrounding area

Fig. 5: The draft concept is demonstrated using contrasting materials.

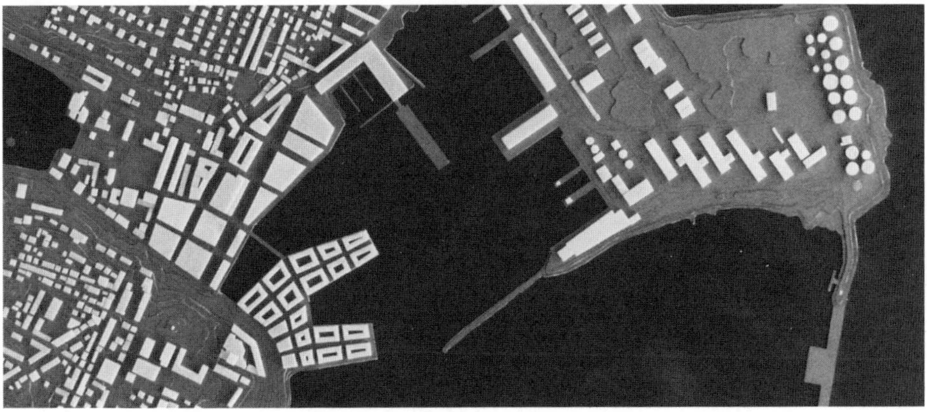

Fig. 6: Urban design model of Reykjavik showing the city and water

and depicted, in the chosen material, as a level plain. If the landscape slopes, it can be broken down into horizontal layers that are stacked on top of each other in the model.

Raised-relief models

If the model is meant to reproduce uneven landscapes, the first step in building it is to conceive of the irregular natural terrain as a stack of horizontal layers. The more finely layered the material, the more precise and homogeneous the resulting model will be (width of the elevation layers: 1.0 mm or 2.0 mm). The work is based on a plan that shows contour lines or, at least, provides information on elevation. Once the real topographic situation is known, contour lines (curved, straight or polygonal) are drawn. Depending on the material, the modeller can cut out each layer with a utility knife or saw before arranging the layers on top of each other.

Insert models

A single assignment might include several designs, and urban design models are often constructed as "inserts" or group models to reduce the amount of work required to present them. Only one model of the surrounding area is made, and each participant is given a mounting board for the section on which he or she is working. This particular section is omitted from the urban design model so that the inserts can be interchanged.

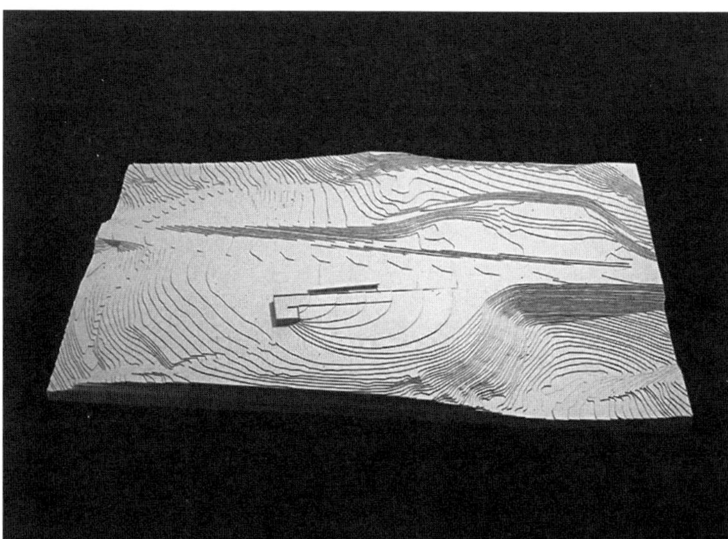

Fig. 7: Three-dimensional raised-relief model

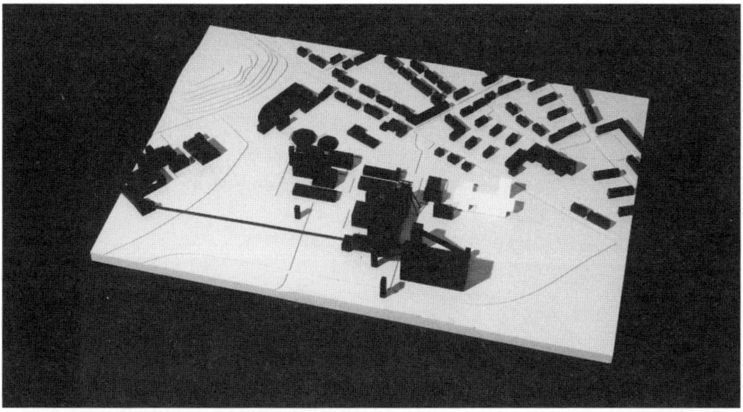

Fig. 8: The same design on a scale of 1:1,000 ...

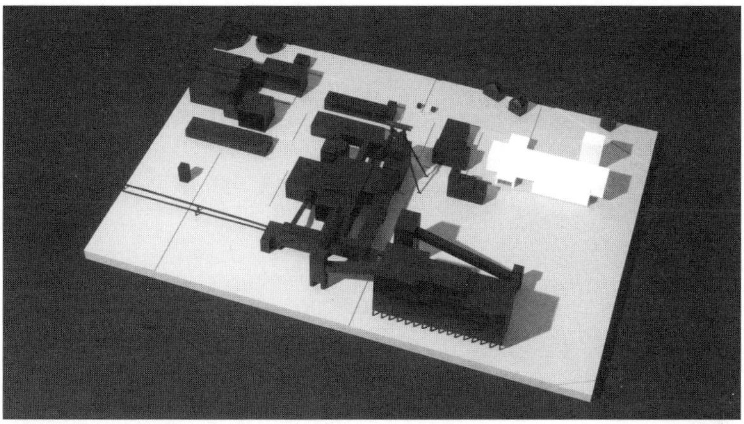

Fig. 9: ... here at 1:500

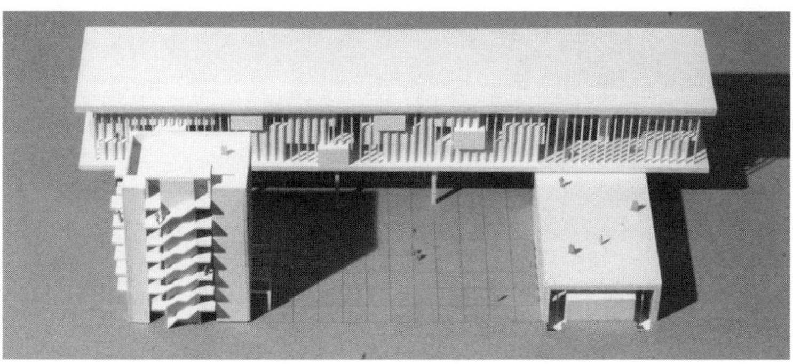

Fig. 10: ... and at 1:200

ARCHITECTURAL/BUILDING MODELS (SCALE 1:200, 1:100, 1:50)

The building model is a common illustrative tool for simulating an architectural design. While larger objects such as museums, schools and churches are usually represented on a scale of 1:200, 1:500 is common in competitions. In addition to three-dimensional forms and volumes, the design's many and diverse features play a more significant role here than in urban design models.

From drawing to model

Facade design is extremely important. On a reduced scale, the elements that are visible on the building exterior catch the eye, including:

- The facade - surface, structure, features, material qualities
- Apertures and what fills them (windows) - embrasure, wall widths
- Roof type and design - specific details such as roof overhangs or parapets

The building model can also convey information on the interior space and building structure. For example, a sectional model (divided into two parts built on separate mounting boards) can provide views of important interior rooms. In combination with removable floors and other interior components, a modeller may alternatively use a removable roof element that affords a glimpse into the model from above.

Fig. 11: Representation on different scales: 1:200 building model and 1:50 structural model

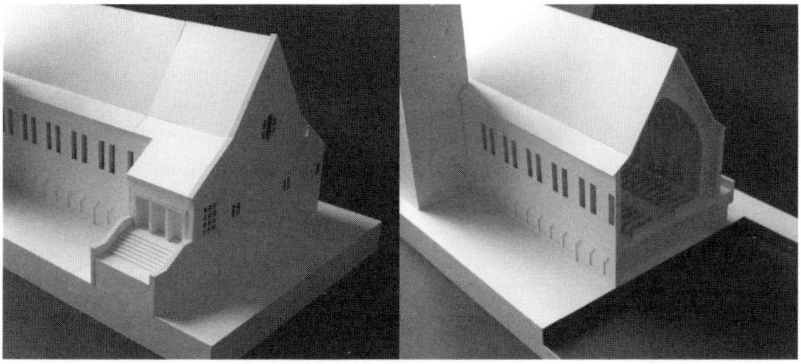

Fig. 12: Sectional model of a church (closed and open)

Fig. 13: Sectional model of a church (view of interior space)

Depending on the purpose of the design, the model can also be reduced to its structural or conceptual components for greater illustrative effect.

INTERIOR MODELS (SCALE 1:20, 1:10, 1:5, 1:1)

When spaces such as bars, chapels or living areas are depicted, it is often advantageous to use a model to provide an accurate and detailed simulation of a real situation. Abstraction plays only a subordinate role in these models. The overriding goal is to portray real objects and materials on a small scale.

How can surfaces, elements and objects be reproduced on a small scale while maintaining the effect they have on the structure as a whole? Let us use the model of a chapel interior to explain the process. The design uses just a few materials for the finished building. Combined in a simple way, they possess the specific properties that are crucial for the spatial atmosphere and the overall concept. The linoleum floor of the real building is reproduced with linoleum in the model. Wood composite board is painted white to represent the real white plaster surfaces. Glass is used for glass. The resulting construction is both a three-dimensional model and a collage of materials.

The best way to simulate a real material is to use it in the model. For instance, model builders can reproduce fair-faced concrete in a large-scale model using concrete. They need only to build miniature formwork, fill it with a fine mixture of cement and sand, pack it down and let it dry.

Fig. 14: Model of chapel interior – scale 1:10

Fig. 15: Modelled interior of a tea salon – scale 1:20

The results are impressive! In this case, modelmaking scales down the entire construction process, simulating not only the finished object, but the process itself.

The general rule is: the factors that have the greatest influence on the effect of the real building must be successfully reproduced in the model. This will make the model an effective representation of designed space. Modellers often achieve a stunning effect with their interior models, making it impossible for viewers to distinguish between a photograph of the modelled space and the real spatial situation.

DETAILED MODELS (SCALE 1:20, 1:10, 1:5, 1:1)

Detailed models are not only used in the field of interior design but also as structural or technical models (details). In principle, these models can be made on a scale of up to a 1:1, although in this case it would probably be more accurate to call them "prototypes." Model builders must first decide whether they wish to include furniture, lamps and similar details, and how they can do so most effectively. Creativity knows no bounds when it comes to putting old objects to new uses. Such objects can provide a basis for 1:10 scale models of tables and chairs or serve as simple building blocks or abstract volumes.

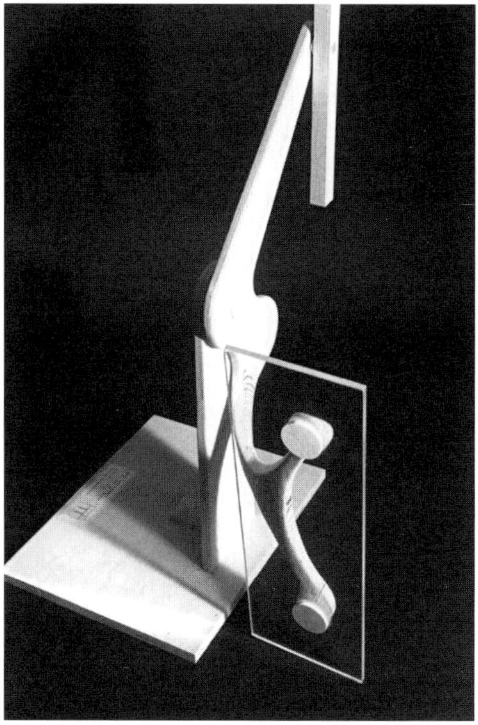

Fig. 16: Mounting points of adjustable sun screen – scale 1:1

Fig. 17: Multiplex plywood cabinet handle – scale 1:1

Design and concept development

Even a model needs a concept

Modelmaking is a creative process that requires a design concept in addition to the right tools and materials. > Chapter Equipment, tools and techniques The finished architectural model must be an aesthetic object that impresses people with its content and design. The following explanations are offered to help students develop designs:

- Color - monochrome or polychrome models
- Material contrasts - differing material properties
- Composition
- Proportions
- Level of detail ("abstraction")

COLOR AND MATERIALS

Monochrome models

After deciding whether a model should be built of wood, cardboard, metal or plastic, modellers must determine how many different materials they need in total. Generally speaking, one material will suffice if it can be modified in different ways. The advantage of surfaces with a uniform texture and color is that the represented space will remain the focus and not compete with the material or the model itself for attention. Building monochrome models is a common approach. Most models in architectural competitions are executed as "white models" of plaster and polystyrene plastic: the goal is to direct the viewer's eye exclusively to the architectural or urban design project. Wooden models usually require only one type of wood. It goes without saying that the aesthetics of the selected material will be shown to best effect if other components do not detract from them. If it is nevertheless important to differentiate between components or elements, modellers can use paints, clear varnishes etc. > Chapter Materials

Differentiating elements and surfaces is part of the design concept. Accurately simulating the combination of elements in the model is thus a time-tested method of modelmaking.

A few architectural examples:

- Smooth plaster surfaces can be combined with a roughly textured brick wall.
- Solid concrete and stone elements can be used to contrast light, delicate structures of wood and steel.
- Transparent or translucent elements (glass building envelope) can be combined with opaque sections.

Fig. 18: A three-color building model: the terrain is grey, the building anthracite black and natural brown (scale of complete model 1:200; detail 1:50).

If contrast is part of the architectural idea, it should generally be featured in the model. In such cases, representing materials in a simplified way to create a more abstract impression does not give the necessary clarity and precision. However, if different materials are combined, modellers should stick to what is absolutely essential to avoid a hodgepodge of materials.

COMPOSITION AND PROPORTION

Modelmaking replicates a process that has already taken place during the design work. The most important question is how materials can be combined to exploit their contrasts, whether hard or soft, dark or light, heavy or light, rough or fine. A great deal of experimentation may be necessary to make the final selection and to ensure that the composition of materials captures what the modeller wishes to convey. It is only after these issues have been resolved that the actual modelmaking should begin.

Interplay of elements

How do we "compose" a model? The goal is to enhance the design concept using the methods of modelmaking.

Modellers should first consider the following questions:

- How can the detail be selected so that the building model is in proportion to the dimensions of the overall representation?
- Will the project be positioned at the center of the representation, or are there reasons to abandon this principle?
- What are the relationships between the individual elements within the model (color, material qualities, proportions)?

■ **Tip:** The size and format of the mounting board has a large influence on the effect of the model. You can hardly go wrong by choosing a square, the golden section, side proportions of 1:2, or by adapting the board to the format of architectural plans. Another option is to base the shape of the mounting board on that of the building: the effect of a long narrow building will be enhanced if a long, narrow mounting board is used.

ABSTRACTION AND LEVEL OF DETAIL

Along with the right materials, the mode of representation plays a key role in determining the final result. It is essential that all parts of the model have the same degree of abstraction. For example, there is no sense in accurately reproducing the site and the surrounding buildings if the model of the new building remains abstract.

Establishing the scale of the model will determine the level of abstraction. In modelmaking, abstraction means stripping things down to their essentials. Non-essential items can be ignored or left out. But what exactly are the essentials?

Abstraction = interpretative freedom

In this context, it is important to consider the effects of the selected level of abstraction: a precise, detailed model lays claim to portraying a sound, thought-out design. If the model is meant to provide a great deal of information, viewers will be given relatively little freedom in imagining it. A detailed, miniature version of the real structure will convey a very concrete idea of the intention of the design and keep viewers from imagining their own details. As a rule of thumb, a high level of detail is an advantage when dealing with clients and laypeople. The more realistic the model, the clearer the impression people will have of the building and the architecture.

What degrees of detail are possible in modelmaking? In principle, the only limits are what is technically possible, or what is possible within the given deadline. If a window is too small to be cut out with a utility knife at the selected scale, it should be left out.

Fig. 19: Examples of different levels of abstraction

A more abstract model tends to convey principles and ideas, with details fleshed out at a later stage. The model remains conceptual. Architects often prefer this type of minimalist representation to grant free rein to the imagination and to enable various interpretations of the subsequent building. They are not forced to commit themselves.

Accessories

The use of trees, figures, cars and other accessories in modelmaking must also be considered in conjunction with the level of abstraction. It is often easier to convey a concrete idea of a design to a lay audience if the model depicts not only the architecture and the site but also elements that are familiar to them from daily life, such as cars, trees, plants and people. "Human scale" is the most important yardstick in real life, but it is not always apparent in a model. > Chapters Materials, Accessories: trees, figures and cars

Precision

Modelmaking is often associated with terms like perfectionism, exact workmanship and precise execution. These standards are generally justified when presentation models are made, but precision on its own does guarantee a good model. It is not even the prerequisite for one. An idea can be portrayed clearly without a lot of work. More important than perfection is the modeller's "signature" style, which we have mentioned above, and which gives the model the required expressive power. As a creative approach, a broad stroke can be as effective as the detailed representation of the large object on a miniature scale.

Equipment, tools and techniques

When building small spatial objects, many students will feel the same passion that drew them to architecture as a profession in the first place. Others will prefer pencils and drawings to the tools of the modellers' trade. Whatever their preference, all architectural students will be confronted with the demands of modelmaking in their very first semester. What is the simplest way to build a model?

CUTTING

The simplest method is to work with a utility knife and a piece of paperboard or cardboard. The utility knife is an essential modelmaking tool since it can be used to cut a variety of materials in their original form. It is simple and inexpensive, and many different versions are available for different cutting tasks. We recommend purchasing a high-quality knife instead of the simple carpet knives found in many home improvement stores. The blade must be firmly attached and must not move during cutting. Ideally, the knife will fit comfortably in the hand so that it can be held and guided effectively. The selection of a knife is just as important ○ as the choice of a good pencil.

In addition to the universally deployable utility knife, a variety of other cutting tools are available at speciality shops. The scalpel, the well-known surgical instrument, can be used to make fine cuts in materials or cut out ■ very small windows from cardboard.

○ **Note:** Many modellers have had painful experiences with the utility knife, especially when working under time pressure. To minimize the risk of injury, you should always handle tools with the utmost care and only use them for the work for which they are intended. For instance, you should not to try to cut a hard piece of wood with a utility knife due to the danger of slipping.

■ **Tip:** When using a utility knife to cut cardboard, you should hold the knife as close to the surface as possible in order to make precise, clean cuts. If this is not done correctly, the material may tear and increase the risk of injury since the sharp blade is more likely to slip.

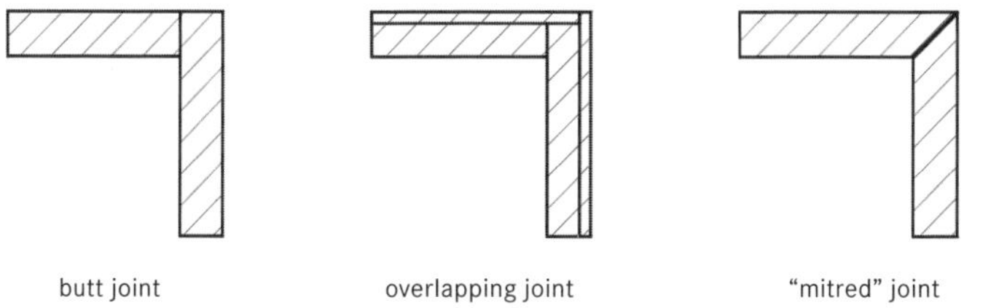

Fig. 20: Ways of joining materials at corners

Fig. 21: Corners – examples and approaches

How should cuts be made? First, the required edge should be marked with a thin pencil; after cutting, this thin mark will no longer be visible. The edge should then be cut at a 90° angle to the surface so that the individual parts can be butt-jointed or glued together.

At corners the edges of the material can also be cut at a 45° angle to form mitred joints. Special utility knives with slanted blades are available to make such cuts. Another method is to make a wooden board with a 45° edge and use it as a kind of a template for guiding the blade of a standard utility knife.

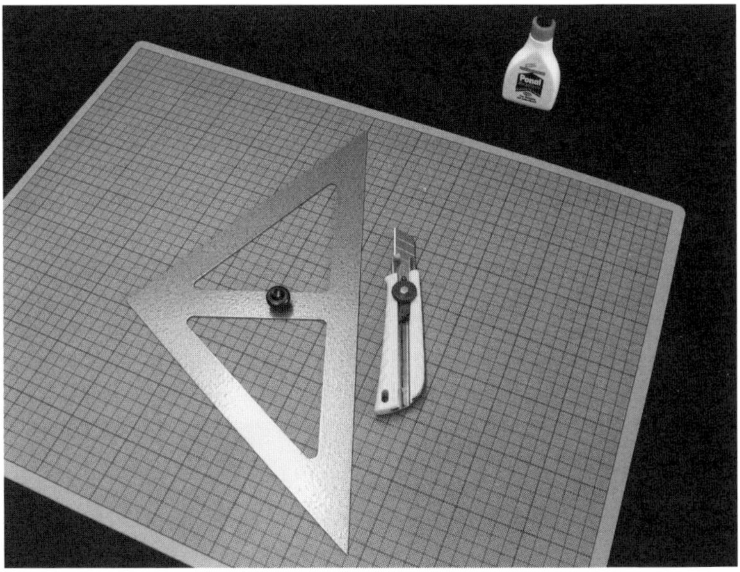

Fig. 22: Basic equipment for building architectural models – utility knife, cutting ruler, cutting mat and glue

In other cases, a metal-edged ruler can be used to guide the knife and ensure a straight cut. Another important tool is a hard cutting mat, which not only protects the tabletop but also makes for a better quality cut than a soft base. We recommend plastic cutting mats.

These are the only tools a modellers needs to build simple, practical working models out of cardboard and pasteboard. But other tools are necessary to intensively work the material, including:

- Sandpaper: required to smooth surfaces, finish cut edges and remove sharp pieces from cut-out holes. If sandpaper is wrapped around a firm, stable base such as a sanding block, it is easier to move back and forth over the part that needs sanding.
- File: excellently suited for finishing the corners and edges of a variety of materials. Files are available for both wood and metal. It is generally possible to use the same tools when working on plastics or metals – for instance, a fine iron saw lends itself well to cutting plastic.

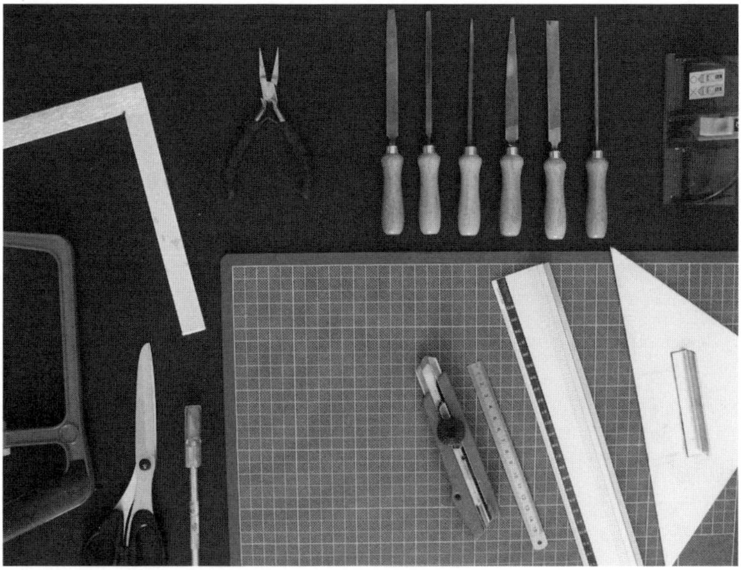

Fig. 23: Simple tools for architectural modelmaking

- Tweezers: increase the precision of the human hand and allow modellers to work on even the smallest parts. Small-scale models may contain parts that are only a few millimeters in size and nearly impossible to grasp with the fingers.
- Measuring instruments ("sliding calipers"): are used to measure diameters and cross sections accurately. Since the trained eye can detect even the tiniest size differences on a small-scale model, precise measurements are an important aspect of modelmaking. Precision extends to one tenth of one millimeter, a unit that cannot be measured with normal rulers.
- Measuring tools (ruler and measuring stick): for the precise measurement of lengths and dimensions.

■ **Tip:** Before gluing the model together, you should first find out about the most suitable glue. Most glues are sold in containers and do not include a tool for applying the glue properly. As a result, you may apply too much glue and leave unsightly stains.

One way to remedy this situation is to buy a standard syringe with a wide canula from a pharmacy and fill it with the selected glue. This method can be very useful when gluing transparent plastic films since stains on these materials are eye-catching and bothersome.

An even simpler method is to apply daubs of glue using a toothbrush or a thin wooden stick.

GLUING

Depending on the materials to be glued, modellers have a wide range of products at their disposal. Whereas all-purpose glues can be used universally for many different materials, white glue is the perfect choice for all types of wood, wood-based materials and cardboard.

Tab. 1: Overview of glues

Glue	Properties	Application
All-purpose glue	Generally a solvent-based artificial resin adhesive that is transparent, viscous and may become stringy when applied. Reacts with some plastics (e.g. Styrofoam), melting their surfaces. Usually dries in just a few minutes. A light irritant; non-aging	Can be used for various materials (e.g. cardboard, wood, plastics, metals, glass, fabric etc.). Parts can be glued to the same or different materials. The glue does not cause cardboard to buckle and is often all that is needed in modelmaking thanks to its great diversity.
White glue (wood glue)	Has a white, viscous consistency and dries by absorbing the moisture in the bonded material. Transparent and slow drying, meaning the glued surfaces can be moved for a while after application. Fast-drying "express glue" dries in 3–5 minutes.	Ideal for woods, wood-based materials, cardboard and paperboard. The parts must be pressed together for an effective bond. The glue's high moisture content may change the shape of the material and cause cardboard to buckle. Not suitable for plastics, metals or materials that cannot absorb moisture.

Contact glue	Used to bond large surfaces. The glue is applied to both parts and bonds with itself. After application, the parts must dry for a few minutes before they are bonded together, and it is important to apply firm pressure. Contact glue should only be used in well-ventilated rooms.	Ideal for gluing large surfaces (e.g. cardboard) in raised-relief models. Since the glue is applied to both parts and the room must be ventilated, this is a time-consuming method, but it has the advantage of not buckling the materials. Can be used for wood, cardboard, a large number of plastics, metals and ceramics.
Plastic-bonding adhesives	A fluid, usually clear glue containing solvent. Specially designed for plastics and the single-sided application of glue. The parts must be joined quickly while the glue is still wet, and the surfaces must be free of dust and grease.	Can be used for many thermoplastics, including polystyrene, PVC and perspex, but not suitable for polyethylene or polypropylene. Can also be used to bond wood or cardboard (see all-purpose glue), and are more effective than all-purpose glue for plastics.
Super glue	Transparent, very fast-drying glue; viscous and non-dripping.	Ideal for connections that cannot be held together and that require an instant bond.
Spray glue	Colorless, UV-resistant, CFC-free glue that comes in a spray bottle and does not change color when applied. Due to its low moisture content, it does not permeate the material. Spray glue should only be used out of doors or in well-ventilated rooms.	Ideal for application to large surfaces, such as in cardboard raised-relief models. The materials may buckle or warp slightly, but do not usually wrinkle. Can also be used to glue paper or cardboard to different backgrounds, especially when large surfaces must be glued.
Solvent	Used to bond plastics. The solvent melts the surface of the material, and pressure is applied to "weld" the two parts together. Example: dichloromethane (methylene dichloride), which like all organic solvents is extremely harmful to human health.	For gluing polystyrene, perspex or polycarbonates; bonds both parts without residue by dissolving the thermoplastic resin. Use only in very well-ventilated rooms.
Rubber cement	An elastic adhesive that is easy to remove, normally without any residue. If applied to both parts, it creates a permanent bond.	Can be used for various materials including paper, cardboard and plastics. Ideal for use in working models or montages.

Double-sided tape	A basic alternative to fluid bonding agents, useful because of its instant bond. The properties of the bonded materials are not adversely affected by moisture.	Can be used for bonding large surfaces, and ideal for all types of materials, including PE and PP, which cannot be joined with other adhesives. The materials do not buckle, warp or wrinkle. Not suitable for joining small points.

MODELLING, SHAPING AND CASTING

Working with modelling clay

An alternative method for building working models is to use plasticine or another modelling clay.

Plasticine is usually sold as a greyish-green modelling material whose plasticity varies with temperature. It is hard to knead plasticine at room temperature, but it becomes softer and easier to work once it is slightly warmed up (e.g. on a warm radiator). Plasticine can also be heated in a pot, and in fluid form, it can be applied to a surface with a putty knife or brush.

Modelling clay lends itself well to experimental work with a model. It is excellently suited to studies of urban space and enables modellers quickly to build many different versions of the same object. Small structures can be quickly and easily cut off with a knife.

By working the clay with their hands or tools, modellers can gain a feel for the manual work and its results. The finished object may not be a very precise model, but the modelled form can be a very expressive way of representing space.

Plaster and pouring compounds

Plaster (gypsum) is an inexpensive material that is very easy to work with. Even so, making a plaster model is a time-consuming process because it requires two steps:

- First, an exact negative mould is made of the subsequent three-dimensional object and liquid gypsum is poured into it. The precision of the mould determines the quality of the final result.
- After the plaster dries, the cast object is removed from the mould.

Fig. 24: Plasticine models

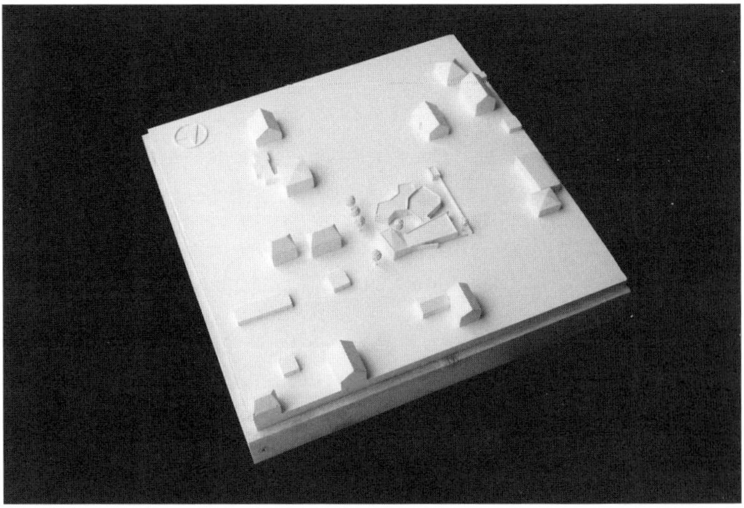

Fig. 25: Urban development model made of white plaster and spray-painted subsequently with a white latex paint

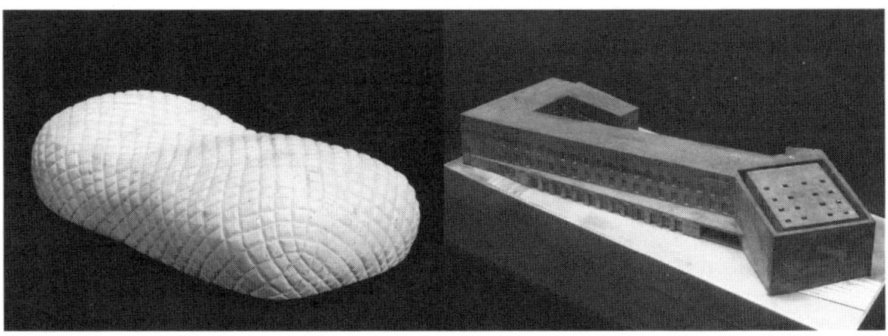

Fig. 26: Plaster models showing the form of the building (white), colored with pigments

Fig. 27: Concrete model portraying a solid concrete building

Plaster models are often used in architectural competitions, particularly for urban design models, since here the same site model must be made several times and using a single mould is convenient. Colors can be portrayed by adding pigments or liquid paint to the plaster or by smoothing and painting the surface after it dries. These models not only create a solid, heavy impression, but are solid and heavy themselves.

It goes without saying that other pouring compounds can be used besides plaster. If fair-faced concrete needs to be represented, modellers can use concrete in the model.

MACHINES IN THE MODELLING WORKSHOP

The simple tools and methods described here are sufficient for working with easily processed materials. However, many materials require the use of machines and professional tools in order to achieve the desired result. Working with machines

Many professional architectural modellers use the same tools that can be found in most carpenters' workshops: Tools in the carpenter's workshop

- Handsaws
- Files, rasps and sanding blocks
- Planes
- Chisels and mallets
- Set squares

A power saw is commonly used when a utility knife is no longer sufficient. Although a knife can be used to work on veneer, wood is a material that usually requires the use of a saw. Sawing

Fig. 28: Typical handheld tools in a wood workshop

Fig. 29: Circular saw

Fig. 30: Jig saw

In addition to the usual commercial table saws – saws with round blades and benches – table saws of a smaller size, called micro table saws, are also available for (professional) modellers. If the correct blade is used, these fine power tools can be used for cross cutting and profiling wood, as well as for cutting plastic. It is very helpful to have precisely these kinds of tools at hand when building wooden models. With the use of the fence, it is possible to cut materials both across and with the grain. It should be noted, however, that students will require a certain amount of training and time to become familiar with such saws and the specific features of materials to be worked.

In addition to the table saw, which is useful for straight cuts, the band saw is an important tool for curved and free-form cuts. This machine is useful for sawing solid wood cross sections. Jig saws are also useful for cutting free-form and curved lines.

Planing

A plane is used to reduce the thickness of wood or to modify the surface of cross sections. By planing the surface of terrain models, the modeller can make differences in elevation more apparent.

■ **Tip:** Using wood for architectural modelling is extremely attractive, as the result lives from the aesthetic of this material. Even so, use of the required machines like the table saw or grinding machines should be supervised by professional joiners or modellers, particularly at the beginning.

■ **Tip:** In addition to tools available in hardware stores and DIY centers, creative modellers can often make their own tools using very simple materials. A good example is a miniature file consisting of a thin piece of square iron pipe and fine sandpaper. It is also possible to use everyday items. For instance, a clothespeg works well as a clamp when gluing.

Fig. 31: Band saw

Fig. 32: Table saw

Fig. 33: Micro table saw for precise cutting

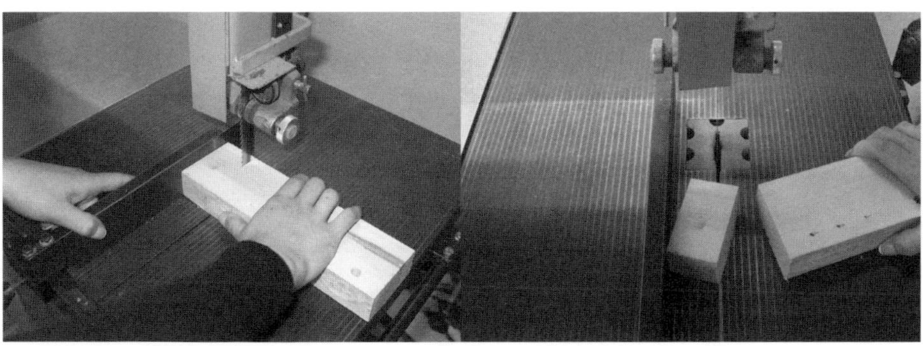

Fig. 34: Sawing wood using a band saw

Fig. 35: Planing a surface using either a traditional smoothing plane or an electric one

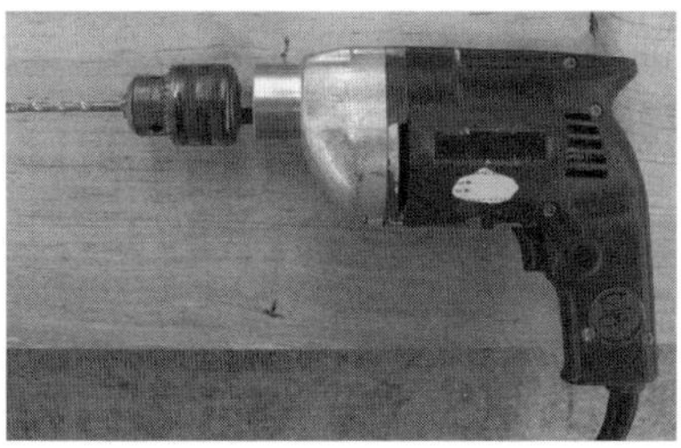

Fig. 36: A handheld power drill with no type of guidance system

Drilling

A drill is useful for making connections, for example when dowels are used on the base of a model to represent columns or trees. Holes bored in the base material are perfect connections for these elements and increase stability as well.

Of utmost importance when using a drill is the correct guidance of the tool. In workshops, drills are usually clamped into a drill stand so that the angle at which the drill enters the material can be set precisely and locked in place. The micro drills available for modelling have very small chucks and can be used with drills with a diameter of less than one millimeter.

Milling

A milling machine enables a modeller to cut into the surface of wood.

The different types of milling bits > Fig. 37 that can be attached to the machine allow modellers to cut roads, rivers, depressions and other features into the surface of a raised-relief model. This machine offers new woodworking options in addition to those possible with the saws outlined above.

Fig. 37: A drill in a drill stand – for precise and right-angled drilling

Fig. 38: A milling machine

Sanding

There are various ways to sand an object in order to produce the final shapes and surfaces. Power tools make the work much easier than manual sanding with sandpaper. It is of fundamental importance when sanding that the proper type of sandpaper – e.g. for metal or wood – be used for each material. Coarse sanding can be done using coarsely grained sandpaper, and a finely grained paper should be used afterwards. A power disc sander is a very helpful tool. A rotating sanding disc is combined with a flat work surface so that large surface areas can be finely sanded. Just as with table saws, micro sanders are also available to carry out the fine and precise operations necessary for precise modelmaking.

In addition to flat disc sanders there are also tools with rounded sanding surfaces, which are useful for the smoothing off round shapes. They include belt sanders and oscillating sanders, which are guided by hand across the surface in question.

HOT WIRE CUTTERS

A hot wire cutter (Styrocut) is a common tool among architecture students. It allows for the simple, fast and precise cutting of thick polystyrene foam and can be used to make individual pieces for an urban design model or mass models during the planning process. The hot wire

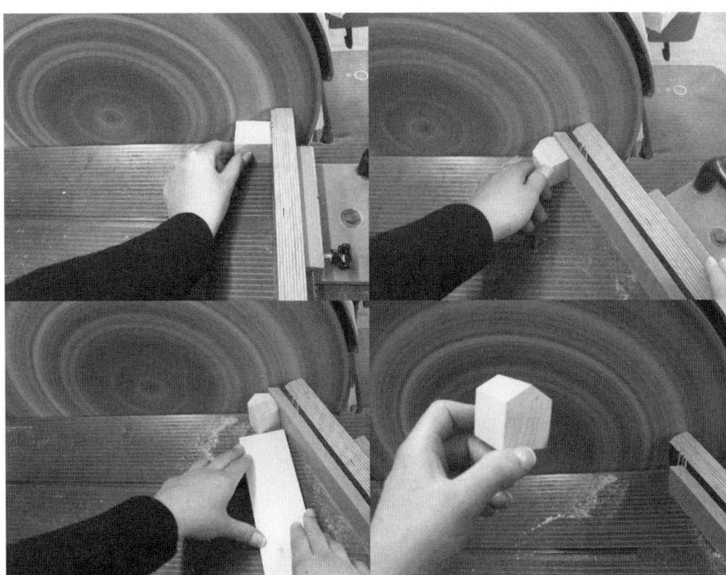

Fig. 39: The fine sanding of wood with a disc sander, here for an urban design model

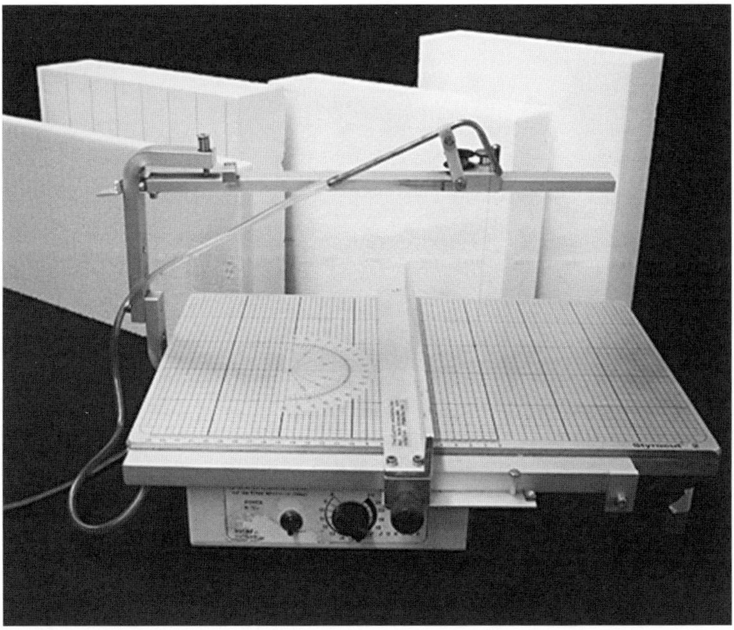

Fig. 40: Hot wire cutter and polystyrene foam

cutter consists of a cutting table and a fine wire, which is heated up by a low voltage energy supply and slices through the foam material.

COMPUTER MILLING

The use of computers has transformed the field of architecture, particularly in representing complex organic forms and structures. CAD software and CNC (computerized numerical control) milling machines – a modern digital tool for architectural modelling – have played the biggest role in this change. Strictly speaking, the use of CNC milling for three-dimensional representation involves nothing more than the use of CAD software for two-dimensional drafting. Just as the draughtsperson's methods have been digitalized, so has architectural modelling by the CNC milling machine.

Technically, CNC milling machines, which are usually controlled along three spatial axes (x, y and z) by the computer, are able to produce models with an extremely high degree of precision and perfection. The cutting and engraving bit cuts out geometrically and spatially complex shapes from a variety of suitable materials, just as a digital plotter can produce finer and more accurate line drawings than can be made using manual

○ **Note:** Depending on the design, CNC milling machines can speed up the modelling process enormously, particularly when reproducing facades with many apertures. Colleges, professional architectural modellers and companies that make moulds and prototypes commonly offer the use of their machines at fixed hourly rates.

methods. In addition, models can be produced as often as desired, and the individual parts are always identical. This machine therefore opens a broad field of possibilities for graphic representation that were not available before. Some passionate modellers nevertheless feel that items produced using CNC milling machines have no character of their own.

Many universities now offer these new digital methods in addition to traditional modelling workshops as part of architectural studies. Depending on the type of machine, all necessary modelling data (base topography or information about a building, including the structure of the facade in vectorized form) must be available before any milling can take place. These data enable the machine to cut the correct shapes out of the material. Problems occur if the milling machine's software cannot adequately translate the CAD file (due to older file standards, for example). This means that everything has to be drawn once again.

Fig. 41: CNC milling machine

■ **Tip:** During the milling process, which involves digitally converting the two-dimensional drawing into a three-dimensional spatial object, all mistakes in the drawing will become visible. It is thus important to consider the following points:

- Lines must always be cleanly and precisely connected at their endpoints.
- Double lines cannot be used.
- Lines must be assigned colors in such a way that the milling machine is able to define the right and left sides of a line.

To achieve optimum results with CNC milling machines, modellers must allow sufficient time for test runs with this modern technology. It is important to note whether the cutting head moves to the left or right of a pre-defined line, or directly on the line itself.

Not all materials are suited for use with a CNC machine. Aluminum, brass, steel and stainless steel can be used in sheet form (a thickness of 3 mm to 5 mm is common). Perspex of superior (moulded) quality can be used in thicknesses of up to 10 cm, as is the case for plastics such as polystyrene. Wood products such as plywood (e.g. birch and multiplex plywood, and MDF) can also be used.

3D PLOTTER

Many universities and professional model-building workshops now use 3D plotters in addition to CNC milling machines. A 3D plotter enables replication of three-dimensional CAD volumes. This is particularly useful in the case of amorphous and sculptural forms. The equipment generally functions in a similar manner to the layers of cardboard in a terrain model, with the plotter computationally dividing the CAD model into thin slices. Viscous plaster equivalents of these layers are then laid one atop the other on a foundation plate, in the form of viscous plaster. The three-dimensional form is successively constructed, layer by layer. Disadvantages of this model building process include costs being higher than for conventional models due to the materials used and the need for the raw CAD data to be free of errors. Where 3D bodies are not fully defined, lines are not solid or non-differentiated interpenetrations exist, processing the CAD data quickly becomes problematic.

Materials

Which material for which model?

Strictly speaking, a model is nothing more than a scaled-down version of an existing situation or a future building. In the practice of modelling this means that actual surfaces are transformed into a model through a process of abstraction. An attempt is nevertheless made to retain the specific qualities of materials and the effect they might have, because in the end a building's appearance comes primarily from the sum of the materials from which it is made. Materials are matte or shiny, rough or smooth, heavy and solid or light and filigree. This raises the question of which materials the model should incorporate in order to simulate reality best. In this regard modelling is the same as real construction. A wide variety of materials are available. Some have been used in architectural modelling for a long time and are considered "classic" materials; others are new; and others still were originally intended for different purposes. Specific characteristics are necessary to create particular effects. Glass can be simulated using transparent materials, water by reflective materials, and walls can be reproduced using layered materials made of small modules with a regularly or irregularly structured surface.

Below, materials are described together with their uses and methods of preparation. Materials can be categorized on the basis of their specific sources:

- Paper, paperboard and cardboard
- Wood and wood-based products
- Metals
- Plastics

Other important materials are:

- Paints and varnishes
- Plaster and clay
- Plasticine and modelling clay
- Prefabricated parts for modelling such as figures, vehicles and other accessories

○ **Note:** Most projects can be easily built using these materials. In addition their ease of use, they have the advantage of being inexpensive and readily available in many places.

Fig. 42: Modelling paperboard – a selection of different colors and textures

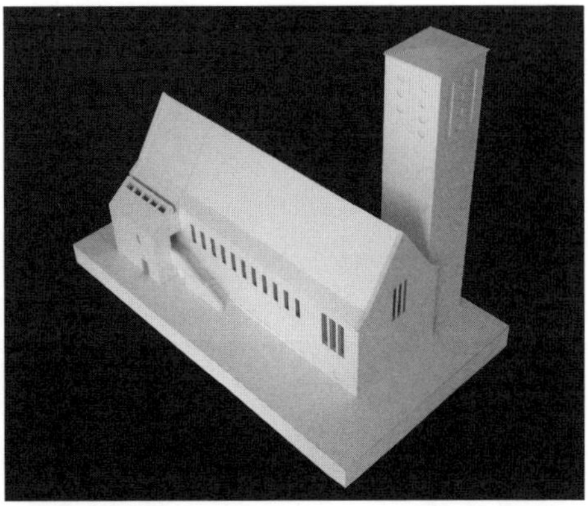

Fig. 43: Paperboard model – all parts are made of the same material

PAPER, PAPERBOARD AND CARDBOARD

A wide variety of these materials exist on the market, and there is no limit to the creativity with which they can be used in architectural modelling. Many products, including grey paperboard, were actually developed for the packaging industry but are nonetheless very popular among modellers.

Table 2 (page 287) gives an overview of the most common types of paperboard. Paper, including colored paper or tracing paper, is also a useful material for modelling. Cardboard, sold under names such as Mill blank, colored board, glossy board or Chromalux board, can also be used, as can paper and cardboard with structured surface textures. ○

Photo cardboard

Photo cardboard, like thinner colored paper, is particularly well suited for representing different colored surfaces. It is available from many manufacturers in a wide variety of colors, and is a stable material for the work due to its thickness.

Glossy cardboard

Glossy cardboard's name leaves little doubt as to the material's special feature. Because of its glossy exterior this cardboard is always suitable for representing reflecting or mirrored surfaces. Its many different colors are also an advantage in addition to its shine.

Fig. 44: Model made of grey paperboard

Fig. 45: Model made of Finnboard

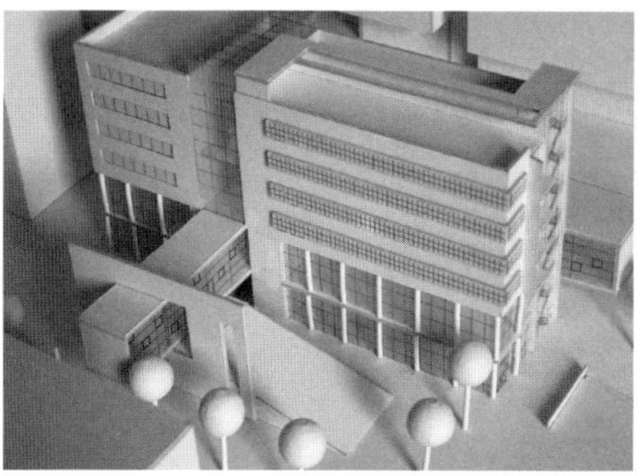

Fig. 46: A model made of white-coated paperboard

Fig. 47: A model made of dyed white paperboard (Chromalux)

Corrugated cardboard/wellboard

Materials that are inexpensive or available for free are always very practical for building working models. Corrugated cardboard is primarily produced and used for packaging and can be "recycled" and used for modelling. The advantages that the material brings to packaging also apply to modelling:

- It is easy to cut using a utility knife
- Thicknesses of up to 6 mm make it easy to work with
- The structure of this material (corrugated cardboard core, covered on both sides with smooth cardboard) means that it keeps its shape and remains stiff despite its light weight
- It is also suitable for use with raised-relief models

Tab. 2: Paperboard – uses and characteristics

Material	Properties	Use	Processing
Finnish wood pulp board (also known as Finnboard)	Made of wood fibres; beige, woody color; darkens when exposed to sunlight (yellowing); smooth and rough textures; available in thicknesses approx. 1.0–4.0 mm	General use for topographic layers and buildings, interior models with simulated daylight (due to its light surface)	Easy to cut; easy to stick together using white or all-purpose glue; surfaces can be varnished or painted to prevent yellowing or aging
Grey paperboard	100% recycled; warm grey tone; smooth and rough textures; available in approx. 0.5–4.0 mm thicknesses according to manufacturer	General use for topographic layers and buildings	Easy to cut; easy to stick together using white or all-purpose glue; surfaces can be varnished or painted
Serigraphy board	Wood fibreboard with bonded texture; available in approx. 1.0–3.0 mm thickness	Ideal for spatial models (scale 1:50); simulation of light due to white surface color	Easy to cut; easy to stick together using white or all-purpose glue; surfaces can be painted with acrylic paints or printed with silk-screen dyes

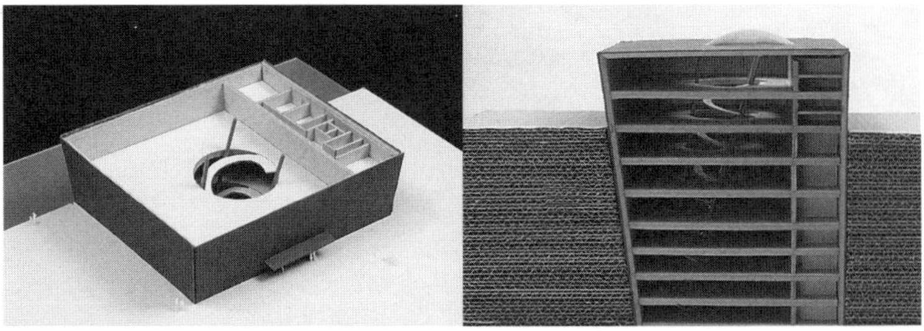

Fig. 48: Model made of corrugated cardboard showing a building extending below a site's surface (layers of earth)

Fig. 49: Combination of grey board (site) and birch plywood

Fig. 50: Urban design model made of one kind of wood (homogenous)

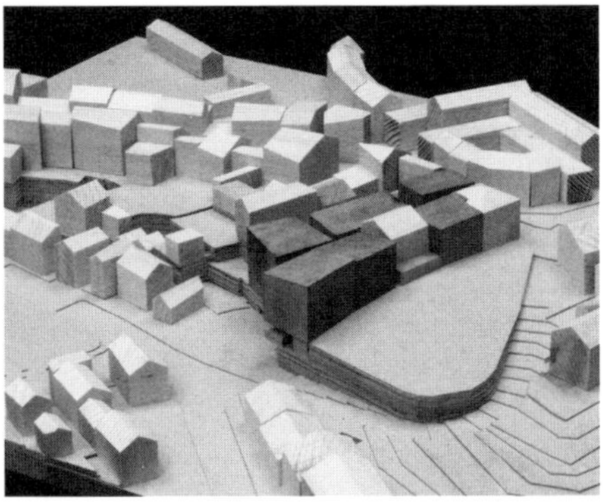

Fig. 51: Urban design model made of different kinds of wood (contrast)

Fig. 52: Wood: Veneer boards and strips

WOOD AND WOOD-BASED MATERIALS

Wood has been used longer than any other "construction material" for building architectural models. Even Michelangelo used the wood of a linden tree to make a model of Saint Peter's dome. Wood is much more work-intensive than paperboard; the results, however, are much more impressive. Wood is used above all for presentation models. As a natural raw material, wood has its own aesthetic, which is expressed independently of an architecture model's shape, design and finish. Nuances in color and the structure of the grain give wood the appearance of a "living" component of a model.

There are two basic categories: naturally grown and dried wood, and industrially processed wood-based products. Both are used in modelling. ■

■ **Tip:** A wide variety of good-quality wood is available at timber yards as well as in small carpentry workshops and wood-processing firms. An overview of the various types of wood from all over the world is nearly impossible, but professionals are usually happy to advise architects and students about the correct choice of wood for modelling. It may also be possible to observe carpenters and cabinetmakers as they work, and learn about how they deal with wood.

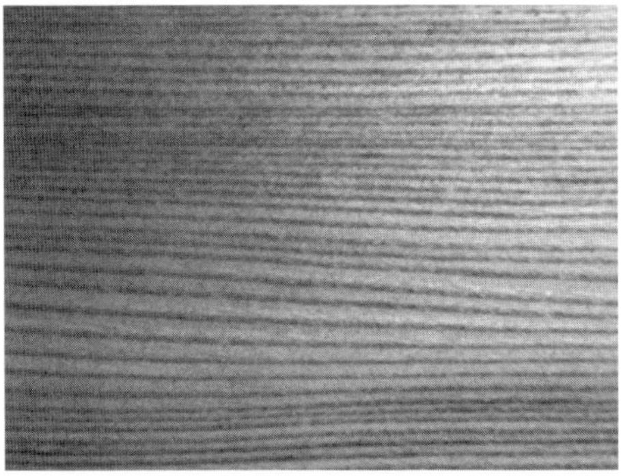

Fig. 53: Rich in contrast, with an even grain (e.g. elm)

Fig. 54: Dark and finely grained (e.g. wengé)

Fig. 55: Grainy, yellow-beige wood (e.g. oak)

Fig. 56: Strongly grained wood, "busy" surface (e.g. zebrawood or Macassar ebony)

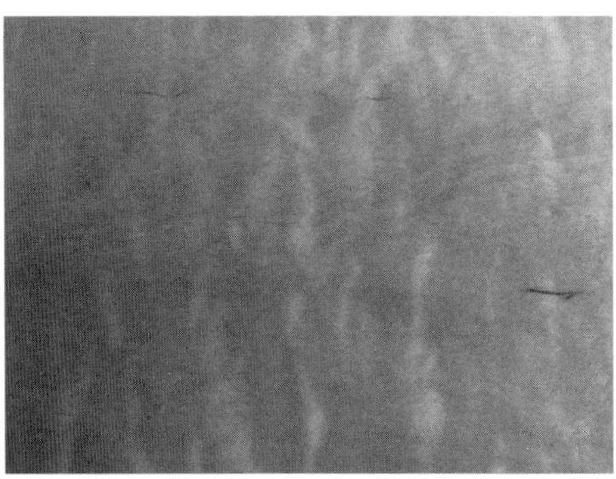

Fig. 57: Light-colored wood with a cloudy grain (e.g. birch)

Fig. 58: Even, light-colored wood with a fine grain (e.g. pear, reddish, or maple)

Tab. 3: Wood – uses and properties

Tree species	Properties	Use	Processing
Abachi	Soft, light hardwood, low strength, light colored, straw-yellow, slightly structured surface	Used for making decks in model ships. Veneer strips are used to represent wood surfaces (grooved, structured)	Veneer strips can be easily cut with a utility knife (along the grain). They bond excellently with white glue, or with an extensively applied spray adhesive
Balsa	The lightest of all commercial timbers. Shines slightly, has a whitish surface and a soft, velvety, homogenous structure	Especially suitable for making model aircraft. Veneer strips are used to represent wood; wood profiles to represent buildings	Simple to cut with utility knife or saw. The wood can break easily along the grain; very easy to bond with white glue
Beech	Strong hardwood, fine, uniform grain structure, light brownish-red color	Suitable for all kinds of models: wooden blocks for representing urban developments; veneers for surfaces and model buildings	With standard wood-processing tools. Can be sawn and sanded. Very easy to bond with white glue
Linden (lime)	Short-fibred, soft hardwood, plain surface, yellowish, light color	One of the woods most commonly used in model construction. It is suitable for most purposes	Depending on dimensions, linden is very easy to process with a utility knife and saw
Mahogany	Very hard tropical wood, slightly shiny surface, dark, reddish-brown color	Used to contrast with all light-colored woods and modelling materials	Owing to its hardness it can only be processed with a saw and sanding tools

Maple	Soft hardwood, yellowish natural white color; fine, differentiated grain pattern	Can be used for all types of models, wooden blocks in urban planning models and veneers for surfaces and models of buildings	With standard wood-processing tools, sawing and sanding. Very easy to bond with white glue
Pear	Evenly structured hardwood, light reddish-brown with a fine surface	Suitable for all sorts of models: wooden blocks for representing urban development schemes, veneers for surfaces and model buildings	With standard wood-processing tools, sawing and sanding. Very easy to bond with white glue
Pine	Long-fibred softwood with a typical, striking surface structure, yellowish color	Its dimensional stability makes it very suitable for wood profiles in frame structures and construction models	Depending on dimensions pine is very easy to cut with both a utility knife and a saw
Walnut	Depending on origins: fine or coarse grain, deep dark brown color	Used to contrast with all light-colored woods and modelling materials. Very fine appearance	With standard wood-processing tools, sawing and sanding, very easy to bond with white glue

Wood and tree species

When a modelmaker is working with natural wood, he or she must use a kind that is also suitable for small-scale models. Coarse-grained wood species with distinct markings, such as Macassar ebony and zebrawood, are unsuitable. > Fig. 56 The surface should look smooth and plain. The woods given in Table 3 are highly recommended.

Wood-based materials

Wood-based materials, which are usually supplied as panels, are made from the waste wood generated by the timber-processing industry. In the building industry, they are used for finishing furniture and interiors as well as for making architectural models. The boards are also used for making bases, such as the loadbearing substrates of models, and for large-scale models of interiors.

Tab. 4: Wood-based materials – uses and properties

Wood-based material	Properties	Use	Processing
Chipboard	Reasonably priced wood panel, manufactured from wood shavings and glue, rough surface, material thicknesses: 6.0–22.0 mm	For making mounting boards, for depicting rough and structured surfaces with surface treatment	Processed like wood (sawing and sanding), very easy to bond with white glue. Can warp if exposed to excessive moisture
MDF	Hard, high-density wood fibreboard with homogenous, smooth board structure, high dimensional stability, flat surface, "natural brown" color or stained in many different colors, including black	For mounting boards, raised-relief models and complete, large-scale (1:50) building models	Processed like wood, very easy to bond, the surface is treated by painting or staining
Plywood (birch, beech, poplar)	Glued-laminated wood panels made of several layers of one of these species, visible grain, same color as that of the wood used	For raised-relief models and model buildings. Used as an alternative to models made of wood only, as plywood with small cross sections is also stable	Easy to process with utility knife or saw and, in some cases, with a milling machine (birch). Very easy to bond with white glue
Coreboard	Plywood made of glued wood; visible grain, same color as that of the wood used	Suitable for mounting boards and bases	Processed like wood. Owing to its composition (glued rods) it can generally bear loads in one direction only

Fig. 59: Wood as a panel material: birch multiplex boards, chipboard, MDF

Fig. 60: Model to a scale of 1:50, made of MDF panels

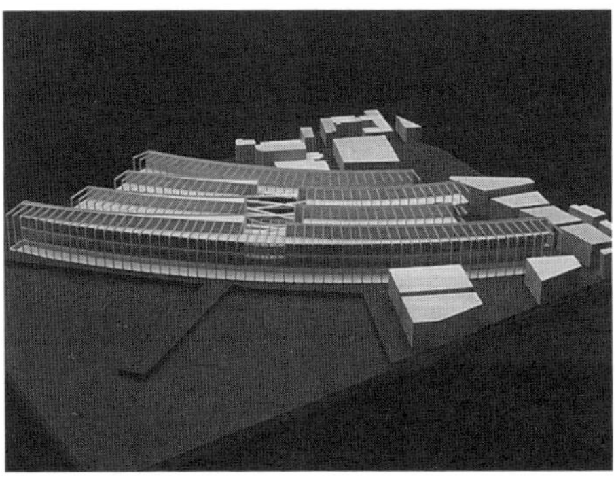

Fig. 61: Model made using MDF (painted black) for the site and linden for the design (contrast in material and color)

Fig. 62: Model made of wood profiles to show the skeleton structure and MDF for the mounting board

METALS

Special care must be taken when representing metals, since their specific properties cannot be faithfully simulated with other materials. If a material is intended to convey the aesthetic idea behind the concept, it will also affect the impression created by the model too. Filigree steel columns and tension ties are ideal for representing thin metal profiles in situations in which the specific properties of other materials would cause these to fail.

Tab. 5: Metals – uses and properties

Metal	Properties	Use	Processing
Aluminum	Silvery white, air- and water-resistant owing to thick, opaque, oxide layer that forms on the service, non-magnetic	Aluminum sheets and profiles can be used to represent metal building elements, e.g. corrugated sheet for the roof	Cannot be soldered. Bonded with glues (all-purpose glues), easy to polish, malleable
Brass	Alloy of copper and zinc. Red to light red, depending on the proportion of copper used. A golden color can be produced by using a higher proportion of zinc	Brass sheets can be used to simulate shining gold surfaces; profiles can be used for loadbearing models (girders and columns)	Can be soldered. Bonds well. Depending on strength of material, it can be processed with metal tools. Polishes well
Copper	The only red metal, oxidizes in contact with the air, turning first red and then green	Copper sheeting and profiles should be used to represent copper in the model	Can be soldered; glues well. Depending on strength of material, it can be processed with metal tools. Polishes well
Iron and steel	Dark silvery color, corrodes in contact with moisture and oxygen, resulting in formation of reddish-brown rust; magnetic	Steel sheets can be used to simulate metal surfaces, profiles can be used for loadbearing models (girders and columns)	Can be soldered and welded or bonded with all-purpose glues. Materials are corrosion protected (e.g. galvanized) or later painted. Cut with tin snips or metal-cutting saw

Nickel silver	Alloy of copper, nickel and zinc, silver color and surface, good air-corrosion resistance	Nickel silver sheets are suitable for representing metallic and shining building elements	Can be soldered; bonds well. Ideal for chipless processing (swaging)
Stainless steel (V2A)	Silvery grey, smooth, fine surface, non-magnetic. The material can be processed to stop it rusting.	Suitable for use in areas exposed to moisture (e.g. exteriors)	Bonded with glues (all-purpose glues)

Metal sheeting and profiles are used in architectural models. Smooth sheets, in thicknesses of approx. 0.2–4 mm can be used. There are also structured sheets such as channelled plates, corrugated sheeting and chequered plates; and sheets with round-hole, square-hole or elongated perforations, as well as expanded meshes.

To represent steel profiles realistically, it is also possible to buy miniature solid round profiles, round tubes, T-, L-, H- and I-profiles, square and rectangular profiles.

Fig. 63: Model of a building with a facade of very fine perforated sheeting

PLASTICS

There are so many different plastic products that it is difficult to describe them in general terms. Most plastics are malleable synthetic materials made of macromolecules. Carbon (an organic material) is one of the main constituents. All plastics can be processed easily and with a high degree of precision. Their light weight and stability combine to make them very useful in areas where other materials would be out of the question.

Polystyrene models

The most common plastic used in modelling is polystyrene (PS). Being mass-produced, polystyrene – like polypropylene (PP) and polyvinylchloride (PVC) – is inexpensive and has a wide variety of applications. Many architects and modellers work with nothing but polystyrene. As a result, a special type of design and presentation has been developed for constructing architectural models. Polystyrene is white and smooth. It is ideal for doing precision work and making filigree forms. Models made solely of polystyrene offer the desired degree of abstraction and also provide plain and simple examples of three-dimensional architecture.

Nearly perfect results can be obtained using plastics, a feature that sets them apart from other materials. It is possible to work precisely to within fractions of a millimeter, which is a great advantage when making urban planning models, for example. Furthermore, it is possible to simulate transparent elements such as glass by using thin, transparent PVC foils. Plastics are an indispensable modelling material. Polystyrene is the

Fig. 64: Plastics – a wide range of choices for modelling

○ material most widely used by architects in competition projects and in modelling in general.

Acrylic glass in modelling

After polystyrene, acrylic glass (chemical name: polymethyl methacrylate, PMMA; also known as perspex and plexiglass) is the plastic most widely used in architectural modelling. Being a thermoplastic material, it displays excellent thermal ductility. Furthermore, many of the varieties manufactured are ideal for representing glass panes, as well as glass and transparent building elements (e.g. in urban planning models). The surface can be modified. Satin matte structures can be made by grinding acrylic glass (so-called "wet grinding," with fine-grain sand paper, for example grain 600). Grid structures and patterns can be made in acrylic ■ glass by milling, grooving or scoring it with a sharp utility knife blade.

There is a very wide range of plastics and plastic products. In modelling, too, far more types are used than are described here. The only criteria for using plastic are the form and color desired and its surface properties. Among the plastic products available for modelling in the form of panels, foils and profiles, special mention should be made of polyester and polyethylene (PE plastics).

In addition to the above-mentioned "raw materials" for making architectural models, a number of other products – paints and varnishes, for instance – are also indispensable modelling materials.

○ **Note:** In modelling, PS rigid foam is often finished in a different color. Unfortunately, some paint solvents – especially if sprayed – react with the plastic compound and can even dissolve it. It is therefore advisable to carry out tests first.

■ **Tip:** Acrylic glass is often very expensive, and difficult to obtain from specialist dealers. It is therefore worth contacting processing companies or the manufacturer directly and asking for waste materials or samples.

Tab. 6: Plastics – uses and properties

Plastic	Properties	Use	Processing
Polystyrene (PS): as a duroplastic, "hard" plastic	Shock-resistant, hard plastic. Matte, white, opaque panels are used in modelling. PS is not UV-resistant. Material thicknesses 0.3–5.0 mm	Universal: in all areas of modelling	Very easy to cut with a utility knife, the surfaces are easy to polish and very easy to mill. They can be easily bonded together using solvents or special PS adhesives and contact glues. Easy to paint or varnish
Polystyrene hard foam (e.g. Styrofoam)	A porous material manufactured in panels and blocks. Not shock-resistant. The surface can be easily depressed. Available in different colors, depending on the manufacturer	For building and urban planning models	Very easy to cut with a hot wire cutter, and to cut or carve with a utility knife. It can also be polished and painted
Polypropylene (PP)	Heatproof, hard and tear-resistant plastic. In modelling, it is generally used in the form of thin, transparent or opaque foils. It has a non-scratchable surface, is UV stable, and available in various thicknesses	As a translucent foil, it is excellent for imitating matte glass surfaces and for designing lamps	Very easy to cut with a utility knife. It can be bent, folded, grooved, welted, moulded and punched. Before bonding, it must be pre-treated, e.g. with Poly-Primer

Polyvinylchloride (PVC)	Depending on the mode of manufacture, either transparent or opaque, various material thicknesses	Transparent foils make good imitation glass in models, and can be used as thin foil in many different areas	Very easy to cut with a utility knife. It can be drilled, milled or turned. PVC surfaces can be bonded together with standard plastic glues and contact glues
Polycarbonate (PC)	Very strong, impact-resistant plastic, weather resistant, fine surface, transparent or milky-translucent plastic foils	Transparent foils make good imitation glass in models, and can be used as thin foil in many different contexts. It generally has a finer and smoother surface than PVC	Very easy to cut with a utility knife. Thick sheets can be scratched and broken. PC surfaces can be bonded together with solvents and contact glue and leave no residues
Acrylic glass (PMMA)	Very transparent and bright, excellent optical properties, similar to glass. Weather-resistant plastic, available in transparent, translucent or opaque form	As a transparent material for representing glass or water	Thin foils can be easily cut with a utility knife, thicker materials must be broken or sawn; moisten before grinding and polishing. Can be easily bonded with solvents, contact glues or special glues for acrylic glass

Fig. 65: Monochrome polystyrene model, sprayed white with latex paint

Fig. 66: The facade of this model was covered with translucent foil to give it a more abstract appearance

Fig. 67: Urban planning model with buildings made of rigid expanded polystyrene

PAINTS AND VARNISHES

The surface of a material is not always the surface that will be visible on the finished model. Coats, films and paint finishes may be applied to many different grounds in order to modify the original design. These products also improve the resistance of the surface (insolation, UV light resistance, water-resistant surfaces, preventing yellowing).

Tab. 7: Paints and varnishes – areas of application

Paints and varnishes	Use	Result
Paint sprays (coloring pigments with adhesives and propellents)	Can be used with most materials. However, care must be taken that chemical reactions do not take place between the solvent and the material (e.g. compatibility with polystyrene foam boards)	Different types of sprays can be used (silk matte or gloss) to match the colors of the surfaces
Clear varnishes	Can be used with many different materials. Applying clear, transparent layers, you can create nuances without the need for additional materials	For example, nuances in sites, topography and the building, varying intensities of color or degrees of brightness on the surface of the material. Varnishes conserve the surface (e.g. of Finnboard, preventing the material from yellowing)

■ **Tip:** When you use paints, varnishes or other surface coats, it is worth doing tests first to see what effect they have. Using samples and testing materials, you will acquire a feel for the products' properties and for different ways of using them. Experimenting can be good fun too. Colors and contrasts are best judged under natural lighting.

Acrylic paint	For painting specific building elements or surfaces on the model. It is easy to mix and the brush can be cleaned with water	The different materials can be made to match by applying a uniform monochrome coat; very intense, bright colors (depending on the pigmentation)
Wood stain	Stains can be used to change the natural colors of the wood surface. The original properties, such as the grain, are preserved	By changing the hue, different shades and nuances can be created. Colored stains make the material look very different.
Oils and waxes	The surfaces of both wood and cardboard can be treated with these products, thus changing coloring and brightness	These protective surface coats can often be applied to intensify the impact of the surface properties of woods

PLASTER, CLAY AND MODELLING CLAYS

Materials such as plaster (gypsum) and clay, like the other materials presented here, form a distinct category of materials. People often limit themselves to using only the material from which the entire model is made. These materials are particularly suitable for presentations that focus not on the exact formal details but on a building's corporeality and massivity. Plaster, it might be added, can be cast in very precise, smooth forms.

Gypsum is used as a building material on a scale of 1:1 (in the form of plaster and stucco, for example). Its chemical name is calcium sulphate, a compound that occurs naturally and as by-product of power stations. Plaster

In modelling, it is used as a pouring compound. First, a mould must be made. This is a time-consuming process, but its advantage is that you can cast a product as often as you wish.

Gypsum, as "modelling plaster," is available as a white powder. It is mixed with water and used either in liquid form or applied in a thicker consistency with a putty knife.

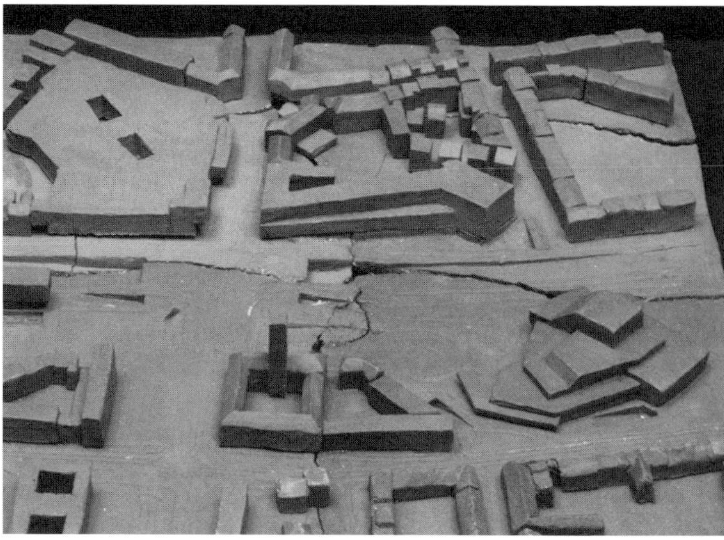

Fig. 68: An urban design model made of fired clay

Liquid plaster quickly sets and hardens. Once it is in this state, it can be sandpapered and painted or varnished.

Clay

Clay has long been used to manufacture a wide variety of objects in different fields.

The history of architectural models shows that clay (also known as loam) has been used in certain areas since models were first built:

- For the construction of forms: free forms, organically formed objects
- Sculptures
- Three-dimensional solid models, e.g. for urban development projects

The great advantage of clay lies in the fact that it is simple to use. Working with clay is also a tactile experience. With clay you can create "corporeal" three-dimensional, sketches, work on entire development processes and make changes quickly and effortlessly. While you are processing clay, make sure that you always keep it sufficiently moist (with water) to prevent it from drying out and cracking.

When a clay model is ready, it has to be fired in kiln to preserve its form. The product is known as pottery or ceramics. It is used the building industry for making bricks and clay roof tiles.

In addition to the classic materials plaster and clay, other products are also available: Plastic modelling clay

- Air-drying modelling clay: its processing properties are similar to those of clay, with the difference that it hardens in the air and can be subsequently processed with sanding tools - like wood.
- Plastic modelling clay/plasticine: a modelling material that basically remains processible and formable, whilst preserving a constant degree of hardness. A typical feature of this material is that it becomes "softer" at higher temperatures, but retains a relatively firm consistency at normal room temperature. Plasticine has a familiar greyish-green color. Plastic modelling clay is available in many different colors.

Assembly units are increasingly often used in modelling.

ACCESSORIES: TREES, FIGURES AND CARS

When clients first set foot in a new building, they often exclaim: "I imagined it would be much smaller (or bigger)." This is hardly surprising, since the only impressions they have of a project's scale before it is built are gained from drawings and models. And this is the crux of the matter: how can architects convey an accurate impression of the size and scale of the final structure? To give the viewer an idea of the real size, they can use "known quantities." Such reference points give the viewer a basis upon which he or she can imagine the finished product. Among the objects that convey an idea of scale are small-scale human figures. We all have an idea of our own height and can relate this to the model. If we read and grasp objects in relation to this "human scale," we find them easier to judge. ●

● **Example:** Modelling figures are available in all scales as injection-moulded products. For the common scale of 1:200, grains of rice can be stuck vertically into the base as an abstract representation of people.

Fig. 69: Materials used to represent trees

Accessories

In addition to figures, there are many other objects that help us visualize the scale of a project. Vehicles, available from specialist dealers, or represented by other objects, are indispensable in a multi-storey car park. The same applies to trees and plants, which must be shown if they are an important feature of the concept (in landscape planning or urban design projects). Balls, rods and simple, three-dimensional blocks can be used to represent trees. However, the best method is simply to use trees themselves. Various dried plants (such as yarrow), which are normally used in flower arrangements, make ideal miniature trees. If trees play an important role in the model design (site design, relationship of buildings to trees and the interior courtyard etc.), the abstract trees must be selected very carefully, since they are often decisive for the overall impression.

In architectural models, the accessories mentioned above are normally all you need. In some cases, however, other objects may be more suitable for illustrating the purpose of the future building:

- Streetlamps as a line-forming element
- Street furniture (benches, advertising pillars, signs)
- Furnishings in interiors such as shops and restaurants
- Trains, ships and aeroplanes, in the case of transport buildings

Fig. 70: Wooden balls

Fig. 71: Branches/twigs

Fig. 72: Foam

Fig. 73: Foam

Fig. 74: High-resistance foam

Fig. 75: Brush trees

Summary: Most of the materials mentioned above are obviously not specifically manufactured for making models. It is up to you, as the modeller, to use your imagination and apply unusual materials to the context of architectural models. ○

○ **Note:** When you choose suitable materials, consider how long you want to use or keep the model. Many materials age – in this respect models are very similar to constructed buildings – changing the appearance of models as time goes by. Sunlight (UV radiation), in particular, darkens cardboard and wood. Finnboard, for instance, turns yellow very quickly. Although ageing affects the aesthetic appearance of wooden models, it has a far more detrimental impact on the durability of cardboard models.

From drawing to model – steps and approaches

Below, we shall examine different methods of making models and show you different ways in which you can make one yourself. These tips are intended as a guide to help you in your creative work.

A FEW PRELIMINARY THOUGHTS

Objectives of the presentation

Before you pick up your utility knife and cutting ruler, you should consider your objectives. Although modelmaking can be a very creative way of designing a building and a very pleasurable activity (e.g. tearing and joining pieces of paper), if you want to make a model for representational purposes, you should avoid proceeding by trial and error from the very start. Hence, you should begin by clarifying your goals.

You should first decide what you want to present. If it is a design principle (e.g. a stone slab with a glass hall), then this will influence your choice of scale, materials and the level of abstraction. If you want to present a concept to, for example, a professorial committee or representatives of building clients, you must decide exactly what you want to communicate to the target group. You should also consider whether they are likely to be very imaginative. In general, people teaching architecture have far more experience in judging designs, and are more likely to be familiar with abstract models than, say, building clients who have had little experience in the field of construction.

Relationship between plans and model

Furthermore, the presentation plans will influence the choice of material and the format of the mounting board, especially if it and the model are meant to form a coherent whole. Hence, you should carefully select the essential elements and graphically explore different levels of abstraction – using sketches, too, if necessary.

Deciding plan detail

The degree of detail shown in your model will depend on spatial relationships and the physical size of the mounting board you intend to use. If some parts of the design (e.g. a striking axis in the immediate surroundings) are very important, but too big to fit on a suitable base, you might have to reconsider the scale of your model.

THE MOUNTING BOARD

If the surroundings and the terrain are to play a decisive role in your concept, you should start by thinking about the mounting board. Although this may not be appropriate for every project, it is always a good place to start. Begin by making a working model of the location. This can, of course, be used for the presentation too. Often, when people start working on a design, they are short of ideas, so it is often worth reproducing the terrain and topography and making a spatial analysis of the site. Very often, the best ideas arise when you get down to work. Another reason for reproducing the terrain at the beginning is that the workload generally tends to grow toward the end of a project. It is therefore worth preparing and finishing this part of the work before you do anything else.

When making the terrain (the "foundation") make sure that the dimensions of the whole model are right: if the model is too large it will be heavy and difficult to transport; if it is too small, it will not communicate enough information during the presentation. Boards manufactured from wood-based materials usually make good foundations. > Chapter Materials

If you already have a suitably sized mounting board for presenting the section you have chosen, you will now need a site plan to transfer the surroundings or the terrain to the mounting board. Once you have done this, you will have to transfer your geometric planning data onto the modelling material. You can use one of the following methods:

- Frottage: copy the drawing as a mirror image, affix it to the material with adhesive tape and then rub it onto the material with the aid of acetone solvent. In the process, the printing ink is transferred from the drawing to the material.
- Tracing with needles: mount the drawing on the material, pierce the key features into the material with a needle or a pounce wheel (a special modelling tool) and then trace the line geometry.
- Drawing: the best way of making simple outlines is to draw a line on the material with a fine pencil. ■

■ **Tip:** Transferring the typography of the terrain to the model is generally very time-consuming. If you are making a raised-relief model, select a material thickness that, in the desired scale, corresponds to the elevation lines on the terrain plan. This approach renders further changes unnecessary. First, make the required number of layers to fit the dimensions of the mounting board and glue an entire layer on to the mounting board. Now cut the first elevation layer out of the site-plan base, which has also been cut to size, and transfer it to the next layer of paperboard. Once you have glued the first layer, cut additional layers and transfer them one at a time to the others until you have created a perfect reproduction of the terrain. Note that you may have to create a new model of the terrain of the new construction site, which will then have to be integrated into the raised-relief model.

MAKING INDIVIDUAL BUILDING ELEMENTS

Modelling is more like constructing a prefabricated building than erecting a complete structure (from the primary construction to the finished product). Generally, it is advisable to finish building elements completely before you join them to others. Typical elements include:

- Floor plate, ceilings, roof top and all of the structure's horizontal building elements
- Walls, shear walls and facades, including the arranged window and door apertures as well as all vertical elements
- Interior walls

Working from plans and sketches

These elements are made on the basis of architectural drawings (in the same way that a building is constructed on the basis of a building plan or work drawing). All we have on paper are the classic two-dimensional projections, e.g. the plan, the section and the elevation. However, the plans and the sections are equally important. They each provide two-dimensional views of a building. Together, however, they create a three-dimensional impression. The best method is to transfer the geometry of the plan to scale onto the material. There are different ways of doing this:

- The walls and supports are mounted as indicated on the plan (three dimensions). This is a quick and easy method, regardless of whether you are using working models or urban design models.
- All the important information in the plan is transferred to the desired material. > see above

Once the information in the plan has been evaluated and applied layer by layer, the height indications in the longitudinal sections and cross sections gradually assume concrete form. ■

■ **Tip:** When you transfer the lengths and heights of the elements to the model, pay attention to the thicknesses of the materials. If you want to mitre a wall corner, both sides must be made to their full length. If the elements are to be butt jointed, however, you must deduct the width of the material of the projecting element.

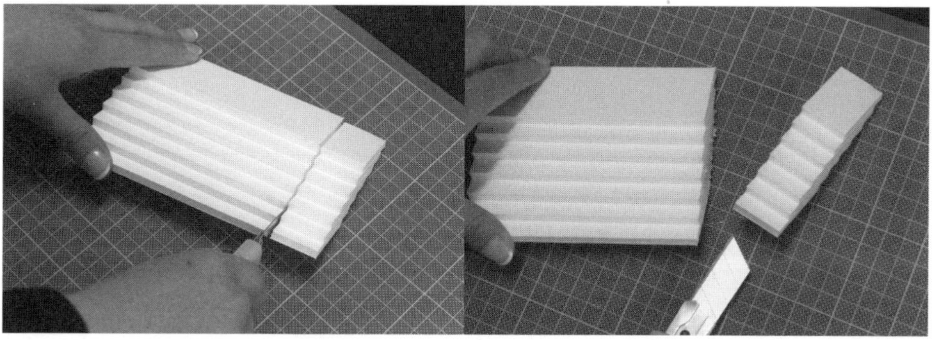

Fig. 76: "Stair boards" cut to the right width

Walls are usually the most important parts of a building. When you are constructing models, you should design them not as single elements, but as part of a whole, and make them accordingly. In this respect, modelmakers can work far more efficiently than builders, since they can cut or saw walls into endless strips and then cut them to the required length when needed.

This method of "endless manufacturing" greatly simplifies the modelmaking process for both urban construction projects (involving rows of houses or buildings with the same cross section as "endless rows"), and for other building elements with the same cross sections (supports, window frames, floors etc.). It is worth making a large number of individual elements and then varying them, especially if you are experimenting with your model.

Stairs

Stairs are often a decisive element in any project and their representation is very important. In working models, stairs are simplified and installed in the form of slanted surfaces (ramps). This work can be done quickly, and everyone knows what the ensuing slopes are supposed to represent. Representing a real staircase with treads and risers is more time-consuming, but it also creates a more impressive result. ●

● **Example:** When you are making stairs, consider how many staircases you are going to have in your model. You can save yourself a lot of work by making the flights (in the case of single flight stairs) much wider and cutting off single sections in the desired width with a utility knife or a saw.

Fig. 77: Transferring the drawing to paperboard

Fig. 78: Cutting out the mounting board

Fig. 79: Measuring out the walls in strips

Fig. 80: Cutting out the apertures

Fig. 81: Gluing the walls together

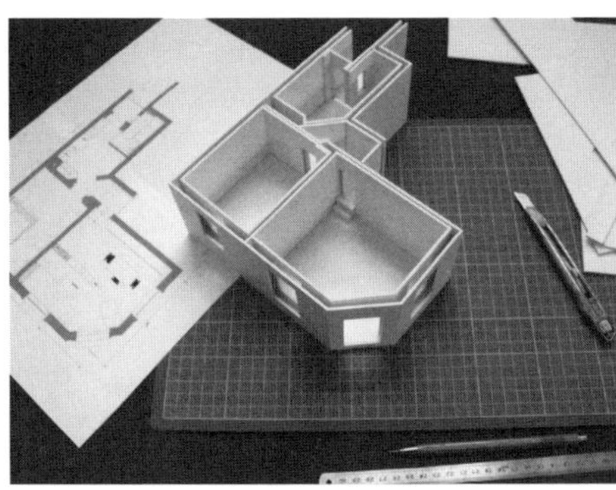

Fig. 82: The finished model

ASSEMBLING THE ELEMENTS

The elements should also be assembled systematically since in most cases you cannot take them apart without causing damage once they have been glued. An effective method is first to mount two exterior walls of a building and then successively glue the interior walls and the ceilings. Finally, you can complete the building by attaching the missing exterior walls.

A detailed simulation of windows and facade elements is also important for the expressive power of a building model. You should install the windows before assembling the exterior walls and facade. The same holds true for ceilings with openings for stairs and for walls and roofs with their apertures.

At times it may make sense to prefabricate all the elements associated with a specific phase of construction – i.e. entire building sections – and to assemble the entire unit afterwards. However, you should first make sure that, should the need arise, you can adjust the connected elements in case the building sections do not fit together with geometric precision. ■

■ **Tip:** You should avoid using a utility knife on a model that has already been glued together since you can never work as precisely as you can on a cutting board. A better approach is to prefabricate as many elements as possible and then glue them together. You can check for measurement errors by temporarily joining the parts together. You can ensure that your model is stable by setting up the pieces at right angles.

FINAL TASKS AND ACCESSORIES

After all the elements have been assembled to form the building, a few final tasks remain before the model is complete. The process must be carefully planned, especially if you want to paint individual elements or the entire model. If, for example, a piece running through the entire building is to be a certain color, you should make this piece and glue it together as a single unit so that you can paint it independently of the rest of the model, using a spray gun if necessary. If parts of the model are a certain color, you should also consider whether it is best to add accessories such as trees and figures before or after painting.

Adding accessories

It is definitely worth considering whether, and how, to use accessories as the model nears completion. Trees are a very popular element and can substantially improve an architectural model. Even so, trees and other accessories should only be included if they are relevant to your concept, but not if they merely serve as ornamentation. Often, modellers make the mistake of "planting" too many trees on the mounting board, which can divert attention from the actual subject of the model. As a general rule, if trees are architectural elements – that is, if they have a space-forming function – they should be part of the presentation, but they are not absolutely necessary (less is often more). ■

■ **Tip:** If the accessories play too prominent a role, they may detract from essential features of the model: viewers will literally not see the architecture for the trees. To minimize this effect, you can paint the chosen materials to match the other materials used. Not only will the elements blend in better with the surroundings, but they will still be perceived in a spatial context. If you execute large public buildings such as concert halls, museums and the like as small-scale models, you can add small abstract figures to indicate paths, emphasize public spaces and give viewers a better understanding of the real context. If you want to create the impression that the structure exerts a magnetic pull, you might consider adding more concentrated groups of figures near the main entrance than those scattered across the grounds.

PRESENTATION

The finished model will usually be part of an exhibition or presented in conjunction with a talk. You should not leave this last step to chance. When pictures are hung on the wall, they are positioned at eye level to achieve the best possible effect. Models should also be presented in such a way that audiences can view them from the right angle. Whereas urban design models are usually viewed from above, you should ensure that people viewing an interior model can look into the spaces without assuming contorted or uncomfortable positions.

Constructing a base

To ensure that the model is exhibited at the right height, you can build a base (e.g. in the form of a pedestal) that conforms to model's shape. A base can be used to support a model conceptually: for instance, if a tall, narrow building is displayed, a tall, narrow base can illustrate the architectural concept from a distance.

The base of a group model is often equipped with wheels so that it can be moved easily from presentation to presentation. All you need to do at the new venue is replace the inserts.

Display cases

High-quality models can be presented in a display case to protect their surfaces and emphasize the object-like character of the architectural representation. A perspex case protects the model from damage at exhibitions and is particularly useful at public shows.

Hanging models on the wall

Urban design models (raised-relief models of landscapes) can be hung on the wall like a drawing or a plan (a kind of three-dimensional plan). Here, it is important to find out in advance what kind of wall is available. If plans are hung on partition screens, they may not be inordinately heavy. ■

■ **Tip:** You will probably be reluctant to throw your models away, but in the course of your studies, you will make so many that you will probably not have the necessary space to store them all. Since models stored in basement or attic spaces can be damaged by moisture and fluctuating temperatures, you might consider hanging your models on the wall after presentation. In this way, you can both store them and use them as wall decoration.

In conclusion

The study of architecture confronts students with a plethora of demands and challenges. Among other things, they must learn to make good models. Many of these models are created for presentational purposes just before an assignment is due. The potential they offer as design and work tools is overlooked. Studying architecture involves learning about technical matters as well as artistic and creative processes. Models are a way to explore space and proportions and to promote three-dimensional thinking. Models show the ramifications of paper sketches and also help students train their ability to imagine the spatial relations of two-dimensional drawings.

Models are also a method of communicating with a lay audience. If a client hires an architect to design a building, it is ultimately the model and not the detailed plans that will give him or her a concrete idea of the architect's "product." The model provides a foundation for approving and rejecting ideas, making improvements and fleshing out details. The different roles that the level of detail plays for architects and clients are reflected in the ways they respond to the model: clients see the model as a finished result and want a high level of detail because they are eager to see the project completed. Architects, on the other hand, prefer a model that is only moderately accurate since it will allow them greater creative freedom.

For both, models round off the ways a project can be represented. As the three-dimensional implementation of a design idea, a model is every bit as important as presentation drawings.

Michael Heinrich

Architectural Photography

Introduction

Architects, urban developers and structural engineers develop their architectural ideas largely with the help of architectural photographs. Such photographs assume a mediating role between architecture and the observer, but they can never completely reproduce a building, since they only show a particular perspective. The photographer selects a specific point of view, deciding what he or she would like to show the observer. It is therefore wise to make a thorough study of the details of an architectural object before photographing it.

Concept

Reproducing a three-dimensional building in a two-dimensional medium confronts the photographer with the fundamental difficulty of depicting interrelationships and spatial impressions. Over and above this, a concept for communicating architectural context needs to be based on an analysis of the structures of a building, the fundamental ideas informing its design and the context in which the building has been positioned. Apart from an understanding of architecture, it is also necessary to have a knowledge of how designs are realized in technical terms, a sense of proportion, and the ability to select the right content for photographs.

> Chapter Image analysis

The chapters below provide insights into the technical fundamentals of photography, image analysis, photographic techniques and the subsequent adaptation and editing of architectural images.

Fundamentals of photography

To exploit the full potential of a camera it is important to have a basic understanding of the way it functions. This chapter explains fundamental photographic concepts such as aperture, focal length and angle of view, while the next chapter outlines their application.

The photographic process is shaped by three essential factors. The first, the science of optics, draws on the theory of light to delineate the process of perception by the human eye. The second, the principles of representation, is additionally determined by the physics of the optical path. The third, recording the image, is required to preserve images for posterity.

OPTICS

The presence of light is essential to visual perception. Light that the human eye can perceive is constituted by electromagnetic radiation with wavelengths ranging from 380 to 780 nanometers (nm). The color of light is defined by its wavelength. Radiation with a wavelength of less than 380 nm (ultraviolet light) or more than 780 nm (infrared light) cannot be detected by the human eye. Light and color

What we actually see is not the object itself but the light rays it reflects. When light strikes a surface, some parts of it are reflected in all directions and other parts are absorbed. Only reflective surfaces allow light to be reflected in a directed manner. In colored surfaces, a particular spectrum of the light is absorbed by the surface while the eye perceives another spectrum as reflected light. When white sunlight hits a green surface, for instance, the red spectrum range is absorbed and the reflected light is consequently perceived as green.

When reflected light rays enter the eye, they pass through the cornea, the pupil and the lens before falling on the retina. In the retina's photoreceptors the absorbed light waves cause changes that are transmitted as impulses along connected neuronal networks to the visual cortex. Here, and in other higher brain centers, the excitation patterns stemming from the eye are processed and transformed into the perception of light and color. The eye

Most of the retina is covered with sensory cells. However, the capacity for acute vision is possessed only by 0.02% of the retinal surface, an area called the macula lutea ("yellow spot"). This area corresponds to only about 2° of the approximately 200° comprising a person's horizontal field of vision. Indeed, the only segment of the visual field seen in sharp focus is the part at which the visual axes of both eyes are directed.

When observing an object, the stationary and focused image is produced by the eye muscles consecutively shifting different segments of the object in front of the macula, a process that is largely unconscious. The eye is thus never at rest during the observation process and is constantly carrying out minute movements. These movements and the choice of fixation points differ between individuals and are connected with the habits and interests of the particular observer.

Although the ocular lens, like a camera, produces a two-dimensional image on the retina, humans are nevertheless able to perceive space. Spatial perception is based on two principles. First, the distance to an object is perceived by focusing both ocular lenses on it and, second, the interpretation of spatial depth is based on knowledge of the world and its objects, which already exists in the observer's brain.

The high visual acuity of the human eye is determined more by its "software" than its "hardware," as shown by optical illusions. The way the brain processes information is key to our understanding of what we see, whether in terms of reality or its representation in a photograph. If the eye permits only a highly subjective form of perception, a photograph can be only a subjective reproduction of that reality. This underscores the importance of the subjective statement that ultimately determines the character of the photographic image.

PRINCIPLES OF REPRESENTATION

Every object, whether it is a light source or reflection of light, emits light rays in all directions. These spread out linearly. In a lightproof chamber equipped with a tiny hole, only a minute part of each beam of rays can pass through the aperture and form a point on the opposite side of the chamber. An image is produced by the sum of all such points. This is the principle that forms the basis of the earliest precursor of the modern camera, the pinhole camera or camera obscura, which is thought to have been discovered by Aristotle in the 4th century BC. > Fig. 1

Lenses

The problem with the pinhole camera is that only a very small amount of light can pass through the aperture, and the larger this aperture is made, the blurrier the image. As a consequence, from the middle of the 16th century onwards, convex lenses were used to increase the amount of light without losing image definition. Convex lenses focus light rays passing through the lens on a point on an imaging plane positioned on the other side. > Fig. 2 Their disadvantage is that they require a fixed distance from the imaging plane. If the distance between a photographic

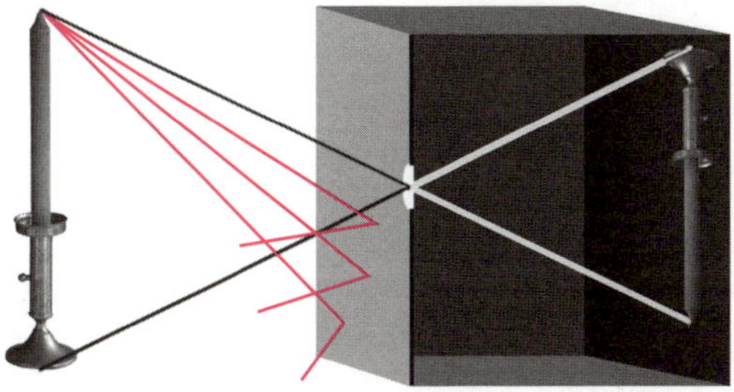

Fig. 1: Principle of the camera obscura

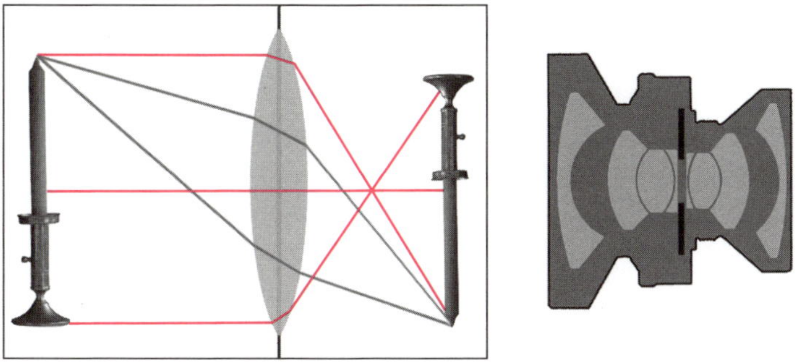

Fig. 2: Principle of a convex lens, cross section of an objective

subject and the lens is varied, the distance between the lens and the imaging plane must also be varied in order to keep the subject in focus. In a camera obscura, all subjects remain in focus irrespective of their distance from the aperture, whereas the distance between a lens and the imaging plane must be coordinated with the distance between the subject and the lens.

Objective

If several lenses are assembled to form an optical system, the result is called an objective, although it is also often referred to as a camera lens. An objective concentrates the incident light and directs it into the interior of the camera, onto the imaging plane. There, the light rays strike either a ground glass screen, on which the image can be seen, or the film or sensor recording the photograph. In order to capture an image of

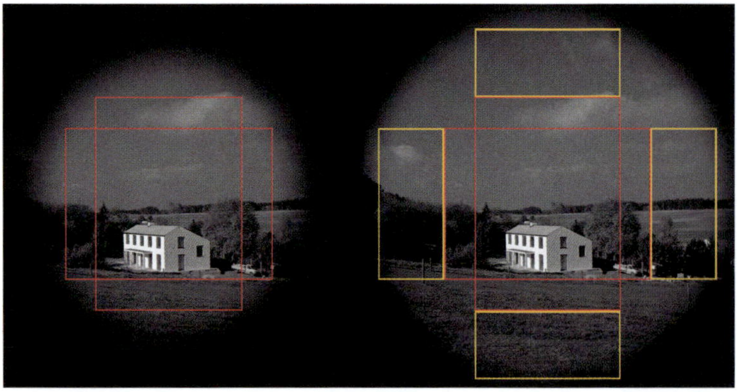

Fig. 3: Shifting the imaging plane in a large image circle (vertical and horizontal format = red field, shift = yellow field)

reality that is as precise as possible, modern objectives are intricately assembled from lenses with different refraction indexes.

The optical characteristics of an objective are defined in terms of focal length (f), light intensity—or speed—and image circle.

Focal length

Focal length refers to the distance between the optical system (objective) and the point on the optical axis at which an infinitely distant object (e.g. the sun) is depicted. The focal length is thus a structural feature of an objective.

Light intensity

Light intensity is calculated by dividing the largest effective aperture of an objective by the focal length. If an objective with a focal length of 50 mm has a lens diameter of 25 mm at its narrowest point (which is usually in the middle of the objective), light intensity will be 0.5. This relationship is expressed as 1:2. In order to regulate light intensity, diaphragms are installed in camera objectives to decrease the effective aperture. > Chapter Fundamentals of photography, Recording the image

Image circle

The image circle—or coverage—is the diameter of the projection on the imaging plane that corresponds to the largest possible representational size. > Fig. 3 The production of a precise photographic image requires an image circle that is larger than the format diagonal of the film or sensor. If the image circle is smaller than the diagonal, the result will be shadowing, or "vignetting," along the image edges. > Chapter Image editing If it is bigger, appropriately designed equipment allows the image to be shifted within the image circle. > Fig. 3 and Chapter The camera

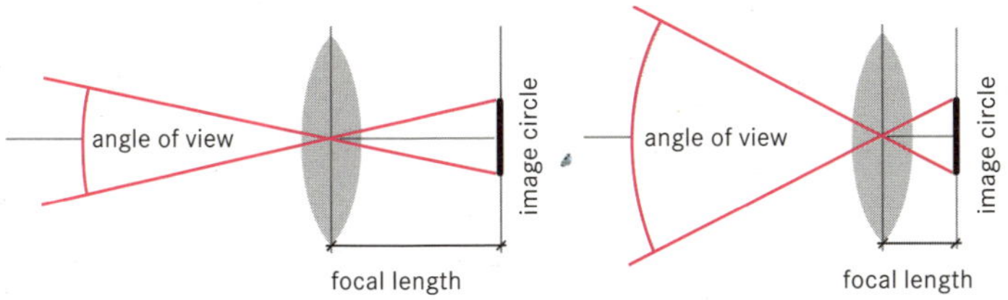

Fig. 4: If the image circle remains unchanged, a short focal length results in a large angle of view, and a long focal length in a small angle of view.

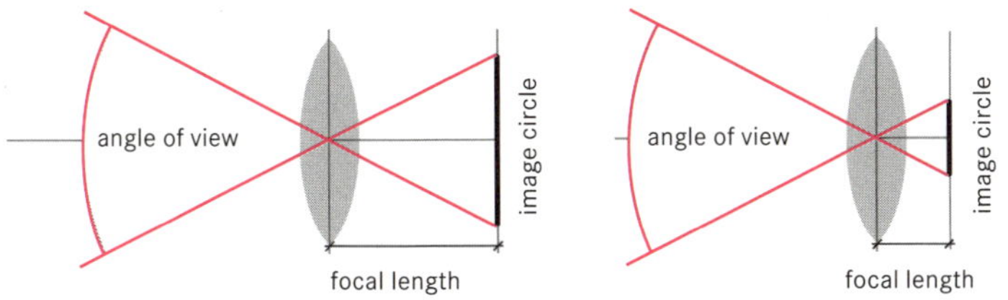

Fig. 5: If the image circle does not remain constant (e.g. different film or sensor sizes), the angle of view may be identical despite different focal lengths.

Angle of view

The segment of the photographic subject that can be depicted with an objective is of paramount importance for the photographic process. It is referred to as the angle of view and is determined by the focal length of the objective and by the format being used (sensor size or film format). > Figs. 4 and 5 The angle of view of an optical system is dependent on both the focal length and the image circle. > Chapter The camera, Objectives

The angle of view is calculated on the basis of the format diagonal and the focal length as follows:

Angle of view α = 2 * arctan (Format diagonal/2 * focal length f)

Depth of field

In addition to the subject, the sharpness of an image is an important aspect of photographic quality. Depth of field refers to the field along the optical axis that is depicted in focus. If the camera is focused on a certain point, then all other points at the same distance from the lens will be in focus, and all other points, whether closer or farther away, will be out of focus. > Fig. 6 The lack of focus within a limited field in front of and behind the depicted plane is compensated for by the human eye. The

Fig. 6: Different depths of field achieved with different apertures

extent of this depth of field is mainly dependent on the reproduction scale and the light intensity. The smaller the reproduction scale (scale of photographed subject to the depiction on the imaging plane), the greater is the depth of field. Reducing the light intensity (small decrease in aperture) ● also increases the depth of field.

RECORDING THE IMAGE

Recording an image requires a light-sensitive recording medium such as film or a sensor as well as a shutter that limits the time during which the medium is exposed to light.

Exposure

A balanced exposure that distinguishes between as many levels of brightness as possible is very important for achieving good technical results. However, it is incumbent upon the individual photographer to support the visual statement of the photograph using different exposure ○ times, irrespective of optimal camera settings. > Chapter Image analysis

● **Example:** When photographing landscapes using a wide-angle lens, the depth of field is usually very large. Objects at different distances are perceived as sharply defined. If the aim is to produce a somewhat blurred background, the aperture must be opened as wide as possible. However, when a stamp is photographed, the depth of field is only a few millimeters. In this case the focus needs to be very precisely adjusted and the aperture reduced to the smallest possible diameter.

○ **Note:** There are limits to how much an underexposed or overexposed image can be corrected in the processing phase. If a photograph is overexposed, for instance, brighter parts of the picture—both white and light gray—will be reproduced as pure white. In the processing phase, the lack of pictorial information will prevent the difference between white and light gray from being restored.

Three factors are decisive when reproducing surfaces of differing brightness: the sensitivity of the medium, the quantity of light entering the objective, and the time the medium is exposed to light.

Sensitivity

The sensitivity of a recording medium, whether film or a sensor, is expressed as ASA, DIN or ISO. ASA is an American industrial standard and DIN the German equivalent. ISO, on the other hand, is the international standard and provides a simple way of expressing both values. ISO 100/21° (100 ASA, 21 DIN) is regarded as the standard level of photosensitivity. If this level is doubled, the ASA value also doubles, while the DIN value increases by three (ISO 50/18°, ISO 100/21°, ISO 200/24°, ISO 400/27°). ○

Aperture

The aperture regulates the amount of light entering the objective. Most objectives have an iris aperture composed of several segments that slide into one another to allow greater or lesser amounts of light through and to increase or reduce the incident light falling on the film or sensor. The quantity of light passing through the objective is expressed by the f-number or f-stop (highest value = smallest opening). Since doubling the diameter of the aperture means quadrupling the size of the imaging surface, the setting *f*8 is actually four times greater than *f*16. An aperture half the size of *f*8 is calculated as follows: $8 * \sqrt{2} = 11$. The series of aperture settings corresponding to a consecutive halving of the quantity of light is as follows: 1; 1.4; 2; 2.8; 4; 5.6; 8; 11; 16; 22; 32; 45; 64; 90; 128, etc. The objective's level of light intensity corresponds to the reciprocal of the smallest aperture number, i.e. the largest relative opening. ●

Contrast

The range of brightness in an image is referred to as contrast. The contrast range describes the difference in intensity between the brightest and darkest point in an image. If an interior illuminated by light coming through a window exhibits a very large difference between the

○ **Note:** Coarse-grained, highly sensitive film (ISO 200/24°, ISO 400/27°, etc.) is used to photograph poorly lit subjects (such as church interiors photographed without a tripod), and rapidly moving subjects requiring a short exposure time. Film with a low photosensitivity is fine-grained (longer exposure times) and therefore provides better photographic quality. The sensitivity of digital sensors is usually controlled by software. In many cameras a high-sensitivity setting leads to a significant loss of photographic quality (image noise).

● **Example:** If the combination ISO 100/21°, *f*8, time 1 sec, provides the correct degree of brightness when photographing a subject, then changing one of these factors will produce an image that is too dark or too bright. If photosensitivity is increased, either the quantity of light must be reduced or the time shortened: ISO 200/24°, *f*11, 1 s; or ISO 200/24°, *f*8, 1⁄2 s. If *f*2 is selected in this case, sensitivity and/or exposure time must be reduced: ISO 25/15°, *f*2, time 1⁄4 s; or ISO 100/21°, *f*2, 1/15 s; or ISO 3200/36°,*f*2, 1/500 s.

Fig. 7: Lower and higher levels of contrast caused by different levels of incident light

brightest and darkest points (e.g. the window and a corner of the room), this is referred to as hard contrast. Subjects without direct lighting generally have low, or soft, contrast. On a sunny day the light falling on a white wall is up to 16,000 times (2^{14}) as bright as that falling on a dark shadowed area, and the difference in brightness amounts to as much as 14 f-stops. On a rainy day this difference amounts to around 5 f-stops, which corresponds to 32 times as much light in the brighter area as in the darker area. > Fig. 7

The camera

The fundamentals of photography described in the previous chapter provide a basis for understanding the extensive range of available cameras and their respective features and accessories. They will also help you evaluate your own work. The most important parts of a camera are the film—or, in digital cameras, the sensor—the objective, and the control elements, each of which is discussed below.

IMAGE QUALITY

Photographic technology provides an important foundation for developing design concepts in architectural photography. For instance, large-format images are often best suited to reproducing details and particularly intricate structures. Important factors in the production of high-quality images include lens quality, resolution, the sensor or film size, and the editing of image data.

Resolution

In digital photography, the resolution factor is often presented as the absolute standard for evaluating image quality. Resolution is measured in terms of the number of individual pixels. For example, if a sensor has 2112 × 2816 individual photosensors, this is usually rounded up to 6 million and expressed as 6 MP (megapixels). The individual photosensors on a sensor unit can measure only one color channel. Almost all image sensors use the so-called Bayer matrix, which groups together one photosensor for red light, two for green light and one for blue light. Although technological developments are producing ever higher resolution levels, improvements to image quality are not keeping apace. The number of photosensors is only one factor among many. The image qualities of the objective and signal conversion within the camera are of at least equal importance.

When using analog film, resolution is determined by the composition of the film. Slow—or less sensitive—film has a higher resolution than fast—or more sensitive—film. This is due to the fact that the surface of slow film contains a larger number of flat silver grains than fast film. While the flat grains require less light in order to react, they produce a more coarse-grained image. In analog cameras, film size is more important than film resolution for the quality of images. The different types of analog cameras are therefore defined in terms of standard film sizes. 95% of all analog cameras use 35 mm film (with a standard frame measuring 24 × 35 mm^2), although roll film (56 mm wide, varying lengths) and sheet film (102 × 127 mm^2, 205 × 254 mm^2) are also used. > Chapter The camera, Camera types

Sensor sizes

In contrast to film, the sizes of sensors used in digital cameras are not standardized. The spectrum ranges from 2 × 3 mm sensors for mobile telephones to 36 × 48 mm for medium-format cameras. The sensor size is usually not indicated, but at the same resolution a larger sensor almost always produces better results. The angle of view can be calculated on the basis of the sensor size and focal length. > Tab. 1, page 334, and Chapter Fundamentals of photography

OBJECTIVES

Apart from imaging capability the most important aspect of an objective is the angle of view. The imaging capability of an objective is defined as its measurable capacity to reproduce very fine lines. The structure of an objective is highly complex and every objective has "aberrations." The fewer aberrations an objective has, the higher its imaging capability.

An objective with an angle of view over 90° is referred to as super wide angle, > Fig. 8 one with an angle of view between 90° and 60° as wide angle > Fig. 9 and one with an angle of view between 60° und 30° as a normal objective. > Fig. 10 Due to the confined spaces often involved in architectural photography, wide-angle objectives are the most important. Objectives with an angle of view under 30° are referred to as telephoto objectives or lenses, although this term is often also applied to non-telephoto lenses with a long focal length. > Fig. 11 Objectives with a variable angle of view are called zoom objectives. Due to their intricate construction and the need to accommodate different angles of view, the imaging capability of zoom objectives is usually lower than that of objectives with fixed focal lengths.

Unfortunately the angle of view is seldom indicated on objectives, and it can only be calculated if both the focal length and the sensor format are known. > Chapter Fundamentals of photography For this reason the focal length supplied is usually converted to the 35 mm format. > Tab. 1, page 334

O **Note:** In reflex cameras, an exposure factor is sometimes indicated along with the 35 mm equivalent focal length. A factor of 1.5, for example, means that a 22 mm objective on the camera in question corresponds to a 33 mm objective on a 35 mm camera or a camera with a "full format" sensor (35 mm size).

Fig. 8: Super wide-angle objective, angle of view 100°

Fig. 9: Wide-angle objective, angle of view 85°

Fig. 10: Normal objective, angle of view 45°

Fig. 11: Telephoto objective, angle of view 10°

Distortion

Architectural photography is often required to depict straight horizontal and vertical lines. When these lines are not depicted as straight but appear curved, especially on picture edges, the effect is known as distortion. > Fig. 12, page 335 Distortion is an imaging defect that stems from the design of the objective and has nothing to do with the type of distortion resulting in divergent lines. > Chapter The photograph, Divergent lines

Tab.1: Focal lengths and angles of view

	Compact camera	Reflex	Reflex	Digiback	Roll film	35 mm equivalent focal length
	e.g.: 1/2.5 in	APS-C	KB		4 × 5 inch	
Sensor size mm	6 × 4	23.7 × 15.6	36 × 24	49 × 36	124 × 100	
Diagonal mm	7.2	28.4	43	61	160	
Factor to KB	6	1.5	1	0.7	0.27	
Angle of view 120°	2 mm	8 mm	12 mm	17 mm	43 mm	12 mm
Angle of view 100°	3 mm	12 mm	18 mm	26 mm	64 mm	18 mm
Angle of view 85°	4 mm	16 mm	24 mm	34 mm	86 mm	24 mm
Angle of view 75°	5 mm	19 mm	28 mm	40 mm	100 mm	28 mm
Angle of view 65°	6 mm	23 mm	35 mm	50 mm	125 mm	35 mm
Angle of view 45°	8 mm	33 mm	50 mm	70 mm	180 mm	50 mm
Angle of view 30°	13 mm	53 mm	80 mm	115 mm	285 mm	80 mm
Angle of view 20°	20 mm	80 mm	120 mm	170 mm	430 mm	120 mm
Angle of view 10°	41 mm	170 mm	250 mm	350 mm	900 mm	250 mm
Angle of view 5°	82 mm	340 mm	500 mm	700 mm	1800 mm	500 mm

Negligible distortion can be corrected on a computer. However, many wide-angle objectives distort to such an extent that a residual defect remains. > Chapter Image editing In such cases the only option is to use a higher quality objective.

CONTROL ELEMENTS

Exposure control

Exposure can be controlled in different ways. In the case of fully automatic exposure, time and aperture are determined by a light meter in the camera and are set automatically. In a semi-automatic camera, the time or aperture is manually selected and the parameters required for correct exposure are set by the camera itself. In manual cameras, time and aperture need to be set manually.

Fig. 12: Pronounced barrel distortion

Fig. 13: Without distortion

Whereas in fully and semi-automatic cameras images are usually correctly exposed, the photographer has to establish the correct exposure for manual cameras. This can be done with the help of an external light meter—though it must be added that many types of manual cameras already indicate whether the photograph is over- or underexposed. If the aim is to achieve special effects such as a shallow depth of field by means of a wide aperture > Fig. 6, page 328 or specific motion effects > Chapter Image analysis the corresponding parameters need to be set manually. ■

■ **Tip:** Optimal working aperture: An aperture that is open too wide results in shallow depth of field, whereas an aperture that is closed too far results in diffraction. The aperture setting that achieves the sharpest focus depends on the design of the particular objective and can be identified only by experimenting with different settings.

Shutter delay

Shutter delay refers to the time between pressing the shutter release button and the actual exposure. Shutter delay can last a matter of milliseconds or several seconds. Although this factor is not very important for architectural photographs, you should consider it when selecting a camera.

Self-timer

In order to avoid camera "shake" that blurs the image, a tripod and a cable release should be used. If the camera is not equipped with an attachment for a cable release, the camera's self-timer can be used. Even in photography involving short exposure times, it can improve the sharpness of the image. Use of a tripod is advisable for all photography involving exposure times longer than 1/60 of a second.

Apart from the main functions that can usually be activated by buttons on the camera, digital cameras feature menus that display numerous auxiliary functions. Of these, white balance and the histogram function are particularly important.

White balance

White balance (WB) refers to the adjustment of the relative amounts of color in the image that is recorded by the camera. The human eye also has the capacity for chromatic adaptation. In a camera it is usually achieved by recording a white or gray surface, which is initially rendered in color and, after correction, as neutral. Depending on the time of day, weather and location, sunlight has different colors, which can of course also be consciously exploited (e.g. during sunset). In analog cameras, such chromatic adjustments can be achieved only through time-consuming color analysis and the use of appropriate filters.

Histogram

The histogram function of many cameras is also very helpful. > Fig. 14 Histograms graphically represent the frequency scale of brightness values in the image. The histogram allows for a more accurate assessment of correct exposure than the camera's viewing screen, since this is affected by ambient light. If the distribution of brightness (256 levels for 8-bit images) does not conform to a normal distribution but is skewed to the right (underexposure) or left (overexposure), this is an indication of incorrect exposure. However, the precise interpretation of this data is ● dependent on the nature of the subject.

● **Important:** The histogram provides an accurate indication of exposure. If brightness levels reach 0 or 256 (at 8-bit color depth), it means that these parts of the motif are outside the range of the sensor and cannot be reproduced effectively. The image is either underexposed or overexposed, or the contrast range is too high.

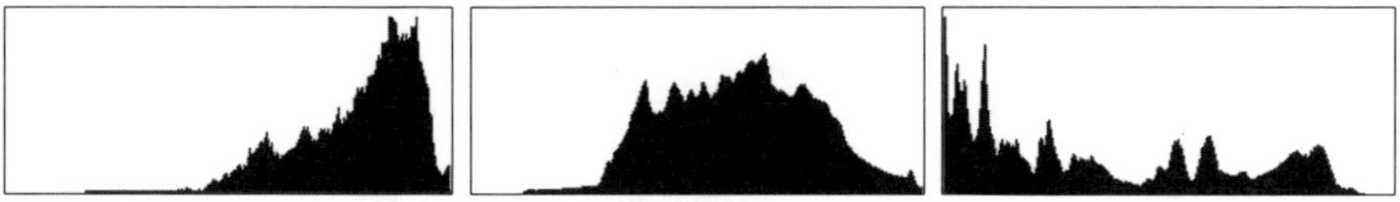

Fig.14: Histogram: overexposed (left), correct (center), underexposed (right)

Another important criterion concerns how easy or difficult a camera is to handle. The camera should be easy to hold and operate. Ergonomic buttons and simple menu design cannot be taken for granted and should be checked prior to purchase. Handling

CAMERA TYPES

Digital compact cameras

Today, the most popular camera is the digital compact camera. Since compact cameras do not have interchangeable lenses, zoom objectives are usually built into them and often produce a high level of distortion. It is therefore important to check whether a camera has the specific qualities required for architectural photography. These include a wide-angle objective with a 35 mm equivalent focal length of 24 mm (angle of view 85°) or less (greater angle of view). In nearly all compact cameras the shortest focal length is 35 mm (angle of view 65°), which is not sufficient for most architectural motifs. > Fig. 15 Apart from an optical zoom, many compact cameras are also equipped with a digital zoom. Since this function only interpolates the center of the image a significant loss of quality must be expected.

In compact cameras exposure control is usually completely automatic. Only a few models allow manual control. Ideally, a camera will be equipped with an over- and underexposure function that can be operated directly via a button (+/−). It is also imperative that a compact camera have a tripod socket. All other features such as image stabilizer, film mode and screen size can be considered secondary. Exposure methods

Mirrorless system cameras

In what are known as system cameras the optical viewfinder is replaced by an electronic viewfinder or the display. As, on account of the smaller flange focal distance, these cameras can incorporate almost all the lenses of a reflex camera by means of an adapter, they can be used for the same purposes. However, the difference in chip size from system to system must be taken into account.

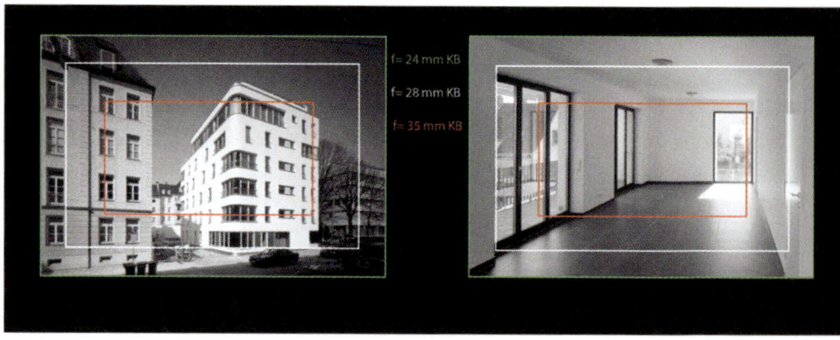

Fig. 15: 35 mm focal lengths compared

Digital single-lens reflex cameras

Single-lens reflex cameras (SLR) are distinguished from compact cameras by their automatic mirror system and prism viewfinder, as well as by their interchangeable lenses.

Interchangeable lenses

If photographers can interchange camera lenses, they can use very short focal lengths, which is a great advantage in architectural photography. They can also select specialized lenses such as shift lenses. > Figs. 16 and 70, page 363 In a shift objective, the lens unit can be moved parallel to the imaging plane without tilting the camera. > Chapter The photograph, Divergent lines However, for this to be possible the image circle must be larger than the format diagonal of the recording medium. > Fig. 3, page 326 In a tilt objective, the lens can be moved horizontally or vertically around an axis in order to achieve a focus plane that is not parallel to the imaging plane.

Since the objective makes up a considerable part of the overall cost of a camera, it is wise to consider keeping the objective from your old camera when purchasing a new one. Of course, this only makes sense if the two cameras have compatible systems, and where sensor sizes differ, even the same brand of objective may be incompatible.

Prism viewfinder

Apart from interchangeable lenses, the other main feature of the reflex camera is its prism viewfinder, which allows the user to see an exact representation of the subsequent photograph. The light rays entering the objective are directed via a mirror and a glass prism onto a viewing screen. A magnifying glass at the back of the camera then allows the image to be assessed. When the photograph is taken, the mirror flips up and the shutter in front of the sensor opens. After exposure has been completed, the shutter closes and the mirror flips back into its original position. > Fig. 17

Fig. 16: Digital single-lens reflex camera with shift objective

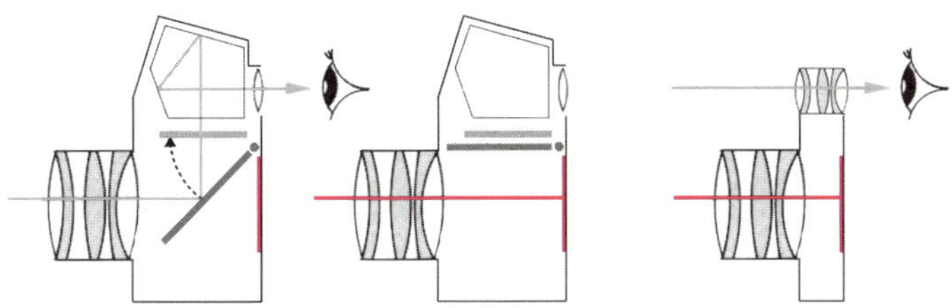

Fig.17: Single-lens reflex camera during and after exposure, rangefinder camera

Analog 35 mm cameras

Analog 35 mm cameras use a 35 mm wide film with a perforated, lateral guide strip. The film format is $24 \times 36\,mm^2$ (35 mm format). 35 mm cameras have now been almost completely pushed out of the market by digital cameras. However, analog systems will persist above all in the black-and-white and large-format fields, where they offer clear advantages. Both technical and non-rational factors play a role in the preference for analog cameras. Digital photographs and film photographs have different characters. Moreover, digital and analog equipment offer different options when it comes to image composition. Due to the higher cost of film, photographers must select motifs with greater care on an analog 35 mm camera.

Medium-format cameras

Medium-format cameras use 60 mm roll film, which has far better imaging qualities than the 35 mm format. The size of the exposed image ranges from 45 × 56 mm^2 to 175 × 56 mm^2 depending on the camera. In contrast to a 35 mm camera, the film casing of a medium-format camera can be separated from the camera body at any time. As a result, the same subject can be shot on slide film and on negative film, to name two examples.

Digital back cameras

Since these camera systems can accommodate film cassettes, instant film cassettes and digital sensor elements (i.e. digital backs), they can be used for both analog and digital photography. > Fig. 18

There is no standard sensor size for medium-format digital backs. The highest resolution is currently 80 MP (sensor size 40 × 54 mm^2), and this will certainly be exceeded in the coming years.

Most models function like a 35 mm reflex camera, and are mainly used for advertising and fashion photography. The models available for professional architectural photography are equipped with objectives that can be shifted vertically and horizontally. The degree of shift is limited only by the image circle of the objective used. > Fig. 18 In addition, these cameras are highly suited for use with super wide-angle and wide-angle objectives and glass viewing screens. Built-in levels allow the cameras to be mounted quickly on a tripod. Furthermore, a modular principle allows digital backs and objectives made by different manufacturers to be mounted on large format and reflex cameras made by the same manufacturer.

Large-format cameras

Large-format cameras are the oldest type of camera system. > Fig. 19 The modular structure of this type of camera consists of a lens element and an element for the film, which also includes a glass viewing screen. The objective plane and the film plane can be shifted in relation to each other in order to set distance parameters and adjust the focal length in relation to different objectives. “Bellows” is the technical term for the connection between the objective plane and the film plane. The two elements are integrated into a unit known as the optical bank.

Since these cameras are constructed on a modular principle, the type and size of the film used can vary. Modern large-format cameras can accommodate film sizes of between 6 × 9 cm and 20 × 25 cm as well as instant film and digital backs. Due to their adjustability and image quality, large-format cameras are still widely used in architectural photography. Along with vertical and horizontal shift capacities, they also offer the possibility of rotating objectives and the film or sensor element. Large-format cameras require a tripod, and function purely mechanically.

Fig. 18: Professional digital architectural camera with digital back

Fig. 19: Petzval camera from 1857 and large-format camera from 2007

They therefore do not have a light meter, an autofocus or an eyepiece, and image composition and focus are achieved using a viewing screen. This is removed after the camera has been focused and replaced by the film or sensor.

Scanbacks

Large-format cameras can accommodate not only film and digital backs but also scanning backs. These are back sections that function using a mobile row of sensors, as in a scanner or copier. An exposure can therefore take several minutes. For this reason this technology is suited only to completely stationary subjects such as pictures or plans. Its use in architectural photography is restricted to subjects devoid of people or mobile objects. However, in technical terms, scanning backs offer the highest resolution of all digital systems (up to 700 MP).

ACCESSORIES

Tripod

A tripod is indispensable to high-quality architectural photography; only by using a tripod can a viewpoint be precisely fixed and maintained during a shot. It also allows photographers to take their time to study a subject and, if necessary, to correct the camera position down to the last centimeter. If a test shot is taken followed by alterations to the exposure and the subject, the use of a tripod is essential to guarantee the shot and the viewpoint can be replicated. It also allows series of shots to be taken using different exposures. > Chapter Processing the image One disadvantage is that it involves carrying extra gear and, to a certain extent, it also slows the working process. Nevertheless, it has the major advantage of allowing the photographer to spend more time considering the image and its parameters. > Chapter Image analysis Use of a cable release with a tripod is highly recommended. A lens hood should also be used to prevent side-light interference. Another highly practical accessory is a small level that can be attached to a camera's flash socket. Since most architectural photographs require a perfectly level camera, such an accessory can be used to quickly establish the correct camera position. A number of camera types allow a laptop, a tablet or a smart phone to be connected by cable or wireless. This is known as "tethered shooting" and is recommended for photographs of interiors and models.

Filters

Filters play an important role in analog photography, not only when shooting in black and white but also in fine-tuning color contrasts. However, due to the way sensors are constructed, color filters have only a very limited application in digital photography. Moreover, most filtering effects can be simulated when digital images are processed. One exception is the polarization filter, which reduces reflections from smooth surfaces.

Accessories such as remote shutter releases, external flashes and devices for radio data transmission and computerized process control can all be integrated as modules into reflex, medium-format and large-format cameras, but this is almost impossible in compact systems.

Image analysis

As a rule, architectural photography is neither purely rational documentation nor purely free artistic expression. As a means of depicting constructed architecture, its special character is based not only on the camera's technical potential, but also on conceptual and creative factors. Although there are no hard-and-fast rules on how to create architectural photography, we can identify a range of typical factors that impact image quality. The analysis of these factors and the illustration of their potential can help each and every photographer to refine their visual language and develop their own specific concepts.

A time-honored way of analyzing architectural photographs is to look at these different factors separately so that photographers can deal more effectively with the complexity of the various parameters in different pictures. The following chapter describes 24 factors that are key to analyzing images. They can be grouped in three categories: content, reproduction, and graphics.

Photographic content is the most important element in architectural photography since a photograph is always an interpretation of the observed subject. Architecture is presented primarily through images, and it is through this visual medium that architects usually first become acquainted with particularly noteworthy buildings. Nevertheless, a photograph of a building can never convey the wealth of information taken in by the person visiting the building, since the architectural experience often includes the path to the building, the interior space, and the immediate environment. Furthermore, photography does not convey sensory perceptions such as smells and sounds, nor it does address the sense of touch. Photographs can therefore only convey selected impressions. Even so—or precisely for this reason—they can be deliberately used to express specific ideas. This is why it is not unusual for people to be disappointed by the reality of a building after first viewing photographs of it.

Reproduction refers to the technical implementation and quality of a photograph. Brightness, contrast, colors, focus and reproduction of detail play an important role in this regard, but reproduction also depends heavily on the purpose for which the image is used. For many of the photographs shown on the Internet, reproduction quality is of secondary importance and can even be achieved by the standard digital cameras in cell phones. At the other end of the spectrum are the fascinating large-format images that convey such a density of information that viewers get the impression they could almost "stroll" through the depicted worlds.

The third category, graphics, applies the graphic principle of proportion to photography—as to all other two-dimensional representations. What is decisive here is the reduction of reality by one dimension and the limited "detail" that a photograph represents.

The factors described above are a good starting point for understanding the aims and methodologies of architectural photography. The selection of a specific viewpoint, a specific type of light, a specific color palette and a specific photographic composition often says much more about an image than do technical data. By dint of precise analysis, photographers can even discover new things in their own photographs. Although many elements may be used unconsciously, the effects can be analyzed and thus replicated in the future.

There are many parallels between photographic composition and architectural design. The primary goal of image analysis is to distinguish the different compositional elements and to understand their effects.

The photographic examples in this chapter have been selected primarily to illustrate these different factors and to simplify their analysis. Although all the photographs have been chosen with a specific factor in mind, each of the factors can be examined in each photograph.

IMAGE FACTOR: CONTENT

Viewpoint

Viewpoint is one of the most important factors determining the effect of an architectural photograph. The orientation of a building or room strongly influences the photograph's spatial effects. It is therefore essential to take the time to choose the correct viewpoint and, if necessary, to consider different concepts for conveying photographic content. The viewpoint is naturally often restricted by technical specifications. For example, if the camera or lens has a small angle of view, the photograph must be taken at a greater distance from the subject in order to capture the entire building or the entire space. Spatial possibilities are often limited, and may only permit extremely wide-angle photographs or reproductions of selected details. > Chapter The camera

Photographers should also refrain from using a large number of randomly selected viewpoints. Rather, a close examination of the subject should lead to a conscious choice of the location from which to take a shot. Photographs with similar viewpoints often express indecision and should therefore be avoided. Every image in a photographic series should also contain a new piece of information. The selection of a viewpoint is often influenced by additional factors such as building axes, lateral edges, the horizon, or light. It is nearly impossible, when looking through the

Fig. 20: Frontal view of motif

Fig. 21: Diagonal view of motif

Fig. 22: Upward view

Fig. 23: Downward view

viewfinder, to keep all these factors in mind. Using a tripod can facilitate the choice since the factors can be observed one after another without changing the view. > Figs. 20 and 21

Line of sight

The tilt of the camera and its angle to the subject determine the perspective, the height of the horizon and the resulting vanishing points. A closer shooting position with an extremely wide angle of view creates a low-angle shot that has a much more dynamic and aggressive effect than a normal view (with the horizon at eye level). Photographers often attempt to align the shot horizontally in order to avoid diverging lines. > Chapter The photograph, Divergent lines It can be helpful to use a tripod in combination with an attachable or integrated level, since even small deviations can lead to clearly visible distortions of parallel lines, at least in wide-angle photographs. However, depending on the photographic concept and subject, unusual diagonal, upward or downward views can have a breathtaking effect. > Figs. 22 and 23

Fig. 24: Overall view

Fig. 25: Selection of a segment

Fig. 26: Sunrise

Fig. 27: Morning fog

Cropping

There may be graphic or thematic reasons to crop or trim a photograph. On the one hand, building sizes can be reflected graphically in the selection of a format. On the other, a high-resolution image file may have to be reduced to a detail view. Parts of an image may also have to be cropped if they would otherwise disrupt its effect.

Important aspects of photographic detail are the format and orientation of the photograph. Even if cameras nearly always have an aspect ratio of between 3:4 and 2:3, the cropping should be taken into account when the photograph is taken (e.g. a panorama format of 1:2). Common aspect ratios such as those of the DIN formats ($1:\sqrt{2}$) and TV formats have a less obtrusive effect, while unusual aspect ratios such as the square format draw the eye and must therefore be carefully considered. A horizontal or vertical format can also be selected to support thematic statements. Vertical formats are generally perceived as more natural and calm in image composition, while horizontal formats have a more dynamic effect. > Figs. 24 and 25

Fig.28: People in a photograph

Fig.29: People moving in a photograph

Lighting design

Lighting design refers to the controlled use of light and lighting to support thematic statements. In general, natural lighting cannot be influenced, but the atmosphere created by light falling on a subject can nevertheless be controlled by deliberately choosing to shoot at a particular time of day or during particular weather conditions. Photographers should study the subject at different times of the day in order to be able to tell when the best time for shooting is. Sunrise > Figs. 26 and 27 and sunset are especially popular times. The light is as mellow as on a cloudy day, but colors are bold and the sky bluish. If weather conditions are good, noon is mainly associated with dark shadows and stark contrasts, particularly in southern countries, making it a less favorable time for photographs.

If additional lighting is available, a conceptual decision must be made as to whether this lighting is helpful or disruptive. For interior shots, lighting equipment may be used in addition to the light fittings already present in order to illuminate and emphasize specific areas. > Chapter The photograph, Interior shots

Orchestrating people

Architectural photography is often devoid of people. Many photographers are quite dogmatic on this subject. While some always include people in their photographs in order to illustrate the relationship between buildings and users, others leave people out as a matter of principle, not wanting to divert the viewers' attention. As a rule of thumb, photographers should carefully consider what effect people are meant to have, and make conscious choices—as with all other photographic content. Living creatures draw the eye more strongly than objects. If people are included in an image, it can be helpful to use a tripod to maintain the camera position until the right moment to take the shot, particularly in outside areas where little can be done to control events or cordon off areas. > Figs. 28 and 29

Fig. 30: Subject in a room

Fig. 31: Subject in front of a building

Fig. 32: The foreground as a contrast to the surroundings

Fig. 33: The foreground emphasized by surroundings

Composing subjects

Even if photographers cannot change the actual subject, there are always single elements that can be modified. For example, windows can be opened or shut, and cars can be left where they are parked or removed from the scene. Arranging furniture and personal objects within an interior is time-consuming but is almost always necessary to some extent. Interior spaces tend to look smaller and messier in photographs than they do in reality, and steps should be taken to counter this impression. Objects must be positioned in specific places in order to block or open up views. > Figs. 30 and 31

Foreground

Objects in the foreground tend to generate a sense of disquiet, especially along the periphery of the image. Attention is diverted above all by objects that are cut off by the picture frame. Often objects are perceived as disruptive in a photograph that we would hardly notice when walking by: flowerpots, park benches, garbage cans, newspaper stands, street signs, etc. Photographers can often create a calmer foreground by choosing a favorable viewpoint or by temporarily removing objects.

Fig. 34: Building with surroundings in the background

Fig. 35: Building with no background

Fig. 36: Reflections as repeated patterns

Fig. 37: Window reflections

Naturally, it is also possible to use foregrounds such as the surrounding architecture as a deliberate stylistic device to emphasize a building's special character. > Figs. 32 and 33

Background

It is often impossible to eliminate high buildings, landscape formations or other structures from the background, and as a result they inevitably flow into image composition. Backgrounds can also be seen as a kind of stage creating a link to the environment. They can be used to build thematic tension, particularly in contrast to isolated shots of a building. > Figs. 34 and 35

Reflections

Water, glass and many facade materials create reflections > Figs. 36 and 37 that can dominate a photograph. Depending on wind movement, water surfaces can have a flat or agitated look. On bright days, glass is made opaque by reflections, and the reflections on its surface influence its appearance. Due to their complexity, reflections can hardly be planned for, yet they can cause the effect of architecture to vary widely.

Fig.38: Light generates atmosphere

Fig. 39: Atmospheric photograph

A polarizing filter can be used to counteract disruptive reflections—and in extreme cases to eliminate them completely. > Chapter The camera

Mood

Even if moods are difficult to grasp and analyze, nearly every photograph expresses one. Often this mood is created by different image factors working in combination, but a single factor such as light can also produce the impression of calm or even of coldness. Although it is difficult to define mood as a factor, photographs can be judged by their moods, and photographers can intentionally create them. > Figs. 38 and 39

IMAGE FACTOR: REPRODUCTION

Brightness

If a photograph depicts an area with the same brightness that was measured when the shot was taken, we speak of proper lighting. However, it is nearly impossible to guarantee proper lighting for all photographic content. Whether a dark area in a photograph is shown as gray, dark gray or black is naturally dependent on lighting, but lighting is not selected for these individual areas. It is chosen for the entire photograph and determines its overall effect. > Fig. 40 In some cases, overexposing or underexposing the entire photograph > Fig. 41 can also be an effective strategy, one that supports the visual statement made by the picture.

Contrast

Even if different degrees of brightness can be reproduced to suit the motif, the contrast between the different degrees of brightness is often not replicable. Furthermore, it is essential to distinguish between motif contrast and the contrast created by lighting. As a motif, a white wall provides virtually no contrast at all, but if sidelight is used, even small irregularities in the surface create contrasts. Diffuse, shadowless light and glaring sunlight are effects that produce entirely different degrees of brightness and color contrasts. When taking a series of several images,

Fig. 40: Dark background

Fig. 41: Deliberate overexposure

Fig. 42: Low contrast to surroundings

Fig. 43: High image contrast

photographers should pay attention to creating similar contrasts. > Figs. 42 and 43

Colors

The human eye is capable of distinguishing the finest color differences, and the reproduction of a single hue is technically possible, but every photograph will always remain an approximation of reality since an infinite number of colors can be present in a motif. No reproduction medium (screen, print, projector, etc.) is capable of showing all the colors found in nature. > Figs. 44 and 45 Since a realistic representation of all the colors of a motif is not feasible, photographers should concentrate on conveying their own impression of color. The only reason a color photograph seems more realistic than a black-and-white image is that it contains more elements that need to be interpreted.

Fig. 44: Color created by artificial light

Fig. 45: Color created by reflections on materials

Fig. 46: High color saturation

Fig. 47: Low color saturation

Color saturation

Aside from hue and brightness, colors are also defined by saturation. High saturation results in bold, brilliant and eye-catching colors. > Fig. 46 In extreme cases, an image with low color saturation resembles a black-and-white photograph. Even if factors such as saturation and color can be modified in image editing, the shooting process should seek to capture the specific sensory stimuli produced by the subject and its environment. Color saturation can be used effectively to convey local moods as well as the photographer's impressions. As a result, low color saturation can itself become a theme in architectural documentation. > Fig. 47

Focus

Focus can also be used to emphasize single objects within the depicted space. From a technical perspective, focus refers to the adjustment of the focal distance of the camera. > Chapter Fundamentals of photography

Fig. 48: Background blur

Fig. 49: Selected focus

Fig. 50: Entire motif

Fig. 51: 1% reproduction of detail

In architectural photography, the entire picture area usually falls within the depth of field. If photographers decide to deviate from this rule, they should do so for a well thought-out reason. It is worthwhile to analyze the use of focus and blurs in cinema films in order to become acquainted wlth their potential. Upon closer inspection, it is easy to recognize different visual languages and effects. A blurry background can help emphasize motifs, particularly architectural details. > Figs. 48 and 49

Reproduction of detail

The resolution of an image is influenced by many factors. > Chapter The camera, Image quality The size of photograph when it is used ultimately plays the most important role in determining the required resolution. Sophisticated photo systems such as medium- and large-format cameras are usually needed to reproduce the tiniest details in very large pictures.

Fig. 52: Reproduction of a surface covered by shadows

Fig. 53: Reproduction of a surface with sidelighting

However, not every photographic concept calls for the maximum resolution of detail. When photographs are produced for purposes such as presentations, resolution of detail is subject to extensive limitations. However, if high resolutions and high image quality are required, details or sections can be adopted from general views without reducing their quality. > Figs. 50 and 51 This should be considered when pictures are taken, especially if they will subsequently be cropped.

Material qualities

Architecture often uses materials, surfaces and structures that are best experienced by touch. To depict these structures, photographers should carefully study the subject's surface and pay special attention to the use of light and the reproduction of detail. A popular method for emphasizing fine structures is the use of sidelight—that is, rays of light falling across the structure at a low angle. Many materials require high resolution of detail, while others require additional light or the precise reproduction of different hues. A thematic analysis of the materials used can help determine the required technical implementation. > Figs. 52 and 53

Movement

In contrast to frozen movements created by short exposure times, speed can be depicted by motion blurs. Blurs are created by incorrect focus or by a motif that moves during shooting. The factors determining motion blurs include the speed of the object, the direction it is moving, and exposure times. A human face can easily become an attention-grabber in a photograph, transforming the architectural depiction into a portrait. Motion blurs can be used to avoid this problem. Vehicles that would otherwise disrupt the photograph can be made less obtrusive in the same way. Here, too, a tripod must be used. The proper exposure time for a balanced graphic representation of movement can only be

Fig. 54: Motion blurs left by vehicles

Fig. 55: Motion blurs left by people

determined by trial and error. The moving objects should generally remain recognizable, with only their details appearing blurry. > Figs. 54 and 55

IMAGE FACTOR: GRAPHICS

Proportions

The area taken up by the sky in relation to the subject, the subject itself in its environment, the use of vertical or horizontal format—proportions play an important role in both color photography and architectural design. For the study of photographic proportions, image elements can be divided into points, lines and planes. The principle of proportions assigns different weights to individual building elements.

For example, if a building with a gable roof is photographed close up, the roof will look smaller in relation to the outside wall than if it is shot from further away. However, it is only at a theoretically infinite distance that the same relations are shown as in a plan view. Proportions assign every element a place in the image. Even a small element can be made to look large and important if it is positioned in the foreground, and an unimportant element can be made to look important if it is skillfully arranged it on a homogenous plane.

Like all graphic works, photography is subject to basic rules of proportion such as the Golden Section. > Figs. 56 and 57

Proportions: points

Many photographs contain individual points that catch the eye. Photographers should only use such points selectively and as part of a well thought-out concept since they have the potential to disturb even a balanced photographic composition. Reducing the number of elements usually produces a calmer picture. An appropriate visual focus can help

Fig. 56: Proportion of sky and building

Fig. 57: Proportion of floor, ceiling and walls

Fig. 58: Individual element as a color accent

Fig. 59: Focal point in a room

guide the viewer's gaze. A person shown in a photograph will always be a point of visual focus and can serve as a yardstick, compensate for large, uniform areas, or act to grab attention in a busy environment. In order to evaluate the proportions of an image, photographers may find it helpful to place a piece of tracing paper over the image and mark out the compositional elements. > Figs. 58 and 59

Proportions: lines

Perspectives, visual axes, paths and edges are always key elements in architectural contexts. They, too, are part of the graphic compositional element and must be considered. The horizon is the predominant line in most general views of buildings. When several pictures are taken of the≈same building, the series will have a much calmer overall effect if the horizon is located at the same height and does not vary. With the

Fig. 60: Line important for photograph

Fig. 61: Railing line generates asymmetry.

Fig. 62: Proportions of plane and sky in relation to one another

Fig. 63: Proportion of plane and background sky

exception of the horizon, the lines essential for the image do not need to be straight. Bent and curved linear elements are also categorized as lines. > Fig. 60 The dynamic nature and depth of an image is usually the result of the lines therein. If a railing or other line running out toward the viewer is diagonal, it will have an entirely different effect from a vertical line. > Fig. 61

Proportions: planes

Various elements in the photograph are also perceived as planes. These can include facades, the sky, streetscapes, and landscape areas. Large, uniform planes direct the viewer's gaze to the rest of the composition. In a photograph that consists almost exclusively of the sky or a meadow, the eye will inevitably fall on elements that break up this homogeneity and enhance its effect.

Fig. 64: Brightness proportions: low key

Fig. 65: Brightness proportions: high key

Planes should be used in a way that suits the depicted architecture. In our modern age, planes are used differently compared with other historical periods such as the Baroque: two-dimensional, homogeneous elements are viewed as "calm" in a positive sense. This fact must be borne in mind in photography. Nevertheless, the serenity and balance of well-proportioned planes are perceived in a photograph only if the same design principles are applied when the picture is taken. > Figs. 62 and 63

Proportions: brightness

The distribution of light and dark areas across a photograph also represents a graphic element like the reproduction elements described above. This becomes particularly evident when extremes are viewed. Photographs that consist primarily of low-key > Fig. 64 or high-key > Fig. 65 areas have a very distinct character and cannot easily be combined with others. Dark areas with light patterns arouse curiosity or can have a threatening effect. Light areas often have a flat, lightweight effect. The distribution of brightness across a photograph is also important. In painting, the illusion of spatial depth is created by a sequence of increasingly light visual elements. This effect can also be used as a deliberate stylistic device in photography. > Figs. 30, page 348, and 41, page 351 By contrast, a light room with dark vanishing points has a much more two-dimensional effect.

Proportions: colors

It is also advisable to explore the effect of colors and their proportions. The large blue areas of the sky and the green of the natural environment can be as effective visually as the gray of cities. If complementary colors predominate—e.g. blue and yellow > Fig. 66, or red and green—they can create effects that differ from those of monochrome images containing color accents. > Fig. 58, page 356 It is usually easier to alter

Fig. 66: Effect of blue, yellow and green planes

Fig. 67: Effect of red and yellow planes

the colors of the environment than those of the subject itself. A white building depicted in combination with a green field and a blue sky has an entirely different effect from the same building presented with a white sky and snow. Like individual colors, which are always important in themselves, color proportions must be tailored to the subject. A boldly colored building should be depicted differently from a building in subdued colors. > Fig. 67 The photographer's experience, concept and aesthetic perceptions are of great importance in this regard.

The photograph

To create architectural photography that captures a building's visual statement and the way it is perceived, the photographer should study the structure's architectural content and the image-analytical factors discussed in the previous chapter. Ideation and subject analysis are required to determine how best to cope with the problems inherent in nearly all architectural photographs.

THE SERIES

In magazines, books, lectures and presentations, photographs are shown in a series, the overall effect of which often overrides that of the individual images.

It is only by combining several images that photographers can transform an individual shot into a thematic work. If the same subject appears in all of them, the result will be a series. Nevertheless, the overall impression is likely to be inconsistent and confused if the subject is shown on a sunny day in one, in black-and-white in another, in a detail view in yet another, and finally from an aerial perspective. Photographers should therefore select specific photographic factors to be used as constants to give the series a common thread. Any of the factors described in the "Image analysis" chapter can function as constants in this sense. The selection of certain factors as constants and others as variables is often of paramount importance for the visual statement made by the entire architectural documentation. To develop a concept for a series, photographers must first examine the qualities, strengths and weaknesses of the motif, as well as the architectural statement the building makes. This provides a basis for the guiding principle behind the series. Black-and-white images are especially well suited for creating a thematic context for highly diverse motifs. ● ■

● **Example:** The figure on page 360 shows student work produced in Valencia. The students chose a single factor as a constant for each theme. In one series it is color saturation, in another, the detail shown, in a third, point of view. You can easily recognize the individual works as part of a series if you imagine reshuffling the photographs and grouping them in another way.

■ **Tip:** If photographers plan to show images on a projector, they can illustrate the function of moving parts by taking several slightly varied shots using a tripod and presenting them in succession like a film. The series will convey a clear spatial impression of the building.

DIVERGENT LINES

One problem in architectural photography is the depiction of vertical lines that run parallel to each other or diverge. These divergent lines are non-parallel vertical lines that result from a three-point perspective. They always appear when the camera is tilted and the horizon is not at eye level. The problem of divergent lines is a result of geometry and has nothing to do with image errors or distortion.

Architectural photography nearly always uses two-point perspective with parallel vertical lines. > Figs. 39, page 350, and 42, page 351 Since viewers know that the lines (e.g. the edges of a highrise) are parallel in reality, they also expect them to be so in a photograph. Non-vertical lines are disturbing, especially in relation to the edges of the photograph, which are always vertical. In addition to two-point perspective, architectural photography often uses a central perspective with one vanishing point. This best approximates the plan view. > Figs. 20, page 345, and 66, page 359

Local conditions are often so cramped that it is impossible to optimally photograph a building due to the limited angle of view in the photograph. If the camera is tilted upward and positioned close to the subject, the entire motif can be photographed, but the result will exhibit divergent lines. > Fig. 70 left If a lens with a wider angle of view is used and the camera is held horizontally, the building lines will appear straight in the photograph, but this photograph will show a great deal of the surroundings, especially below the level of the horizon. The problem can be solved by cropping, yet poorer image quality will often result. > Fig. 70 center The best solution is to use a shift lens or a camera with a vertically adjustable lens. > Fig. 70 right With this equipment, only part of the picture area is depicted, and adjustments can be made by shifting the lens. However, it is crucial that the image circle be considerably larger than the film format. > Chapter The camera

Divergent lines can also be corrected and made parallel in the image editing phase, but this usually leads to poorer image quality as well. > Chapter Image editing

ORDER

A second and equally important topic is that of order. Cities consist of more than buildings, streets, and nature. They also include a large number of other objects that, while hardly noticed in everyday life, can prove highly disruptive in a photograph. Parked cars, garbage cans, cyclists, pedestrians, street signs, power poles, street lights, billboards and many other elements can draw the eye in a picture.

Fig. 68: Divergent lines

Fig. 69: Corrected lines

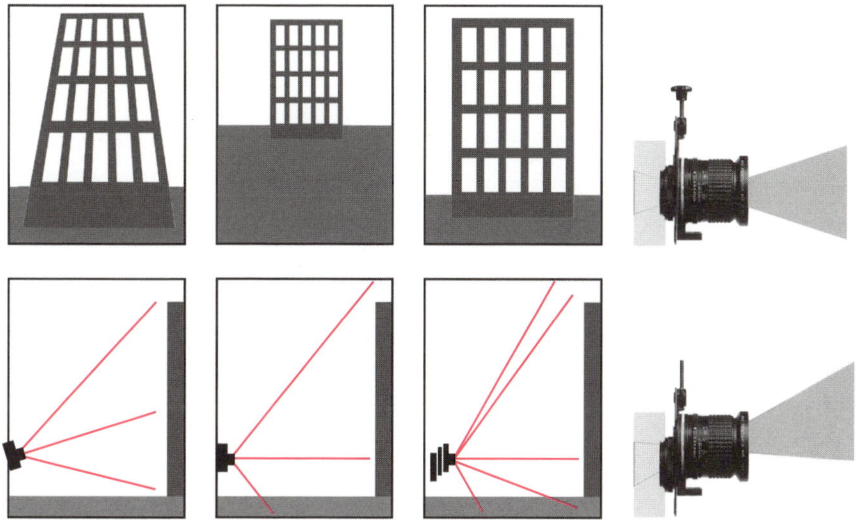

Fig. 70: Divergent lines and correction options

Moreover, architecture is often hidden by furnishings and decoration in interior spaces. The given state of the motif and the photographic concept will determine whether this state should remain unchanged as the natural one or whether photographers should attempt to restore the order shown in plans and animations.

Photographs in architectural magazines often seem over-tidy and ordered, to the point of emptiness. As described in the "Image analysis" chapter, photographers should duly consider which image elements undermine the visual statement and which strengthen it.

Many disruptive elements can be eliminated by selecting a favorable viewpoint, while others can be made less obtrusive by applying different aspects of image composition. A slightly raised viewpoint may also be a solution. Using a ladder, photographers can easily raise eye level to a height of 3 or 4 m, which will remove parked cars from the area around the motif. Using a camera box as a base and a suitably tall tripod can also considerably expand options.

Smaller elements such as flowerpots, chairs and pieces of fabric can be temporarily removed or rearranged. Even the decision to partially close or open building windows can be decisive for a photograph's effect.

It is nearly always necessary to create order in inhabited interior rooms. As a result of their greater density, interior spaces almost always look messier in a photograph than they do in real life. In addition, individual objects tend to dominate the view and divert attention from spatial proportions.

If necessary, the effect of disruptive objects can be diminished by longer exposure times. In some cases, parked cars can be concealed by photographing cars driving by. If the exposure time is longer than a quarter of a second, cars driving by will appear as stripes and will be thus perceived as much less disruptive than parked cars. Passers-by are also perceived differently if they are in motion, and they may possibly not be noticed at all if exposure times are long enough.

The proper exposure time depends on the object's speed. It is always wise to take several shots with different settings—which is of course only possible with a tripod. If there are too many passers-by or moving vehicles in a photograph, multiple exposures may offer a solution. With the camera on the tripod, three, five or ten photographs are taken at different time intervals with the same camera setting (the color settings and exposure must be the same). In the image editing phase, all the images are placed on top of each other, and the disruptive elements are removed from the individual layers. Since the moving objects are never in the same place in the different shots, all the parts of the photograph can be depicted without the disruptive objects. This process can naturally also be carried out in reverse if, for example, the photographer wants to turn an empty shopping arcade into a lively meeting point. There are programs that can automatically assemble the image from the individual shots.

Fig. 71: Photograph in twilight

Finally, there is the option of retouching images, but this should only be used sparingly. More often than not, viewers will be able to see that something has been altered in the image, especially since exaggerated retouching can distract viewers and prevent them from thoroughly engaging with the constructed environment.

WEATHER

Weather plays a decisive role in architectural photography, especially in exterior shots, but is often impossible to predict. As a result, there are limits to the photographer's capacity to plan for it. If facades have been dampened by rain, they look very different from how the appear in sunny weather, due to the kind of light created by the overcast sky, the changed surfaces, and surface reflections. It is crucial to observe the building in different kinds of light in order to achieve the proper effect. Fine weather and blue skies are not always a must—other weather conditions can also support a concept. > Chapter Image analysis

Snow is always a special case. Pictures of snow are nothing out of the ordinary in winter, but in summer they can seem strange. By contrast, summer images often exude a positive atmosphere even in winter. Images including snow should therefore only be used in exceptional cases. It is also difficult to combine them with other images. Snow

Photographs taken at twilight have a special look. They often make dark window surfaces appear bright or generate a lively atmosphere based on the quality of the light. Twilight photographs should be taken Twilight

Fig. 72: Interior space with natural light

just after sunset so that the sky has sufficient residual light. > Fig. 71 Since it is difficult to select the right point in time for an optimal balance between lightness both outside and inside, it is advisable to mount the camera on a tripod just before sunset in order to monitor camera settings and to take pictures at regular intervals until it is completely dark. Twilight photographs are usually too difficult for the camera's automatic exposure mode to handle, making it necessary to manually adjust and control exposure times.

INTERIOR SHOTS

The same image composition principles apply to interior shots as to exterior ones, but there are a number of additional lighting and proportioning factors that must be considered in concept development. > Fig. 72

Proportions

It is nearly impossible to photograph even a single wall of a standard square room using a normal lens (angle of view approx. 50°, 35 mm, focal length 50 mm). Wide-angle lenses are essential for interior shots, but even an extremely wide angle will at best capture only one wall and parts of the adjacent ones. The human eye is also incapable of taking in the entire room, but people can sense its proportions. In a photograph, this can be conveyed only if the interior space is very large. A tiny room may also be well proportioned, but the photograph will have to convey this spatial atmosphere by other means. Creativity is required to find a suitable concept. > Chapter Image analysis

ARTIFICIAL LIGHT

Artificial light is usually present in interior rooms together with natural light. Most light sources look white to the eye. Only candlelight is so

Fig. 73: Interior space with artificial lighting

Fig. 74: Interior space with mixed lighting

yellow that it is perceived as such. However, cameras can register even slight differences in the color of light. Every light source (light bulbs, halogen lamps, gas discharge lamps, fluorescent lamps, etc.) has its own color. > Figs. 73 and 74

One disadvantage of fluorescent lamps is their discontinuous color spectrum. While the human eye perceives fluorescent light as white, sensors or film often show it as green. If the room has several different light sources that are not carefully combined, the photographic moods will be heterogeneous and unpleasant.

There are different ways to compensate for discrepancies in the color of light. Digital cameras offer a white balance function for uniform discrepancies. > Chapter The camera, Control elements Colors can also be adjusted to a certain extent in the image editing phase. Nevertheless, if the room contains a colored light source, some colors will not be depicted. For example, if a light bulb is green, the red shades will be shown as dark gray to brown, since the red components are not present in the light and cannot therefore be reflected from the surface. This problem is caused not only by very colorful light but also by neon tubes. If wood is illuminated solely by neon light, it will be poorly reproduced without additional lighting.

Fig. 75: High contrast

Fig. 76: Corrected contrast

Flash

The flash device often integrated into digital cameras is unsuitable for interior shots since its direct, harsh light does not modulate the room, but makes it look flat and lifeless. Additional indirect lighting should always be used since the hard shadows produced by direct light are always unpleasant. If the lamp is directed at a wall not photographed by the camera, a much more even light will result. Construction site spotlights, floor lamps or a small handheld flash can all be used, depending on the desired color of light and the necessary illumination.

Contrast range

One common problem with interior shots is the high contrast range. The differences between the dark corners of the room and the light windows can be so great in the photograph that the windows will be completely washed out, or the unlit parts of the room will be entirely black. This problem can be solved with digital technology using HDRI (high dynamic range imaging) > Chapter Image editing or with the layer technique. In the latter case, exposures are taken with different degrees of brightness—a darker image in which the window or perhaps the outside space is properly depicted, and a brighter image to pick up the dark areas of the room. The images are then combined manually so that the contrasting areas are evenly illuminated.

However, these techniques should be used sparingly to produce natural-looking images. In publications one often finds photographs in which the landscape seen through windows appears as it would if the viewer were standing outside, or a deep interior space is lit with the intensity of daylight. Even though the technical editing process makes this possible, photographs with a washed-out window or slight corrections can at times convey spatial impressions much more effectively. > Figs. 75 and 76

CONSTRUCTION SITES

Construction site documentation is a special case since it records daily construction activity in order to preserve evidence. The architect's responsibility to document the construction process takes precedence over the composition of individual shots. Important aspects of documentation include image archiving, their chronological sequence, and their completeness. Efforts should always be made to document all the components of the subject since it is impossible to tell at the time of shooting what photographs will be required at a later point in time in order to document possible errors. "Establishing shots" are also necessary to properly categorize detail shots. It is advisable to use a zoom lens with a small wide angle in the lower zoom area in order to photograph the different motifs in interior and exterior space.

Lighting

As long as natural light is an adequate source of illumination, photographers should refrain from using additional lighting. If it is not possible to illuminate the space using a construction site spotlight, and the camera's flash must be used for reasons of time, an external flash with a diffuser should be used. A diffuser is a diffusing reflector that softens the harsh light of the flash such that shadows are not rendered flat in the photograph but appear structured by the objects they fall on.

Digital photographs are favored for construction site documentation due to their quick availability and because costs are not dependent on quantity. A disadvantage is that they can be manipulated and must be archived with great care. If digital photographs are used for documentation, the photographer must have a data security concept to prevent data loss. The data must be saved and stored as backups on secure data storage media in several places. ■

■ **Tip:** A good medium for securing documentation data is the camera's memory card since it has no moving parts and a very long lifespan. If JPEG data are used with manageable resolutions, large quantities can be stored on memory cards at an acceptable cost.

Photographers should refrain from editing site documentation images in order to ensure that different versions of one photograph do not exist, as they could lead to mix-ups and the suspicion that images have been manipulated. It is also wise to save images in JPEG format rather than as RAW data > Chapter Image editing, Storage formats since JPEG is both format- and software-independent and can be used by all participants.

PHOTOGRAPHING MODELS

Architectural photographers do not take pictures of construction sites and completed buildings alone: a common motif is the architectural model. > Fig. 77 Architectural photographs are nearly always taken at eye level, but when models are photographed, this choice depends on the model itself and the camera's technical features. The bird's-eye view is the most popular perspective, especially for urban design models. Here it is wise to use a normal lens since the shot should not be taken too far away from the model. The strong perspective lines resulting from a short distance will otherwise make it difficult to assess the model's proportions. A wide-angle lens is better suited for taking shots from the viewer's height and for ensuring a wide angle of view from a close-up position—similar to the position assumed by the subsequent visitor to the building. To achieve this end, the camera can be placed directly on the base of the model, or shots can be taken from a tripod set up before the table. ■

Models should not be photographed in daylight since the direction and angle of the sun is difficult to influence and the light is often too harsh. If models are photographed in a room, a simple light bulb is often all that is needed as a light source, but it is important to position it properly. To avoid double or triple shadows, the model should never be directly illuminated by more than one light at the same time. Flashes should generally be avoided since they produce unforeseeable shadows

■ **Tip:** If the camera is properly focused, depth-of-field problems rarely arise in architectural photography, but they should be kept in mind when photographs are taken of models at eye level due to the spatial depth that needs to be represented. The aperture must be reduced to increase depth of field. It is also possible to take shots with different focus settings and to assemble them into sharply defined images using special programs.

Fig. 77: Eye-level shot of a model

and lighting effects. If shadows are too dark, the photographer can create adequate lighting conditions with an indirect lamp aimed at the ceiling. Furthermore, shadows can be lightened by means of a light homogeneous surface such as white cardboard positioned opposite the lamp. The reflections lighten dark spots without creating shadows. The optimal position can be determined by moving the surface about.

The basic rule is: the further away the light source, the harder the shadows. If the light is too harsh, transparent paper should be placed in front of the source in order to create more mellow light. Photographers must maintain a safety distance between the lamp and the paper, especially for light sources that become very hot. In the event of longer exposure times, the light source can also be moved to avoid hard shadows.

In most cases, a light or dark fabric will suffice as a background for the model. If necessary, the background area can also be modified in the image editing phase.

Processing the image

After a photograph has been shot, another crucial phase begins for image quality: selecting the most suitable shots and processing them to produce the end product. Save for a few exceptions, this processing phase is carried out on a computer, and for this reason an ever-increasing number of analog photographs are being digitized. An essential part of processing is ensuring workflows are structured and comprehensible.

SCANNING

There are a number of ways to digitize analog film material. The most common method involves using a flatbed scanner, which functions in a similar way to a photocopier. As a general rule, flatbed scanners result in some loss of image information. Better results are achieved by film scanners, which are usually designed for traditional 35 mm film strips or framed slides. However, the quality of the scan varies depending on the particular model. Professional equipment, such as that used in photo laboratories, includes drum scanners, virtual drum scanners and industrial scanners. These systems allow more information to be extracted from a slide than can be seen with the naked eye. However, operation is a very complex process and requires several years of training, and the quality produced depends on the skills of the individual operator. If the maximum amount of information is to be extracted from the analog original, a professional scan, although costly, is essential.

IMPORTING IMAGES

Photographs taken with a digital camera are transferred directly to a computer through a cable or a radio signal. It is also possible to remove the camera's memory card and transfer the data using a reading device. ■

■ **Tip:** An enormous range of programs is available to import, manage, analyze, edit and publish image data. Finding the best program is not as important as identifying, developing and perfecting individual workflows. It is therefore is helpful to take note of which standard storage and editing procedures are generally used for which types of image.

Backing up data

Apart from data transfer between camera and computer, workflow includes the storage and backup of original data and their various image versions. It is a good idea to save the camera's raw data separately so that selected and edited images are not mixed with raw data and do not destroy them. Original camera data cannot be retrieved if information is deleted during post-processing. Even small corrections such as changes to brightness result in a loss of detail information. In some cases, loss that cannot be discerned on a computer screen becomes evident when the results are printed. At the very minimum, backups should be made of the raw data and the edited images so that any loss of data by the storage medium can be rectified.

SELECTING IMAGES

Experience shows that working with a digital camera commonly produces many more photographs than are ultimately needed. Results range from different versions and series of the same motif to variations within the motif (e.g. mobile objects depicted differently in every picture). Image selection and management therefore play an important role in the processing phase and must be integrated into the workflow. In principle this is precisely what the numerous image management programs now available on the market allow photographers to do. Images can be preselected, sorted, renamed and supplemented with comments and keywords. EXIF data can be altered and small corrections can be made to images. Images can also be labeled with keywords to establish an image archive equipped with a search function. Another very practical aspect is the capacity of such programs to create contact proofs, which are files that depict several motifs together.

EXIF files

Exchangeable image file format (EXIF) is a standard file format in which digital cameras store information about photographs (metafiles). Apart from exposure time, aperture and camera default settings–which are already recorded when the photograph is taken–this file format also allows additional information to be listed, such as the photographer's name and the subject of the images.

Image editing

RESOLUTION

The size of a digital image can be described in terms of resolution, pixel count, file size, dpi (dots per inch), or simply photograph size. One important factor for image quality is the distinction between absolute and relative resolution.

Absolute resolution

Absolute resolution refers to the amount of data—defined as the number of depicted pixels—and thus determines the potential reproduction quality of these data. Although image processing software can be used to increase the absolute number of pixels, it cannot improve the quality of the image since it merely extrapolates and interpolates the pixels making up the base data.

Relative resolution

The relative resolution refers to the number of pixels per length unit and is generally measured in terms of pixels or dpi.

Since the relative resolution can be changed during processing without increasing information density, it is merely an indicator of the subsequent production quality of a particular size. The resolutions listed in Table 2 indicate the required relative resolutions for different reproduction media and sizes.

The relative resolution in dpi can only be used to describe the resolution of an image in conjunction with the absolute resolution or the reproduction size. If a 600 dpi file is printed at a size of A4, the resolution on an A2 printout will be 300 dpi because the number of pixels is the same. Only the size and thus the distance between the pixels will have changed.

Tab.2: Relative resolutions for different reproduction media and sizes

72 dpi	Screen resolution
160 dpi	Minimum resolution for large print, DIN A0 and higher
200 dpi	Minimum resolution for large print, DIN A1 and higher
300 dpi	Minimum resolution for simple print
600 dpi	Maximum resolution for most printing technologies—a higher resolution is seldom used

COLORS

Color depth

The bit depth or, more accurately, color depth refers to the fineness of the gradations with which a color channel of a single color is shown, irrespective of how this color is stored as a pixel.

A color depth of 1 bit would mean that precisely two states—e.g. black and red—are possible in a color channel (a computer screen, for example, has red, green, and blue channels). In the case of the conventional color depth of 8 bits, 256 states are possible, i.e. 256 individual hues per color channel. In a color space with three channels, such as conventional RGB, 8 bits per channel mean that 256^3, or 16,777,216, colors are theoretically possible. Most computer monitors can generate only 8 bits per channel. A greater color depth such as 16 or 32 bits (HDR) > Chapter Image editing, Special techniques allows finer color and brightness gradations, but also increases the amount of data. Such images are scaled down when the image data are represented on a monitor (tone mapping).

Color spaces

The color space refers to the system used to represent colors. The same hue has a different designation in each color space. The difference between the color spaces is based on the limits of representation capacity. Not all colors can be represented in every color space; their representations are merely similar. The most important color spaces are:

- RGB (red/green/blue)
- CMYK (cyan/magenta/yellow/black)
- L*a*b* (color axis system)
- HSV (hue saturation value)

Digital cameras, scanners and practically all screens use RGB color spaces, which are based on an additive system made up of red, blue and green. Ideally, lighting in these three colors combines to produce white light. This principle can be observed by looking at a white area on a monitor through a magnifying glass. sRGB, Adobe RGB, Apple RGB and Color Match RGB are different industrial standards, with different representational applications. sRGB is commonly used for screens, the Internet and semi-professional fields. As in many areas, it is not possible to make a clear recommendation here. However, it is important to establish a clear and concise workflow and not to constantly switch standards.

CMYK is a subtractive color space and is the established standard in print media. If the RGB colors were to be printed over one another, the result would be a dark brown. For this reason the color space used in print media is made up of cyan, magenta, yellow and black, since they allow nearly all colors to be represented with the exception of white.

L*a*b* and HSV are larger color spaces that are used in scientific and graphic fields.

Color profiles

Color profiles are essential for professional work. Put simply, a type of calling card (profile) is produced for each of the devices involved in producing an image (scanner, monitors, printer, print media, printing presses, etc.). Such profiles help ensure that colors, brightness and contrast levels in the end product correspond to the original motif. ●

Since profiling requires calibration of the individual devices with a gauge, this field is accessible only to advanced users. The systematic application of profiles is referred to as color management. Non-professional users should also establish a constant workflow and always endeavor to use the same equipment (scanner, monitor, printer, plotter). This will allow them to become acquainted with the particularities of the equipment and keep color deviations to a minimum even without professional color management.

STORAGE FORMATS

Apart from resolution and color depth, storage formats for image data also have a decisive influence on image quality. The initial form of data storage in the camera is of prime importance, as is the data format of the end result.

RAW

RAW or raw image format refers to a data format that varies with different types of cameras and contains minimally processed data from the image sensor. Although the digital image sensors made by different manufacturers essentially function in the same way, the corresponding RAW formats are not compatible. The information content of a RAW format is always greater than that of a processed data format, even if that format is larger. The processing of RAW files is also referred to as RAW development because it has similarities with the development of analog color negative material. RAW development is carried out by programs produced by the camera manufacturer or by plug-ins in the image processing software.

● **Example:** If a data file were printed on two different printers using two different types of paper, it would be a mere coincidence if the resulting color impressions were the same. However, if the profiles of the printers in relation to the types of paper are known, the reproduction can be manipulated using the image editing software to produce almost identical results.

■ **Tip:** To achieve an optimal result, processing in RAW development is preferential to work with an image editing program. In addition, post-processing should be kept to a minimum. Editing image data can reduce or at best maintain the density of information, but it can never increase it.

DNG (digital negative) is a raw image data format developed by Adobe to replace the different RAW formats. In the case of long-term storage this standard is preferable to the camera-specific RAW formats and the standard TIFF and JPEG formats, which are susceptible to data loss. It is still not clear whether DNG will actually become widely established as a standard. DNG

Image files with the suffix jpg are stored using the JPEG standard (JPEG = Joint Photographic Experts Group). JPEG is used to achieve what is known as lossy image compression. The particular advantage of this standard is that it allows photographers to reduce data volume as desired, although this of course affects the density of information. Due to the low data transmission rates involved, nearly all images on the Internet are stored in this image format. JPEG

In image files with the suffix tif or tiff (Tagged Image File Format) every pixel is stored individually, and the file size thus indicates the level of resolution. TIFF is the standard format for image storage without compression. TIFF

PARAMETERS

Raw data can be adjusted, distorted, adapted and retouched in numerous ways in the image processing phase. Of course, images should never be modified simply because it is technically possible to do so. Furthermore, in view of the enormous number of commands, filters and options in photography software, it is easy to forget that there are actually only a handful of key parameters for image editing. For this reason the following section focuses on these parameters and refers readers back to the chapter on image analysis. ■

It is important that a photograph be shot at the right exposure since missing image information cannot be added after the fact. However, a certain tolerance is possible in the RAW development phase. It is also important to keep in mind that brightness should be altered using the gradation curve instead of the brightness and contrast command. Brightness

Similarly, the adjustment of contrasts requires a series of finely graduated changes. When altering contrast, photographers can mistakenly delete light (the bright areas in the image) and shade (the dark areas in the image). This results in the gradations within the image field being irreversibly lost. Contrast

Increasing the contrast on non-homogeneous surfaces is known in digital technology as sharpening. Digital images are nearly always sharpened, either by the camera software itself or during the subsequent Sharpening image processing phase. However, this later correction only increases the impression of sharpness. A blurred area produced during the shooting process cannot be corrected. There are special programs and plug-ins for sharpening. If sharpening is too extreme, artifacts (disturbances) and awkward transitions are produced. For optimal sharpening, photographers also need to consider the target medium (print, screen, etc.) and the output size. For this reason images should be sharpened only at the end of the process.

Colors

The fine adjustment of colors should always take into account the intended end result. It is impossible to precisely determine colors without consistent color management and calibrated hardware. In addition, it is advisable to create a data sample on the different output devices as a guide for achieving the desired result. Printing out a data sample in a specialist laboratory can help determine the consistency of private equipment compared with professional standards. If the colors produced by a printer clearly deviate from the monitor image, a macro should be created to correct the deviation. However, the original data should not be altered too much. ■

If the picture shows color-neutral surfaces, white balance adjustment can be used, as in black-and-white photographs. > Chapter The camera, Control elements

CORRECTING IMAGE ERRORS

Image editing is commonly required due to errors in the image caused by lens problems. > Chapter The camera, Objectives Specialized correction programs are available to deal with almost every kind of error. Some also offer a correction procedure designed for the most common lenses. In addition, every image processing program includes a variety of options for correcting image errors. Typical settings should be stored or noted down so that a particular lens problem can be corrected for all images. Some errors, such as those involving colors on the edges of an image, occur frequently but are difficult to correct. Others, such as the Moiré

■ **Tip:** If you find yourself unsure about changing colors or brightness levels, there is a trick to correct brightness problems and color error. For example, if you need to alter an interior that has been tinted orange by artificial lighting, you should alter the color balance toward cyan until you reach a point where a cyan color error appears. Halving this value will give you a satisfactory alteration measure.

effect (i.e. overlap between a fine grid structure in the motif and the image sensor grid) are almost impossible to correct after the photograph has been shot.

Vignetting

A loss of brightness along the periphery of an image is known as vignetting. Most RAW converters are equipped with a compensation setting that can be used to influence the brightness intensity and gradient. Correcting the brightness gradient manually in the image processing program is a far more laborious process.

Linear distortion

Linear distortion should not be confused with image distortion. The former refers to the arched or barreled representation of parallel lines. > Chapter The camera, Objectives Wide-angle lenses almost always produce this error. Since the distortion is often not regular throughout the image, correction methods may be unable to eliminate the entire effect. It can be helpful to superimpose lines or a grid onto the image when dealing with this problem in the processing phase.

Image distortion

There are many ways of correcting undesired distortions in the three-point perspective. A superimposed grid is also required here.

Dust retouching

Dust is a constant problem in photography and inherent to SLR cameras. It is easier to take measures to avoid it in the first place than to deal with it during the processing phase. Constant checks for dust are particularly important when using interchangeable lenses. In order to test lenses for dust, it is advisable to take a shot of a homogeneous surface (e.g. the sky) with the smallest aperture, and expose for light gray. If dust particles are visible on the images, manual retouching will almost always be necessary. Automatic correction programs tend to wash out the image because they cannot distinguish between tiny image elements and dust particles.

RETOUCHING

The process of retouching images applies not only to the elimination of image errors caused by dust and scratches but also to deliberate changes to images. Digital technology has made it even easier than before to completely transform images. Construction fences, flower pots, cars, and entire houses can now be removed from photographs in order to reduce the content of an image as desired. Given that architectural photography is increasingly being used in advertising, this is a logical development. There is also a growing perception that certain building elements, such as power sockets, lighting outlets, fire alarms, switches and access hatches, tend to disrupt otherwise homogeneous images. Although current image processing programs offer a greater number of retouching options, these should be utilized only when they are really necessary. If a photograph does not accurately reflect a motif, it no longer constitutes a documentation of architectural reality.

SPECIAL TECHNIQUES

Stitching

In photography, stitching refers to the production of one large image from several smaller ones. Using this method, a panorama can be composed from several photographs taken from the same shooting position. Whereas normal image processing may involve joining two or three images, special software is now available to combine even several hundred images. Combining spatial bodies that have not been photographed from the same perspective > Fig. 78 produces an image that does not accurately depict reality. For example, the same elements may appear in different places in the background. Only parallel shifting of the exposure plane or swiveling around the nodal point enables pictures that match reality to be achieved.

Mapping

In nature we sometimes encounter differences in brightness that cannot be represented by film and digital sensors, and that cannot be processed by the eye. Nevertheless, the eye is able to perceive a far greater degree of contrast than a film or a sensor. Furthermore, a printed image is able to show a far lower level of contrast than a computer screen. For this reason contrasts as well as colors are condensed in a process known as gamut or color mapping. This process often operates in the background of other processes–for example, during printing with printing software–but it can also be consciously controlled, as in high dynamic range imaging.

HDR

High dynamic range imaging (HDR) attempts to represent extreme contrasts within an image. In a dark room with small windows, the landscape outside can be easily discerned with the naked eye, like the objects in the room. But the range of contrast is extremely difficult to depict in a photograph. Either the representation of the room will correspond to its perception by the naked eye and the window will appear white, or the landscape will be recognizable but the room will appear black. The eye compensates for differences in brightness by changing its aperture (pupil) and through other visual processes. Indeed, we do not see everything at the same time but in succession. The HDR technique attempts to reproduce these extreme contrasts by combining images produced at different exposures. This technical possibility is fascinating but the end product usually looks artificial. Viewing habits can change but they only do so very slowly. A washed-out window in a dark room is perceived as more natural in an image than a window that separates an equally bright interior from an exterior space. In the latter case, the window is perceived as a light box. Such techniques can be applied if they actually improve the impression made by the image.

Fig.78: An image composed from 40 individual photos

THE IMAGE AS END PRODUCT

Application data

Every application places specific demands on the type of data used. On the Internet or in a beamer presentation, data size is the decisive factor. Different printers often require different color spaces or operate with different resolutions. To convert data into the appropriate format it is therefore necessary to be aware of the special requirements of the particular application. To ensure flexibility it is also essential to have access to specific kinds of application data as well as the master file. It makes no sense to incorporate a 30 or 40 MB file stored in 16 bit into a beamer presentation. Here, the maximum resolution is usually only 1024 × 768 pixels, and large quantities of data will only hold up proceedings. Many image processing programs also include a batch processing function that can convert several images at the same time.

Data formats

Another important aspect to bear in mind is the need to ensure that file formats are convertible and that any processing done on Mac is compatible with PC systems. High compression rates should always be avoided when using data formats prone to information loss (e.g. JPEG). A better approach is to first reduce the size of the images and then to compress them.

Image transmission

If image data need to be transmitted to others (postcard printers, journals for publication, etc.), consistent color management is a must. > Chapter Image editing, Colors If this is not possible, it is advisable to pass on samples of the original material that show the desired effect.

Printers

Every printer and every type of paper has its own characteristics. Photographers should limit themselves to a small range of media once they have identified the equipment and material best suited to their purposes. With regard to printer workflow, it should be noted that printer software often includes automatic functions that carry out color corrections in the background. Photographers aiming to control this process themselves need to disable these functions in advance. Inkjet printers and the appropriate type of paper can now achieve such impressive results that it is easy to forget that it is ultimately the user who must decide what the final colors will look like—and color assessment requires a trained eye.

Light resistance

If an inkjet printer is used, the question of light resistance should also be considered. Some systems use special pigments to provide protection from light, while others favor particular types of paper. These are relatively new techniques and there is no basis as yet for judging longevity or identifying a particularly effective system.

The architect and communications media

Today, architects are expected to be familiar with a range of specialist areas and peripheral fields. Even though they are not able to replace a particular specialist, they are expected to communicate with that person at an advanced technical level. In recent years, media and advertising, in particular, have posed additional challenges to architects. Collaboration with photographers, writers, editors, journalists, and PR specialists is increasingly becoming part of everyday architectural work. For this reason alone, it is advisable for both students and practitioners to develop an insight into the field of architectural photography. While architects are not supposed to replace photographers, they need to be able to evaluate and, if necessary, direct photographic input into a project.

Auteur photography

At its best, architectural photography is auteur photography, which exhibits the photographer's trademark style and has an additional level of quality based on his or her competence. The field of architecture most closely related to photography is that of design. Design is also based on principles and learned techniques, but it is only by virtue of the author's personality that an individual work is produced.

Such authorial images are preferred in most of the specialist media connected with the practice of architecture. In recent years promotional photography has been gaining increasing importance in the architectural field. In this case it is the image and its effect on the observer that is the focus of attention, rather than the built object itself.

All architects should thus consider the ways in which they intend to market their work. In addition, the use of images produced by professional photographers requires architects to be familiar with photo copyright.

Photo copyright

Copyright on images lies exclusively with the author of the images concerned. However, usage rights are transferable. These are the rights that architects must acquire from photographers if they want to use–i.e. publish–the latter's images. Usage rights can be transferred both for a particular purpose such as an Internet presentation and for general use of the material. Usually photographers grant architects simple usage rights, which are, however, not transferable to third parties. The architect is thus free to use the images to market his or her own work in brochures and on Internet sites. However if a third party, such as a publisher or a specialist firm, would like to publish the images, this party is obligated to pay the photographer for usage rights. In most countries the fee involved is set by agreements between the relevant professional associations. Apart from the arrangement whereby every user pays the photographer for specific use of the latter's images, photographers also have the option of granting exclusive usage rights. In this case the user is completely free to decide how the images are to be used. Since this arrangement, which corresponds to the model used in the field of promotional photography, often entails considerable cost to architects, they seldom use it. Furthermore, using such a model makes little sense in this context, since most specialist media outlets have fixed fees for the reproduction of images, which they pay to the photographer but not the architect.

In conclusion

Once the technical hurdles have been cleared, photography can become a wonderful tool for the architect. Furthermore, training the art of seeing through the analysis of photographs and their intent is itself extremely helpful for architectural work. It is only when one can see details and interconnections that these aspects can inform one's own work. Although the camera is not an indispensable part of this kind of sensitization, apart from the sketch pad it provides the best form of practice. Representation is always reduction and thus interpretation. It is only through the interpretation of what already exists that something new can emerge.

Furthermore, there are many interesting conclusions to be drawn from the differences between the concrete experience of building and the image of it disseminated in the media.

Students should begin as early as possible to compile their own picture archives, comprising both examples from publications and their own images. Even the seemingly infinite variety of examples available on the Internet cannot replace an individual's own collection.

In later professional life, advertising and public relations also play a significant role for architects. Being able to convey information about the work one has done is vital to securing contracts. Since a client's introduction to the work of an architect is often through Internet presentations and brochures rather than a direct viewing of buildings, photographs can play a key role in shaping a potential client's initial impressions. Moreover, the kudos enjoyed by architects within their profession is almost always based on effective representations and photographs of their work.

It is thus very important for an architect to engage with the photographic medium in order to be able to assess its representational possibilities. The design concept for a building can only be communicated when the photographic image takes it up and mediates it.

Appendix

Literature

FREEHAND DRAWING

Jonathan Andrews: *Architectural Visions. Contemporary Sketches, Perspectives, Drawings,* Braun, Salenstein 2010

Alejandro Bahamón: *Sketch: Houses,* Loft Publications, Barcelona 2008

Herman van Bergeijk and Deborah Hauptmann: *Notations of Herman Hertzberger,* Nai Publishers, Rotterdam 1998

Matthew Brehm: *Sketching on location,* Kendall Hut Publishing Company, Dubuque 2012

Gabriel Campanario: *The Art of Urban Sketching,* Quarry Books, Beverly 2012

Francis D. K. Ching: *Architecture: Form, Space & Order,* John Wiley & Sons, Hoboken 2007, 3rd edition

Magali Delgado Yanes and Ernest Redondo Dominguez: *Freehand Drawing for Architects and Interior Designers,* Parramon Paidotribo, Barcelona 2005

Brian Edwards: *Understanding Architecture Through Drawing,* E & FN Spon, London 1994

Danny Gregory: *An illustrated life. Drawing inspiration from the private sketchbooks of artists, illustrators and designers,* How Books, Cincinnati 2008

Eric Jenkins: *Drawn to Design. Analyzing Architecture Through Freehand Drawing,* Birkhäuser, Basel 2013

Cathy Johnson: *Artist's Journal Workshop. Creating your life in words and pictures,* F&W Media, Newton Abbot 2011

Natascha Meuser: *Construction and Design Manual. Architectural Drawings,* DOM publishers, Berlin 2012

Grant W. Reid: *Landscape Graphics. Plan, Section, and Perspective Drawing of Landscape Spaces,* Watson-Guptill Publications, New York 2002

James Richards: *Freehand Drawing and Discovery: Urban Sketching and Concept Drawing for Designers,* John Wiley & Sons, Hoboken 2013

Francesca Serrazanetti and Matteo Schubert: *La mano dell'architetto. The hand of the architect,* FAI – Fondo Ambiente Italiano/ Moleskine srl/Editrice Abitare Segesta, Milan 2009

TECHNICAL DRAWING

Balder Batran et al.: *Bauzeichnen: Architektur, Ingenieurbau, Tief-, Straßen- und Landschaftsbau,* Holland + Josenhans, Stuttgart 2013

Jörg Breuer, Thomas Kesseler, Uta Pottgiesser, Verena Wriedt: *Architektur- und Plandarstellung,* UTB, Paderborn 2007

David Dernie: *Architectural Drawing,* Laurence King Publishing, London 2014
Hansjörg Frey et al.: *Bautechnik Technisches Zeichnen,* Europa-Lehrmittel, 2010
W. Otie Kilmer and Rosemary Kilmer: *Construction Drawings and Details for Interiors: Basic Skills,* Wiley, Hoboken 2008
Gernot Störzbach: *Architektur zeichnen: Ein Arbeitsbuch zum Selbststudium,* Springer Vieweg, Wiesbaden 2013

MODELBUILDING

Nick Dunn: *Architectural Modelmaking,* Laurence King Publishing, London 2010
Wolfgang Knoll and Martin Hechinger: *Architektur-Modelle: Anregungen zu ihrem Bau,* DVA, Munich 2006
David Neat: *Model-Making: Materials and Methods,* Crowood Press, Ramsbury 2008
Eva Pascual i Miró: *Advanced Architectural Modelmaking,* W. W. Norton & Co, New York 2010
Megan Werner: *Model Making*, Princeton Architectural Press, New York 2012

ARCHITECTURAL PHOTOGRAPHY

Götz Adriani: *In Szene gesetzt, Architektur in der Fotografie der Gegenwart,* Hatje Cantz, Ostfildern-Ruit 2002
Gabriele Basilico: *L'esperienza dei luoghi,* Art& Verlag, Tavagnacco (Udine) 1997
Robert Elwall: *Building with Light. An International History of Architectural Photography,* Merell, London 2004
Joachim Giebelhausen: *Architectural Photography,* Nikolaus Karpf, Munich 1965
Klaus Kinold: *"Ich will Architektur zeigen, wie sie ist," Klaus Kinold, Fotograf,* Richter Verlag, Düsseldorf 1993
Jost J. Marchesi: *digital Fotokollegium 1–3,* Verlag Photographie, Schaffhausen 2007
Cervin Robinson, Joel Herschman: *Architecture Transformed. A History of the Photography of Buildings from 1839 to the Present,* MIT Press, Cambridge, MA 1987
Karl-Hugo Schmölz: *Hugo Schmölz, Fotografierte Architektur 1924–1937,* Mahnert-Lueg, Munich 1982
Julius Shulman: *Modernism Rediscovered,* Taschen, Cologne 2013
Julius Shulman: *Photographing Architecture and Interiors,* Balcony Press, Glendale, CA 2000
Susan Sontag: *On photography,* Anchor Books, New York 1990

TECHNICAL DRAWING

Typical abbreviations

A	area
ANC	anchor
a.g.	above grade
a.s.l.	above sea level
B/	bottom
BC	blind cases
BESF	bottom edge shell floor
BSMT	basement
CAD	Computer-Aided Design
CEL	cellar
CH	clearance height
CHL	channel
CIRC	circumference
CLG	ceiling
CLR	clearance
cm	centimeters
CND	conduit
DIN	Deutsches Institut für Normung
FD	floor drain/fire-resisting door
FDN	foundation
FFL	finished floor level
FLR	floor
GDT	gradient
LNTL	lintel
m	meters
mm	millimeters
m^2	square meters
MO	masonry opening
MSL	mean sea level
OPG	opening
R	radius
RAD	radiator
Roll	roller blind
RSR	riser
SH	sill height
SSL	structural slab level
T/	top
TECF	top edge complete floor
TESF	top edge shell floor
U/S	underside
W	wall
ZL	zero level

Symbols

Symbols for sanitary fittings

Item	Symbol
Hand basin	
Basin	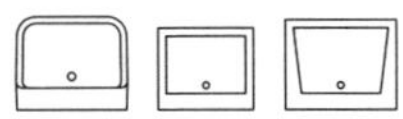
WC with cistern	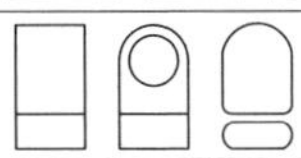
WC without cistern	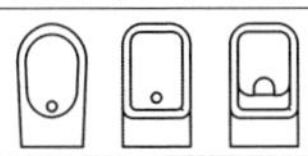
Bidet	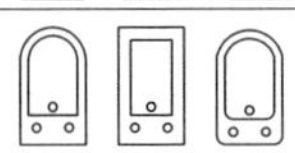
Urinal	
Shower-base	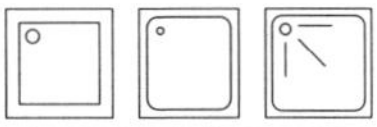
Bathtub	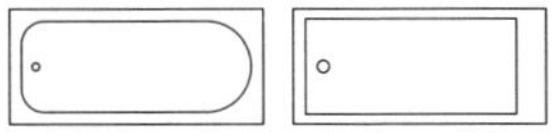
Washing machine	
Tumble dryer	
Corner bathtub	

Symbols for kitchen fittings

Item	Symbol
Cupboard under	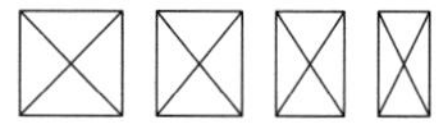
Cupboard over	
Cupboard under and over	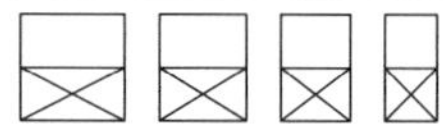
Sink with draining board	
Gas cooker	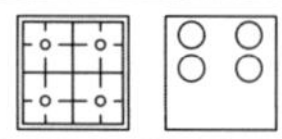
Electric cooker	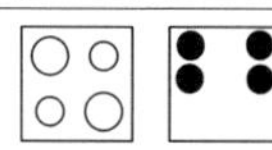
Cooker with oven	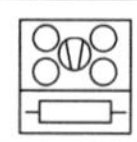
Built-in oven	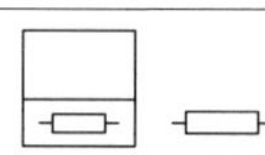
Worktop	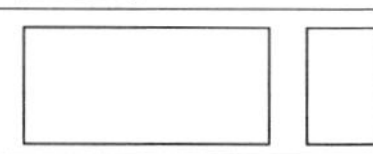
Refrigerator	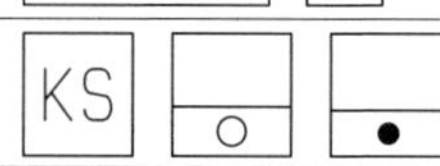
Freezer	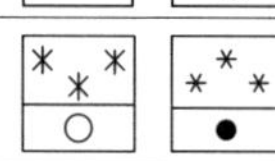
Dishwasher	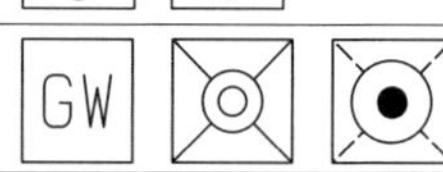
Microwave oven	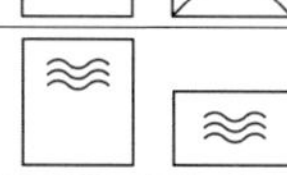
Extractor hood	
Chair	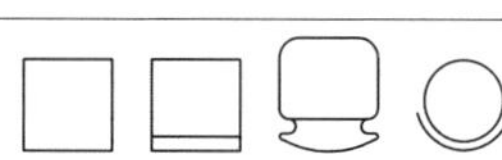
Table	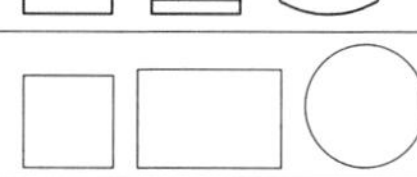

Symbols for furniture

Item	Symbol
Cupboard	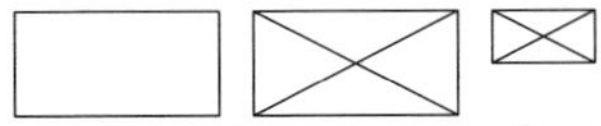
Armchair	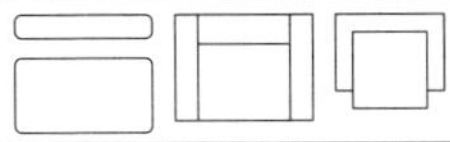
Sofa	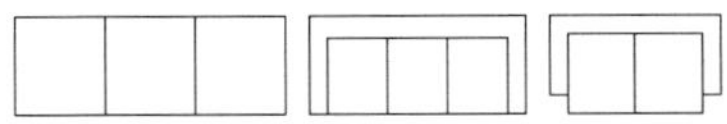
Table	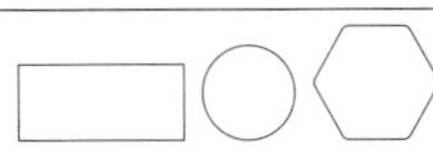
Chair	
Grand piano	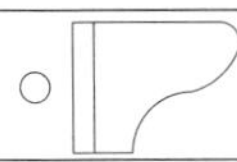
Upright piano	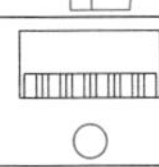
Desk	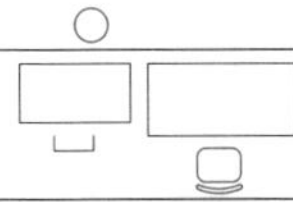
Wardrobe	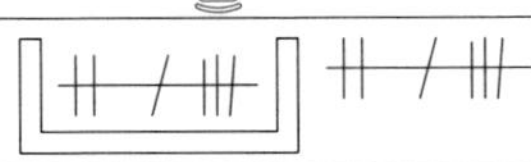
Single bed	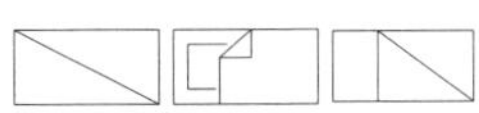
Single bed with bedside table	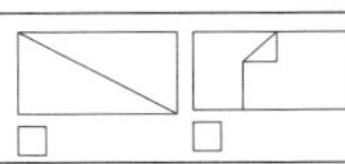
Double bed	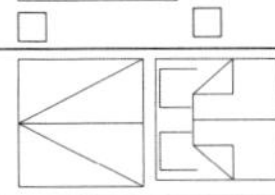
Double bed with bedside table	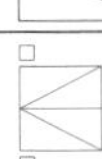

Standards

Large areas of Technical Drawing are covered by international standards. For this reason, they are standardized by ISO standards, which are recognized in most countries. The following table gives the valid ISO standards, which have generally been adopted by the national standardization institutions (ISO 128 would then be called DIN ISO 128 in Germany, for example).

Relevant ISO standards

ISO standards	Description
ISO 128	Technical drawings. General principles of presentation
ISO 216	Writing paper and certain classes of printed matter. Trimmed sizes. A and B series
ISO 2594	Building drawings - Projection methods
ISO 3766	Construction drawings. Simplified representation of concrete reinforcement
ISO 4067	Building and civil engineering drawings - Installations
ISO 4069	Building and civil engineering drawings - Representation of areas on sections and views - General principles
ISO 4157	Construction drawings - Designation systems
ISO 5455	Technical drawings. Scales
ISO 5456	Technical drawings. Projection methods
ISO 6284	Construction drawings - Indication of limit deviations
ISO 7518	Construction drawings. Simplified representation of demolition and rebuilding
ISO 7519	Construction drawings. General principles of presentation for general arrangement and assembly drawings
ISO 8048	Technical drawings. Construction drawings. Representation of views, sections and cuts
ISO 8560	Construction drawings. Representation of modular sizes, lines and grids
ISO 9431	Construction drawings. Spaces for drawing and for text, and title blocks on drawing sheets
ISO 10209	Technical product documentation. Vocabulary. Terms relating to technical drawings
ISO 11091	Construction drawings. Landscape drawing practice

CAD

Checklists and overview of software

Sample layer structure for designing a building

Environment	Building
	Development
	Trees
	Piece of property
Design	Design grid
	Layouts
	Views
	Sections
Loadbearing structure	Construction grid
	Foundations
	Exterior walls
	Interior walls
	Columns
	Beams
	Stairs
	Ceilings
	Roof structure
Building finishing	Grid
	Lightweight construction
	Electrical installation
	Heating and plumbing
Furnishings	Bathroom fixtures
	Furniture
	Objects
	Flooring
Drawing information	Dimensioning
	Labelling
	Areas and rooms
	Room label
	Hatches
	Patterns
	Fillings
	Symbols
	Markers
	Fixed points

Plan layout	Frame
	Illustrations
	Scans
	Renderings

Checklist for a computer visualization

Capacity	Hardware performance
	Software options
	Timeframe provided
Purpose of visualization	Design tool
	Intermediary presentation
	Final presentation
Level of detail in visualization	Close-up
	Building portrait
	Extended context (e.g. aerial shot)
Rendered scene	Choice of perspective, camera settings
	Image format
	Rendered object
	Lighting scenario
	Background or surroundings
Rendering parameters	if needed, rendering type (e.g. Raytrace, Phong, Gouraud, OpenGL, Z-Buffer etc.)
	Resolution
	Anti-aliasing
Surfaces	Colours
	Textures
	Reflexions
	Transparency

Overview of CAD software

Program	Homepage
Allplan	www.nemetschek.com
ArchiCAD	www.graphisoft.com
ArCon	www.arcon-software.com
AutoCAD / Architectural Desktop / Inventor / Revit Building	www.autodesk.com
BricsCad IntelliCAD	www.bricscad.com
CAD	www.malz-kassner.com
CATIA	www.catia.com
ideCAD	www.idecad.com
MicroStation	www.bentley.com
Reico CADDER	www.reico.de
RIB ARRIBA® CA3D	www.rib-software.com
SketchUp Pro	www.sketchup.com
Spirit	www.softtech.com
Solid Edge	www.ugs.com
TurboCAD	www.imsi.com

Overview of rendering software

Programm	Homepage
3ds Max/VIZ	www.autodesk.com
Artlantis	www.graphisoft.com
Cinema 4D	www.maxon.net
Maya	www.alias.com
mental ray	www.mentalimages.com

Picture credits

FREEHAND DRAWING

Figs. 2, 22, 57: Ulrich Exner
Figs. 6, 44, 45, 51: © 4a Architekten GmbH | Florian Afflerbach
Figs. 7, 8, 15, 88: Martin Schäpers
Figs. 19, 54: © kadawittfeldarchitektur | David Baros
Figs. 23, 53: © 4a Architekten GmbH | Ernst Ulrich Tillmanns
Fig. 48: Boris Szélpal
Fig. 58: © Volkmar Nickol Architekten | Omar Jaramillo
Fig. 66: Gottfried Müller
Figs. 92, 93: Arno Hartmann
Fig. 12 shows sketchbooks by Arno Hartmann, Tina Jacke and Florian Afflerbach
Fig. 59 contains sketches by Ulrich Exner and © 4a Architekten GmbH | Florian Afflerbach
Figs. 70 and 71 contain drawings by Adrian Fischer, Alexander Görg, Arno Hartmann and Florian Afflerbach
All other figures: Florian Afflerbach

CAD

Figs. 1, 4a, 12, 65, 88, 93: Nemetschek AG, Munich - Allplan 2006
Figs. 2, 3, 4b, 10, 11, 24, 69, 71, 92: Graphisoft - ArchiCAD 10
Figs. 4c, 9, 25, 68, 94: Autodesk GmbH Deutschland - Architectural Desktop 2007
Figs. 53–55: Bert Bielefeld, Isabella Skiba
Figs. 73, 74, 76, 77, 78: ch-quadrat architekten
Fig. 75: Frank Münstermann
Fig. 81: HKplus architekten
Figs. 82–87: HKplus architekten/the author
Fig. 89: Maxon Computer GmbH - Cinema 4D R10
All other figures: The author

MODELBUILDING

The following photographs were generously provided by the Chair of Building Theory and Design, Professor Arno Lederer/Professor Daniele Marques, at the University of Karlsruhe. Professor Lederer supervised the designs. The research associates were Kristin Barbey, Roland Kötz, Peter Krebs and Birgit Mehlhorn. Manfred Neubig oversaw the model-making that accompanied the design process. If not otherwise indicated, photographs were taken by Thilo Mechau, on staff at the photography workshop of the Department of Architecture.

Fig. 1: Student project, design, Reykjavik harbor, Florian Bäumler
Fig. 6: Student project, design, Reykjavik harbor, collaborative urban design model
Fig. 19: 1st row: student project, design, "Do it again," Steffen Wurzbacher
3rd row: student project, design, "Do it again," Matthias Rehberg
4th row: student project, design, "Do it again," Ioana Thalassinon
Fig. 24: End-of-term project for building theory course, collaborative model made of plasticine, photo: Cornelius Boy
Fig. 26: Left: student project, design, Palace of the Republic, Marc Nuding
Right: student project, design, Islamic community center, Axel Baudendistel
Fig. 27: Master's project, seaside resort in Barcelona, Philip Loeper
Fig. 48: Student project, design, Reykjavik harbor, Holger Rittgerott
Fig. 49: Student project, design, "Do it again," Lisa Yamaguchi
Fig. 50: Student project, design, "Do it again," Andrea Jörder
Fig. 51: Student project, design, "Do it again," Lisa Yamaguchi
Fig. 60: Student project, design, "Do it again," Benjamin Fuhrmann
Fig. 61: Student project, design, Reykjavik harbor, Markus Schwarzbach
Fig. 62: Student project, design, Reykjavik harbor, Kuno Becker, Tina Puffert, Holger Rittgerott
Fig. 66: Student project, design, Palace of the Republic, Matthias Moll
Fig. 67: Student project, design, Reykjavik harbor, collaborative model
Fig. 68: Student project, design, Islamic community center, Axel Baudendistel

The following photographs were made available by Büro für Architektur Peter Krebs in Karlsruhe.

Fig. 4: Competition model, Mainhardt community center
Figs. 12, 13, 43: Competition model, Church of St Augustine, Heilbronn
Fig. 14: Competition model, Stella Maris Chapel, Stuttgart
Fig. 25: Competition model, St George's parish hall, Riedlingen
Fig. 65: Competition model, community center, Schwetzingen

The following photographs were made available by Christoph Baumann, Karlsruhe:

Figs. 70, 71, 72, 73, 75: Details from study models

The following photographs were made available by Bert Bielefeld, Dortmund:

Figs. 11, 16, 45–47, 74

The following photographs were made available by Isabella Skiba, Dortmund:

Figs. 8–10, 44

The following photographs were made available by Stefanie Schmitt, Stutensee:

Fig. 18: Study model, St Francis Kindergarten
Fig. 19: 2nd row: Master's project, Olympia station, Stuttgart
Fig. 63: Master's project, Olympia station, Stuttgart

The author has supplied Figs. 2, 5, 15, 17, 20–23, 28–42, 52–59, 64, 69, 76–82

ARCHITECTURAL PHOTOGRAPHY
Photographs: technical information

Figure p. 320 Technique:	Kemeter warehouse, Eichstätt, Germany, Hild & Kaltwasser Linhof Kardan GT 8 × 10 in, color slide, 200 mm lens
Figure p. 322 Technique:	House in Aggstall, Munich, Hild und K Architekten Linhof Kardan GT, color slide 13 × 18 cm, 300 mm lens
Figure 7 Technique:	Concrete test pavilion, Kaiserslautern, Germany, architects Matthias Castorph, Dagmar Jung, Marten Ulpts Technika V, color slide 13 × 18 cm, 150 mm lens
Figures 8–11 Technique:	Laimer Würfel, Munich, architects Frick, Krüger, Nusser, Plan2 Figure 8: Digital SLR, 12 MP, left-hand image 18 mm lens, perspective correction during editing Figure 9: Digital SLR, 12 MP, stitch from 2 images, 35 mm shift lens Figure 10: Digital SLR, 12 MP, 45 mm shift lens Figure 11: Digital SLR, 12 MP, 250 mm lens
Figures 12, 13 Technique:	Pullach office building, Germany, architect Franz Riepl Linhof Kardan GT 13 × 18 cm, color slide, 110 mm lens
Figure 15 Technique: Technique:	Left: Low-energy building, Munich, architect Martin Pool Linhof Technikardan, color slide 4 × 5 in, 72 mm lens Right: Fuchs building, Ramstein, Germany, Bayer Uhrig Architekten Digital SLR, 12 MP, stitch from 3 images, 35 mm shift lens
Figure 16	Canon single-lens reflex camera, Zörk shift adapter, Pentax 35 mm lens
Figure 18	Sinar ArTec camera with Sinar 33 MP digital back

Figure 19	Linhof Kardan GT
Figures 20, 21 Technique:	Ramstein residential building, Germany, Bayer Uhrig Architekten Linhof Technikardan, color slide 4 × 5 in, 72 mm lens, twilight
Figure 22 Technique:	Public housing, Kempten, Germany, Hild & Kaltwasser Linhof Kardan GT, roll film 6 × 9 cm, 58 mm lens
Figure 23 Technique:	Weimar University library, Germany, Meck Architekten Linhof Technikardan, roll film 6 × 9 cm, 47 mm lens
Figures 24, 25 Technique:	Research center, Ingolstadt, Germany, Fink + Jocher Linhof Kardan GT, slide film 13 × 18 cm, 110 mm lens
Figure 26 Technique:	Cemetery, Finisterre, Galicia, Spain Technika III, color slide 13 × 18 cm, 110 mm lens, dawn
Figure 27 Technique:	Research center, Ingolstadt, Germany, Fink + Jocher Linhof Kardan GT, color slide 13 × 18 cm, 90 mm lens
Figures 28, 29 Technique:	Education center, Riem, Munich, Spreen Architekten Linhof Technikardan, roll film 6 × 9 cm, 58 mm lens
Figure 30 Technique:	Aircraft paint shop, Erding, Germany, Lux Architekten Linhof Technikardan, roll film 6 × 9 cm, 35 mm lens
Figure 31 Technique:	Kemeter warehouse, Eichstätt, Germany, Hild & Kaltwasser Linhof Technikardan, color slide 9 × 12 cm, 47 mm lens, MB 220/8
Figure 32 Technique:	Student apartments, Garching, Germany, Fink + Jocher Linhof Kardan GT, color slide 13 × 18 cm, 90 mm lens
Figure 33 Technique:	Building, Steinwenden, Germany, Bayer Uhrig Architekten Linhof Technikardan, roll film 6 × 9 cm, 90 mm lens
Figures 34, 35 Technique:	Research building in the central university sports complex, Munich, Hild und K Architekten Plaubel Proshift, color slide 6 × 9 cm, 47 mm lens
Figure 36 Technique:	Multi-story car park, Riem, Munich, Hild und K Architekten Linhof Kardan GT, sheet film 4 × 5 in, 72 mm lens
Figure 37 Technique:	Munich City Utilities (SWM) administration building, Munich, Meck Architekten Linhof Technikardan, color slide 4 × 5 in, 150 mm lens
Figures 38, 39 Technique:	Multi-story car park, Riem, Munich, Hild und K Architekten Linhof Kardan GT, color slide 13 × 18 cm, 110 mm and 300 mm lens
Figure 40 Technique:	Residential building, Ramstein, Germany, Bayer Uhrig Architekten Linhof Technikardan, roll film 6 × 9 cm, 72 mm lens
Figure 41 Technique:	Challenger for Air Independence Technika V, color slide 13 × 18 cm, blurring due to tilting of lens plane, 300 mm lens
Figure 42 Technique:	Nuwog administration building, Neu-Ulm, Germany, Fink + Jocher Digital SLR, 12 MP, stitch from 8 images, 35 mm shift lens
Figure 43 Technique:	Secondary school, Aschheim, Germany, Bär, Stadelmann, Stöcker Architekten Linhof Technikardan, color slide 6 × 9 cm, 72 mm lens, polarizing filter
Figure 44 Technique:	Bauzentrum, Munich, Hild und K Architekten Linhof Kardan GT, color slide 13 × 18 cm, 300 mm lens, night shot, 5 sec exposure

Figure 45 Technique:	Gillet house, Liège, Belgium, architect Jacques Gillet Linhof Technikardan, color slide 4 × 5 in, color correction filter
Figure 46 Technique:	Barn Linhof Technikardan GT 4 × 5 in, 210 mm lens, f16, 1 sec
Figure 47 Technique:	Research building, Ingolstadt, Germany, Fink + Jocher Linhof Kardan GT, color slide 13 × 18 cm, 480 mm lens
Figure 48 Technique:	Bus shelter, Landshut, Germany, Hild und K Architekten Linhof Kardan GT 8 × 10 in, color negative, Lens 200 mm
Figure 49 Technique:	Challenger for Air Independence Technika V, Color slide 13 × 18 cm, blurring due to tilting of lens plane, 500 mm lens, open aperture
Figures 50, 51 Technique:	"Transplant," Kunst am Bau, artist Matthias Castorph Technika V, color slide 13 × 18 cm, 110 mm lens
Figures 52, 53 Technique:	Concrete test pavilion, Kaiserslautern, Germany, architects Matthias Castorph, Dagmar Jung, Marten Ulpts Technika V, color slide 13 × 18 cm, 72 mm and 300 mm lens
Figure 54 Technique:	Linde administration building, Aschaffenburg, Germany, Ritter Bauer Architekten Digital SLR, 12 MP, image composed from 2 individual shots, each with a forklift, 35 mm shift lens
Figure 55 Technique:	Consulate General of the Netherlands, Munich, Cepezed with Ring Schuster Architekten Linhof Technikardan, roll film 6 × 9 cm, segment, *f*11, 1/2 sec
Figures 56, 57 Technique:	Cemetery, Riem, Munich, Meck Architekten Linhof Kardan GT 8 × 10 in, color slide, 150 mm lens
Figure 58 Technique:	Bauzentrum, Munich, Hild & Kaltwasser Linhof Kardan GT, color slide 13 × 18 cm, 110 mm lens
Figure 59 Technique:	Attic conversion, Baaderstrasse, Munich, Meck Architekten with Susanne Frank Digital SLR, 12 MP, 35 mm shift lens
Figure 60 Technique:	Bauzentrum, Munich, Hild & Kaltwasser Linhof Kardan GT, color slide 13 × 18 cm, 110 mm lens, color correction filter for neon light
Figure 61 Technique:	Temporary bridge, Munich, architect G. Haimerl Linhof Technikardan, roll film 6 × 9 cm, 110 mm lens, *f*11, 3 sec
Figure 62 Technique:	Fellner house, Großnöbach, Germany, Bayer Uhrig Architekten Linhof Technikardan, roll film 6 × 9 cm, 110 mm lens
Figure 63 Technique:	Aufberg 1113, Germany, Meck Architekten Sinar ArTec, Digital back Sinar eMotion 75, 33 MP, Sinaron HR 28 lens
Figure 64 Technique:	Consulate General of the Netherlands, Munich, Cepezed with Ring Schuster Architekten Linhof Technikardan, slide film 4 × 5 in, lens 90 mm
Figure 65 Technique:	Exhibition in Bavarian National Museum, Munich, Hild und K Architekten Linhof Technikardan, slide film 4 × 5 in, 72 mm lens, *f*11, 15 sec
Figure 66 Technique:	Signal school, Starnberg, Germany, architect Gerhard Landbrecht Linhof Technikardan, color slide 4 × 5 in, 72 mm lens, morning mist
Figure 67 Technique:	Parish hall, Lenting, Germany, Meck Architekten Linhof Technikardan, color slide 4 × 5 in, 72 mm lens

Figure p. 360	Seminar, University of Kaiserslautern, 2007, B.O.E. Prof. M. Castorph Above left: Christine Jung, above right: Liu Ruo, middle left: Michael Zach, middle right: Julia Lederle, below left: Oliver von der Heydt, below right: Mira Sasser
Figures 68, 69 Technique:	Secondary school, Aschheim, Germany, Bär, Stadelmann, Stöcker Architekten Linhof Technikardan, color slide 4 × 5 in, 110 mm lens
Figure 71 Technique:	Parish center, Thalmässing, Germany, Meck Architekten Linhof Technikardan, color slide 4 × 5 in, 90 mm lens, *f*11, 8 sec
Figure 72 Technique:	Gillet house, Liège, Belgium, architect Jacques Gillet Linhof Technikardan, roll film 6 × 12 cm, color correction filter
Figure 73 Technique:	Munich city hall canteen, Morphologic Gebhard and Burgstaller Digital SLR, 12 MP, 35 mm shift lens, composed of three images with different exposures
Figure 74 Technique:	Medical practice, Munich, Landau + Kindelbacher Linhof Technikardan, roll film 6 × 9 cm, color correction filter, color correction via filter and subsequent processing
Figures 75, 76 Technique:	Attic conversion, Munich, Unterlandstättner Schmöller Architekten Digital SLR, 12 MP, 35 mm shift lens
Figure 77 Technique:	Model: Platz der Menschenrechte, Valentien + Valentien Digital SLR, 8 MP, 22 mm lens
Figure 78 Technique:	Museum, Manching, Germany, architect Florian Fischer Digital SLR, 12 MP, 35 mm shift lens Each axis is a shot, and together they form an image several meters long. The lack of distance made a frontal shot impossible.

The authors

FREEHAND DRAWING

Florian Afflerbach, Dipl.-Ing. (FH) Architect M. A., is a research assistant at the Chair for Spatial Design at Siegen University and the Chair for the Depiction of Architecture at the TU Dortmund. He is a co-founder of Schaff-Verlag für Architekturvermittlung, Hamburg.

TECHNICAL DRAWING

Bert Bielefeld, Prof. Dr.-Ing. Architect, Professor for construction economics and construction management at the University of Siegen, executive partner of bertbielefeld&partner architekten ingenieure

Isabella Skiba, Dipl.-Ing. Architect, executive partner of bertbielefeld& partner architekten ingenieure

CAD

Jan Krebs, Dipl.-Ing. Architect, works as an architect and lecturer for structural engineering in Dortmund.

MODELBUILDING

Alexander Schilling, Dipl.-Ing. Architect, project architect with the Peter Krebs Architekt BDA architecture firm in Karlsruhe, works independently in the field of architectural model building.

Acknowledgements

Special thanks go to:

Chair of Building Theory and Design, Professor Arno Lederer/ Professor Daniele Marques, University of Karlsruhe (Photographs of models that were built over the last few years for design and end-of-term projects in design theory. Master modelmaker Manfred Neubig provided modeling courses to support the design process.)

Gerstäcker-Bauwerk GmbH, modelmaking materials and art supplies, Thomas Rüde and Marc Schlegel, Karlsruhe (provided advice on materials and assistance when tools and modelmaking materials were photographed)

Wood workshop at the Department of Architecture, workshop supervisor Wolfgang Steinhilper, University of Karlsruhe (assistance with photographs)

Metals workshop at the Department of Architecture, workshop supervisor Andreas Heil, University of Karlsruhe (assistance with photographs)

Christoph Baumann, Karlsruhe (model photographs)

Verena Horn, Karlsruhe (assistance with photographs)

Peter Krebs, Büro für Architektur, Karlsruhe (model photographs)

Stefanie Schmitt, Stutensee (model photographs)

ARCHITECTURAL PHOTOGRAPHY

Michael Heinrich, Dipl.-Ing., is a freelance architectural photographer in Munich, where he also runs photography seminars for students of architecture. He trained as a photographer at the Bavarian State Academy of Photography and also studied architecture at Munich University of Technology.

ALSO AVAILABLE FROM BIRKHÄUSER:

Design
Basics Design and Living
Jan Krebs
ISBN 978-3-7643-7647-5

Basics Design Ideas
Bert Bielefeld,
Sebastian El khouli
ISBN 978-3-7643-8112-7

Basics Design Methods
Kari Jormakka
ISBN 978-3-03821-520-2

Basics Materials
M. Hegger, H. Drexler, M. Zeumer
ISBN 978-3-7643-7685-7

Basics Spatial Design
Ulrich Exner, Dietrich Pressel
ISBN 978-3-7643-8848-5

Basics Barrier-Free Planning
Isabella Skiba, Rahel Züger
ISBN 978-3-7643-8959-8

Construction
Basics Facade Apertures
Roland Krippner,
Florian Musso
ISBN 978-3-7643-8466-1

Basics Glass Construction
Andreas Achilles,
Diane Navratil
ISBN 978-3-7643-8851-5

Basics Loadbearing Systems
Alfred Meistermann
ISBN 978-3-7643-8107-3

Basics Masonry Construction
Nils Kummer
ISBN 978-3-7643-7645-1

Basics Roof Construction
Tanja Brotrück
ISBN 978-3-7643-7683-3

Basics Timber Construction
Ludwig Steiger
ISBN 978-3-7643-8102-8

Professional Practice
Basics Tendering
Tim Brandt,
Sebastian Franssen
ISBN 978-3-7643-8110-3

Basics Project Planning
Hartmut Klein
ISBN 978-3-7643-8469-2

Basics Site Management
Lars-Phillip Rusch
ISBN 978-3-7643-8104-2

Basics Time Management
Bert Bielefeld
ISBN 978-3-7643-8873-7

Basics Budgeting
Bert Bielefeld, Roland Schneider
ISBN 978-3-03821-532-5

Urbanism
Basics Urban Building Blocks
Thorsten Bürklin,
Michael Peterek
ISBN 978-3-7643-8460-9

Basics Urban Analysis
Gerrit Schwalbach
ISBN 978-3-7643-8938-3

Building Physics/ Building Services

Basics Room Conditioning
Oliver Klein, Jörg Schlenger
ISBN 978-3-7643-8664-1

Basics Water Cycles
Doris Haas-Arndt
ISBN 978-3-7643-8854-6

Landscape Architecture

Basics Designing with Plants
Regine Ellen Wöhrle, Hans-Jörg Wöhrle
ISBN 978-3-7643-8659-7

Basics Designing with Water
Axel Lohrer, Cornelia Bott
ISBN 978-3-7643-8662-7

Series editor: Bert Bielefeld
Concept: Bert Bielefeld, Annette Gref
Layout, cover design and typography:
Andreas Hidber
Typesetting and production: Amelie Solbrig
Project management: Petra Schmid

Translation from German into English:
Foreword: James Roderick O'Donovan
Basics Freehand Drawing: James Roderick O'Donovan
Basics Technical Drawing: Michael Robinson
Basics CAD: Adam Blauhut, Joseph O'Donnell
Basics Modelbuilding: Adam Blauhut, Robin Benson
Basics Architectural Photography: Adam Blauhut, Joseph O'Donnell

English copy editing: Monica Buckland

Library of Congress Cataloging-in-Publication data
A CIP catalog record for this book has been applied for at the Library of Congress.

Bibliographic information published by the German National Library
The German National Library lists this publication in the Deutsche Nationalbibliografie; detailed bibliographic data are available on the Internet at http://dnb.dnb.de.

This book is also available in a German language edition (ISBN 978-3-03821-528-8).

P.O. Box 44, 4009 Basel, Switzerland
Part of De Gruyter

Printed on acid-free paper produced from chlorine-free pulp. TCF ∞

Printed in Germany

ISBN 978-3-03821-527-1

9 8 7 6 5 4 3 2 1

www.birkhauser.com